POLICING &
SOCIETY

A GLOBAL APPROACH

POLICING & SOCIETY

A GLOBAL APPROACH

MICHAEL J. PALMIOTTO

Wichita State University

N. PRABHA UNNITHAN

Colorado State University

DELMAR
CENGAGE Learning™

Australia • Brazil • Japan • Korea • Mexico • Singapore • Spain • United Kingdom • United States

DELMAR
CENGAGE Learning

Policing and Society: A Global Approach
Michael J. Palmiotto, N. Prabha Unnithan

Vice President, Career and Professional Editorial: Dave Garza

Director of Learning Solutions: Sandy Clark

Senior Acquisitions Editor: Shelley Esposito

Managing Editor: Larry Main

Product Manager: Anne Orgren

Editorial Assistant: Danielle Klahr

Vice President, Career and Professional Marketing: Jennifer Baker

Marketing Director: Deborah S. Yarnell

Marketing Manager: Erin Brennan

Marketing Coordinator: Jonathan Sheehan

Production Director: Wendy Troeger

Production Manager: Mark Bernard

Senior Content Project Manager: Betty L. Dickson

Senior Art Director: Joy Kocsis

For product information and technology assistance, contact us at
Cengage Learning Customer & Sales Support, 1-800-354-9706

For permission to use material from this text or product,
submit all requests online at **www.cengage.com/permissions.**
Further permissions questions can be e-mailed to
permissionrequest@cengage.com

Library of Congress Control Number: 2010920063

ISBN-13: 978-0-534-62343-2

ISBN-10: 0-534-62343-3

Delmar
5 Maxwell Drive
Clifton Park, NY 12065-2919
USA

Cengage Learning is a leading provider of customized learning solutions with office locations around the globe, including Singapore, the United Kingdom, Australia, Mexico, Brazil, and Japan. Locate your local office at: **international.cengage.com/region**

Cengage Learning products are represented in Canada by Nelson Education, Ltd.

To learn more about Delmar, visit **www.cengage.com/delmar**

Purchase any of our products at your local college store or at our preferred online store **www.CengageBrain.com**

Notice to the Reader

Printed in the United States of America
1 2 3 4 5 6 7 14 13 12 11 10

CONTENTS

4

POLICE AND THE CRIMINAL JUSTICE SYSTEM   61

7

POLICE, ORDER MAINTENANCE, AND SERVICE   112

8

POLICE DISCRETION   129

11

POLICE AND CRIME PREVENTION   188

14

POLICE USE OF EXCESSIVE FORCE   249

15

POLICING THE GLOBE   265

16
THE FUTURE OF POLICING 287

PREFACE

Policing and Society: A Global Approach provides comparative information on policing as a component of criminal justice that is guided by current sociological perspectives and an international understanding. Currently, there exists no text book similar to *Policing and Society: A Global Approach* that discusses the study of law enforcement sociologically and cross-nationally.

Policing and Society: A Global Approach is intended to be used as a main text for undergraduate students, both in community colleges and four-year institutions. It could also be utilized as a major text for international programs and curricula with a global approach to the topic. The other major feature of *Policing and Society* is its sociological perspective. Courses on the police that adopt a macrolevel or societal outlook toward law enforcement issues will find *Policing and Society* a good fit in that it is based on a sociological view of policing.

In recent times, the world has seen a greater trend toward internationalism and globalization. No longer can Americans shut off the rest of the world, and carry on academically in isolation. As a consequence, more and more university students are expected to study abroad for a semester or two, and comparative criminal justice courses have proliferated. *Policing and Society: A Global Approach* not only provides information about American policing, but also compares and contrasts it with policing in other countries. Each chapter has a major section on policing in another country, along with a box written by a police authority connected with, or an individual who has expertise in, policing in that nation.

We collaborated and wrote *Policing and Society: A Global Approach* because we saw the need for such a book, and because of our dissatisfaction with standard texts on the topic that do not address policing in other countries. We also believe that trends in higher education favor more courses that include an international view of the criminal justice field. Given this reality, a sociological approach committed to explicitly comparing and contrasting American policing with practices in other countries becomes necessary. We developed this book based on our years of teaching criminal justice and policing courses, research in the police field, along with attending international conferences and meetings.

Students using this book should have a basic understanding of the criminal justice field, and have a basic knowledge of all three components of the system: police, courts, and corrections. It is also recommended that students should have taken an Introduction to Sociology course, or be familiar with the sociological approach to studying crime and criminal justice.

The major features of this book include the following. Initially, each chapter has an objective section to assist the students in learning the major points associated with the chapter. After describing and discussing the central topics and associated concepts, each chapter then deals with three sociological perspectives (functionalism, conflict, and interactionism) on them. Each chapter then has an international perspective on policing, along with a box or insert on policing dealing with a foreign country written by a police expert on (and in many cases, from) that country. Every chapter concludes with a chapter summary, a list of key terms that students should know, review questions to assist students studying for the examination, and discussion questions that the instructor can use in class to obtain student feedback and participation. The authors and articles cited are listed in the references section.

All of us have had more than a quarter century of experience in the field as professors teaching policing courses, police trainers, and researchers. One of us has worked as a police officer (Palmiotto) early in his career, while the other (Unnithan) has lived and studied abroad for a long time. The authors are familiar with policing in foreign countries, having written books and manuscripts, having attended international conferences on policing, and having made formal presentations to audiences abroad.

Professors, instructors, students, and users of *Policing and Society* can contact the authors with questions, suggestions, and comments about the text or supplements at the following addresses.

Dr. Michael J. Palmiotto
Professor of Criminal Justice
School of Community Affairs
Wichita State University
Wichita, Kansas 67260

Dr. N. Prabha Unnithan
Professor of Sociology
Director, Center for the Study of Crime and Justice
Department of Sociology
Fort Collins, Colorado 80523

ACKNOWLEDGMENTS

Policing and Society: A Global Approach is the product of the efforts of many individuals. The authors are grateful to Anne Orgren, product manager for Delmar/Cengage Learning, for her suggestions, assistance, patience, and encouragement throughout this process. We thank Caroline Henderson, senior acquisitions editor at Wadsworth/Cengage Learning, who worked with us for several years, and Shelley Esposito, senior acquisitions editor at Delmar/Cengage Learning, for their support. We would also like to thank all the reviewers for their suggestions in making our text a better book for the classroom:

Matthew Atherton,
Central Connecticut State University

Paul R. Bowdre,
Western Nebraska Community College
Mengyan Dai, *University of Baltimore (Maryland)*

Gregory J. DeLone,
University of Nebraska at Omaha

Patrick J. Faiella,
MA. CAGS, Massasoit Community College (Massachusetts)

Greg Galardi,
Peru State College (Nebraska)

Dr. Brian A. Kinnaird,
Fort Hays State University (Kansas)

Dr. Jacqueline L. Schneider,
University of South Florida—St. Petersburg

Hallie E. Stephens, Ph.D.,
Southeastern Oklahoma State University

Ivan Y. Sun,
University of Delaware

Gennaro F. Vito,
University of Louisville (Kentucky)

DEDICATION

We dedicate this book to our spouses for
their unstinting love and support:
Emily Palmiotto
Shashikala Unnithan

LIST OF CONTRIBUTORS

The authors thank the following colleagues who have contributed their expertise to this book in the form of Boxes on policing in a specific country or region:

Sebastián Sal on Argentina,

Tonita Murray on Canada,

Keith N. Haley and Theodora Ene on Romania,

Chris Braiden on Canada,

Ibrahim Cerrah and Murat Yıldız on Turkey,

Arvind Verma and T. K. Vinod Kumar on India,

Branislav Simonovic on Serbia,

John Scott and Patrick C. Jobes on Australia,

Lucía Dammert on Chile,

Larry French on Native Americans,

Steven Tong on Great Britain,

Tim Prenzler on Australia,

Tara O'Connor Shelley on the Czech Republic, and Milan Pagon on Europe.

ABOUT THE AUTHORS

Michael J. Palmiotto, Ph.D., is a professor of criminal justice in the School of Community Affairs at Wichita State University, Kansas. He is a former police officer of New York State, and has experience in establishing and operating a police training facility. He has a master's degree from John Jay College of Criminal Justice (City University of New York), New York, and a doctorate from the University of Pittsburgh, Pittsburgh. Professor Palmiotto has published ten books, numerous book chapters, and articles on policing and criminal justice.

N. Prabha Unnithan, Ph.D., is a professor of sociology at Colorado State University in Fort Collins, and the director of the Center for the Study of Crime and Justice there. He was born and brought up in Malaysia, and studied in India before coming to the United States, where he completed his doctorate from the University of Nebraska-Lincoln. Professor Unnithan has published more than sixty research articles and book chapters on crime and criminal justice, coauthored two books, and serves as the editor of the *Social Science Journal.*

CHAPTER 1

For the better part of the 20th century, law enforcement was not a primary concern in mainstream America. Racketeers and gangsters, whose power and wealth grew from the bootleg whiskey trade during Prohibition, were the jurisdiction of federal law enforcement agencies, and local police departments, which once were comprised of remarkably few officers even in large urban centers, existed as peacekeepers and caretakers of public safety. In addition to being relatively few in number, local police forces operated solely in a reactive fashion, that is, they responded to crimes already committed. Any description of community police work today would not be as uncomplicated. A greater degree of training and professionalism is demanded of today's police officers, whose responsibilities far outstrip those of their forerunners. (Fitzgerald, 2000: vii)

A police officer searches for explosives during an exhibition of cars that will race in the Argentina Dakar Rally 2009 in Buenos Aires, Wednesday, Dec. 31, 2008. The 2009 edition of the Dakar rally will run Jan. 3-18 in Argentina and Chile. (Credit: © AP Photo/Christophe Ena)

PERSPECTIVES ON THE POLICE

OBJECTIVES:

1. The student will understand the sociological approach to policing.
2. The student will understand the functions of police in the social order.
3. The student will understand conflict theory as applied to the police.
4. The student will understand the interactionist approach to policing.
5. The student will learn how to study policing on an international level.

A t the beginning of the twenty-first century, both the nature of policing and its tangled relationship with the societies that it serves force us to conceptualize, analyze, and describe an array of issues, challenges, and strategies. A remarkable series of transformations have taken place in the structure and functioning of police agencies that were largely created by governments in the middle part of the nineteenth century. These agencies were originally created as targeted responses to the problems (industrialization, urbanization, rural–urban migration) attendant on the widespread social changes taking place in European societies. Similar changes in American society in the late 1800s and early 1900s spurred the development and expansion of policing in the United States. After a period of time in the twentieth century that was characterized by greater and deeper involvement of governments in the policing of their citizens, police scholars David Bayley and Clifford Shearing (2001) suggest that contemporary policing has become **multilateralized**. By this they mean that governments no longer monopolize the provision of policing services to the public. Many groups in society have chosen to protect and secure themselves (e.g., through gated communities, building monitoring, video surveillance), and nongovernmental entities often provide security and safety services (e.g., private security companies, corporate executive protection firms) to the public when needed.

As a practical matter, however, we still continue to think of the police as primarily a governmental agency. There are two reasons for this. First, while certain areas of policing (patrolling private grounds, protecting important individuals, providing computer security, etc.) may have been ceded to private groups, governmental police remain the agency of final resort for crime-fighting purposes. When computer hackers invade a company's corporate records over electronic networks, the immediate warnings to the company and its employees may come from its internal security providers; however, local, state, or federal law enforcement organizations are going to be the ones investigating and arresting the perpetrators. Second, the residual powers to deal with situations that threaten public order or violate the law also remain with governmental police agents. For example, let us assume that private security agency personnel have detained a vandal at night on the grounds of an industrial unit they have been contracted to provide security for. It is likely that they will inform the police to arrest and process the criminal case against that individual. The private agency lacks the authority to detain the vandal, frame charges against that individual, and hold him or her for the purposes of identification and interrogation. Therefore, as students of policing in its many forms, it behooves us to pay attention to both the governmental and nongovernmental (or multilateral) aspects of this ubiquitous feature of contemporary societies.

There are many possible ways to approach, study, and understand the police. For example, we could catalog all the activities that police organizations engage in and describe them in administrative and operational terms. We could specify the major issues and controversies that confront the police as they carry out their defined mission of protecting and serving the public and examine typical policies and solutions for them. We could identify patterns of interaction between the police and other sectors of the criminal justice system, levels of government, and various groups of stakeholders in society.

multilateralize

The process by which governments no longer monopolize the provision of policing services to the public and where many groups in society have chosen to protect and secure themselves.

While all of the above are viable ways of approaching the study of policing, we are more ambitious in this book. It is our objective to touch on and illuminate all of the above; however, our approach will be distinctive in two ways. First, while we use insights gained from various social sciences (economics, history, political science, and psychology) our primary standpoint will come from the field of **sociology**. Sociology is defined as "the study of group life and those aspects of individual lives that are affected by social interaction" (Walton, 1990: 4). Second, we will approach police topics and issues internationally and comparatively. This means that while our primary focus will be on American policing, we will include in our descriptions and analyses information and examples about policing from other countries of the world. As we contemplate the similarities and differences of policing in many countries, we can begin to reflect critically and innovatively about the issues that confront American policing. At the same time, the growth in transnational forms of policing (INTERPOL, EUROPOL, etc.) will enable us to consider the problems of crime and criminal justice globally. Let us turn our attention first to the sociological approach.

SOCIOLOGY AND POLICE STUDIES

Individuals with ideas and explanations about social life and behavior, or social philosophers, have always existed. Most observers, however, identify the formal beginnings of sociology in the mid-1800s and early 1900s. Sociology, as a discipline, arose in response to several historical processes that occurred during this period in Europe (Giddens, Duneier, and Appelbaum, 2007). These included political revolutions such as the French Revolution and increased democratization; the Industrial Revolution and the rise of capitalist economies; the emergence of socialist thought as a reaction to the excesses of capitalism; urbanization and rural–urban migration; as well as the retrenchment of religious and speculative explanations for human behavior and the substitution of scientific ones (Ritzer, 1988). In general, sociology was seen as a way of understanding and explaining these historical transformations systematically and as a means for social reform and renewal since it solved the problems associated with these changes. These two goals continue to motivate sociologists who, to this day, use scientific methods to (a) study and describe society and social behavior, that is, **pure sociology** and (b) delineate problems that afflict society and test solutions for them, that is, **applied sociology**.

Coincidentally, the social upheavals of the 1800s that combined to give birth to the intellectual discipline of sociology also resulted in the formation and deployment of police forces (as we understand them today) in many of these European societies. This coincidence of births provides us with the opportunity to examine three striking parallels between the discipline of sociology and the study of policing. As mentioned above, sociologists are interested in studying social groups for the purpose of understanding and explaining their behavior. Similarly, we study police organizations and personnel for the purpose of understanding how and why they behave as they do. It should be noted that, historically, several prominent police researchers were trained

sociology

The discipline that is a way of understanding and explaining sociohistorical transformations systematically and as a means for social reform and renewal by solving the problems associated with these changes.

pure sociology

The branch of sociology that uses scientific methods to study and describe society and social behavior.

applied sociology

The branch of sociology that uses scientific methods to delineate problems that afflict society and to test solutions for them.

as sociologists. These include, among many others, Joseph Lohman, who developed community and race relations programs for police departments; William Westley, who pioneered the study of police subcultures; and, currently, Lawrence Sherman who has fielded innovative experiments to help police departments choose among several policy alternatives (see descriptions of their work in Axelrod, Phillips, and Kemper, 1996).

Second, sociologists are interested in finding solutions to social problems. Our purposes in examining police issues and controversies are to examine behavior that is problematic and to identify the means for changing it through policies and programs that help the police serve the public better. Third, sociologists gain their knowledge of human behavior not by intuition, personal experience, and common sense (although these might be starting points) but by using scientific methods (systematic observation, experiments, surveys, analysis of information collected by official agencies, etc.). Often the insights generated by sociological research challenge and subvert conventional wisdom on the topic (Ruane and Cerulo, 1997). In our efforts at describing and analyzing the police, we will rely on critical knowledge generated by social scientific methods (although not necessarily from sociologists alone).

There are three major characteristics to the practice of sociology that are also relevant in studying the police. Let us consider these characteristics using a hypothetical example drawn from the police. First, sociologists attempt to identify social forces that produce the social behavior they are observing by using the **sociological imagination** (Mills, 1959), i.e., they study the influence of the social on the individual. This helps us connect individual behavior to the social structure and culture that produced it. When considered in this manner, an act of police brutality to elicit a confession from a suspect is explainable not solely as the unintended and unsupported behavior of one rogue cop. It may reflect tacit societal support for "tough" crime control measures as well as ambiguous organizational practices and pronouncements regarding the treatment of suspects. The previous tentative statement and relationships suggested therein could be termed the outline of a *theory*, a "set of inter-related propositions, that allow for the systematization of knowledge, explanation and prediction of social life, and generation of new research hypotheses" (Faia, 1986: 134), regarding police brutality. Second, systematic research into a social phenomenon of interest is conducted utilizing a **hypothesis**, a tentative statement that suggests how two classes of phenomena may be connected or related. In the above example, it is possible to test the hypothesis that organizational policies affect rates of brutality among officers in that organization. In other words, those organizations that have clear written policies and training that prohibit treating suspects roughly will have lower incidence of brutal behavior. The opposite, that is, those agencies that do not have such policies and training will have higher numbers of such incidents, can also be tested in this study using this hypothesis. Third, theories and hypotheses regarding social behavior are evaluated using a systematic, scientific method that can be repeated or replicated by another researcher, if needed. In pursuit of the evidence needed to support or disprove the above hypothesis, a sociologist could gather data about the clarity of organizational policies regarding the treatment of suspects (i.e., is it discussed in the department's standard operating procedure manual; is it dealt with in the police

sociological imagination

In studying the influence of the social on the individual, that which helps us connect individual behavior to the social structure and culture that produced it.

hypothesis

A tentative statement that suggests how two classes of phenomena may be connected or related.

academy and during field training; do the chief or other higher-ups mention it in departmental meetings, etc.) and about the number of occurrences of allegations (or findings) of police brutality in a department. The two sets of information drawn from a number of police agencies (usually along with data on other variables that may affect the relationship) can then be subjected to statistical analysis to reveal either the existence or the lack of a correlation between agency policy and the incidence of brutality. It is possible on the basis of this study (and others like it) to conclude whether or not the hypothesis positing a relationship between organizational policy clarity and police brutality has been supported or not.

UNDERSTANDING THE POLICE IN SOCIETY

Sociology is not a monolithic discipline in the sense that there is not simply one accepted way of studying society and social behavior that all sociologists uniformly adhere to. It has been described as a multiple paradigm science (Ritzer, 1975) that uses multiple *perspectives,* that is, broadly competing ways of looking at society and assumptions about the nature of the social world. Therefore, the perspective we use influences the development of theories, research questions, hypotheses, and ultimately the answers we find. One perspective is not necessarily right or wrong or even better or worse than others. Each perspective approaches the study of any given social phenomenon differently, asks different questions, and provides different answers. There are three major perspectives that have come to dominate sociological research and writing. We will consider each of these perspectives by using a situation or event connected with policing that could take place in any given society or community. For our limited purposes, we will ignore relatively minor variations within, and interpretational differences that may exist among adherents to, each of these perspectives.

Functionalism: Police and Social Order

One important sociological perspective that was influential through much of the mid-twentieth century was *functionalism*. The major focus of functionalists is the studying and understanding of how societies develop and maintain social order. First, every element (rules, greeting rituals, language, food habits, religious beliefs, courtship patterns, etc.) and institution (family, education, law, the economy, government, mass media) is, it is assumed, related to the need for societies to organize social life in an orderly way and to thereby ensure their continued survival. Functionalists examine behaviors and interactions that occur in terms of how they contribute to the effective functioning of society. Crime, for example, is seen as dysfunctional because it harms others and violates expectations of orderly behavior and interaction to which all members of society subscribe.

Second, functionalists assume that all parts of an orderly society are integrated with each other and operate in an interdependent manner. Thus, change in one aspect of society will result in changes in other parts of the social structure. For example, economic pressures beginning in the 1970s resulted in more women in the United States joining the labor force and working outside the home. This led to changes in the provision of childcare with the rise of private day-care centers, all day kindergarten, corporate day care, etc. In turn, media and political institutions began paying attention to issues affecting "working women." You may remember, for example, stories in the mass media and policy discussions regarding the "glass ceiling" (how businesswomen were finding it difficult to be promoted beyond a certain level in corporate situations) and the "Supermom" syndrome (the difficulties that faced women who tried to combine working outside the home with playing an important role in the care of their families and the upbringing of their children).

Let us apply the **functionalist perspective** to the police and examine their place in the social order. Consider the following quotation that describes how police go about promoting good relations with the community they serve.

> Visiting school classrooms, bicycle safety presentations, informal bantering with kids on the street, "Officer Friendly" programs, summer camps, "junior police" programs, and scout troops are a few of the police-sponsored programs and activities designed to create constructive contacts between youth and the police, and to reinforce a positive image of the police in the eyes of youth. (Cox and Fitzgerald, 1983: 61)

Remember that functionalists look for how various elements of society contribute to social order and that change in one aspect of society brings about change in the others. From the above example, it is clear that the police are important contributors to order in society. By engaging the young very early in their lives, the police teach them the importance of obeying the law, engaging in conventional activities, and responding to the expectations that society has of them. At the same time, "constructive contacts" and "a positive image" is built up regarding the police (and by extension) the government and polity that they represent. Notice also that by engaging in these activities, the police also can keep tabs on aspects of youth culture that may subvert or threaten the existing social order (e.g., drug use, minors buying alcohol, driving without a license, running away, etc.) if unchecked. Overall, the police act as monitors and guardians who ensure that society's laws are obeyed and that there is an orderly flow of life in the community they serve.

One final point about functionalism needs to be made. Although much of this perspective focuses on what may appear to be obvious and intended, or **manifest functions**, attention is also paid to less obvious, and often unanticipated **latent functions**. The manifest functions of policing have been reviewed earlier. However, it could also be suggested that one latent function of allocating societal resources and maintaining a police force is to provide employment for hundreds of thousands of sworn police officers as well as other civilian support personnel (secretaries, police psychologists, maintenance workers, etc.) in police departments. As a result, all of these people are likely to "buy into" and support the social arrangements that have provided them with their means of livelihood. Considering this their duty and their bread and butter, the police are, therefore, unlikely to question their own belief in the rightness of the laws they enforce.

functionalist perspective

A sociological paradigm that focuses on studying and understanding how societies develop and maintain social order.

manifest functions

Social functions that appear to be obvious and intended.

latent functions

Social functions that are less obvious, and often unanticipated.

Conflict: Whose Side Are the Police on?

In contrast to the functionalist assumption that society represents some sort of consensus on the part of its members, the **conflict perspective** (Collins, 1975) focuses on competition that exists between groups (racial/ethnic groups, tribes, social classes, genders, age groups) in any given society. Conflict theorists examine societies to figure out which groups control scarce resources and which groups do not and who benefits most from the status quo. For example, they point out how the children and grandchildren of the elite appear more likely to become the wealthiest members of society, hold the most powerful positions, and have prestige and celebrity status associated with them. Given all the rhetoric about democracy, fairness, and equality that most contemporary societies engage in, how is it that the elite are almost always drawn from a fairly small number of groups? For example, take the idea that anyone in the United States can grow up to be president; this was proven with the election of Barack Obama in 2008, and it won't be long before America has a women president. Groups that control scarce societal resources such as wealth, power, and prestige do not wish to and are in no hurry to give these up to others who they see as less deserving.

Given that there are likely to be winners and losers in the competition for control of societal resources, conflict theorists focus on how existing social arrangements always represent the powerful against the weaker members of society. If considered in this manner, those on top of the current social setup have every reason to make sure that the legitimacy of social institutions and processes are to be maintained and not challenged, by those below them. Such challenges would serve to question and subvert the privileges enjoyed by them. Ensuring support for the legitimacy of existing social arrangements is carried out in a number of ways. Some token members of the lower classes or groups at the bottom are co-opted and used as examples of how it is possible for anyone to rise to the top. The mass media are filled with messages about how wonderful the American economic and political system is and how rotten other systems (which may be based on other criteria and assumptions) are. Laws are passed by pliant legislatures that discourage and prohibit behavior seen as threatening to the interests of the powerful. Finally, the civil and criminal justice system is utilized to punish those who dare to dissent from or violate these laws (Chambliss, 1988).

Unlike functionalists who see social change as, at best, problematic, and, at worst, undesirable, conflict theorists see social change as necessary and beneficial. Change; whether it is orderly, through peaceful activism (e.g., dissent, civil disobedience), or through revolution can be a positive force if it results in a reduction in inequality, that is, if it enables members of the weaker sections of society to gain greater access to scarce resources. Thus, it is important for conflict sociologists to bring about change in the communities and societies in which they live, resulting in justice for, and the liberation and empowerment of, those oppressed by the weight of existing social arrangements.

We are now ready to apply the conflict perspective to the police and examine how they are viewed in a world of constant group competition. Consider the following quotation that describes what happened to an individual picked up in Belfast, Northern Ireland, suspected of having terrorist connections.

conflict perspective

A sociological paradigm that focuses on the competition that exists between groups (racial/ethnic groups, tribes, social classes, genders, age groups) in any given society.

In the room there was half a dozen soldiers, military police, and one policeman—4162 was his number, ginger hair, he was about twenty-four, twenty-five; if I saw him today, I'd know him—and they just started beating me while I was lying on the camp bed. They beat me with batons, they kicked me all around the place. They were aiming towards my privates and my head and they were making me keep my hands at my sides. I went unconscious a couple of times and they woke me up. (Conroy, 2000: 5)

It is clear from the foregoing quotation that members of the police, from a conflict perspective, are not considered impartial and unbiased enforcers of benign laws that represent societal consensus. The police represent one of the tools that elites use to keep dissenters, protesters, and other troublemakers in line. In this example, the dominant groups are the British allied with the Protestants in Northern Ireland (now a part of the United Kingdom) against Catholics who are struggling to unite the province with their coreligionists (to the south) in the Republic of Ireland. The Protestants in Northern Ireland are, however, not willing to surrender their privileged positions to join the Republic of Ireland where *they* would become a minority. They, therefore, use the military and the police to preserve the status quo. Notice the alignment of the regular police officer with the military and military police; it is as though all of the oppressive arms of a (supposedly democratic) society are joined together to torture this individual. Is a change in this situation that results in greater equality, through peaceful or violent means, needed? Conflict theorists would suggest so, although they are less likely to agree on the means and on what the ultimate fate of Northern Ireland should be. Should it join the Republic of Ireland, which would mean greater empowerment of the Catholics, or should it remain with the United Kingdom, which would mean no discrimination against the Protestants? At the same time, conflict theorists will point out that the police are the least likely proponents of social change. They are more likely to obey the powers that be and enforce whatever the latter want. This can be further clarified by considering American history. During the late-twentieth-century struggles of the civil rights movement that fought prejudice and discrimination against African Americans, the police were at the forefront of putting down protests by arresting peaceful demonstrators and enforcing segregationist laws.

Moving to other areas of policing, conflict theorists note that law enforcement practices are almost always aimed at the poor and powerless in society. While crime in the streets (e.g., property crime, muggings, drug sales, panhandling) is often dealt with harshly and severely, crime in the suites (e.g., corporate crime, environmental degradation, insider trading, stock fraud) is dealt with a slap on the wrist, if at all. This is true even if the harm or damage resulting from the crimes of the upper classes is greater and wider-ranging. Many police departments, for example, designate a unit specifically for the investigation of robberies and burglaries (more likely to be committed by members of the lower classes), but it would be difficult to find a similar unit specifically devoted to corporate crime, medical fraud, price fixing, etc. Further, "the outlawing of violent behaviors increases the likelihood of social tranquility among the underclasses. In turn, these disenfranchised groups are less likely to direct their anger and frustration at the overclasses who exploit them" (Berg, 1992: 10). As the enforcers of these one-sided laws, the police become agents of and one of the weapons used by those in power to keep the powerless in line.

Interactionism: Understanding the Meanings of Police Interaction

So far, in discussing the functionalist and conflict perspectives, we have dealt with what sociologists refer to as *macrolevel analysis*. In other words, we have considered the police as a group or organization that operates within larger collectivities such as classes, communities, and societies. We have, in essence, paid attention to the "big picture." There is another perspective in sociology, known as interactionism, that carries out **microlevel analysis**, that is, attention is paid to the nature and meanings as well as to the details attached to more specific settings and situations within which individuals or groups interact, for example, in a family, classroom, football stadium, police station, courtroom, supermarket, boot camp, etc.

Similar to functionalism and conflict theory, there are many varieties of interactionism that have attempted to tease out the patterns and meanings that are created when individuals associate with each other. However, the form of interactionist theory that has dominated this perspective is known as **symbolic interactionism** (Manis and Meltzer, 1978; Charon, 1985). Let us explore this particular style of interactionist analysis. Here, we will use an example that shows the importance that symbolic interactionists place on **socialization**, the process by which individuals learn, through interaction with others, how to think and behave, in general, and as members of a group or culture, in particular. The symbolic interaction perspective is based on the premise that human beings, while born with the capacity for thought, will have that capacity molded by a series of interactions with others. These interactions help individuals learn what is meant or symbolized. For example, we learn in the course of interacting with parents, teachers, and friends that a particular facial expression indicates anger or happiness. Learning these meanings and symbols allows us to act and react to other human beings when the facial expression of these emotions is called for. We can experiment with using what we have learned about these particular facial expressions to indicate our own anger or happiness. Meanings and symbols may be modified on a situational basis; and this is due to the human ability, in an ongoing sense, to contemplate both our actions and ourselves. We learn, for example, that our employers prefer that, in serving clients or customers, we use facial expressions that indicate happiness and not use facial expressions that indicate anger, because we may lose business. These interconnected series of actions and interactions help constitute social groups, communities, and ultimately, societies. Using this facial expression example, when it is repeated over and over again by many individuals, we can show its utility in and effect on groups such as the family, peers, and the educational and economic institutions of society. It is possible to see the extensions of this example into other institutions such as the media (e.g., how an actor portrays anger or happiness on film or in the theater) and politics (e.g., a candidate for office showing that he or she is annoyed or pleased with a question or his or her opponent's answer during a debate), among others.

macrolevel analysis

Studying the police as a group or organization that operates within larger collectivities such as classes, communities, and societies.

microlevel analysis

Studying the police with attention to the nature and meanings as well as the details attached to specific settings and situations within which individuals or groups interact.

symbolic interactionism

A form of the interactionist perspective that is based on the premise that human beings, while born with the capacity for thought, will have that capacity molded by a series of interactions with others which help individuals learn what is meant or symbolized.

socialization

The process by which individuals learn, through interaction with others, how to think and behave in general, and as members of a group or culture.

This perspective suggests two major conclusions regarding human behavior. First, people do not necessarily respond directly to everything they are likely to encounter in everyday life. Words, physical objects, gestures, situations, and everything else is assimilated and interpreted actively, both mentally and subjectively. Second, given these ongoing subjective interpretations of both human behavior and the physical world, that which is thought of as "reality" is socially constructed. Consider the following example taken from the work of Peter Manning, who is well known for his interactionist analysis of police work:

> Several basic facts must be understood about crime statistics. If the police know about the event, they can exercise discretion in response to it, in terms of whether it will be defined as a crime ('founded'), what law (or laws) is (are) said to be violated, which of several violations to charge a person with (if a suspect is apprehended), whether to bargain with the person over the charge (for example, in drug cases, persons are often released on their own recognizance if they promise to inform on other users or dealers), what information to turn over to the prosecuting attorneys, and what charges to recommend to them (Manning, 1997: 123).

The microlevel analysis that interactionists typically engage in is shown in the above example even though it deals with what we would take to be the sum of a series of objective decisions, that is, since offenses are statutorily defined, behaviors and actions that go into police statistics should be clear cut, and not based on subjective individual interpretations. However, it is clear that meanings understood or imputed at the situational (or micro-) level affect the process of categorization and counting of crimes. The two key conclusions regarding human behavior discussed above are also illustrated in this example using police behavior. First, police officers do not respond directly to every instance of offending behavior by immediately labeling it a crime and proceeding in terms of the absolute dictates of the law. Instead, they use their discretion (characterized here as their mental and subjective interpretations of the situations they confront and the many statutes that are possibly applicable to them) to decide how to react to what they encounter. Second, the "reality" of police activity and criminal statistics is actively constructed through a series of social interactions and individual interpretations based on these interactions.

It is clear from the above example that interactionists are unlikely to attach any "hardness" or objectivity to the numbers or statistics generated by this entirely subjective process. Interactionist estimations of the relative worth of these numbers may fall along a continuum from mildly positive to negative. At the mildly positive end of the continuum, police statistics may be considered indicators of what various individual officers decided as a result of their interactions with others in the agency, both higher-ups and peers, prosecutors, victims, witnesses, informants, and suspects, and their interpretations of legal statutes as taught to them during training and modified through their experience. At the negative end of the continuum, police statistics may be summarily dismissed as nothing more than the easily manipulated results of whatever priorities (e.g., local prosecutors and the chief of police are currently emphasizing a "crackdown" on drug offenses) and current pressures (e.g., the public is perturbed by a series of burglaries and the local newspaper is suggesting that the police department is failing at the job of nabbing the burglars responsible) members of police organizations have to deal with.

Thinking Sociologically about the Police

The discipline of sociology provides us with tools, particularly in the form of systematic scientific research methods and incisive theoretical perspectives, to study and understand police organizations and police officers. Using the theoretical perspectives identified above, it should be possible for us to analyze specific police activities in communities and countries and to gain additional insights and explanations regarding them. As a result, you will find that the subsequent chapters in this book use the functionalist, conflict, and **interactionist perspectives** to explore and explain particular police issues. These insights are incorporated throughout the text of each chapter and are not segregated in particular sections that deal with "sociology only."

However, it is our hope that you will recognize the utility of a sociological analysis of the police and, as needed, will incorporate them into your own approach to understanding policing. For example, you could think about the police recruitment and selection process using the three sociological perspectives. From a functionalist perspective, the written and physical tests, the psychological examination, and background investigation are all important to find the best candidates who will fit into the department and meet community expectations regarding performance and professionalism. If the wrong individuals get into police departments, these organizations can become dysfunctional. From a conflict perspective, we may ask who benefits from the current qualification process and selection criteria. Further, who, among a variety of applicants, are more likely to be selected to become police officers? What resources do those successful individuals have (appropriate schooling, family connections, prior knowledge of testing procedures, race/ethnic backgrounds) that others lack? From an interactionist perspective, we may contemplate the subjective dynamics of making a good impression on the hiring board (what combination of individual characteristics, spoken words, physical gestures, etc., is likely to bring this about) in a selection situation. Beyond the basic qualifications, what interactional strategies do some applicants use to convince the board of their superiority?

Finally, it is often possible to combine two of the above perspectives for a fuller understanding of a particular form of social process or interaction. In particular, given that interactionist analysis operates at the microlevel, it can be combined with one of the other two macrolevel perspectives. In the police selection example above, you can utilize a combined functionalist/interactionist or conflict/interactionist perspective. However, it would be difficult to use both functionalism and conflict theory together, given the stark differences in their underlying premises and what they deem to be of importance in the study of human behavior. Having established the utility and relevance of a sociologically informed analysis of policing, we now turn to the second leg of the approach we have taken in this book. We identify and describe next, the elements and advantages of an international and comparative description of our subject matter.

interactionist perspective

Studying the police with a view to tease out the patterns and meanings that are created when individuals associate with each other.

globalization

The increasing interconnectedness of the economies, peoples, and to a lesser extent, the politics of various countries of the world.

comparative (cross-national) approach

Analyzing information from the United States and at least one other country on various police topics.

koban

Small, continuously staffed, neighborhood ministations in Japan that allow continuous police interaction with residents.

INTERNATIONAL PERSPECTIVES ON POLICING

It is commonplace in recent times to hear that we live in a global society or global village and work in a global economy for multinational corporations. The term **globalization** used in these discussions is meant to draw our attention to the increasing interconnectedness of the economies, peoples, and to a lesser extent, the politics of various countries. In the United States, we have, given the varying origins of most people living here, a basic understanding of how groups from different parts of the world have shaped this country after migrating here. However, a visit to the local supermarket or clothing store with the objective of finding out where the products we buy and use come from will convince us of how people living in other countries shape our product consumption patterns (e.g., coffee from Colombia, clothes from China, and so on). More recently, as a further sign of our global economic interdependence, even services used by Americans have been outsourced to other countries, for example, interpreting medical imaging such as x-ray film to India and corporate customer-assistance lines to various Caribbean countries. It is thus curious that policing and the field of police studies (perhaps because it is identified with governments) have been less involved in discussions of globalization.

In this text, we have consciously adopted a **comparative or cross-national** approach to studying the police. This means that we analyze information from the United States and at least one other country on various police topics. (We use "comparative" and "cross-national" as interchangeable terms, although they are not exactly the same; see Ragin, 1987; Oyen, 1990.) In every chapter of the book, we will discuss the issues being dealt with using information from other countries (similar to our earlier use of a vignette from Northern Ireland to discuss conflict theory). For example, in Chapter 13, our discussion of police deviance, while based on the United States, benefits from comparative information drawn from India on the same topic. To further understand the issue of police corruption, look at the box in this chapter that deals with Argentina. Although cultural and historical differences do exist between countries, there are several advantages to this approach. One is the simple matter of curiosity: once we become familiar with how the police go about their business in our own country,

we become interested in learning how they do it in others. There are several other reasons. David Bayley (1999), an expert on comparative policing, enumerates four benefits to using a cross-national approach in studying the police. We draw extensively from his discussion in the next few paragraphs.

First, studying police practices in other countries allows us to extend our knowledge of various possibilities. This means that we refuse to accept certain problems as unsolvable. We also refuse to accept what we know to be less-than-optimum solutions to other problems as something we cannot do much about. Instead, we can try to learn from the experiences of other countries. Waddington (1999: 151), for example, suggests, "Americans and the British have a mutual fascination for each other's police, at the heart of which is their contrasting relationship with the gun." In other words, the problem of armed versus unarmed policing can be explored using these two police forces. Do the police always have to be armed (as in the United States) or alternatively, would it not be dangerous for them to be unarmed (as in the United Kingdom)? In recent times, we have seen experimentation in the United States with unarmed community service officers who carry out order maintenance duties, such as crowd control, traffic enforcement, and first aid to traffic accident victims. Without the existing examples of other countries where the police do not carry guns, it is difficult to imagine American police departments attempting to "disarm" some aspect of their functions.

Second, cross-national analyses allow us to develop greater insights into human behavior in general. Bayley (1999: 8) points out that in studying the police we are interested in two questions: the effect of the police on society and the effect of society on the police. Most of the time, research focuses on the first question, that is, whether preventive patrol on the part of the police reduces crime in a given community or society. However, the second question is equally relevant and important. In relation to this, we can examine the effects of various national characteristics by cataloging the range and types of policing and police practices. For example, how does a country's shift from agricultural to an industrial and then to an informational society change the nature of social control in general, and policing in particular? Further, many African countries, such as Nigeria and the Ivory Coast, only recently became independent after centuries of colonialism, under the United Kingdom and France, respectively. How do their police systems adapt to the changed social arrangements of independence, particularly since many of these forces were, for a long time, in charge of keeping the colonized Africans in line? The quote at the beginning of this chapter captured some of the effects that these society-wide changes have had. However, by considering the comparative experiences of various countries that, in historical sequence, have undergone or are currently undergoing these transformations, we can arrive at a convincing answer to this question.

Third, considering the experiences of other countries allows us to increase the chances for success in our own reform efforts. Bayley (1999: 10) cites the Japanese police use of **kobans** (small, continuously staffed, neighborhood ministations that allow continuous police interaction with residents) as an example. Other countries (including the United States) have imported and utilized these neighborhood ministations as part of a thrust aimed at promoting partnerships between the police and the community in carrying out police work.

Another example is the recent popularity, in the United States, of citizen police academies. These programs allow ordinary citizens to experience, through a series of weekly classes, some aspects of police preparation and training. The premise underlying these academies is again to build bridges between the police and the public, such that the former are seen as an integral part of the community and not as outsiders who show up only when there is trouble. The original idea for these academies was derived from the United Kingdom.

Finally, Bayley (1999) notes that by studying the police forces of other countries we gain a better perspective on our own. In a sense, the police forces of all countries embody the varying results of a negotiated balance between the extent of intrusiveness of governmental power and the importance placed on individual citizens, their liberties, and their privacy. Cultural and historical forces shape much of this balance. When we visit other countries, we often wonder about the demeanor and attitudes (officious, threatening, and suspicious in some countries versus pleasant, correct, and friendly in others) of the police personnel we encounter and our own reactions to those attitudes. The suspicion that Americans have for untrammeled governmental power manifests itself in how we have chosen to order our policing (mostly locally controlled and subject to major legal and constitutional constraints in carrying out their duties). Yet, at certain points in history and in the interests of our own security and safety, we are willing to renegotiate the balance, for example, as a result of airplane hijackings and bombings, no one objects to going through security checkpoints at airports and being subjected to body searches. Sometimes, we may not be so willing, for example, the growing opposition in recent times to the use of camera radar by the police to nab speeders and those running stoplights at traffic intersections. Studying the police from other countries helps us learn a little more about our own police officers and the historical and cultural forces that have shaped them, their interactions with us, and ultimately, American society.

The police are a social group that operates in society, often in support of the existing social order, interacting everyday in countless ways with other groups and individuals. Both the structure of police organizations and the process of policing need to be analyzed sociologically and comparatively. This is the ultimate goal of this textbook, and we view it as the opposite of technical and insular presentations about policing. Join us and let us get to work.

As mentioned earlier, to get a sense of the comparative sociological approach in studying policing, consider the issue of police corruption in Argentina in the following box. As you go through it, consider the differences and similarities with United States policing (e.g., centralized versus decentralized police departments, differences and similarities in corrupt practices, as well as measures to instill police accountability in the two countries, etc.) and see what you can conclude overall with regard to the phenomenon of police corruption, an issue that we will return to in Chapter 13.

 ## SUMMARY

Policing, which was created in the mid-1800s, has undergone many changes and developments in the twentieth century. Although nongovernmental entities have begun to carry out some policing functions, we continue to think of it as a government agency. Given the complex nature of contemporary policing, it is necessary to use both a sociological and an international (or comparative) approach to studying it.

There are three reasons for using a sociological approach. Several prominent police researchers were trained as sociologists and this informs their contributions. Sociologists are interested in studying social (which are often police) problems and offering possible solutions for them. Finally, sociologists use systematic scientific research methods to arrive at their conclusions. In carrying out research on social behavior, sociologists use a combination of the sociological imagination that links social forces to individual behavior, stated hypotheses about the behavior in question and its causes, and verifiable methods for testing those hypotheses.

Sociologists use three major perspectives in analyzing the police in society. Functionalism focuses on how the police as a group act in ways that promote social order and cohesion. Conflict theory assumes that the police represent the interests of the elite in any given society. In contrast to the macrolevel analyses of functionalists and conflict theorists, interactionism studies events and situations at the microlevel and pays attention to the importance of meanings in these interactions. It is possible to use one or more of these perspectives to analyze policing fruitfully.

Although we live in a global society, police researchers have tended not to analyze policing using this approach. We intend to incorporate the experiences of the police and police forces in other countries into this text. In addition to simple curiosity, there are several other important reasons. These include the following. By studying the police cross-nationally, we may extend our knowledge of various policing possibilities. It will help us develop greater insights into human behavior. Looking at the experiences of other countries may increase the chances of success with our own policing reform efforts. Finally, we will end up gaining a better perspective on our own society and ourselves.

 ## KEY TERMS

Applied sociology: The branch of sociology that uses scientific methods to delineate problems that afflict society and to test solutions for them.

Comparative (cross-national) approach: Analyzing information from the United States and at least one other country on various police topics.

Conflict perspective: A sociological paradigm that focuses on the competition that exists between groups (racial/ethnic groups, tribes, social classes, genders, age groups) in any given society.

Functionalist perspective: A sociological paradigm that focuses on studying and understanding how societies develop and maintain social order.

Globalization: The increasing interconnectedness of the economies, peoples, and to a lesser extent, the politics of various countries of the world.

Hypothesis: A tentative statement that suggests how two classes of phenomena may be connected or related.

Interactionist perspective: Studying the police with a view to tease out the patterns and meanings that are created when individuals associate with each other.

Koban: Small, continuously staffed, neighborhood ministations in Japan that allow continuous police interaction with residents.

Latent functions: Social functions that are less obvious, and often unanticipated.

Macrolevel analysis: Studying the police as a group or organization that operates within larger collectivities such as classes, communities, and societies.

Manifest functions: Social functions that appear to be obvious and intended.

Microlevel analysis: Studying the police with attention to the nature and meanings as well as the details attached to specific settings and situations within which individuals or groups interact.

Multilateralize: The process by which governments no longer monopolize the provision of policing services to the public and where many groups in society have chosen to protect and secure themselves.

Pure sociology: The branch of sociology that uses scientific methods to study and describe society and social behavior.

Socialization: The process by which individuals learn, through interaction with others, how to think and behave in general, and as members of a group or culture.

Sociological imagination: In studying the influence of the social on the individual, that which helps us connect individual behavior to the social structure and culture that produced it.

Sociology: The discipline that is a way of understanding and explaining sociohistorical transformations systematically and as a means for social reform and renewal by solving the problems associated with these changes.

Symbolic interactionism: A form of the interactionist perspective that is based on the premise that human beings, while born with the capacity for thought, will have that capacity molded by a series of interactions with others which help individuals learn what is meant or symbolized.

REVIEW QUESTIONS

1. What does knowledge of sociology as a discipline contribute to the study of policing?

2. Analyze policing using the three sociological perspectives that you learned in this chapter. How do they differ?

3. How does learning about police corruption in Argentina help us understand similar corruption in the United States?

DISCUSSION QUESTIONS

1. Which sociological perspective on policing discussed in this chapter do you most agree with? Please explain.

2. Discuss the benefits of studying policing comparatively using other countries.

3. Discuss the idea mentioned in this chapter that policing is now a global activity.

REFERENCES

Axelrod, Alan; Charles Phillips and Kurt Kemper (1996) *Cops, Crooks and Criminologists*. New York: Facts on File.

Bayley, David H. (1999) "Policing: the World Stage." Pp. 1–12. In R. I. Mawby (ed.) *Policing Across the World: Issues for the Twenty-first Century*. London: UCL Press.

Bayley, David H. and Clifford D. Shearing (2001) *The New Structure of Policing: Description, Conceptualization and Research Agenda*. Washington, DC: National Institute of Justice.

Berg, Bruce L. (1992) *Law Enforcement: An Introduction to the Police in Society*. Boston, MA: Allyn and Bacon.

Chambliss, William J. (1988) *Exploring Criminology*. New York: Macmillan.

Charon, Joel (1985) *Symbolic Interactionism: An Introduction, an Interpretation, an Integration*. Second Edition. Englewood Cliffs, NJ: Prentice Hall.

Collins, Randall (1975) *Conflict Sociology: Towards an Exploratory Science*. New York: Academic Press.

Conroy, John (2000) *Unspeakable Acts, Ordinary People: The Dynamics of Torture*. New York: Alfred A. Knopf.

Cox, Steven M. and Jack D. Fitzgerald (1983) *Police in Community Relations: Critical Issues*. Dubuque, IA: Wm. C. Brown.

Faia, Michael A. (1986) *Dynamic Functionalism: Strategy and Tactics*. Cambridge, UK: Cambridge University Press.

Fitzgerald, Terence J. (2000) *Police in Society*. New York: H. W. Wilson.

Giddens, Anthony; Mitchell Duneier and Richard P. Appelbaum *(2007) Introduction to Sociology*. New York: W. W. Norton.

Manis, Jerome and Bernard Meltzer (eds.) (1978) *Symbolic Interactionism: A Reader in Social Psychology*. Third Edition. Boston, MA: Allyn and Bacon.

Manning, Peter K. (1997) *Police Work: The Social Organization of Police Work*. Second Edition. Prospect Heights, IL: Waveland Press.

Mills, C. Wright (1959) *The Sociological Imagination*. London: Oxford University Press.

Oyen, Else (1990) *Comparative Methodology: Theory and Practice in International Social Research*. London: Sage.

Ragin, Charles C. (1987) *The Comparative Method: Moving Beyond Qualitative and Quantitative Strategies*. Berkeley, CA: University of California Press.

Ritzer, George (1975) *Sociology: A Multiple Paradigm Science*. Boston, MA: Allyn and Bacon.

Ritzer, George (1988) *Contemporary Sociological Theory*. Second Edition. New York: Alfred A. Knopf.

Ruane, Janet M. and Karen A. Cerulo (1997) *Second Thoughts: Seeing Conventional Wisdom through the Sociological Eye*. Thousand Oaks, CA: Pine Forge Press.

Waddington, P. A. J. (1999) "Armed and Unarmed Policing." Pp. 151—166. In Rob I. Mawby (ed.) *Policing Across the World: Issues for the Twenty-first Century*. London: UCL Press.

Walton, John (1990) *Sociology and Critical Inquiry: The Work, Tradition and Purpose*. Second Edition. Belmont, CA: Wadsworth.

Sebastián Sal

POLICE CORRUPTION IN ARGENTINA

Police corruption in Argentina has been increasing over the last thirty years. During the 1970s, police forces were given more weapons, autonomy, and a military organization to fight terrorism. After the 1976 "coup d'etat," militarization of the Argentinean police force increased. This served to elevate corruption. No organization or individual, except the army, which was also corrupted, could control the police. When democracy arrived in 1983, new administrations attempted to solve corruption problems in the police with varying levels of enthusiasm. However, in parts of Argentina, the police and politicians continued to treat each other as *partners*. "This phenomenon has existed and is historic," said Mr. León Arslanian, former minister of public security of the Buenos Aires province. "The political class has contributed to the phenomenon of police corruption in various ways," he maintained in an interview (Rohter, 2004). Some have hinted that part of the money collected by the police from illegal activities supports the Peronistas (former ruling party) (Rohter, 2003).

The pace of demilitarization or withdrawing the armed forces from police duties, and removing many personnel from temporary assignments to law enforcement duties has quickened. (This also took place in other Latin America countries.) For example, in the Province of Buenos Aires, Argentina, there are frequent "purges" of police officers and deputies. Many unemployed police and deputies afterwards form criminal gangs called "*mano desocupada*." In 2003, President Néstor Kirchner pledged to cleanse the Buenos Aires Provincial Police, a 47,000-member force that he described as "oozing with pus." Purges were conducted there and within the troubled Federal Police leading to the removal of hundreds of officers. Corruption in the police force (federal and provincial) is still very high. In the last Transparency International Report (2007), the Argentinean police was labeled one of the most corrupt institutions in the country, scoring 4.3 points out of a possible high of 5 points.

Anecdotes of petty bribery related to traffic violations are legion. In December 2006, a local police commander was suspended for demanding payment from a local business in exchange for security. Overall, in 2006, 269 serious allegations of police corruption were received in Mendoza City, in western Argentina, and 31 officers, a record number, were fired. Alleged offenses included charging for the return of stolen property, helping a gang of youths rob a mall, "trigger happy" shooting sprees, and demanding money from families of homicide victims in return for advancing investigations (McMahon). The Argentinean Institution against Discrimination (INADI) stated that Contraventional Codes in most provinces give the police discretionary powers to stop people for supposed infractions against public morals. These practices "legitimize every class of abuses and police corruption." A simple manifestation of affection between people of the same sex in the street is a motive for detention. Arbitrary arrest—to investigate criminal records—is a discriminatory action taken against these minorities. National Law #23.950 allows police agents, in very few and exceptional cases, to arrest people on the grounds of serious circumstances or "suspicious behavior" ("suspicious behavior" is not an objective question. People can be stopped for identification, because police functions include the prevention of crimes. The "stopping for ID" must be done with prudence and fairness) (see Dell Aquila, 1991) that makes the officer presume that a crime was, has been, or would be committed by a person. Police officers often abuse that law against illegal residents because they know that these people do not have any identification. Police officers collect bribes from that minority (CEL, 2001), a clear violation of basic human rights.

Strong governmental policies to eradicate corruption in the country's police departments are lacking. The administration needs a long-term policy to deal with police corruption, one that uses judicial power, prosecutors, special financial units, and anti-corruption offices. The government cannot fight police corruption by itself. It needs the Argentinean media and people on its side.

References

CELS report about Illegal Arrest (2001) *Detenciones por Averiguación de Identidad. Argumentos para la discusión sobre sus usos y abusos*. Tiscornia y otros.

Dell Aquila, S. G. Cámara Nacional en lo Criminal, Sala II. Published in Boletín de Jurisprudencia, 1991, Nro.3.

McMahon, Luke Hard Graft http://www.wine-republic.com/articles.php?id_cat=5&id_art=102 (accessed August 18, 2009).

Rohter, Larry (2003) Argentine Moves Against Police Corruption. http://query.nytimes.com/gst/fullpage.html?res=9D05E3DC1138F934A25752C1A9659C8B63.

Rohter, Larry (2004) Police Corruption Plagues Argentines and President. http://www.globalexchange.org/countries/americas/argentina/2386.html.

CHAPTER 2

Public policing as we recognize it today may be a recent historical development, but social control is as old as human societies. Social control is a fundamental requisite for the survival of any society, whether the society is from the past, present, or future. Although human beings are by nature social creatures and choose to congregate with others for mutual protection and emotional satisfaction, eons of evolution have demonstrated how social living requires considerable compromise, adaptation, and forced civil behavior. (LaGrange, 1993: 76)

A fire department rescue chief, left, stands watch at an annual samba carnival parade while police officers block a crossing on a street in Tokyo, Saturday, Aug. 25, 2007. (Credit: © AP Photo/Junji Kurokawa)

POLICE AND SOCIAL CONTROL

OBJECTIVES:

1. The student will understand crime in relation to values, beliefs, and norms.
2. The student will understand crime as a form of deviance.
3. The student will understand the three levels of social control and policing as a form of formal social control.
4. The student will understand the functionalist, conflict, and interactionist approaches to policing and social control.
5. The student will learn about policing and social control on an international level.

We often curse and rail while driving our vehicles on the roads, for example, for having to wait at a stoplight or for pedestrians who are crossing the street and when we have to reduce our speeds in residential neighborhoods. However, imagine for a minute whether contemporary American urban life would be possible if we did not have traffic signals and signage that "force" us to conform and be civil to others. What would happen? No one would be available to tell us when to turn left or right, what the appropriate speed level is in different parts of town or on the highway, when to stop for or yield to other vehicles and pedestrians, and when not to do so. Chaos would be an understatement for the resulting problems. Throughout history, human beings have wrestled with an analogous issue: how to regulate the "social traffic" among all members of their societies. Regulating human social interaction and thereby maintaining internal order is of extreme importance. Order leads to predictability in the many dealings that individual members of society engage in with each other through the course of their daily lives. In contemporary society, the ultimate responsibility for ensuring that "social traffic" flows smoothly in an orderly and predictable manner and that major problems in social life are taken care of has been given to paid professionals (e.g., doctors, lawyers, psychologists, social workers, police officers, and alcohol or drug counselors). Historically, this is a fairly recent development. The regulation of, and control over, the conduct of members of a society has historically been carried out in two ways. First, it was done by religious proscriptions (e.g., the god given admonition "Thou shalt not kill" in the Ten Commandments) that individuals were supposed to learn and absorb. Second, it was accomplished through the active guidance of families and clans to their own members especially when young, along with their reactions to wrongdoing. Only in certain specific or extreme circumstances (failure to pay taxes or tributes, rebellion, war) did the rulers or government interfere in everyday situations, often using soldiers or royal guards to do so.

Policing involves the use of a specialized set of paid, uniformed individuals who are members of a paramilitary organization (acting as an arm of the government) and who have been given a monopoly over the use of force for the purposes of enforcing **criminal laws**, maintaining order, and serving the public during peacetime. Paraphrasing Goldstein (1977), an authority on the place of police in society, their functions are as follows. The police are expected to:

- prevent and control behavior that threatens life and property;
- help individuals in danger of physical harm, for example, victims of violence;
- maintain the orderly movement of people and vehicles;
- help those who have difficulty in taking care of themselves, such as those who are drunk or high, those who are mentally ill, those who are physically disabled, the elderly, and the very young;
- reduce or resolve conflicts between individuals and groups, or between individuals, groups, and the government;
- identify issues that may eventually turn into serious problems; and,
- contribute to a feeling of safety and security in the jurisdictions they are responsible for.

criminal laws

Definitions of violations that are deemed to be important enough for society to join with the victim in the official reaction against the offender.

As we will see in Chapter 4, this type of specialized organization is a fairly new phenomenon in human history, having been first developed in England in the early 1800s. How is this organization embedded in a large social structure and culture? In this chapter, we discuss two interrelated matters that are answers to this important question. First, we show how a society's culture, specifically, in the form of its **values**, beliefs, and **norms**, affects expectations regarding the behavior of its members (including what is to be expected of the police). Second, we show how the police are an important (though not necessarily the only or even the major) part of wide-ranging system of social control employed by contemporary societies. We characterized social control earlier (in somewhat general terms) as a given society's mechanisms for regulating the behavior of its members and for ensuring order and predictability in the social interactions that occur within it.

values

The abstract standards that cultures use to communicate to members what is ideally expected of them.

norms

The rules and expectations by which society instructs and directs the behavior of individual members.

VALUES, BELIEFS, NORMS, DEVIANCE, AND CRIME

Many students of criminal justice are no doubt familiar with the character Dirty Harry, portrayed in a number of movies in the late 1970s and 1980s by the famous Hollywood actor Clint Eastwood. The character, a police officer who (often acting alone) flouted official departmental policies and rules for the sake of getting the "bad guys" most of whom he often killed or made to suffer in creative ways, proved immensely popular. This reveals something about the characteristics we deem to be admirable (or that we value) in American society and culture. Dirty Harry did not bother with rules and paperwork; he was a practical man of action. He worked alone. He kept busy doing detective work and was efficient and successful, that is, as a result of his tenacious and single-minded efforts he always got his "bad guy." Sociologists suggest that this character (and others like him in the movies, on television, and in best-selling print fiction) remains popular in the United States because he reflects certain assumptions regarding the standards that Americans make about how an "ideal" man would think, feel, and act.

The term, values, is used to denote such criteria. Values are defined as the abstract standards that cultures use to communicate to members what is ideally expected of them. Values are derived from the culture of a given society. The culture of a group of people generally reflects their geography, that is, where they are located (the United States occupies much of the North American continent with lots of space available for human expansion and use); form of society (the United States developed into a democratic industrial/information society with a capitalist economy), and history (the United States was relatively isolated from the rest of the world during its formative years). These values will instruct us on what to look for in terms of what is considered correct, just, and beautiful. Although the large size and heterogeneous, multicultural population of the United States make it difficult for sociologists to identify core American values, there have been many attempts over the years to do so. The sociologist Robin Williams (1970) made the most famous of these attempts to define core American values. He designates ten values that he sees as being central to American society and culture.

1. Equal opportunity. We like society to guarantee not equality of outcome, but (as much as possible) for individuals to be given equal chances to get ahead in life.

2. Achievement and success. Winning and individual competitive accomplishment is prized above all in our society, as opposed to cooperation and group solidarity.

3. Material comfort. It is important to have money and to enjoy the goods and services that flow from it. Self-sacrifice and the lack of material goods are less valued.

4. Activity and work. We think that individuals should be busy and not spend too much time thinking and worrying about problems and issues.

5. Practicality and efficiency. We are forever interested in quicker and more effective ways of getting things done, often without regard for the consequences, for example, even if it means people that may lose jobs or that the natural environment may be affected.

6. Progress. We believe in novelty, continuous improvement, and generally assume that the present is better than the past, and that the future will be better than the present.

7. Science. We think that science and technology (applied science) can be employed to solve all our problems. Reason, logic, and systematic analysis are valued over intuition, emotion, and personal belief.

8. Democracy and free enterprise. The bases for our political and our economic institutions are individual rights (to choose our leaders) and to make market choices (regarding what to buy and sell).

9. Freedom. We believe that individuals should be free from major societal constraints to make their own choices and live their own lives (e.g., "the pursuit of happiness" as an individual right).

10. Racism and group superiority. Although there are countervailing values of equal opportunity and individualism, people in American society are often classified and evaluated on the basis of racial and group characteristics, for example, skin color, gender, ethnicity, and socio-economic status.

This is obviously not an exhaustive list. For example, patriotism, many would argue, is an important American value. It is not to be found on this list, although group superiority (as in the superiority of the United States and the American way) may cover this. However, using Williams's list, we can see several values that we expect members of the police to possess and ascribe to them. Entry into policing as an occupation is supposed to be based on equal opportunity (i.e., merit), while promotions are decided on the basis of how successful one has been in carrying out police work. We want police officers to be actively out and about enforcing the law and to constantly look for ways to improve reaction times, case processing, and in dealing with the public. We expect the police to use scientific methods (fingerprints, DNA analysis, psychological profiling) of crime detection. At the same time, the police are often perceived to be high-handed and biased in dealing with minorities and sexist in terms of valuing male police officers over female ones. You will notice that some of the values (e.g., group superiority vs. equal opportunity) are in conflict with each other, and that these conflicts can be found in policing as well. Thus, policing in America is found to follow the values and reflect the value conflicts of the larger American society.

While values tend to be abstract, **beliefs** (which are based on the former) are explicit and more concrete statements that members of a society accept as true. For example, we believe, on the basis of our values, that the American form of government or economy is the best. We are likely to similarly assume on the basis of our values regarding individual freedom (and related privacy) that the police should not intrude too much into our private affairs and transactions. Such a belief was sorely tested in the aftermath of the September 11, 2001, attack on the World Trade Center in New York and the Pentagon in Washington, D.C. If we had a more intrusive law enforcement presence that aggressively targeted and watched people who entered the country (i.e., including the terrorists), some will argue, we could have prevented the plane hijackings and terror attacks. Similar arguments were made again in the wake of the failed plot to blow up American airliners over the Atlantic in 2006, although ironically, the British police were successful in acting on a tip from a concerned community member, a typical law enforcement tactic. However, we would have difficulty squaring our beliefs regarding the importance of freedom and privacy with such an effort that would result in much greater police involvement in and surveillance of the daily lives of citizens and residents of the United States.

Flowing from the values that societies hold dear and the beliefs that they foster are rules that help members navigate through a variety of situations that occur in society. In other words, we are taught in the process of growing up in (or moving to) a particular culture, how we are to negotiate various events and happenings in daily life that we encounter. For example, we have learned that we should not interrupt people who are busily going about their jobs (unless it is really crucial), whether it is waiting tables at the restaurant, counting cash at the supermarket, or a business executive making a presentation. This is based on the value of activity and work and the belief that the individual's job is more important than anything else. The rule of not interrupting someone on the job is derived from applying these values to workplace situations. Such rules are referred to as norms. Norms are the rules and expectations by which society instructs and directs the behavior of individual members. Some norms tell us what to do (you should study and get good grades while in school) while others tell us what not to do (you should not smoke marijuana).

Sociologists beginning with William Graham Sumner (1959 [1906]) have identified two major types of norms. These are differentiated on the basis of the importance that is attached by society to adhering to each type and the reactions that would follow from violating them. Minor, or less important norms, are known as **folkways**. For example, if in response to the question "How are you?" you were to give the questioner a detailed, blow-by-blow account of your current physical, mental, and emotional state, you would be violating a folkway. The questioner may think you are a little strange, and avoid you (or minimally, avoid asking that question again) as a result. You do not suffer major consequences for this violation. The same cannot be said if you were to flout the major, more important norms that are known as **mores**. For

beliefs

Explicit and concrete statements that members of a society accept as true.

folkways

Minor, or less important norms.

mores

Major, or more important norms.

example, if an adult were to engage in sexual relations with a person below the age of responsibility, that would violate a more. The violator, if discovered is likely to be punished both legally (a long prison term) and socially (labeling and shunning). Laws are very important mores that have been codified, that is, they have been written down in penal codes through legislation, and are enforced by the police, prosecutors, courts, and correctional authorities acting in the name of society. At the same time, there are mores that are not laws (e.g., we understand that we should not drink to excess, but if we were to do this at home and not in public and were reasonably quiet about it, we would not be subject to arrest by the police).

Deviance is behavior that violates norms, both folkways and mores. We are taught at an early age that it is rude to interrupt someone who is speaking (violation of a folkway) and also that it is illegal to steal someone else's money (violation of a more that has been codified as a law). Acts of deviance that are minor are generally dealt with informally (people may avoid the violator, or laugh at him or her) while those that are major are taken seriously and dealt with formally (arrest, charging, trial, sentencing, prison term, etc.). It is possible therefore to see that the police are in the business of dealing with major forms of deviance that society has specifically codified in the form of criminal laws. Acts of deviance that violate criminal laws (or **crimes**) are deemed to be important enough for society to join with the victim in the official reaction against the offender. This is the reason why criminal cases are identified, for example, as "The state of California versus Jones." This is because criminal deviance is seen as a violation against society.

From a legal perspective, there are other forms of deviance which are also codified, but which the police do not deal with, given that they are only one cog in the system of social control. These are **violations** of **civil laws** often involving conflicts between individuals living and interacting with each other in society. For example, there are contractual disputes between landlords and tenants, or between employers and employees. While the state is interested in settling these disputes, it does not take the side of either party. If approached by one of them, the state arbitrates and renders judgment finding for either the plaintiff (the complainer) or the defendant (the person alleged by the former to have done something wrong). As a result, civil cases are usually designated in the form "Hernandez versus Smith."

Returning to the forms of deviance that the police are specifically required to deal with, that is, crimes, we can see that there are further divisions (in terms of seriousness) among these. Generally, societies accord the highest level of criminal seriousness to **treason**, for example, acts that involve the overthrow of the government and collaborating with the enemy in times of war and hostility. Since it threatens the very existence of the reacting government, it draws the most amount of reaction and punishments are likely to be severe. More than likely, punishment for treason will include consideration, and often imposition, of the death penalty. The next level of criminal seriousness is given to the acts designated as **felonies**. The third level of seriousness is for **misdemeanors**. At the bottom of the heap are petty offenses, often called violations. Differences in the seriousness with which these offenses are viewed also means that there are differences in the police powers that go along with officially dealing with various incidents that exemplify these levels of crime.

deviance

Behavior that violates norms, both folkways and mores.

crimes

Acts of deviance that violate criminal laws

violations

Petty offenses; the last level of serious crimes.

civil laws

Definitions of violations involving conflicts between individuals living and interacting with each other in society.

treason

Acts that involve the overthrow of the government and collaborating with the enemy in times of war and hostility. These are defined as the most serious crimes.

felonies

Second level of serious crimes.

misdemeanors

The third level of serious crimes.

Before moving away from the topic of where crime as a form of deviance fits overall in the context of a society's culture and **socialization**, we should make two associated observations. First, the police (as a sector of the criminal justice system) are, as we have seen, only one possible form of reaction to deviance. Others such as priests and ministers (representing religion) as well as physicians and mental health professionals (representing medicine) may also be (and historically have been) pressed into service in this social enterprise. The major difference between the police on the one hand and religious and medical personnel on the other is that the police have a monopoly over the use of force, extending to deadly force, in dealing with deviant behavior (e.g., killing someone in a hostage situation). Clergy and medical professionals are not allowed to use killing as a means of solving problematic situations; and, in fact, are encouraged to preserve life, to the extent possible.

For much of recorded history, crime was not distinguished from sin and evil, and the clergy were the major group involved in dealing with human beings who were lying, cheating, stealing, killing each other, etc. Such behaviors invoked moral judgments of sinfulness, evil, and immorality from the formal representatives of various religious traditions. Religious means of dealing with these problems took the forms of torture, pain, and sometimes, death for the offender. They justified the utilization of these cruelties on the assumption that the devil or some other evil spirits were the root causes of the bad behavior in question.

Peter Conrad and Joseph Schneider (1992) refer to the use of medical diagnoses for nonconforming behavior as the **medicalization of deviance**. Here, certain forms of deviance, although resulting in criminal acts, are defined as arising out of an individual's illness and pathology. This approach exists side by side with the current conceptions that some forms of deviance are criminal and ought to be dealt with by the police and the rest of the criminal justice system. This means that nowadays, rather than (and also often in addition to) arresting and ultimately punishing that individual, he or she is seen as needing to be treated for their sickness or ailment. Thus, someone who steals to support his or her drug and/or excessive alcohol consumption habit, is diagnosed and classified as needing specific counseling and medical treatment for their proneness to dependence on these substances.

Second, police reactions to acts of criminal deviance are not always uniform. For example, the police, in order to arrest a drug seller, may ignore or even support the drug usage of an informant. They may ignore the illegal and severe beating and assault of a criminal suspect by a fellow police officer (see our discussion of Police Deviance in Chapter 13) or those usually committed by persons of high social status (e.g., Medicare fraud by physicians). This means that reaction to criminal behavior is often subject to a variety of contextual influences. Of course, everything else being equal, there are certain crimes (e.g., homicide) that the police are going to react to in a much more forceful manner than others (e.g., vice and traffic offenses). It is possible to observe here that even among crimes that are supposed to be major norm violations, there are levels of seriousness in the responses they evoke. These are often based on perceptions shared by members of a society about the seriousness of certain crimes as opposed to others. Some classes of crimes, referred to as **high consensus crimes** (e.g., crimes against persons,

socialization

The process by which society inculcates values to its members through a variety of institutions that act as agencies in teaching, modeling, and encouraging them to behave along expected lines.

medicalization of deviance

Certain forms of deviance, although resulting in criminal acts, are defined as arising out of an individual's illness and pathology.

high consensus crimes

Classes of crimes (e.g., crimes against persons, property crimes) evoke more reaction and commitment of resources than others.

property crimes) evoke more reactions and commitment of resources than others. The latter lower-priority offenses, or **low consensus crimes**, are typically ones that both the public and the police are conflicted about and are controversial politically (e.g., drug offenses, gambling, prostitution, jaywalking, etc.). There is often disagreement as to whether these behaviors ought to be criminalized and whether police resources ought to be expended in enforcing such controversial laws.

SOCIAL CONTROL: PERSONAL, INFORMAL, FORMAL

Sociologists have shown that society inculcates values to its members through a variety of institutions that act as agencies of society in teaching, modeling, and encouraging them to behave along expected lines. When we assimilate these values and behave according to the norms that flow from them, we are less likely to commit acts of deviance, both large (e.g., murdering someone else or stealing their money) and small (e.g., wearing our clothes backwards in public or eating mashed potatoes with our fingers). Sociologists refer to such transmissions of values and norms to individual members as successful socialization. This is the most efficient and effective form of control over deviance (i.e., it occurs even before the individual acts). Another name for the almost unconscious rejection of deviant behavior is **personal or self-control.** An individual who has been successfully socialized by society has developed an internal mechanism that rejects outright the possibility of his or her engaging in lying, cheating, stealing, or killing someone else. While it may be argued that self-control is not social, in the sense of involving others, nevertheless it is the values and norms we learn from important others that affect us so much that we censor or control our own behavior.

However, as we know, personal control over deviant behavior sometimes does not happen. If socialization proved to be successful in every case, we would not be talking about dealing with various major and minor forms of deviance, including criminal behavior. To ensure that those who will not or cannot personally control (in other words, those who would contemplate) the possibility of engaging in deviant behavior, another level of control exists in all societies. This level is known as **informal social control**. Notice the two features of this term. First, it includes the word "social." This means that at this level of control, it is no more a personal matter; others in society have become involved. Next, there is the implication of a lack of formality. This means that it occurs at an interpersonal, interactional level between people who know each other. This level of control occurs when we do not do something deviant because we fear the negative judgments of those who are close or dear to us (what sociologists would refer to as significant others), for example, parents, spouses, ministers, teachers, conventional friends, etc. We, therefore, do not engage in deviance since we generally want to be thought of in a positive way by those who are important to us.

Obviously, if all people avoided doing anything deviant because they were afraid of the negative evaluations of significant others whenever they personally contemplated it, there would be no need for the next level of control. This is known as **formal social control**. Again, note two characteristics of the term. First, while it occurs socially, it is

---

low consensus crimes

Lower-priority offenses that typically both the public and the police are conflicted about and are controversial politically (e.g., drug offenses, gambling, prostitution, jaywalking, etc.).

personal (or self-) control

Individuals are less likely to commit acts of deviance because they have assimilated societal values and behave according to the norms that flow from them.

informal social control

When individuals do not do something deviant because they fear the negative judgments of those who are close or dear to them.

formal social control

Particular individuals and agencies designated to maintain control and order in society become involved in reacting to deviant behavior.

certainly not informal anymore. Formal social control means that particular individuals and agencies designated to maintain control and order in society become involved in dealing with deviant behavior. These agencies include the police (dealing with criminal deviance), mental hospitals (dealing with mental illness), and others. Usually, these agencies operate on a fairly long-term basis and use personnel (e.g., police officers) who have a monopoly of powers in reacting to or dealing with a specific form of deviance, that is, crimes.

Let us use an example that will be familiar to most college students to illustrate the three levels of social control. Think about the way you and your classmates approach the issue of cheating on tests. For some (we hope, all the readers of this text) cheating on a test would be unthinkable. This is personal control at work. Others would be tempted to cheat, but would fear the negative perceptions of their professor (we know some of you will find this fear of your instructor downright humorous) or their parents if they were caught. Now we have informal social control operating. Yet others among your classmates, would not worry about these negative perceptions, but would be deterred from cheating because they would think about the official consequences if they were caught. They would be punished by their college or university after disciplinary hearings and given failing grades in that course which would then become part of their academic records. Notice the involvement of designated authorities (heads of departments, college deans, student disciplinary committees, registrars) in the formal process of dealing with this form of deviance.

It should be clear from the above, that the police function as agents of the state (Melossi, 2009) and as authorities of formal social control who deal with particular forms of deviance: the violations of major norms (or mores) that have been legally codified and are officially enforced by the criminal justice system. At the same time, the police do not have a completely free hand in democracies (as opposed to totalitarian and authoritarian countries) to control crime and do away with deviance using any method or means. As Berg (1992: 3) puts it, "Free societies depend upon a balance between a person's ability to act independently and without fear of official reprisal and a person's responsibility not to infringe upon other's abilities to act independently as well." This balance is held, ever so gingerly, in the hand of that society's police.

POLICING AS FORMAL SOCIAL CONTROL: THREE SOCIOLOGICAL PERSPECTIVES

In Chapter 1, we described three perspectives that sociologists use to analyze and make sense of the social phenomena that exist in any given society. Let us take each one of these in turn.

Functionalists are interested in analyzing what any given social institution or practice contributes to that society's continued survival and functioning. From their point of view, having the police around allows ordinary members of society to operate in an orderly way by dealing with criminal deviants and other "trouble makers" who refuse to follow the rules and regulations of the community that they live in. Given that the police is the only public agency available and operating twenty-four hours a day and seven days a week dealing with a host of problems and issues that others cannot or will not, they are therefore, vital to the smooth functioning of society. The police contribute to social order by making sure that people meet interactional expectations in everyday life (e.g., obeying traffic rules, not robbing or assaulting fellow citizens) and by carrying out other activities such as patrol (a visible reminder of police presence) and investigation (leading to the arrest and punishment of criminals). These activities affirm and reaffirm the importance of social norms and strengthen important cultural values.

Conflict theorists believe that society is composed of competing groups and are generally interested in which group benefits from social arrangements, as they exist. If society is an arena in which various groups fight for the control of scarce resources, who really benefits from having the police around as "social controllers" and "behavioral regulators"? Conflict theorists will identify the powerful in society as the ones who stand to gain from having all forms of social control, particularly those involving the police. Inequalities in surveillance, arrest, and in what constitutes police priorities are major concerns of conflict theorists who therefore conclude that the police are not impartial but biased in their enforcement of the law. Typical police activities almost always target the poor and the powerless, people who are often the primary focus of attempts at controlling deviant behavior. For example, a homeless vagrant, who is drunk and snoring in a library, is likely to be removed by the police when complaints are received from the library staff. However, the police will not (or cannot) do the same to the drunken president of a neighboring bank who is behind closed doors in his office. At a more concrete level of regulating individual behavior, is there any satisfactory legal reason why possession of "rock cocaine" (generally associated with the poor and minority groups) is likely to be punished more severely than possession of "powder cocaine" (associated with the rich and majority group)? Needless to say, police are much more active and interested in stopping, questioning, and arresting suspected minority drug traffickers. Reiner (1991) notes that various studies of the police have shown that most of their work consists of maintaining order in public places, especially among the less privileged members of society. Thus, the social control of behavior overall, and the involvement of the police, always takes the form of a dagger aimed on behalf of the elite toward the powerless. Parks (1970: 76) notes, for example, that the "morality enforced [by the police] is always the morality of those in power and it is primarily enforced upon those without power."

The third sociological perspective, interactionism, pays attention to the microlevel of human behavior. For them, the many interactions between individual members and social control personnel, such as the police, make up the experience of social control. Thus, situational characteristics are very important in figuring out how social control of deviant behavior takes place and, specifically, how the police operate in their day-to-day encounters with the citizens. Wiley and Hudik (1974) test a variety of interactionisms that focuses on exchange relations in encounters between the police and the public. Exchange theory holds that interactions between human beings involve various costs and rewards for the parties involved. The study assumed that in any given police-citizen encounter, the more rewarding it was for the citizen (e.g., if the police officer took the trouble to explain why the citizen was being stopped), the more willing the citizen was to cooperate with the police. The less rewarding and more costly the interactions (e.g., when officers did not explain the purpose behind stopping and questioning), the less cooperative the citizen was. Situationally, therefore, rather than treating every individual being stopped and questioned as a potential criminal, a more productive use of the officer's time, particularly in an American cultural context (with its emphasis on freedom and equality), would be to explain the crime being investigated (e.g., there was a call about a gunshot and a loud scream) and to enlist the citizen's assistance. The citizen would perceive this encounter as a satisfying and rewarding form of cooperation with the authorities (i.e., the social control system).

We have emphasized the importance of cultural values as the basis for the form of the police in that society as well as their interactions with the public that they serve. Let us take a look at policing in a society with a different set of cultural values, Japan, to understand how both the nature of criminal deviance and the organization of the police's reaction are shaped accordingly there.

POLICE AND SOCIAL CONTROL INTERNATIONALLY: JAPAN

Japan has enjoyed an enviable reputation as a country with low rates of crime (Adler, 1983) even in the face of rapid economic development, industrialization (most of it occurring in the latter half of the twentieth century), and high population density. It continues to maintain its strong reputation as a "country with safe streets" (Leishman, 1999: 117). Many researchers attribute this to specific Japanese cultural values that act together and help the police prevent criminal behavior and to respond to it as and when it occurs resulting in relatively high clearance rates. Recall what we learned about the various sources of culture. The culture of Japan reflects, among other influences, its geography (Japan is an island nation without much immigration in the past, but affected by its proximity to China and Korea), form of society (Japan's democracy and capitalist economy are relatively recent in origin), and history (Japan's martial and monarchical traditions and its defeat and occupation in World War II). Three major Japanese cultural values (among others) have been invoked in connection to police operations and effectiveness.

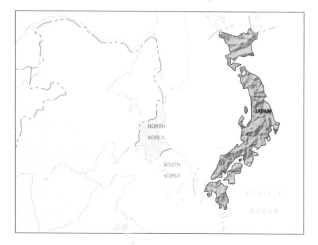

Japanese society and its culture are characterized by a very high level of ethnic homogeneity. Historically, other than a very small Korean minority, almost everyone in Japan was Japanese. This similarity among its people (in contrast to American heterogeneity) makes acceptance of, understanding for, as well as cooperation with the Japanese police easier, given that the latter may be viewed as "one of us." Westermann and Burfeind (1991; 152) note that there are fewer people in Japanese society who feel that they are separated from the mainstream of Japanese life than in other cultures. This contributes to a lower crime rate overall and in turn ensures that there will be very few (what we have come to call) hate crimes against marginalized groups. It should be noted that in recent times, people from other parts of Asia and Europe have migrated to Japan, primarily for employment, and this may change the mix of ethnic groups in a more heterogeneous manner.

Harmony is another major value promoted in Japanese culture. Many observers have suggested that Japan is a society where getting along with other members of society takes precedence over individual feelings and individualism. "The ethnically homogeneous Japanese stress conformity to group norms" (Westermann and Burfeind, 1991; 149) and "the individual's interests are best served in the context of the group and its welfare" (148). The Japanese are likely to stress the importance of duty and responsibility to the group. If one were successfully socialized into Japanese culture, the overwhelming importance of meeting one's obligations and not violating expectations (resulting in deviant behavior) would operate at the level of personal control. In addition, the overpowering influence of parents, relatives, teachers, and other adults, would work at the level of informal social control to induce conformity and to engender shame and guilt in members who have engaged in deviance. As a result, the police would have to deal with fewer instances of individuals breaking criminal laws overall and would have a greater likelihood of receiving confessions (leading ultimately to higher crime clearance rates). In addition, given the general importance attributed to harmony, members of the Japanese public are more likely to cooperate with the police when problems (including crime) do crop up.

A third value, hierarchy, can be added to explain Japanese society's hospitable relations with the police. Japan has a tradition of formal hierarchy wherein four classes (warriors, farmers, craftsmen, and merchants) existed during the seventeenth through the nineteenth centuries. While more recently, "age and tenure as well as education, specialization, and office" (Westermann and Burfeind, 1991: 123) are important to the ranking process, such social stratification does not lead to resentment, but provides members with an understanding of social relationships and everyone's place within a structure. As we can recognize, being part of a hierarchy requires that one willfully submit to those possessing a higher ranking. The resulting respect for authority is especially useful in the promotion of harmonious police relations with the public. People in Japan are more likely to do what they are told by the police, given that they see the police officer as having a higher ranking in a hierarchical structure where everyone, including the person obeying, has a stake.

The inculcation of these three values in individual members of Japanese society means that the police will have a relatively easy time in gaining and keeping the cooperation of the public. This does not mean that there are no acts of deviance in Japan. However, the occurrence of major norm violations, for example, the attack using poisonous gas by members of the Aum Shinrikyo religious cult on subway passengers in Tokyo, are relatively few and far between (see Lifton, 1999). In general, the public does not see the police as interfering "others." When crimes take place, they are more likely to be reported to the authorities and this makes clearing them by arrest and conviction of those responsible easier. Requests for help in dealing with maintaining order or solving crimes are also likely to be heeded under this setup. While all police forces are dependent on the cooperation of individual citizens for their effectiveness, homogeneity, harmony, and respect for authority allow the Japanese police to receive such support with fewer associated problems.

Now that we have learned how a country with a culture that is fairly distinct from that of United States affects its policing, please read the box, which deals with the relationship between culture and policing in Canada, a country that is closer to the United States.

SUMMARY

We began this chapter with a consideration of why it is important for societies to control the behavior of its members such that order and predictability ensue. We identified how historically this was done through the use of religion, family, and clan. Next, we learned how the police came to be involved in this societal undertaking. The importance of a given society's culture as consisting of its values, beliefs, norms, laws, and types of crimes in the shaping of its police organizations and personnel was discussed next. In particular, we looked at how values usually ascribed to American society affect the nature of policing in the country. We followed this with a consideration of the three levels of control (personal, informal social, formal social) that operate to discourage deviance in society and located the police at the third or highest level. We next discussed what the three sociological perspectives (functionalism, conflict, and interactionism) have to say about existing forms of social control from their analytic points of view. Functionalism emphasizes the role of the police in helping maintain social order by contributing to the social control system. Conflict theory focuses on the inequality and lack of fairness in law enforcement. Interactionism looks at situations wherein police and the public interact to deduce clues regarding how the social control system operates at the microlevel. Finally, the case of Japan, which has shown lower rates of crime and higher rates of clearance was subjected to cultural analysis and found to fit the overall proposition of this chapter, that is, the social control system of a society is heavily influenced by its cultural characteristics, particularly in terms of what members are commonly socialized into.

KEY TERMS

Beliefs: Explicit and concrete statements that members of a society accept as true.

Civil laws: Definitions of violations involving conflicts between individuals living and interacting with each other in society.

Crimes: Acts of deviance that violate criminal laws

Criminal laws: Definitions of violations that are deemed to be important enough for society to join with the victim in the official reaction against the offender.

Deviance: Behavior that violates norms, both folkways and mores.

Felonies: Second level of serious crimes.

Folkways: Minor, or less important norms.

Formal social control: Particular individuals and agencies designated to maintain control and order in society become involved in reacting to deviant behavior.

High consensus crimes: Classes of crimes (e.g., crimes against persons, property crimes) evoke more reaction and commitment of resources than others.

Informal social control: When individuals do not do something deviant because they fear the negative judgments of those who are close or dear to them.

Low consensus crimes: Lower-priority offenses that typically both the public and the police are conflicted about and are controversial politically (e.g., drug offenses, gambling, prostitution, jaywalking, etc.).

Medicalization of deviance: Certain forms of deviance, although resulting in criminal acts, are defined as arising out of an individual's illness and pathology.

Misdemeanors: The third level of serious crimes.

Mores: Major, or more important norms.

Norms: The rules and expectations by which society instructs and directs the behavior of individual members.

Personal (or self-) control: Individuals are less likely to commit acts of deviance because they have assimilated societal values and behave according to the norms that flow from them.

Socialization: The process by which society inculcates values to its members through a variety of institutions that act as agencies in teaching, modeling, and encouraging them to behave along expected lines.

Treason: Acts that involve the overthrow of the government and collaborating with the enemy in times of war and hostility. These are defined as the most serious crimes.

Values: The abstract standards that cultures use to communicate to members what is ideally expected of them.

Violations: Petty offenses; the last level of serious crimes.

 ## REVIEW QUESTIONS

1. Describe the relationship between values, norms, and crime?

2. What are the three levels of control over deviant behavior? Where do the police fit in among these levels?

3. Describe how Japanese policing, as a part of their system of social control, relates to their cultural values.

 ## DISCUSSION QUESTIONS

1. Discuss how the major American values as identified by Robin Williams affect policing in the United States.

2. Discuss how the American police may or may not be involved in the medicalization of deviance.

3. What is deviance? Provide examples that may be criminal or noncriminal in the United States. Do the same for another country of your choice.

 ## REFERENCES

Adler, Freda (1983) *Nations not Obsessed with Crime.* Littleton, CO: Fred B. Rothman.

Berg, Bruce L. (1992) *Law Enforcement: An Introduction to Police in Society.* Boston: Allyn and Bacon.

Conrad, Peter and Joseph W. Schneider (1992) *Deviance and Medicalization: From Badness to Sickness.* Philadelphia: Temple University Press.

Goldstein, Herman (1977) *Policing a Free Society.* Cambridge, MA: Ballinger.

LaGrange, Randy L. (1993) *Policing American Society.* Chicago: Nelson-Hall.

Leishman, Frank (1999) "Policing in Japan: East Asian Archetype?" Pp. 109–125 In Rob I. Mawby (ed.) *Policing Across the World: Issues for the Twenty-First Century.* London: UCL Press.

Lifton, Robert Jay (1999) *Destroying the World to Save It: Aum Shinrikyo, Apocalyptic Violence and the New Global Terrorism.* New York: Owl Books/Henry Holt and Company.

Melossi, Dario (2009) *Controlling Crime, Controlling Society: Thinking about Crime in Europe and America.* Cambridge, UK: Polity Press.

Parks, Evelyn (1970) "From Constabulary to Police Society: Implications for Social Control." *Catalyst* 5: 76–97.

Reiner, Robert (1991) "Policing and Criminal Justice in Great Britain." *Coexistence* 28: 107–117.

Sumner, William Graham (1959 [1906]) *Folkways.* New York. Dover.

Westermann, Ted D. and James W. Burfeind (1991) *Crime and Justice in Two Societies: Japan and the United States.* Pacific Grove, CA: Brooks/Cole.

Wiley, Mary G. and Terry L. Hudik (1974) "Police-Citizen Encounters: A Field Test of Exchange Theory." *Social Problems* 22: 119–127.

Williams, Robin M. (1970) *American Society: A Sociological Interpretation.* New York. Alfred A. Knopf.

THE CANADIAN POLICE AS AGENTS OF SOCIAL CONTROL

Tonita Murray

Canada shares the North American continent with the United States of America and in many ways a similar society, culture, and values as well. But there are some substantial differences between the two, not the least being the differences between their systems of government and attitudes to authority.

Canada is a parliamentary democracy. Its government is not founded on revolutionary or rational ideals but is based on an evolved model of the English government. It recognizes the British monarch as its head of state, and its executive authority is not separate from but responsible to the House of Commons, which is the legislative arm of the government. In theory, the sovereign authority does not flow from the people to the government, as in the United States, but is vested in the government itself.

Given the evolutionary process, this concept of government in Canada has been undergoing a change, most noticeably since 1982 when the Canadian constitution was repatriated from Britain. The repatriation allowed the incorporation into the *Constitution Act* of a new *Charter of Rights and Freedoms*. As a result, there is now more legal and social emphasis on individual as opposed to collective rights. Nevertheless, Canadian society remains more deferential to authority and more conservative and stable than American society. The strength of these social characteristics is well illustrated by the fact that the Royal Canadian Mounted Police (RCMP) is a widely recognized symbol of Canadian identity. Moreover, public confidence in all Canadian police departments, not just the RCMP, is repeatedly reaffirmed by public opinion polls. The use of the police to protect Canadian social values is thus strongly supported by the public.

The police's role in social control is supported by their possession of their original powers as peace officers. This means that peace officers derive their authority from the common law and legislation, not through delegation from a government (Ceyssens 1.16 1.3b). A considerable body of literature in a number of common law countries has accrued over the years discussing exactly what such authority means for the independence of the police from political direction. In practice, it is generally accepted that the police can receive policy direction from the government, but are operationally independent. While their independence is subject to the *Charter*, to the law, to some civilian oversight, and to the requirement to be accountable for the use of authority, it means that sworn peace officers are able to exercise, without warrant but on reasonable and probable grounds, the powers of detention, entry, arrest, search, seizure, and the use of force, including deadly force. Moreover, with some important exceptions, police and not attorneys are responsible for the laying of criminal charges (Stenning, 1986). Their independence to coerce, intervene, and lay charges thus makes them very effective agents of social control.

The effectiveness of the police in maintaining social control is further enhanced by their use of discretion. This power was not expressed in law and is still little discussed or defined. It is a natural concomitant of the duty to act on reasonable and probable grounds and means that police officers can make their own judgment on whether to act or not, according to circumstances. While what they judge to be reasonable and probable can be challenged in court, discretion gives them a certain amount of influence and flexibility in deciding what socially important values to control and how to control them. When governments do not want police to exercise discretion, they have to develop specific policies to direct the police to act in a certain way. An example of this is in the matter of spousal violence, which is discussed below.

Another measure that enables the police to be effective social control agents is community policing. Canadian policing is locally based. Through a system of contracting to provinces and municipalities, even the federal RCMP is locally accountable when it carries out general policing duties. Community policing is thus practiced with varying degrees of fervor and success throughout Canada and incorporates many community values and requirements. Police in different localities may therefore enforce support values. One community may wish for the police to suppress illicit drug activity or other vice problems, another may be more concerned with traffic laws, a third with noise violations, and yet another with youth in conflict with the law. Yet, while the community may influence the focus of police attention, it is left to police discretion to decide the means by which community priorities are attained.

The effectiveness of an interplay of public deference to authority, the original powers of the police, police discretion, and the community policing approach in the exercise of social control can be seen in the examples discussed below. They describe situations where mainstream, modern society frequently has strong requirements and is not ready to tolerate deviance.

In recent years, Canadian society has become preoccupied with preventing youth crime and discouraging violence. The police have an array of programs for dealing with youth in conflict, or in danger of being in conflict with the law. One of the most nationally prevalent of these programs is the placing of police officers in schools as youth liaison officers. Their role is largely one of awareness, education, and role modeling but, as social disapproval of youth violence has grown, they have developed and implemented programs against bullying, fighting, and other forms of violence in schools. Police are also major participants in restorative justice, family counseling and other alternative forms of justice for dealing with youth in conflict with the law.

The *Youth Criminal Justice Act (2002)* affirms the important role of the police and of the use of police discretion in dealing with youth in conflict with the law. The Act suggests that police are more than agents of the criminal justice system. The implications are that police have a pervasive community role in dealing with young people, have the discretion to make independent judgments, and can apply a whole range of remedies before even considering the formal justice system. Most importantly, the police decide when the formal system of youth justice will be invoked. They are, in fact, the only agents who have a role in all of the options provided by the act.

Spousal violence is another area in which the police are relied on to effect and maintain strong social values related to the family. But in this case, most Canadian jurisdictions have removed police discretion and have directed the police to lay criminal charges in all cases. In this situation governments still rely on the police as the social control agent but decide themselves on the mechanism of control.

In their community policing role, the police have developed cooperative relations and protocols with other community agencies and volunteer organizations to ensure that the needs of the victims of family violence are met. When this is combined with their role in youth justice, it means that the police rather than the church, social workers, schools, doctors, or other community agencies are often the major players in ensuring that community standards are upheld against deviance. While the intention is benevolent, the immediate recourse to police authority to bring about such social aims suggests a growing trend in communities, albeit largely inadvertent, to bypass other means of ensuring conformity in favor of coercion.

Current treatment of the mentally ill shows a similar pattern. Community care of the mentally ill, often a fiscal rather than a medical policy, means that if the mentally ill become self-destructive, vagrant, or disruptive, they are a police problem rather than a medical one and are dealt with coercively. This has occasionally led to tragic consequences where mentally disturbed people have been injured, killed, or otherwise inappropriately treated by the police who have not recognized their medical conditions. Some police officers are now receiving training in the recognition of mental illness, but given that police decisions to use force are often made rapidly and under pressure, differentiating between deviant behavior caused by mental illness as opposed to other causes may not always be possible.

It might be argued that relying heavily on the police rather than on more appropriate agencies to respond to some forms of social deviance, particularly when it is done for financial or other expediencies, is too crude a form of social control.

An example where the police have developed a more subtle form of social control is in their responsibility for the maintenance of order during public demonstrations. In early antiglobalization demonstrations, the outbreak of violence led to criticism of how the police handled demonstrators. In one demonstration, there were indications that the hasty police use of pepper spray had been the result of a political order. In the subsequent public inquiry, it was suggested that political encroachment on the independence of the police had led to mishandling of the situation. This was a clear reiteration that the police had the authority, the responsibility, and the accountability to maintain order.

Understanding that, while wanting order, both the government and the public wanted it to be achieved without violence, the police had to rethink their operational strategies. More than a year of very careful preparation therefore went into maintaining order at the G8 summit meeting of 2002. Because the federal government decided to hold the summit in a remote location to protect visiting heads of state, a number of large and potentially dangerous demonstrations were held in a number of major cities across Canada, rather than at the summit site. This had been anticipated by the police. Using the techniques of community policing, police services in different jurisdictions consulted intensively with special interest and protest groups across the country to develop strategies to ensure that legitimate protest was not stifled but order was maintained. In lieu of riot gear, pepper spray, tear gas, and perimeter fences, they used bicycle and foot patrol police in ordinary uniform along the parade routes. Their stated aim was to enable protestors to demonstrate legitimately without incident. Their efforts at community cooperation to neutralize the trouble makers were entirely successful. There was no violence in any city and, where there had been some threat of it breaking out, it was the legitimate protestors who prevented it without confrontation.

This example of public order maintenance perhaps represents a new approach in social control for the Canadian police. It is preventive, proactive, and cooperative and entails winning the trust and support of the protest minority who would normally be labeled as deviant. Moreover, it means the police have to work honestly with those who could be so labeled. In many ways, it was an act of faith on both sides, but it has perhaps set a new norm for managing public demonstrations. It is possible that it succeeded in part because of the inherent conservatism and deference of Canadians, because Canadians on the whole respect their police, and because the demonstrators ultimately knew that the police had considerable powers to contain any violence, but it also probably worked because the police co-opted those they were expected to control.

Reference

Stenning, P. C. (1986) *Appearing for the Crown*. A study conducted for the Law Reform Commission of Canada. Cowansville, Quebec: Brown Legal Publications.

CHAPTER 3

In Western liberal-democratic societies such as ours, there has always been a certain amount of distrust of the police. After all, the police are highly visible representatives of the state, symbolizing state power and control over the lives of people. While nearly two centuries of "successful" public policing has allayed most of the deeply felt skepticism toward the police, a residual distrust still lingers. (LaGrange, 1993: 98)

Traffic police officers are seen in front of Singapore's financial district, re-directing traffic due to road closures in a bid to heighten security around the venue where The International Monetary Fund meets in Singapore next week, Monday Sept. 11, 2006 in Singapore. The IMF meets, the first time in Asia since the 1997 financial crisis hit the region, intent on vamping itself to give greater power to emerging economies in hopes of enhancing the legitimacy of the 61-year-old institution. (Credit: © AP Photo/Wong Maye-E)

POLICE AND SOCIAL INSTITUTIONS

OBJECTIVES:

1. The student will learn about six major social institutions.
2. The student will learn how social institutions relate to policing.
3. The student will learn how policing affects major social institutions.
4. The student will learn how functionalism, conflict theory, and interactionism relate to social institutions and the police.
5. The student will learn to view social institutions and policing on an international level.

social institution

A set of well-established, widely held rules and procedures that are prescribed for meeting important needs in a society and as a result pattern social relationships and interaction.

family

Social institution that makes sure that societal members channel their sexuality for the purpose of procreation and that they then bring up their children such that the society does not die out due to the lack of new members or their neglect.

education

Social institution that provides for teaching each new generation of members the history, culture, or way of life of a society as well as to train them for future work.

economy

Social institution that ensures that needed goods and services are produced and distributed and that workers who will contribute to this end through their labor are integrated into relevant occupations.

government (or polity)

Social institution that relates to power within a society and its exercise in terms of who will play leadership roles at various levels and how they are selected and replaced.

Consider the following hypothetical news items (all based on real events) that constitute a variety of law-enforcement activities that could take place in the course of any given day of the week. Following his arrest, the former dictator of an East European country is being tried by the World Court in The Hague (Netherlands) for ordering the "ethnic cleansing" of a region of his country when he was in power. The Federal Bureau of Investigation (FBI) in the United States is investigating the workings of an organized crime group that is involved in stealing cars from various locations and selling them in other states. The State Bureau of Investigation in the capital of your state is interviewing witnesses and preparing a case against state education officials involved in mismanaging the state's education budget. Sheriff's department personnel are responding rapidly to a 911 phone call from a home, in an unincorporated part of your county, that appears to involve severe domestic violence. The local police in your city are presenting a request to a magistrate asking her to issue a search warrant for the living quarters of the pastor of a prominent city church who has been accused of child sexual abuse. These disparate occurrences may appear to have nothing in common other than that they are crime-fighting activities that involve police organizations at the international, national, state, county, and city levels. However, sociologists will also note that these actions taken by the police implicate several important social institutions.

SOCIAL INSTITUTIONS

A **social institution** is a set of well-established, widely held rules and procedures that are prescribed for meeting important needs in a society and as a result pattern social relationships and interaction. Every society confronts a number of vital needs that have to be dealt with in order to ensure its survival and continuation. These include, first of all, making sure that its members channel their sexuality for the purpose of procreation and that they then bring up their children such that the society does not die out due to the lack of new members or their neglect. The institution of **family** is generally designated for this purpose. Next, each society has to provide for teaching its new generation of members the history, culture, or way of life of that society as well as training them for future work. The institution of **education** takes care of this critical need. Third, each society will have to make sure that needed goods and services are produced and distributed and that workers who will contribute to this end through their labor are integrated into relevant occupations. The **economy** is the institution that fulfills this need. Fourth, the question of power and its exercise in terms of who will play leadership roles at various levels of a society and how they are selected and replaced is important. The **government or polity** is the institution that serves this purpose. Finally, every society is faced with certain residual questions that are important to the lives of its members. These include providing meaningful answers to important questions regarding our origins, the reasons for our human existence, and our ultimate destinations (including after death). **Religion** is the institution that provides answers that satisfy these eternal and spiritual questions.

Sociologists generally identify the family, education, economy, government or polity, and religion as the Big Five of social institutions. Thus the examples that we began this chapter with relate to these important social institutions. The government or polity (in the case of the former dictator); the economy (in the case of the interstate automobile theft ring); education (in the case of state education officials); the family (in the domestic violence case); and religion (in the case of the minister) are all affected by the actions of the police at various levels. However, we must recognize that additional institutions that deal with other critical needs also exist in any given society. These include the institutions of medicine (as it relates to the health and physical well-being of members); law (the rules and regulations that channel behavior into predictable and acceptable paths); the military (which ensures protection and survival by defending the society when aggression and war threaten it); and the media (to provide information and entertainment as needed for the members of a society).

Three points need to be made about social institutions. First, although they are unobservable and only dimly perceived, the social institutions of a society exert an enormous impact on our behavior by specifying how to go about doing what needs to be done in our lives. We are likely to be reared in family settings by parents who also socialize us into society; we go to school (elementary through high school, for eleven years) and college (for an additional four); we work in an occupation or profession (in a capitalist economic system); we vote in partisan elections (in a presidential/executive democratic system as opposed to a parliamentary democracy or the stage-managed elections of a dictatorship); and go to church (or a mosque or temple, although most likely not to a witches coven).

Second, institutions are our main sources of information regarding the values (what is important, what is right, what is correct, etc.) that we carry around within ourselves. The reason that your parents were willing to bring you up and socialize you (while putting up with the innumerable demands you placed on them in the process of growing up from a newborn to infant, toddler, child, teenager, and young adult) is because they have assimilated the message of the "rightness" or "correctness" of having children and becoming good parents. Society, through the institution of family, has instilled these values in them. As another example, think about the importance of activity and work in American society (recall our discussion of core American values in Chapter 2). As a result, it is to be expected that parents, teachers, and bosses want to see us "working" and to evaluate the products of our constructive occupational activity. Notice at the same time that these individuals represent the institutions of family, education, and the economy, respectively. There is the added implication that, in general, social institutions reinforce values that are commonly held in a society. Social institutions join together to form a nexus of values that are mutually supportive and influence the behavior of all individuals enmeshed within them.

Third, since social institutions have developed and existed in their predominant current forms over long periods of time (think about the lengthy history of each of our major religious traditions), they generally tend to be conservative in nature. This means that a lot of weight is placed on "the way things were" and "the way things are" as opposed to "the way things will be" or "the way things ought to be."

religion

Social institution that provides meaningful answers to certain residual questions that are important to the lives of a society's members, for example, questions regarding our origins, the reasons for our human existence, and our ultimate destinations (including after death).

This is understandable. Given that these institutions have stood the test of time, people who are used to them are likely to be resistant to major innovations or changes in them (e.g., think about the controversy surrounding marriages or civil unions for gays in the United States). It should therefore not surprise us that police actions in respect to social institutions may be twofold in their implications. Sometimes the police act to shore up the existing conservatism of institutional structures and attitudes (e.g., the Chicago police beating up demonstrators wanting an end to the Vietnam War at the 1968 Democratic National Convention after labeling them a threat to the existing institutions of government). At other times, the police may be attempting to force the pace of change on these otherwise reluctant institutions (e.g., enforcing mandatory arrest policies with regard to domestic violence, the home being previously considered an area that was exclusively in the private domain of the institution of family).

INTERACTION OF THE POLICE WITH MAJOR SOCIAL INSTITUTIONS

The relationship between the police and various social institutions is reciprocal, that is, they affect and influence each other mutually. As in all human interactions, mutual influences and effects can be for good or for ill. Police agencies and their personnel operate in societies that are dominated by these social institutions and therefore, similar to other groups and individuals, are likely to be affected by these institutions. That is to say police officers are likely to have personal religious and political affiliations; have undergone the process of education in schools and colleges; participate in the economy as consumers, investors, and taxpayers; and will marry, have children, and engage in family life (in addition to having grown up in some kind of familial setting). The impact of social institutions upon officers and the organizations that they serve is clear. Police organizations in their activities and police officers in their daily lives reproduce the dominant and preferred forms prescribed by the social institutions of their society.

It is also true that police organizations and their personnel affect social institutions (Forest, 2006). Think about the examples that we started out with. The first case involved political crime, that is, illegalities committed, in this case, for the purpose of wiping out opponents and staying in power. The second is a case of crime that was carried out in a manner that impinged upon the working of the economic system, in this case, a capitalist economy based on competition and free trade, which the auto-theft ring attempts to sabotage. The third example of financial improprieties concerning a state education budget obviously affects the running of public schools and the lives of schoolchildren and teachers negatively. The fourth case involved domestic violence and affects the institution of family negatively, particularly spousal relations and possibly the care and welfare of the young. Finally, the last case affects faith and trust in an institution, that is, religion, which shapes the values and spirituality of a community and society. Inevitably, while carrying out their functions of fighting crime, maintaining order, and providing service, the police as "the most visible representatives of the state" are going to affect the nature and functioning of these institutions. The role of the police in each of these cases, as we have noted earlier, is mixed. In some cases, they serve to reinforce the existing values of social institutions (e.g., preventing the auto-theft ring from subverting free trade; making sure those who sabotaged the smooth running of schools were on their way to being punished; arresting those who brought ill-repute to religion), and in other cases they bring about change (e.g., hastening the end of those who abused the political system and, as a result, changing it for the better; upsetting traditional conceptions of what used to be considered private and familial and nobody else's business, least of all the state as represented by the police).

We now turn our attention to the interactions between the police and particular institutions. The institutions we will analyze in this manner are the Big Five of social institutions that we have become familiar with: the family, education, the economy, the government or polity, and finally, religion. In the case of each institution we will first examine how it affects the police and then consider how the police, in turn, affect it.

POLICE AND THE FAMILY

As we have noted above, the family is the institution in society that allows for the regulation of sexuality such that children are produced and are then nurtured and socialized to become productive members of society. Depending on the society and culture, there may be variations in how people marry and form families. For example, societies may practice monogamy (one wife per husband), polygamy (more than one wife per husband), polyandry (more than one husband per wife), or group marriage (more than one wife for more than one husband). Values and norms will develop and support the preferred form of marriage and family. In the United States, the dominant form of marriage and family is monogamy (although given the high divorce and remarriage rates, some observers refer to Americans as practicing serial monogamy). As a result, the police–family institutional interaction we will discuss here refers to this familial form.

How the Family Affects the Police

Again as we have learned, police personnel, just like other members of society, marry, have children, and raise them, and sometimes get divorced. As a result, they will play important roles as spouses or ex-spouses, parents, and parents-in-law. These allow police officers to share in the lives that society prescribes for all of its members and the resultant joys and happiness of weddings, births, and the ups and downs of married life. However, their status and occupation as police officers results in a number of unique challenges that have been the subject of research. A large majority of married male police officers have acknowledged that their occupation and its routines affect their home lives negatively, while a smaller number have mentioned the difficulties involved in spending enough time with their children (Kroes, Margolis, and Hurrell, 1974). Spouses of police officers also report difficulties in their lives together that can be traced to job situations (Alexander and Walker, 1996). Swanson, Territo, and Taylor

(1988: 274) have commented that "marital and family strife, discord and unresolved emotional problems affect a police officer's development, motivation, productivity, and effectiveness in ways that we are only beginning to appreciate and understand."

Prominently mentioned among such difficulties are, according to Swanson, Territo, and Taylor (1988: 276–278), their:

- changing work schedules (e.g., shift work and the need to be available at all times, including nights and weekends);
- emotional exhaustion (e.g., the frustration and wearing thin of patience that goes with much psychologically draining police work);
- negative public image (e.g., perceived hostility and disrespect from members of the public);
- overprotectiveness of their spouses and families (e.g., increased concern regarding the welfare of family members and suspicion of others);
- hardening of emotions (e.g., the tamping down of feelings and emotions as a result of an occupation that exposes them mostly to the seamy and undesirable sides of life);
- issues relating to sexuality (e.g., the difficulties inherent in correlating varying work schedules and a satisfactory sex life);
- identity conflicts (e.g., between spouses and partners regarding each other's roles and contributions to the marriage); and
- the aforementioned problems with child rearing.

How the Police Affect the Family

In carrying out their functions of crime fighting, order maintenance, and service, the activities of the police are likely to impinge upon the institution of family. When, for example, the police stop, question, investigate, or arrest someone, we should remember that he or she is likely to be enmeshed in a number of familial relationships, for example, son or daughter, parent, spouse, and sibling, all having implications for that individual's family (in its extended sense).

One major area where the police have a direct impact on the institution of family in the United States is when they intervene in cases of domestic violence. A family setting is typically not one we associate with violence given its "home sweet home" image and our idealized conception of it as our ultimate haven and refuge. However, domestic violence is more common than we expect (Straus, 1995). The rationale for aggressive police intervention in such cases is based on the Minneapolis Domestic Violence Experiment (Sherman and Berk, 1984). In this famous study, police officers were randomly assigned one of the following outcomes in dealing with domestic calls: counseling or mediating the dispute, separating the individuals involved by escorting the offender from the home, or arresting the offender. Researchers demonstrated, as a result of this field experiment, that arresting perpetrators of domestic violence was twice as effective as the other interventions in reducing subsequent battering. While subsequent replications did not provide clear-cut findings regarding the effectiveness of arresting batterers, as a result of political pressures, mandatory arrest policies were adopted nationwide. Regardless of whether mandatory arrest will reduce future domestic violence or not, it can be seen that the threat and possibility of police arrest has fundamentally altered the nature of spousal and domestic partner relationships within the family setting.

POLICE AND EDUCATION

Education is the institution in contemporary society that is connected with teaching the young and developing their skills and career aspirations and that operates to continue their socialization with the goal that they will become well-adjusted and productive citizens of society. Educational systems can be either elite (beyond a certain level, education is only for a few, based on merit or some other distinctive status) or mass based (education for everyone regardless of their backgrounds). They can also be controlled locally (i.e., important decisions regarding textbooks, curricula, hiring teachers, etc., are made by school districts) or centrally (the highest government in the land makes all important decisions regarding schools). In the United States, the system of education is mass based with free and guaranteed public education, and varied higher education choices available in the form of community colleges, four-year liberal arts colleges, public and private universities, etc. Further, as you are no doubt well aware, although the federal and state governments have a financial and guidance role in education, local control is the norm. Let us now examine how this important institution affects and is affected by the police.

How Education Affects the Police

Education affects the police in two direct ways. First, many offenders have a history of school failure, and it has been noted by correctional researchers that two-thirds of offenders do not have a high school diploma or equivalent (Harlow, 2003). The argument is therefore made that if only we had spent some more time and effort in dealing with students who are struggling, not doing well academically, and in danger of dropping out of school, we would help prevent or reduce the creation of future criminals that the police would then have to deal with. Second, the nature and level of education (as opposed to job training) that are needed for future police officers have been subject to debate and research for some time. The assumption that police officers should have certain educational qualifications is, of course, uncontested and more recent controversies have revolved around the content and level; specifically, whether a college degree should be required of police applicants. However, you should note that buried underneath the above-stated assumption is the idea that the institution of education (specifically, higher education) does have important and lasting positive effects on those who have been subjected to it.

Berg (1992: 296) argues in support of the need for college-educated police officers as follows:

> If it were the intention of police agencies to acquire warm bodies, then fixing the minimum requirement at a high school diploma or equivalent might be adequate.
>
> Police work, however, simply cannot be equated with dock work, automobile repairing, operating computer terminals, laboratory technical work, or any other semiskilled occupation for which a high school education might suffice at entry level.

In a study of around 500 police executives, Carter, Sapp, and Stevens (1989) found that based on their experience, the advantages of having a college education outweighed the disadvantages. Among the advantages they mentioned are better communication, better report writing, more effective job performance, fewer citizen complaints, more initiative and professionalism, wiser use of discretion, and so on. Among the few disadvantages mentioned are the greater likelihood that college-educated officers will leave policing, question orders that they receive, and request other assignments. Three other pieces of information speak to the positive effects of greater education for police officers. First, the proportion of police officers possessing baccalaureate degrees has continued to increase substantially, and master's degrees are becoming frequent at higher levels (lieutenant, captain, chief) as well. Second, many police departments provide incentives for officers to acquire educational qualifications beyond the levels that they were hired at. Finally, the Police Corps, a federal program is now available that in exchange for a four-year service commitment pays those selected to get a degree or reimburses those selected who already possess a degree.

How the Police Affect Education

Given the general wariness with which democracies have treated extensions in the reach of the police, it should not surprise us that efforts to involve the police in educational activities have generally been greeted with some suspicion. Traditionally, therefore, the two agencies and their personnel did not interact. The question often asked is why do the police want to be involved with schools and students? Is it to spy on them or, worse still, to gather incriminating information about their parents and home life? Or is it to expand police powers into areas in which they were previously unwelcome?

Regardless of these suspicions, the police have become more involved in schools and with students over time. Although the police have carried out programs involving children and young adults (e.g., Police Athletic Leagues and Officer Friendly school liaison programs) for quite some time, the two most prominent recent examples of this are the DARE (Drug Abuse Resistance Education or Drug Awareness Resistance Education or Drugs and Alcohol Reduction Education) programs and the School Resource Officer (SRO) programs. The DARE programs, initiated in the 1980s, began as a joint effort between the Los Angeles police department and school district and spread across the country. It involves assigning police officers to teach a seventeen session classroom course that focused on providing information about drugs, ways of resisting peer influence leading to drug use, and alternatives to such use. Thus, police officers became teachers for a short period of time. Students completing the program went through a graduation ceremony, received a diploma and a T-shirt, and pledged to be drug-free in the future. Unfortunately, for a program that had considerable hope and fanfare attached to it, rigorous evaluations that were subsequently performed found little to no lasting effects on drug use or beliefs related to drug use (Rosenbaum, Flewelling, Bailey, Rigwalt, and Wilkinson, 1994; Rosenbaum and Hanson, 1998).

SRO programs (also federally funded) began in the 1990s in response to perceived increases in violence among school students, culminating in the killing spree at Columbine High School in Littleton, Colorado, in which thirteen people, including the two gunmen who were students in the school, were killed. These programs are also extensions of the philosophy of community-oriented policing and are intended to enhance the feelings of personal safety in those attending school. School resource officers are considered members of the school faculty and interact with students on a daily basis (walking the hallways, patrolling the parking lots, having lunch with the students), investigate crimes occurring on campus, and serve as a resource for various school-related groups regarding laws. While these programs have yet to be subjected to systematic and rigorous evaluations, initial reports do speak positively about them. In any case, the two programs we have mentioned in this section both promise and seek greater involvement by the police in education, a trend that we are more likely to see in the future.

POLICE AND THE ECONOMY

Anytime the police investigate and arrest property crime offenders (and sometimes, even with a violent crime, especially kidnapping and robbery), they are interacting with the economy. Larceny, theft, burglary, automobile theft, vandalism, check or credit card fraud, forgery, counterfeiting, and a variety of everyday property crimes have a clear implication for the economy if left uninvestigated and unchecked. Assume for a minute that there are a large number of residential burglaries in a particular town. People who intend to move there may not be willing to buy real estate because that particular locality has a reputation for being "unsafe." As a result, the prices of houses decline, and consequently there is less by way of property taxes collected by the city. Further, as residents move away and are not replaced by newcomers, local businesses will have less of a customer base and may close, leading to less competition among the remaining few. The city will again be collecting less in terms of sales taxes. So you can see how crucial it is to the local economy that the police do their crime-fighting duties well. It is also important to remember that a plethora of white-collar "crimes in the suites," such as price fixing, false advertising, polluting the environment, bid rigging, violations against health and safety of employees, and selling unsafe products, all have similar negative implications for the macroeconomy (state, regional, national) as well. Similarly, the economic well-being of a community or region affects police services.

Dempsey (1994: 47) found that the economic recession of the late 1980s and early 1990s resulted in the merging of some neighboring police departments and the closing of others: "In Ohio in 1992, the St. Clair Township Police Department was virtually disbanded when its five part-time officers were laid off due to budgetary problems, leaving the police chief as the only officer in the township." Keeping this in mind, let us consider the two aspects of this interaction.

How the Economy Affects the Police

The state of the economy holds a number of implications for the police. In general, as a country undergoes **modernization** (i.e., it becomes economically developed or industrializes itself), crime rates show an increase. The majority of the offenses that fuel this increase are property crimes, mainly because there is much more in terms of property to steal. In advanced industrial societies (such as the United States) property crimes, rather than violent crimes, make up a large proportion of total crime. At the same time, economically developed countries are also likely to professionalize their police forces into bureaucracies that focus on better record keeping. Thus, some of the increase in crime can be attributed to the police doing a better job of documenting their activities. Very few countries have been able to escape the positive correlation between crime and economic development, Japan, Sweden, and some Middle Eastern countries being the exceptions (Shelley, 1981). The exceptions are generally due to the continuing importance placed in these countries on cultural factors, including values such as adherence to tradition and tribalism. However, for our purposes here, note how at the macroeconomic level, there is a relationship between the state of a country's economy, crime rates, and police activity.

The relationship between crime and the economy operates at other levels as well. There is a body of research in criminology that ascertains the relationship between **relative deprivation** and crime. Relative deprivation is the term that economists and sociologists use to describe the gap between people's expectations regarding what they feel they are entitled to (e.g., in terms of goods and lifestyles) and what is actually available to them given their current capabilities and place in a society (Gurr, 1970). The idea is that the greater the relative deprivation (e.g., when there is a bigger gap between expectations and reality), the higher the likelihood of crime. The police as the crime-fighting and order-maintenance arms of society have to deal with such situations. If the society they serve is one marked by ostentatious wealth and conspicuous consumption on the part of the few members of the elite, and there is a relatively large mass of people who feel that despite all their efforts they will not have access to the desirable things out there, the police are going to have a big problem on their hands. Given the conservative bent of all institutions, including the economy, the police will be struggling to maintain existing arrangements in the face of a large number of people who want to overthrow it.

A third aspect of the relationship between the economy and the police is what Manning (1995: 378) finds is the increasing use of economic and business-related concepts in discussing and evaluating policing.

modernization

The process by which societies become economically developed, or industrialized, which in general leads to increases in crime.

relative deprivation

The gap between people's expectations regarding what they feel they are entitled to (e.g., in terms of goods and lifestyles) and what is actually available to them given their current capabilities and place in a society.

The currently fashionable language of economics and management used by command personnel to describe police functions, command obligations and planning creates a picture of policing as a business. Innovations such as computer-assisted dispatching are advocated on the grounds that they will increase efficiency or reduce costs. Police programs (community policing, for example) are claimed to be a cost-effective means of delivering "service" to "customers" while remaining sensitive to community needs.

Again, the economic structure of a society affects the role, function, and rhetorical basis of the police work.

How the Police Affect the Economy

At the beginning of this section, we learned that all crimes have economic implications and consequences. John Conklin a sociologist–criminologist has specified six different **costs of crime** (Conklin, 1995: 62–63). In some of the six costs, the police are directly involved and in others, indirectly. Let us look at these costs and note how crime and related police actions in each case affect the larger economy, one way or the other.

costs of crime

The economic implications and consequences of crime, some of which are connected to the police.

- Direct loss: The immediate, generally enumerable cost of a crime. For example, arson results in a destroyed building that has a real value. Depending on the effectiveness of the police, direct losses may be higher or lower.

- Transfer of property: As a result of a robbery or burglary, property is transferred from one person to another. One loses and the other gains. Again, police actions will affect the frequency and total amount of property transfer upwards or downwards.

- Costs related to criminal violence: When someone is injured in a violent crime, there are costs associated with his or her loss of wages, productivity, unemployment, insurance, etc. While the police may be unable to do much about the costs once the crime is committed, rapid response on their part may be helpful in minimizing it.

- Illegal expenditures: This pertains to money that changes hands for the purchase of illegal goods (drugs, pornography) and services (prostitution, gambling). Police effectiveness in the area of public order crime enforcement can move this money away from the underground illegal economy to the legal economy.

- Enforcement actions: Money has to be spent to pay police officers, prosecutors, judges, probation officers, etc. This is money that can be considered taken away from other important societal needs or simply (if not used for enforcement) to reduce the burden on taxpayers. Of course, this money is pumped back into the economy by those with police (and other criminal justice system) jobs in the form of consumer spending (e.g., homes, cars, groceries, cafes, and restaurants).

- Prevention and protection costs: Conklin mentions the money spent on alarm systems, locks, and other crime-prevention devices and services. Of course, the police spend money and pay personnel to deal with crime prevention as well (e.g., programs such as Neighborhood Watch, Operation ID, and security audits).

POLICE AND THE GOVERNMENT/POLITY

Unlike most of the other institutions that we examine in this chapter, the connection between the government (or polity, which means the entire political structure of a society, including but not confined only to those who happen to be governing at any given time) and the police is a direct and intimate one. As we have seen, the police are the most visible representatives of the government and one of the few that ordinary citizens are likely to encounter on a daily basis. In addition, they are also one of the few that are available around the clock and are equipped with the resources needed to investigate events and people. Thus it should not surprise us that while the two aspects of the relationship between the police and the government are clear, they are also subject to controversy. The controversy stems from the suspicion that LaGrange (1993) alluded to in the quotation that began this chapter. As residents of a representative democracy that originated with a historical distrust of the means and motives of government, we do not wish to give the police too much power. More bluntly, we do not wish to live in a police state where the government (through the power of its police forces) feels free to spy on and interfere in the private affairs of its citizens.

How the Government Affects the Police

We have mentioned that governments typically begin the movement toward a professional police force. Earlier models of policing essentially involved using the military or the palace guard to carry out some of the functions that we associate with police agencies nowadays. In addition to the establishment of a full-fledged police force, a government broadly defines and sets the structure, tone, and tenor of police agencies and their activities. In Chapter 4, we will discuss the police bureaucracy and will learn about the differences between highly fragmented systems of policing, such as what we have in the United States, and more centralized ones that we find in other countries. The American political system is based on a division of responsibilities among the federal, state, and local governments; it also emphasizes local control over many governmental topics. Thus, the political system of the United States makes it more likely that policing will be divided among the federal (e.g., Departments of Justice, Treasury, and Homeland Security), state (State Police, Highway Patrol), and local (County Sheriff, Municipal Police Departments) governments. Similarly, given the emphasis on local control, most of the policing action in the United States is at the county, city, or municipal levels.

Second, what goes on at all levels in terms of police activity is a product of the nation's political institution. After the terrorist attacks in New York and Washington on September 11, 2001, various parts of the American polity began to pay a great deal of attention to these problems using various police organizations. Legislative changes (e.g., the USA Patriot Act), nationwide sweeps and arrests of suspected terrorists and their sympathizers, training and additional resources for tracking organizations suspected of terrorist funding or sympathy, the creation of new organizations (e.g., the Transportation Safety Administration), and the development of emergency plans to deal with terrorist events all followed. Police organizational activity thus paralleled the immediate political priorities of the government. Inasmuch as democratic governments reflect the interests and concerns of their citizens, perhaps it is only fitting that police organizations follow suit. However, it is possible for governments (if left alone and unchecked) to overstep their bounds and to misuse police powers to strike at those who are opposed to them. Thus, the former Soviet Union and East Germany were both totalitarian countries in which the government actively spied on a large number of its citizens using far-reaching police apparatus. Both governments harassed, banished, or, in some cases, did away with political opponents as a result. This was based on an ideology that insisted that the government needed such powers to safeguard the welfare of the people and the revolutions that brought them to power against those who would sabotage it. Giving the police (as representatives of the government) too much power, just because the political leaders at some point wanted it that way (or successfully argued that they needed extraordinary powers over the life and liberty of residents of the country) is therefore fraught with a number of dangerous possibilities.

How the Police Affect the Government

Police agencies do the bidding of the government or carry out the wishes of the polity. However, there is a feedback loop between the police and the government. Here we are focusing on the fact that how the police carry out governmental mandates which in turn affect public perceptions and feelings toward the polity. If the police are too mild and tentative in their enforcement activities and do not seem to be making much headway, lack of faith in a perceived ineffective political system is likely to ensue. On the other hand, if the police are overzealous in the pursuit of all (even minor) wrongdoing, and pay no attention to public opinion, the government is likely to be perceived as unsympathetic and inauthentic. In democracies, both kinds of perceptions can be fatal to the legitimacy of the government. If carried on too long, people may begin the process of overthrowing the existing political order and replacing it with an alternative form (e.g., what happened as a result of the American and French Revolutions).

Let us take the example of camera radar that many local governments have turned to in recent times as a mechanism for nabbing speeding drivers to illustrate how the police affect public perceptions of government. Traffic enforcement via camera radar uses a parked or moving vehicle equipped with radar that clocks a passing automobile's speed along with a camera that takes photographs of the driver and the automobile's license plate. If the automobile is speeding, a ticket is mailed to the person in whose name it is registered. (So even if it were someone else to whom you loaned the automobile who was speeding, you would be responsible for paying the ticket, although it would be fair to note that some cities have done away with this particular provision.) While those who characteristically do not speed would likely hail this more "objective" and "sensible" way of ticketing speeders, others are not going to agree. Charges that the police are engaging in this to enrich city coffers and that the police have misplaced priorities and would be better off chasing "real criminals" such as robbers and burglars are likely to be heard. Active attempts to restrict the use of such devices (e.g., not on main thoroughfares) and their confinement to narrow areas (e.g., school zones, residential areas, through road construction projects, or adjacent to municipal parks) by applying pressure on legislators have been successful, for example, in the Colorado legislature. While everyone agrees that speeding over posted speed limits is illegal, the political will to punish people like you and me is lacking, and so we send a mixed message to the police: enforce the law, but not too vigorously; otherwise, we will make our legislators change the rules.

POLICE AND RELIGION

Unlike many of the other institutions that we have studied so far, there is very little research that focuses explicitly on the contemporary relationship between the police and religion as a social institution. Therefore, much of what we will be discussing in this section is somewhat anecdotal. Religion generally functions to preserve social order by instilling obedience to rules (e.g., "Thou Shall Not Kill") that are based explicitly on morality. The police are in a similar business: that of making sure people obey rules, usually secular ones. Religious rules have an advantage over human laws (but see Newman [1977], for contrary findings) in that they are believed to be divinely inspired. Thus, the believer who violates religious proscriptions and sins is doomed here and in the afterlife. The police, of course, are interested in finding and punishing criminal wrongdoers, here and now. Another striking parallel between the police and religion is that the two often deal with what are viewed as "residual" issues in society, that is, those areas of social life that are left over because other institutions are unable or unwilling to deal with them. For example, a pastor or a priest from a religious denomination of our choice provides us with help and guidance in our times of need (the death of a loved one, marriage, divorce counseling, etc.). While the police may deal with more mundane questions, police personnel as first responders in crisis situations also provide comfort and assistance to people during difficult times in their lives by, for example, counseling the surviving relatives of a homicide victim and helping those injured in an automobile accident. Let us examine two aspects of the relationship between religion and the police.

How Religion Affects the Police

As we have seen with regard to other institutions, the police as part of a society are also likely to be affected by the institutions of that society. Thus, police personnel are likely to hold religious preferences as individuals, although in general in the United States (given the wall of separation between church and state) this is unlikely to affect how they go about their occupational activities. However, heeding the parallels that we have described between the two groups, religion may affect the police in more subtle ways. Swanson, Territo, and Taylor (1988: 43) assert:

> The religious leaders and congregation members of a community's church groups represent one of the most potentially powerful pressure groups in the community. Their influence can, and frequently does, extend into the voting booth, which assures a high degree of responsiveness from local elected officials.

From an administrative point of view, religion or, more correctly, religious groups affect the police when they act together as a community of believers or as a pressure group on topics of interest to them. Swanson, Territo, and Taylor (1988) cite a number of vice-related issues, for example, prostitution, massage parlors, and adult-oriented businesses, as being ones where religious outrage may result in pressures on the police to do something about them. Historically, the national prohibition on alcohol in the United States between 1919 and 1933 became a law-enforcement problem after a coalition of religious groups led a national movement in support of it and succeeded in having legislation enacted (Gusfield, 1966). In addition, it is also possible to perceive the impact of contentious issues such as abortion and gay rights on police deployment and activity patterns. To keep opposing groups apart (and religious groups are likely to be found on both sides of these and other similar social issues), maintain social order, and, at the same time, avoid impinging on the rights to speech and expression that citizens of democracies enjoy is a difficult challenge.

Thus, religion affects police activity in many ways, although generally indirectly in secular democracies. However, in countries where religion and religious identities are major preoccupations (e.g., Saudi Arabia, Pakistan, Ireland, and Poland) this may not be the case. There have been continuing reports that in Russia and its former province, newly independent Georgia, members of religions other than the state-supported Russian Orthodox Church have difficulty operating. In some instances, it is alleged, the Orthodox Church encourages various wings of the government, especially the police, to harass and shut down other competing religious groups that do not have official recognition, for example, Hare Krishna and Jehovah's Witnesses (see Ochs, 2002).

How the Police Affect Religion

As we have seen in the foregoing section, in most secular democracies where religion and government are officially separate, one has to look for connections between the two because they tend to be indirect and subtle. However, in the case of countries where this kind of separation is not practiced, it is possible to see more direct linkages. In secular democracies, the police affect religion by the manner of their enforcement, lack of enforcement of, or indifference to various laws that are also of interest and concern to religious groups. For example, during the Prohibition era in the United States, one of the questions that had to be dealt with was how wine could be used in Catholic mass, where it is traditionally consumed as representing the blood of Jesus Christ. In time, specific exclusions were made in Prohibition enforcement laws to make an exception in such religious situations. Similarly, after the legalization of abortion, religious groups opposed to it began protesting outside abortion clinics. The police could hurt strongly held religious beliefs and bring the wrath of these groups on them by attempting to throw out protestors too forcefully. At the same time, since the clinics were operating legally, the police could not let their operations be disrupted because some religious group was upset. Throw into this mix the possibility that police personnel may be affiliated with one or more of the religious groups involved, and one can gauge the personal and collective costs of acting or not acting.

In places where religious identity is an important aspect of national identity, it is easier to gauge the impact of the police on religion. Saudi Arabia and Iran are both countries where the strict interpretations of the Sunni and Shia branches of Islam hold sway over all aspects of society, respectively. In both countries, religious police exist who make sure that precepts from the Koran are obeyed in everyday life. Segregating males and females, making sure that women's faces and bodies are covered, and enforcing the requirements for daily prayer and fasting during the month of Ramadan are all strictly implemented by the religious police in both countries. The idea is that by enforcing the observance of these requirements, the religious police serve religious morality and purity. Another example may be taken from the situation in Northern Ireland (the part of Ireland that is not independent and belongs to Britain). Northern Ireland has a majority of Protestants and a minority of Catholics (the latter have long agitated to leave Britain and to join their Catholic brethren to the south). The police forces here are composed of a majority of Protestants. Historically, they have been highly militaristic in the face of a long-running Catholic insurgency and interreligious violence between the Protestants and the Catholics (Drew, 1978). They are perceived by the Catholics to be an occupying force on behalf of the Protestants and are generally unwelcome in Catholic areas of Northern Ireland. In fact, Lee (1981) alleges that the mass media there typically underplays violence by the police against Catholics while overplaying Catholic violence.

In all of the cases that we have looked at so far, the police act to ensure that the dominant religious group and its position is upheld while others (who may belong to other religions or may be dissidents within the same religion) are forced to comply and go along.

POLICE AND SOCIAL INSTITUTIONS: THREE SOCIOLOGICAL PERSPECTIVES

In this chapter we have studied the relationship that the police and policing have with the major social institutions that sociologists say exist in every society: the family, education, the economy, government or polity, and religion. Let us now apply the functionalist, conflict, and interactionist perspectives to these interconnections and evaluate what we learn as a result.

From a functionalist perspective, the police are a major cog in preserving the social order and stability that allow society to function as smoothly as possible. In a sense, this generally parallels the view that police personnel hold of themselves, that is, they are the thin blue line that prevents order from turning into chaos. By working with each of the major social institutions in turn and collectively, the police ensure that deviants who go against the values that these institutions stand for are punished. As a result, police help uphold the values that institutions propagate. In addition, policing allows each of these institutions to carry out their functions in a more orderly and efficient manner. For example, by making sure that traffic flows smoothly, the police ensure that business is able to operate and, ultimately, that the economy functions. Similarly, by providing services such as VIP security to political officials, the police pave the way for the political institution to function. The question that functionalists would ask is not whether the police serve any functions, for if they did not, they would not survive. The alternative formulation that they may prefer is: What would we do if we did not have policing in order to preserve society and social expectations?

Conflict theorists, as we know, are not very interested in exploring the functionality of the police. Their questions are going to be about whom the police represent, and what those people's interests are. We have briefly mentioned the conservative nature of all social institutions. For conflict theorists, this provides a clue as to who benefits from existing social institutions and why the police are deployed to preserve the arrangements that make up the status quo. Who makes the laws that the police uphold? Who benefits, for example, from property laws? Who orders the police to restrain and control those who wish to go on strike and surround a factory? The answer to all these questions is the same: the elite, those who benefit from the way things are currently. Conflict theorists see the police as one of the instruments that members of the elite use to keep everybody else in line who might otherwise join together and threaten them. To add insult to injury, when members of the elite get into trouble (e.g., white-collar crime and corporate crime) their treatment by the police (and the rest of the criminal justice system) is much more lenient and benign than if the concerned offense was more typical of a member of the lower class or a subordinate religious or political minority. From this perspective, the police are not benevolent servants of the general public acting for the good of everybody. They are agents of those in power and all policing has to be seen in this light.

Interactionists are generally interested in what goes on within particular groups when institutions (a concept that they may have difficulty acknowledging, given that it is larger than the level of most interactionist analysis) intersect with the police. For example, in family violence situations, we mentioned above that the police now are subject to mandatory arrest policies. If they go into one of these situations and it is not clear who is responsible for provoking the violence, or who caused the most injury, how do the police know whom to arrest? What characteristics and clues do they use for this purpose? When in doubt, do they automatically arrest the male, as is often alleged? Ultimately, doing their job involves interpreting the mandates of various social institutions as they filter to the police officers on the beat. Do they assume, for example, that mothers on welfare are more likely to abuse their children while an upper-class mother is less likely to do the same? What interests interactionists is to understand how police make sense of the everyday questions that they have to grapple with and the social puzzles they have to solve. Interactionist analysis of the police–social institution nexus will focus on the mundane and continuing task that all police officers have in judging situations and identifying the bases for the making of such judgments and the consequences of either doing so or not doing so.

American social institutions affect policing and are, in turn, affected by them. Let us consider how the same happens in another country, the small South East Asian nation of Singapore.

POLICE AND SOCIAL INSTITUTIONS INTERNATIONALLY: SINGAPORE

In studying the interaction between the police and various social institutions we will use Singapore as a cross-national example. We should be aware of the following pieces of information about the island republic. It is very small in terms of size, although densely populated. British colonialists, who bought it from the ruler of Johore, a neighboring Malay sultanate, founded modern Singapore in 1819. It continued as a British colony until 1963 when it briefly joined Malaysia, and then separated in 1965 to form an independent country. It has a multiethnic (75% Chinese, 15% Malay, 8% Indian), multireligious (Buddhist, Confucianist, Taoist, Christian, Muslim, Hindu), and multilingual (Mandarin, Malay, Tamil, and English are the official languages) population of more than four million people. Although a parliamentary democracy, it has been ruled by one party, the People's Action Party, with only nominal opposition after self-rule was achieved (at that time it was still a British colony) and for all of its existence as an independent country. The British have heavily influenced much of its educational and legal traditions. It also has the enviable record of having moved from a developing country dependent mainly on its port for income to an industrial and postindustrial economy within one generation.

For the sake of comparison let us look at homicide (generally considered the most reliable, cross-nationally) statistics in Singapore, the United Kingdom, and the United States. The homicide rates per 100,000 population were, respectively, 0.8, 1.6, and 5.6 percent. In other words, the homicide rates in the United Kingdom and United States are twice and seven times more, respectively, in comparison to Singapore. Overall, Singapore is considered a safe society. According to many observers, the country's safety and internal security come at a price, in that the government and, by extension, the police intrude in a number of areas of social life. Perhaps we should say that all social institutions are dominated and controlled by the political institution. The Singapore Police Force (SPF) is directly under the Ministry of Home Affairs and has around 7,500 officers. Further to this, there are around 2,500 others who are doing "national service" (a form of mandatory military draft) and nearly 21,000 reservists are also available. A commissioner of police who is assisted by four deputy commissioners heads the organization. There are also two auxiliary police forces that deal separately with port operations and business/industrial security.

The SPF has implemented a form of community policing that involves Neighborhood Police Posts (NPPs, based on the Japanese *koban* system) that allows it to be available and at the same time to keep an eye on various parts of Singapore. Given that most Singaporeans, out of necessity, live in multistory apartments (flats), surveillance by the NPPs is easier than if more land was available and residential areas were less concentrated. A form of decentralized policing that involves Neighborhood Police Centers (NPCs) that provide the full gamut of police services at 32 different locations throughout the island has also been implemented recently. In addition, a scheme known as the National Police Cadet Corps (NPCC) involves secondary students (the equivalent of Grade 7 and above) with the SPF while in school and also a pool of potential recruits after they complete their secondary education. Finally, meritorious police officers are selected to receive scholarships that entitle them to higher education locally or abroad. Certain problems have been identified in Singapore policing. These include the lack of change in dealing with marital violence (Ganapathy, 2002; see also Choi and Edelson, 1995), gangs consisting of minority group members (Ganapathy and Fee, 2002), policing large weekend gatherings of migrant workers, ambiguous relationships with Chinese secret societies (Mak, 1974), and interacting with private security guards (Nalla, Hoffman, and Christian, 1996).

It is possible to see the tight integration of the police with Singapore's political institution (the connection to the Ministry of Home Affairs and the close surveillance of the public). Traditional conceptions held by the police regarding the family act to forestall action on marital violence. The institution of education and students are involved with the police through the NPCC and by the scholarships available for higher education. Much of Singapore's police efforts are to keep the economic institution functioning (notice the specialized forces focusing on the port and business/industrial security). The only institution that is somewhat unconnected to policing is religion, although even here the government has used police powers and actions to curtail religious groups thought to be possible centers of antigovernment sentiment. The close connection with all social institutions, with the government/polity taking a leading role, is clear when we consider the case of Singapore.

Now that we have learned about the impact of various social institutions on policing in Singapore, let us travel to Europe, where we will examine (in the accompanying box) how the police and an institution, the schools, interact in one municipality in Serbia.

 ## SUMMARY

This chapter dealt with the interconnections between the police and major social institutions in society. Sociologists have identified five important institutions that deal with various facets of society. These are the family, education, the economy, the government or polity, and religion. We learned about the tremendous impact these institutions have on our behavior, that they provide members with the values that we learn, and that they tend to be generally conservative. We then examined the interaction between these five major institutions and the police in two ways: how each institution affected the police and how the police affected each institution. We then used three sociological perspectives to shed more light on these interactions. Functionalists focused on the importance of the police in ensuring public order; conflict theorists on how the institutions controlled by the elite used the police to keep themselves in power; and interactionists who are interested in the meanings associated with police–institution exchanges. Finally, we focused on the case of Singapore as an illustration of how closely another country binds the police to the important social institutions in that country.

KEY TERMS

Costs of crime: The economic implications and consequences of crime, some of which are connected to the police.

Economy: Social institution that ensures that needed goods and services are produced and distributed and that workers who will contribute to this end through their labor are integrated into relevant occupations.

Education: Social institution that provides for teaching each new generation of members the history, culture, or way of life of a society as well as to train them for future work.

Family: Social institution that makes sure that societal members channel their sexuality for the purpose of procreation and that they then bring up their children such that the society does not die out due to the lack of new members or their neglect.

Government (or polity): Social institution that relates to power within a society and its exercise in terms of who will play leadership roles at various levels and how they are selected and replaced.

Modernization: The process by which societies become economically developed, or industrialized, which in general leads to increases in crime.

Relative deprivation: The gap between people's expectations regarding what they feel they are entitled to (e.g., in terms of goods and lifestyles) and what is actually available to them given their current capabilities and place in a society.

Religion: Social institution that provides meaningful answers to certain residual questions that are important to the lives of a society's members, for example, questions regarding our origins, the reasons for our human existence, and our ultimate destinations (including after death).

Social institution: A set of well-established, widely held rules and procedures that are prescribed for meeting important needs in a society and as a result pattern social relationships and interaction.

 REVIEW QUESTIONS

1. What are social institutions? List and describe six major social institutions.
2. How do the police interact with any of the six major social institutions that we identified?
3. Describe how the Singapore police are influenced by that country's major social institutions? How do the Singapore police affect the social institutions in turn?

 DISCUSSION QUESTIONS

1. Which sociological perspective on social institutions and their impact on policing do you find most convincing? Discuss why.
2. Which among the six major institutions has the most impact on policing? Discuss why this is so.
3. Which among the six major institutions has the least impact on policing? Discuss why this is so.

REFERENCES

Alexander, D. A. and L. G. Walker (1996) "The Perceived Impact of Police Work on Police Officers' Spouses and Families." *Stress Medicine* 12: 239–246.

Berg, Bruce L. (1992) *Law Enforcement: An Introduction to Police in Society.* Boston, MA: Allyn and Bacon.

Carter, David L.; Allen D. Sapp and Darrel W. Stephens (1989) *The State of Police Education: Policy Directions for the 21st Century.* Washington, DC: Police Executive Research Forum.

Choi, Alfred and Jeffrey L. Edelson (1995) "Advocating Legal Intervention in Wife Assaults: Results from a National Survey of Singapore." *Journal of Interpersonal Violence* 10: 243–258.

Conklin, John E. (1995) *Criminology.* Fifth Edition. Boston: Allyn and Bacon.

Dempsey, John S. (1994) *Policing: An Introduction to Law Enforcement.* St. Paul: West Publishing.

Drew, Paul (1978) "Accusations: The Occasioned Use of Members' Knowledge of 'Religious Geography' in Describing Events." *Sociology* 12: 1–22.

Forest, James J. F. (2006) *Homeland Security: Protecting America's Targets. Volume Two: Public Spaces and Social Institutions.* Westport, CT: Praeger Security International.

Ganapathy, Narayanan (2002) "Rethinking the Problem of Policing Marital Violence: A Singapore Perspective." *Policing and Society* 12: 173–180.

Ganapathy, Narayanan and Lian Kwen Fee (2002) "Policing Minority Street Corner Gangs in Singapore: A View from the Street." *Policing and Society* 12: 139–152.

Gurr, Ted R. (1970) *Why Men Rebel.* Princeton, NJ: Princeton University Press.

Gusfield, Joseph S. (1966) *Symbolic Crusade.* Urbana, IL: University of Illinois Press.

Harlow, C. (2003) *Education and Correctional Populations.* Washington, DC: US Department of Justice, Bureau of Justice Statistics.

Kroes, W. H.; B. L. Margolis and J. L. Hurrell, Jr. (1974) "Job Stress in Policemen." *Journal of Police Science and Administration* 2: 145–155.

LaGrange, Randy L. (1993) *Policing American Society.* Chicago: Nelson-Hall.

Lee, Alfred M. (1981) "Mass Media Mythmaking in the United Kingdom's Interethnic Struggles." *Ethnicity* 8: 18–30.

Mak, Lau Fong (1974) "The Tripartite Relationship of Secret Societies, Police and Subscribers." *National Taiwan University Journal of Sociology.* 10: 87–95.

Manning, Peter K. (1995) "Economic Rhetoric and Policing Reform." Pp. 257–264 In Victor E. Kappeler (ed.) *The Police and Society: Touchstone Readings.* Prospect Heights, IL: Waveland Press.

Nalla, Mahesh K.; Vincent J. Hoffman and Kenneth E. Christian (1996) "Security Guards' Perceptions of their Relationship with Police Officers and the Public in Singapore." *Security Journal* 7: 281–286.

Newman, Graeme (1977) "Social Institutions and the Control of Deviance: A Cross-National Opinion Survey." *European Journal of Social Psychology* 7: 39–59.

Ochs, Michael (2002) "Persecution of Jehovah's Witnesses in Georgia Today." *Religion State and Society* 30: 239–276.

Rosenbaum, Dennis P.; Robert L. Flewelling; Susan L. Bailey; Chris L. Rigwalt and Deanna L. Wilkinson (1994) "Cops in the Classroom: A Longitudinal Evaluation of Drug Abuse Resistance Education (DARE)." *Journal of Research in Crime and Delinquency* 31: 3–31.

Rosenbaum, Dennis P. and Gordon S. Hanson (1998) "Assessing the Effects of School-Based Drug Education: A Six-Year Multivariate Analysis of Project D. A. R.E." *Journal of Research in Crime and Delinquency* 35: 381–412.

Shelley, Louise F. (1981) *Crime and Modernization.* Carbondale, IL: Southern Illinois University Press.

Sherman, Lawrence and Richard A. Berk (1984) "The Specific Deterrence Effects of Arrest for Domestic Assault." *American Sociological Review* 49: 261–272.

Straus, Murray (1995) *Physical Violence in American Families: Factors and Adaptations to Violence in 8,145 Families.* New Brunswick, NJ: Transaction.

Swanson, Charles R.; Leonard Territo and Robert W. Taylor (1988) *Police Administration: Structures, Processes and Behavior.* Second Edition. New York: Macmillan.

POLICE AND SOCIAL INSTITUTIONS IN SERBIA

Sladjana Djurić and Želimir Kešetović

Serbia is located in the central part of the Balkan Peninsula, occupying an area of 88,361 sq. km. with a total population of around 7.5 million. Between 1945 and 1990, Serbia was part of the Socialist Federal Republic of Yugoslavia. The country fell into civil war between 1990 and 1995. Serbia, after spending more than a decade under autocratic rule, took its first steps to democratic transition after the defeat of Slobodan Milošević in October 2000 (Kešetović, 2009).

During the last decade of twentieth century, Serbian police were an instrument of the ruling elite and one of the main pillars of the nondemocratic regime. The only thing that was important to the police was that they be seen in the eyes of the ruling elites as an efficient protector of the existing system interpreted in terms of "constitutional order" and "national interest." The protection of citizen's lives and property were tasks of much less importance—a state of affairs that had tragic consequences for both the police organization and public safety. Besides politicization, processes that devastated police professionalism in Serbia were also

centralization, militarization, criminalization, and ethnicization (Kešetović, 2007). The police force was misused to combat political opposition through surveillance on leaders of the opposition parties, use of excessive force against demonstrators on the streets, etc. The opposition media and emerging Nongovernmental Organization (NGO) sector were treated as enemies, nonpatriots, traitors, foreign payees, and spies, while the issues of minority groups were of no importance at all. The result of these processes was the significant decrease in public confidence in the police, which was seen as politicized, crime prone, brutal, and corrupt (Kešetović, 2000).

Bearing in mind the aforementioned features of the Serbian police and its role in maintaining an autocratic regime in the 1990s, police reform, and reform of the whole security sector as well, became the priority of the first democratic government as a prerequisite for the transition from an authoritarian to a democratic model. Cornerstone challenges of this reform were flagged as the four "Ds"—depoliticization, decentralization, decriminalization, and demilitarization. While high-ranking Serbian police officials are quite satisfied with the course and results of the reform process (Kuribak, 2008), foreign experts (Downes, 2004) and national independent researchers are considerably more critical (Milosavljević, 2004; Kešetović and Davidović, 2007), admonishing that fulfilling the key objectives of reform, the four "Ds," is not a matter of form, new organization, and image, but the essence and a system of values that the police organization is built upon. An analysis conducted by the Organization for Security and Cooperation in Europe (OSCE) concluded that reform was moving very slowly, was subject to variation in direction, and lacked either a clear strategy or a defined time frame (Bakić and Gajić, 2006).

Regardless of those rather contradictory assessments, it should be noted that certain improvements in police–society relations have been made. In cooperation with international organizations and agencies, the Ministry of Interior (MoI) developed a community policing agenda premised upon a bottom-up approach and implemented projects in ten pilot sites across Serbia in June 2003. This implementation of somewhat different community policing models was supported by four international organizations: the OSCE, the Swiss Agency for Development and Cooperation, the UK Department for International Development (DFID), and the Norwegian Police Service. The plan was that the pilot project would last for three to five years, and that the MoI would create a national strategy prior to the development of a community policing model suitable for national rollout. In late 2004, the results of these developments were published in the Joint Evaluation Report conducted by the Serbian MoI and the DFID. Experiences are different and hard to compare because there was no single model of community policing. The report concluded that a great deal has been achieved and that the piloting process has provided a strong foundation for further development and expansion to other parts of Serbia, but that there is still a long way to go before the model can be considered sustainable. On the other hand, the project of implementing a modern and multiethnic police service in the municipalities of Presevo, Medvedja, and Bujanovac in southern Serbia was highly rated.

Connected to the community policing project is the problem-oriented concept that is being implemented with the support of the National Police Directorate of the Kingdom of Norway. Community policing focuses on police–citizens cooperation in indentifying security risks and threats. The community policing concept works toward preventing and eliminating the circumstances and conditions conducive for criminal and civic disorder activities.

Specific attention has been given for the protection of children and juveniles from crime and violent actions. This awareness includes making young people understand the consequences of drug and alcohol use. Making young people aware of poor decision-making has become a joint effort of the Ministry of Interior, Ministry of Education, Ministry of Health, and the Ministry of Labour.

In the municipality of Zvezdara, a suburb of Belgrade, community policing includes educating young people about drug use and personal safety. An advisory board provides the Zvezdara Police Department with input in their crime prevention efforts. These advisory boards comprise pupils, parents, school staff, and police officers.

The Serbian police have made positive changes in their treatment of juvenile offenders. Serbian law requires police protection for juvenile offenders accused of criminal offenses. The law also required that the police must cooperate and work with social welfare centers. Serbian police officers have received training from foreign officers, which has resulted in improvement of police operations. In conjunction with the improvement of police operations, Serbian law has also improved policing by providing them with guidelines in their dealings with families and criminal offenders.

In addition to these improvements, the Serbian police have made progress with the protection of human rights by working with NGOs that deal with the protection of women's and children's rights.

NGOs have not been successful in the protection of human rights. NGOs have been most successful in gaining police cooperation—in decreasing domestic violence, human trafficking, and violence against people with disabilities (Kešetović, 2009).

Relations between the media and the police have improved since the 1990s. Mistrust still exists between the police and media. The lack of trust and cooperation between the police and media can be traced back to the times of the former autocratic regime (Kešetović, 2009).

The police and society in Serbia are not in confrontation, but neither are they partners. Police–community relations are very important and the government must make an effort toward depoliticization and giving the police autonomy. The police must be decentralized and should work toward cooperation and gaining the trust of the community. Only when there is trust and cooperation will a true partnership exist between the police and the people.

References

Bakić, B. & N. Gajić (2006) *Police Reform in Serbia: Five Years Later*, Law Enforcement Department OSCE Mission to Serbia and Montenegro, Belgrade, also available at www.osce.org/publications/fry/2004/01/18262_550_en.pdf.

Downes, M. (2004) *Police Reform in Serbia: Towards the Creation of a Modern and Accountable Police Service*, Law Enforcement Department OSCE Mission to Serbia and Montenegro, Belgrade, also available at http://www.osce.org/publications/fry/2004/01/18262_550_en.pdf.

Kešetović, Ž. (2000) *Odnosi policije sa javnošću*, Police Public Relations, Beograd: Viša škola unutrašnjih poslova.

Kešetović, Ž. (2007) Improving police and media relations in Serbia. *Sociologija Mintis ir veiksmas* 20(2), 92–108.

Kešetović, Ž. (2009) Understanding diversity in policing—Serbian perspective. *Policing* 32(3), 431–445.

Kešetović, Ž. & D. Davidović (2007) 'Policing in Serbia: Challenges and Developments', in G. Meško & B. Dobovšek (eds.), *Policing in Emerging Democracies: Critical Reflections*, Ljubljana: Faculty of Criminal Justice and Security.

Kuribak, M. (2008) 'Police Reform in Serbia', in M. Hadžić (ed.), *Security Sector Reform in Serbia: Achievements and Prospects*, Belgrade: Centre for Civil Military Relations, pp. 51–64.

Milosavljević, B. (2004) 'Reform of the Police and Security Services in Serbia and Montenegro: Attained Results or Betrayed Expectations', in P. Fluri & M. Hadžić (eds.), *Sourcebook on Security Sector Reform: Collection of Papers*, Geneva/Belgrade: Geneva centre for Democratic Control of Armed Forces and Centre for Civil-Military Relations, pp. 249–274.

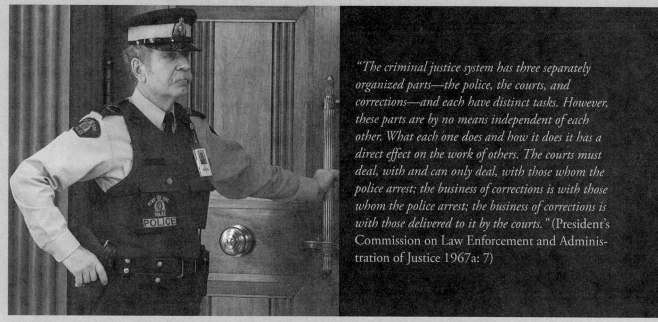

CHAPTER 4

"The criminal justice system has three separately organized parts—the police, the courts, and corrections—and each have distinct tasks. However, these parts are by no means independent of each other. What each one does and how it does it has a direct effect on the work of others. The courts must deal, with and can only deal, with those whom the police arrest; the business of corrections is with those whom the police arrest; the business of corrections is with those delivered to it by the courts." (President's Commission on Law Enforcement and Administration of Justice 1967a: 7)

A Royal Canadian Mounted Police officer keeps the door shut to the federal courtroom in Ottawa Thursday, Jan. 31, 2008 where Mohamed Harkat is appearing to fight his re-arrest after allegedly breaking his bail conditions. (Credit: © AP Photo/Tom Hanson, CP)

POLICE AND THE CRIMINAL JUSTICE SYSTEM

OBJECTÌVES:

1. The student will become familiar with the development of policing.
2. The student will become familiar with the evolution of American policing.
3. The student will understand the structure of American policing.
4. The student will have an understanding of how the American police interact with other sectors of the criminal justice system.
5. The student will learn how functionalism, conflict theory, and interactionism are studied in relation to the police and the criminal justice system.

POLICE IN THE UNITED STATES

The police in the United States trace their roots to the British Isles, and specifically to the London Metropolitan Police. The Peelian Principles were the foundation for the London Metropolitan Police. The premise of the Peelian Principles was that the police were accountable to the people. Since the English settled and claimed the eastern coast of what is now the United States, it seems reasonable that the English settlers would bring their customs, traditions, and culture with them. This would also include the English system of peacekeeping and order maintenance.

During America's colonial period many colonial cities adopted the British constable–night watch system. Boston established a night watch in 1636. New York and Philadelphia followed Boston and established a night watch system. In New York, the night watch carried rattles and was referred to as "the Rattlewatch" (*Task Force on Police*, 1967: 5). The system of the constable night watch remained the primary peacekeeping system of colonial America until the mid-eighteenth century. Like England, America's northern cities were being industrialized and, with the consequent increase in population due to immigration from various parts of Europe and the movement of African Americans from the south. This increased population led to an increase in crime and social disorder because of the lack of job opportunities and density of people living together.

The British in 1829 adopted the "New Police" as the peacekeeping model in their country. The British model was adopted by New York City in 1844 by the New York State legislature and put into place in 1845. Up until 1845, New York City had decentralized policing, a separate day and night watch. This changed in that year and the policing service was centralized in one police department. Other cities followed New York's example: New Orleans, Baltimore, Philadelphia, and Chicago. By the 1860s the New York model was accepted with minor modifications in most of America's larger cities. Although the American police adopted the New Police model of England, there were three major issues that confronted them. These issues were: (1) a controversy over the adoption of uniforms; (2) a concern about arming the police; and (3) using appropriate force in making arrests (Peak, 2009: 17–24).

Continuing Controversies

With regard to the first two issues mentioned above, Americans came to accept police officers wearing uniforms and carrying firearms. In fact, some states prohibit police officers giving traffic citations unless they are wearing a police uniform. As to firearms, it would be unthinkable for an American police officer to be unarmed and it may be difficult to disarm them. Indeed, there is currently no movement to disarm them.

The third issue—the appropriate force in making an arrest—continues to be a major one. Two incidents that have made world news are the Rodney King incident, when Los Angeles police officers on March 3, 1991, used excessive force by beating Rodney King with their batons. A private citizen videotaped the beating, and it found its way to CNN where the videotape was shown not only in America but also throughout the world (http://archievescnn.com/2001.law/3/02/beatinganniversary.king02).

The second incident occurred on December 13, 1999, when New York City police officers responded to a fight outside a club in Brooklyn. By the time the officers arrived, Abner Louima, apparently trying to break up the fight, had been drawn into the melee (Frye, 2001). In the scuffle, Officer Justin Volpe was punched. Volpe believed Louima was the culprit. Louima was taken into custody and taken to the precinct. While at the precinct, Louima had a two-to-three-foot stick forcibly inserted into his rectum (Frey, 2001: 232–234). Obviously, Louima like King received severe physical injuries. Incidents such as King's and Louima's keep the use of abusive force in full view of the public and remind us that this issue has not gone away. In the meantime, other issues have cropped up for the police. Let us take a look at some of them.

Decentralization

Since the initiation of American policing in the nineteenth century, policing in America's cities has been primarily neighborhood oriented. Police in the United States are decentralized unlike many other countries, for example, France and Italy. From the time the English settled on the eastern coast of the United States, policing has always been a local matter. Currently, we find that the decentralized model has not changed from the eighteenth century. There are almost 13,000 local police departments (Hickman and Reaves, 2006a: 7). **Decentralization** means the United States does not have one centralized police department for the country. Policing in America is decentralized because America has three levels of policing: federal, state, and local. At the federal level there are about 50 agencies such as the FBI and secret service. The state level has state police and highway patrol, while on the local level there is the municipal, county, and sheriff's departments. It is the cities, towns, and villages of the United States that organize and carry out policing for the most part. The concept of decentralized policing appears to be integral to the culture of the United States and in all probability will be with America as long as it exists as a country.

decentralization

Multiple police agencies at the local, state, and federal levels of government.

Police Misconduct

A major concern with policing in the nineteenth and twentieth century was the existence of corruption, inefficiency, incompetence, and political influence (*Police Task Force: The Police*, 1967). These nineteenth and twentieth century issues have cropped up in the twenty-first century and may need to be addressed head-on. As a society can we eliminate corruption, inefficiency, incompetence, and political influence from our police departments? Perhaps we may never achieve this, but it does not mean that we as a society should not make an attempt to correct police abuses, inefficiency, incompetence, and unnecessary political influence when found.

Technology

At the end of World War I, technology began to have an impact on policing, mostly with three major technological changes (Shook, 1997: 160). First, the patrol vehicle became an integral part of police patrol, allowing officers to cover wider areas. Second, reactive approach

When the police respond to a 911 call or a crime problem.

the telephone became a valuable tool for citizens who wished to contact the police. Prior to the telephone, police contact was rather difficult. The advent of the telephone may have inadvertently created the **reactive approach** to policing. The term "reactive" is used here in the sense that citizens telephoned the police and the police reacted to the citizen's telephone call by driving over to where their service was needed. Third, the two-way radio also had a major impact on policing. Initially, radio communication was one way, but in the 1930s two-way radios became common in police departments. The two-way radio allowed police headquarters to be in constant communication with their police officers. Now, it would be unthinkable and inconceivable for the police to function without the use of automobiles, telephones, and two-way communication. The equipment used today has also substantially advanced with the incorporation of video cameras and onboard computers into police cars and at headquarters. The Internet is also being employed for community relations, departmental websites, and crime prevention (e.g., posting the names on sex offender registries and for other crime fighting purposes) (Palmiotto, 2005).

Minority Police Officers

The term "minority group" includes women, African Americans, Hispanics, Asians, and homosexuals. While it is now illegal to discriminate against anyone because of gender, race, nationality, religion, or sexual orientation, this was not always true.

African Americans possess the longest history in the policing field. The city of Pittsburgh was the first to appoint black men as special police officers to allow the black community there to defend itself against white mobs (Dulaney, 1996: 4). After the Civil War, southern cities began employing African Americans as regular police officers. An example of this is the city of New Orleans, which appointed black officers in 1867. By 1870, approximately a quarter of the New Orleans police force was black. Similarly, other cities began to appoint blacks to their police departments. Chicago did so in 1872, followed by Philadelphia, Cleveland, Detroit, and St. Louis (Dulaney, 1996: 18–19). By the latter part of the twentieth century, black police officers were more or less integrated into police departments, and sometimes rose to leadership positions. Of course, a great deal of their advancement in equality and opportunity can be attributed to the civil rights movement of the 1960s.

Although Hispanic police officers may have an equally long history of participation in American policing, one of the authors of this book found limited information on this subject when researching information on Hispanic officers. Another minority group lacking a voice in recorded police history is the homosexual community. For most of American police history, they have been discriminated against. It was not until the 1990s that homosexuals could openly declare their sexual orientation and be accepted as police officers. Today, it would be illegal for police departments not to employ qualified homosexuals (Palmiotto, 2005: 247–254).

The minority group, not in a numerical sense, as we make clear in Chapter 12 of this book, that has had the longest documented history of their role in policing are women. Women have been involved in policing since the 1880s (Appier, 1992).

Initially, women were involved primarily as "matrons" in charge of women who had been arrested and female prisoners. The Los Angeles Police Department is credited with introducing the title "police women" when they appointed Alice Stebbens Wells, as the city's first female police officer (Hess, 2009: 27). During the early era of women in policing they were primarily utilized in "preventive roles." Chapter 11 will go into more detail about the role of women in crime prevention.

The Tumultuous 1960s

The 1960s was a decade of turmoil in the criminal justice world. There are several events that not only changed criminal justice but also changed America as a society. There were large-scale race riots in major American cities and the assassinations of President John Kennedy, Senator Robert Kennedy, and the great civil rights leader, Martin Luther King, Jr. The civil rights movement was a major part of the 1960s and many of the rights that African Americans and other minority groups currently enjoy were gained during that decade.

The **hippie** generation or **flower children** confronted governmental authority, specifically the police as the government's representative of the status quo. Hippies were against the Vietnam War, which in the latter part of the 1960s divided America. Protest against the Vietnam War sometimes became violent and this violence was often directed toward the police. The police came under tremendous public scrutiny and the United States Supreme Court expanded interpretations of the Bill of Rights in such court decisions as Mapp v. Ohio (1961) and Miranda v. Arizona (1966). These cases decided that police were accountable when they search an individual and that individuals being questioned by the police must be informed of their constitutional rights to refuse to answer police questions.

President Lyndon Johnson, in response to the violence of the 1960s, created *The President's Commission on Law Enforcement and Administration of Justice* in 1965, often referred to as the President's Crime Commission. In 1967 this President's Crime Commission submitted its report and made recommendations to not only improve policing but also criminal justice as a process. The President's Crime Commission report in *The Challenge of Crime in a Free Society* (1967: 100–119) included the following recommendations among others: police departments should maintain good community-relations; police in minority neighborhoods should have advisory committees; the police should recruit police officers from various minority groups; and training and education for criminal justice personnel should be increased.

hippie or flower children

Young people of the 1960s who dropped out of society. They were against the Vietnam War and the materialism of American society.

Policing Today

As American society changes, so does policing. The police officer of a hundred years ago may not understand today's concepts of policing, nor perhaps would the officer of sixty, fifty, or forty years ago. Police officers are now better trained and better educated. Contemporary police are more diversified. Women police officers generally perform the same tasks as their male counterparts and hold all positions that male officers do. There are female police chiefs as well as African American police chiefs.

There are homosexual police officers, when a decade or two ago this would have been unthinkable. Further, police officers possess technology unheard of even a few years ago. They have computers, video cameras in their police cruisers, and cell phones. They also have the availability of Automated Fingerprinting Identification Systems (AFIS) and DNA. Modern police officers have many tools to help them do their jobs and new technology is being developed and improved upon to make the officers even more efficient and effective.

STRUCTURE OF POLICING IN AMERICAN CRIMINAL JUSTICE

Acting as gatekeepers to American criminal justice, the police in the United States are highly decentralized. Since America's colonial period, the primary emphasis on policing was the maintenance of peace and order at the local level of government. The decentralization philosophy and the cultural value that policing should be a function of local government still holds true today. Since the colonial period, policing in the United States has evolved dramatically.

Policing in the United States can be classified into three large categories: federal, state, and local policing. Since our governmental structure has three levels of government—federal, state, and local—it seems reasonable that policing would fit into this structure. At the national level, the United States Constitution allows the federal government to pass legislation that will protect the federal government and enhance its functions. The Constitution also allows the federal government to create and maintain policing agencies to enforce its laws. The states gain their authority for policing from the Tenth Amendment of the United States Constitution. The Tenth Amendment reserves for the states, or for the people, the balance of the powers not provided to the federal government. The states have the authority to pass their own laws to maintain order and to establish state policing agencies or to allow the local government to establish a policing agency. Generally, the structure of local government policing can be classified into two sections: municipal police, as in cities, towns, townships, boroughs, and villages, depending on the state laws; and the county police and/or the sheriff's department.

Local government has to be distinguished from state or federal government. Any level of government not identified as either federal or state should be considered local. A local police officer works for the local level of government. Local policing agencies therefore include police officers, chiefs-of-police, sheriffs, and deputy sheriffs. They have legal jurisdiction over a specific geographical area that has been defined by law. For example, city police have jurisdiction within city limits and county police of the sheriff's department have jurisdiction within a specific county.

There are approximately 16,661 police agencies at the local and state levels of government. Of this total, 13,524 are local police departments, 3,088 are sheriff's departments, and there are forty-nine **state police** agencies. It has been estimated that there are 556,631 full-time employees who work for local police departments. About

state police

State police who combine traffic duties with law enforcement and criminal investigations.

78 percent or 436,000 of the total employees are sworn police officers (Hickman and Reaves, 2006a,b: 1). Approximately one-third of police officers work in departments with 1,000 or more officers, and about three-fifths of officers work for departments with at least 100 officers. Local police departments that employ fewer than ten police officers account for approximately 5 percent of all local police officers. Around 77 percent of police departments service communities with less than 10,000 residents. However, these agencies employ only about 15 percent of the police officers. Police officers in departments that serve a community of 100,000 or more residents constitute about one-half of all police officers in local government. The largest local department in the country is the New York City Police Department with approximately 36,000 police officers, followed by Chicago with over 13,500 officers (Hickman and Reaves, 2006a: 8).

Generally, local police are assigned a wide variety of functions usually without any degree of government planning. The priorities among various police functions have not been specified. Local police operate on a broad mission with broad functions and often find that they are responding to the influences of larger local, state, and federal governments. The American local police are assigned numerous miscellaneous functions to which no other government agencies are assigned. If local government has a task to be performed and they do not know who to give it to, they generally give it to the local police to carry out. For example, police are required to report potholes they discover while on patrol (Palmiotto, 2005: 36–40).

Most police tasks revolve around noncriminal activity, such as directing traffic and operating holding cells. The usual activities that police encounter include handling traffic accidents, directing traffic, and dealing with a myriad of hazards and dangers. With the use of telephones and two-way radios in patrol cars, the police have often provided a reactive approach to policing. Reactive policing means that police officers are responding to service calls or incidents. A citizen telephones the police and the police dispatchers send a patrol officer to handle the incident. Since the 1970s when 911, the emergency contact phone number, arrived, *response time* became important to policing. The universal 911 number made calling the police easier. The **proactive approach** is the opposite of the reactive approach. In the proactive approach, the police initiate the action and do not just respond to an incident (Palmiotto, 2005: 36–40).

proactive approach

When the police initiate action to solve a crime problem.

County Sheriff

Usually, the state constitution confers that the elected sheriff of the county will be designated the chief law enforcement officer of the county. The legal duties and responsibilities of the sheriff vary from state to state and even from county to county within a specific state. In some counties, sheriffs have almost no responsibilities; in others they are primarily concerned with courthouse security and operating the county jail. In others they function similar to a municipal police department, dealing with the unincorporated areas of a county. The sheriff's office also provides a variety of services to the counties they service and these, too, vary from state to state and county to county. These duties include: (1) providing traditional police service to the unincorporated areas of the county; (2) operating the county jail; (3) executing criminal and civil papers; (4) serving as a court bailiff; (5) investigating public offenses; and (6) serving as tax collectors (Gaines and Miler, 2009: 142).

There are 3,061 sheriff's departments in the United States with approximately 174,000 sworn officers (Hickman and Reaves, 2006b: 5–6). Generally, the county sheriff is elected by the electorate of that county and usually serves a four-year term. In most cases the county sheriff has prior policing experience. The prior experience in many instances often includes being either a state patrol officer or a city police officer. A full-service sheriff's department offers patrol, investigative, court, and correctional services. The Los Angeles Sheriff's Department (LASD) has a national reputation and offers an example of a full-service sheriff's department. LASD provides unincorporated areas of Los Angeles County with police services. The unincorporated areas of the county along with several cities that do not provide their own police services contract with the LASD to do so (Palmiotto, 2005: 46).

State Police Agencies

During the first decade of the twentieth century the modern state police agency was initiated. Due to labor disputes and acts of violence between coal companies and workers, the governor of Pennsylvania established the Pennsylvania State Police in 1905 to maintain order between workers and coal companies (Hess, 2009: 22). Other states used Pennsylvania as a model to establish their state police agencies. State police agencies were established for several reasons including: (1) to assist local police agencies; (2) to investigate crimes that crossed legal jurisdictions; (3) to provide police protection to rural communities; and (4) to be strike breakers (Gaines and Miller, 2009: 142).

Today every state, except Hawaii, has a state police agency. State police agencies have police powers to enforce all state laws. They can patrol all highways in the state and can investigate crimes. State police agencies are often given the power to maintain criminal records, fingerprint files, and crime statistics and oversee police training facilities. One important function given to them is to investigate complaints against local police officers and agencies.

There are basically two forms of state police agencies. The Highway Patrol, which has the responsibility of enforcing the state's traffic laws on highways in the state and land adjacent to the highway (Gaines and Miller, 2009: 142–143). Those states that have **Highway Patrol** agencies (e.g., Colorado, Kansas, Ohio, Georgia, Florida, and California) have state police agencies to investigate crimes in those communities that do not have local police agencies or assist local police in investigations (e.g., Kansas, which has the Kansas Bureau of Investigation, and Colorado, which has the Colorado Bureau of Investigation). States that have one state police agency that is responsible for both traffic laws and general police responsibilities include Michigan, New York, and Pennsylvania.

Federal Law Enforcement

Until the late twentieth century, the federal government was primarily involved in safeguarding the country's revenues and protecting its mail (Siegel and Senna, 2004: 7). In the first decade of the twentieth century, the Attorney General of the United

....
highway patrol

State police officers responsible for enforcing traffic laws on state highways and land adjacent to the highway.

States created the Bureau of Investigation. This agency is now known as the FBI. The bureau was created to investigate corruption and violation of business law.

The Bureau of Internal Revenue within the Treasury Department was established in order to enforce the Harrison Act, designed to regulate the importing, manufacturing, and dispensing of drugs. It was not until the 1960s that the federal government began to take a serious role in policing at the state and local level. In the 1960s the federal government began to provide grants to state and local police agencies for training, equipment, technology, and manpower. For the past several decades, local police officers have been incorporated into federal task forces for the Drug Enforcement Agency (DEA) and the FBI.

Federal law enforcement consists of approximately fifty agencies. Usually, federal agencies have limited powers with a narrow investigative scope. However, they have tremendous amounts of prestige associated with them and are often leaders and innovators that other state and local police agencies follow. Federal law enforcement agencies can be found in every cabinet position of the government. The best-known agencies are found in the Department of Justice, the Department of Treasury, and the Department of Homeland Security.

POLICE INTERACTION WITH THE CRIMINAL JUSTICE SYSTEM

The American legal system of reacting to crime and dealing with offenders has several key components or elements that are referred to as the "criminal justice system," a term that was popularized with the publication of *The President's Commission on Law Enforcement and Administration of Justice* (1967). The organizational components or sectors of the criminal justice system are generally understood to be the police, the courts, and corrections. Each component has specific responsibilities. The police enforce the law; the courts hear the legality of a crime, and corrections holds those convicted of a crime.

Each of the above-mentioned components has distinct tasks and procedures. However, each one of these parts is not completely independent of the other. Since the president's *The President's Commission on Law Enforcement and Administration of Justice*, also known as the *President's Crime Commission*, presented its findings, the juvenile justice system, given its role of diverting the young away from the adult system, has been conceptualized as a parallel component of the adult criminal justice system (see Zimring, 2005). The primary reason for this has been that juvenile offenders are treated, for the most part, in a totally different manner than adult offenders. The juvenile justice process functions in a civil manner with different terminology and types of punishment. The person who has reached the legal age of adulthood will be treated as an adult criminal and go through the adult criminal justice system. The severity of punishments for an adult tried in criminal courts is much greater than for a juvenile tried in a juvenile court.

Each component of the criminal justice system has major effects on the work of the other parts. For example, if the local police department decides to make a drug bust on Friday night and the county jail has no jail spaces, the police have created a problem for the county corrections facility. Most counties have a limited number of judges who are available to hear a specific number of criminal cases at the same time and this affects the volume and flow of cases processed. A large number of arrests by the police or the prosecutor having a large number of cases to be tried can create a backlog for the courts component. In order for the criminal justice system to flow in an efficient and effective manner, the police, courts, and corrections will be required to cooperate with each other. If the corrections component releases sex offenders, recent legislation in a number of states makes it mandatory for them to register with the local police department. That police department then has the job of maintaining and updating these sex offender registries.

The President's Crime Commission (1967) implied that the criminal justice system works as a continuum that consists of an orderly progression of events. Some of the events would receive publicity, such as a trial, while other aspects of the process would receive little or no attention (p. 7). However, as we have seen, the effects of each component of the criminal justice system are not "orderly" as understood in systemic terms but are multifaceted, often unanticipated, and significant. We are used to thinking of the criminal justice system as one entity that begins with the police, flows through the courts, and ends with corrections. It might be more realistic to think of the feedback loops that exist within the system. In other words, we should think of how each sector affects, and is in turn affected by, the other sectors.

POLICE AND THE CRIMINAL JUSTICE SYSTEM: THREE SOCIOLOGICAL PERSPECTIVES

Consider the information presented above regarding how what we now refer to as the criminal justice system developed historically, how it functions in contemporary American society, and the description of the police and the criminal justice system in Canada in the next section. Let us analyze this information using the three sociological perspectives that we have learned.

A functionalist would look at the structure of the American criminal justice system and the police sector within it and marvel at how intricately the federal, state, and local police forces have separate and identified functions, yet can come together to deal with issues as needed. The sequence of steps that lead from the reporting of a crime to arresting the offender (police), charging that individual (prosecution), finding him or her guilty and sentencing them (courts), as well as carrying out the punishment (corrections), would be seen as intricate and representing a machine or system whose parts function together. Further the evolution of policing from policing by members of a tribe or community to its present organization, where matters relating to crime are left to specialized professional police departments, would be viewed as casting off inefficient and unworkable parts of the system. Current problems in the system, for example, the overemphasis on arrest and clearance rates, would also be dealt with by progress and change, problem-oriented, and community-oriented policing.

A conflict theorist would ask uncomfortable questions about the impact of the police in conjunction with the rest of the criminal justice system. Who has the power and control in the system, and when acting together, who are the individuals or groups against whom this power is likely to be targeted? Remember that for a conflict sociologist, competition and disagreements within and among any given set of groups is inevitable, given that each group is seeking to maximize its own standing and access to resources in a given society. For example, the police are likely to target and victimize lower socio-economic classes or subordinate (racial or ethnic minority) groups because they have relatively little power in a society. In doing so, they act in support of the interests of those who are in power and control, that is, the upper classes and superordinate (racial or ethnic majority) groups. The interest of the conflict theorist in exposing and decrying the negative results of imbalances in power, control, and the unequal distribution of resources in society becomes evident.

Those viewing the same phenomenon from an interactions perspective are likely to be interested in the communicated meanings that are created when members of various parts of the system come together. For example, it is often suggested that public prosecutors are the chief actors in a given local jurisdiction's criminal justice system in the United States. Thus, if the prosecutor is running for election or re-election, he or she may want to emphasize "toughness" against drug offenses or other types of crime, because he or she believes this will resonate with voters. How are these changed priorities communicated to other members of the police, courts, and correctional sectors, given that these are supposed to be "independent" entities? What happens if the police department disagrees with prioritizing drug offenses and believes that household burglaries should be targeted? Through a process of interaction and communication between key players, these disagreements may be sorted out through some form of compromise or it may be a continuing source of tension when members of both organizations meet. The interactionist would be interested in how these processes of agreement or disagreement take place and become pervasive among the members of both organizations.

Let us turn our attention to the police and the criminal justice system in Canada, a country that is close to the United States, both geographically and culturally.

POLICE AND THE CRIMINAL JUSTICE SYSTEM INTERNATIONALLY: CANADA

Similar to the United States, Canada, America's northern neighbor has been greatly influenced by the British policing system. Although the French controlled Canada in the seventeenth and eighteenth centuries, it is clear that after the French and Indian Wars in the late eighteenth century, French influence has been confined to the province of Quebec. With Canada being settled by the English, they brought the customs and traditions of their home country to their new home. Like the English settlers who settled in America, they also brought their policing system with them. The police constable, an office that had its roots in England, became an

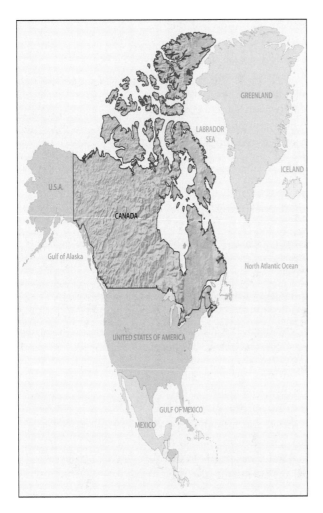

important order maintenance tool in Canada. As cities were formed, they established police constables to maintain social order within their borders. In addition, the night watch was transferred from England to Canada (McKenna, 1998: 3–4).

The Royal Canadian Mounted Police (RCMP) was established to maintain order in the North West territory of Canada as the North-West Mounted Police. Initially, the plan was to disband the mounted police by the Liberal government, which supported provincial and local rights (McKenna, 1998: 10), once order was restored to the territory, but they were so effective that the government decided to continue their authority. They were given additional responsibilities to maintain order during the construction of the Canadian Pacific Railroad and during the gold rush of the Yukon Territory. In 1904, King Edward VII added the name "Royal" to the name as recognition of the service provided by the mounted police. The mounted police were reorganized in 1920 as a national police force and its name changed to the RCMP. Today, the RCMP performs functions beyond their original national mandate. They function as the provincial police in all the provinces, except for Ontario and Quebec. Eight of the provinces, three of the territories, and a few municipalities have opted to contract with the RCMP for police services (Terrill, 1999: 118–119). Although both the American and Canadian police have their roots in their English heritage, they have taken separate paths in their police structure. No organization such as the RCMP exists in the United States.

The RCMP is a federal police service that functions under Canadian laws. At the head of the RCMP is a commissioner, appointed by the Canadian Cabinet. The RCMP is divided into thirteen divisions across Canada. These divisions are further divided into subdivisions. The RCMP has jurisdiction over the Canadian Police Information Centre (CPIC), the Canadian Police College (CPS), the Criminal Intelligence Service of Canada (CISC), the Criminal History and Fingerprint Repositories, and the Forensic Laboratory Services.

Romania, the country whose police and criminal justice system are described in the accompanying box, has a history and culture that is dissimilar to the United States and Canada. Given Romania's recent history of dictatorship and domination by the former Soviet Union, it is interesting to observe a restructured police and criminal justice system taking place. (McKenna, 1998: 48–49).

SUMMARY

The London police became the model of the American police when New York City combined their day police and night police into one police department. Other American cities followed New York City's example and adopted a similar model of policing. Policing in America is decentralized with approximately 13,000 municipal police departments with New York City being the largest, followed by Chicago. Policing in America has had several periods of reform. These include requiring the police to wear uniform, receive training and education, and combat corruption and political influence.

In addition to municipal police officers there are sheriff's departments and every state has a sheriff's department except Connecticut. The sheriff's department's responsibilities vary from state to state and even from county to county. These responsibilities could include operating a county jail, road patrol, criminal investigations, and functioning as a bailiff for the courts.

All states except Hawaii have state police agencies. State police developed in the first half of the twentieth century. They were needed to patrol state highways, the numbers of which were on the increase, to assist local police in the investigation of crimes, and to handle criminal complaints in the rural areas of the state.

The twentieth century saw an increase of federal involvement in the law enforcement arena. The FBI, DEA, and Customs were all federal agencies established to combat lawlessness in the twentieth century. In the first decade of the twenty-first century, the federal government's role in crime control, investigations, and policing in America has become the responsibility of not only local municipal cities but also the state and federal government. Finally, we learned about the similarities and differences that characterize policing in Canada, a system that was also derived from Britain.

KEY TERMS

Decentralization: Multiple police agencies at the local, state, and federal levels of government.

Highway patrol: State police officers responsible for enforcing traffic laws on state highways and land adjacent to the highway.

Hippie or flower children: Young people of the 1960s who dropped out of society. They were against the Vietnam War and the materialism of American society.

Proactive approach: When the police initiate action to solve a crime problem.

Reactive approach: When the police respond to a 911 call or a crime problem.

State police: State police who combine traffic duties with law enforcement and criminal investigations.

REVIEW QUESTIONS

1. Give a review of policing in the United States.
2. How do the police interact with the other components of the criminal justice system?
3. Are the Canadian police influenced by the British System? If so, how? If not, then who influenced the Canadian police?

DISCUSSION QUESTIONS

1. Which sociological perspective discussed in this chapter do you most agree with? Please explain.
2. Do you think the American structure of policing is relevant for the twenty-first century?
3. Do you agree with the functions of the police as outlined by the American Bar Association?

 REFERENCES

Appier, Janice (1992) "Preventive Justice: The Campaign for Women Police, 1910–1940," *Women and Criminal Justice* 4, 1: 3–36

Frye, Richard G. (2001) "The Abner Louima Case: Idiosyncratic Personal Crime or Symptomatic Police Brutality?" In Michael J. Palmiotto (ed.) *Police Misconduct: A Reader for the 21st Century*. Upper Saddle River, NJ: Prentice-Hall.

Gaines, Larry H. and Roger Leroy Miller (2009) *Criminal Justice in Action*. Belmont, CA: Wadsworth.

Hess, Karen M. (2009) *Introduction to Law Enforcement and Criminal Justice*. Belmont, CA: Wadsworth.

Hickman, Matthew J. and Brian A. Reaves (2006a) *Local Police Departments 2003,* Washington, DC: U.S. Department of Justice, Bureau of Justice Statistics, Office of Justice Programs, Law Enforcement Management and Administrative Statistics.

Hickman, Matthew J. and Brian A. Reaves (2006b) *Sheriff's Offices 2003*, Washington, DC: U.S. Department of Justice, Bureau of Justice Statistics, Office of Justice Programs, Law Enforcement Management and Administrative Statistics, 2006.

McKenna, Paul F. (1998) *Foundations of Policing in Canada*. Upper Saddle River, NJ: Prentice-Hall.

Peak Kenneth J. (2009) *Policing in America*. Upper Saddle River, NJ: Pearson/Prentice-Hall.

Palmiotto, Michael J. (2005) *Policing; Concepts, Strategies, and Current Issues in American Police Forces*. Second Edition, Durham, NC: Carolina Academic Press.

President's Commission on Law Enforcement and Administration of Justice (1967a) *The Challenge of Crime in A Free Society*. Washington, DC: U.S. Government Printing Office.

President's Commission on Law Enforcement and Administration of Justice (1967b) *Task Force Report: The Police*, Washington, DC: U.S. Government Printing Office.

Terrill, Richard J. (1999) *World Criminal Justice Systems: A Survey*. Fourth Edition, Cincinnati, OH: Anderson Publishing.

Zimring, Franklin E. (2005) American *Juvenile Justice*. New York: Oxford University Press.

POLICE AND THE CRIMINAL JUSTICE SYSTEM IN ROMANIA

Keith N. Haley and Theodora Ene

If you go by the Piazza Universitatii in downtown Bucharest at 6:30 a.m., you are likely to see a police cruiser facing the National Theater of Romania with two officers inside sipping coffee, waiting for their shift change. They are probably hoping not to get a late call, like all police waiting to get off duty. But beyond this ordinary scene, vast differences exist between the police of Romania and law enforcement in the United States.

The Romanian police are a national police system within the Ministry of the Interior with officers and units deployed throughout the nation. The head of the Romanian police is the general inspectorate who reports to the minister of the interior. Members of the police leadership are graduates of the Romanian police Academy, a freestanding four-year academic unit affiliated with the University of Bucharest and other academic institutions. All graduates possess a baccalaureate degree in law that prepares them for serving as a commissioned officer in the police service and with the credential to practice law should they choose to do so.

To say that the Romanian police are in a state of transition is to truly understate the case. Barely more than a decade ago the Romanian people were subject to the absolute control of one of the twentieth century's most brutal dictators, Nicolae Ceausescu. As is always the case for dictators, the police and its secret branches were the major means of clamping down on any display or personal support of democratic activity. If Romanians are still a little reluctant to express their views in public, consider this: the Securitate, the secret arm of the Romanian police, and its several divisions, had compiled over 700,000 dossiers on Romanian citizens from all walks of life. This is in a nation of twenty-one million people. It paid citizens a few dollars a month to spy on their friends and neighbors, detailing what teachers said in the classrooms, what people listened to on the radio, and what their neighbors and coworkers said against the Communist regime. This secret police organization also took handwriting samples from thousands within the population and supervised the registration of all typewriters and copy machines. The police even set up TV monitors to spy on citizens at many of the street corners in central Bucharest.

A revolution eventually ensued and on Christmas Day in 1989, the dictator and his wife, Elena, were tried and executed. Freedom was reborn and is now prevalent in Romania. President George Bush said in Bucharest on November 23, 2002, "Since those days of liberation, Romania has made an historic journey. Instead of hatred, you have chosen tolerance. Instead of destructive rivalry with your neighbors, you have chosen reconciliation. Instead of state control, you have chosen free markets and rule of law. And instead of dictatorship, you have built a proud and working democracy."

Now the police operate within a democratic society, and it means that old totalitarian tactics had to be abandoned. This transformation has not been easy since many of the former Securitate staff and police officials from the old regime still operate within the Romanian police organization and the Ministry of the Interior as well as the Romanian Intelligence Service (SRI). But monumental progress has been achieved and more is to be accomplished. Democracy now lives in the hearts and minds of the beat police officer on a late night shift, the corrections officer on a prison range, and the judge in a courtroom.

One of the major reform projects was to demilitarize and democratize the police and prison systems. Because Romania has already been approved to enter NATO and entered the European Union in 2007, many of the steps toward demilitarization and democratization are in line with standards handed down by both of these organizations. Policies have been developed, for example, to guide the conditions under which informants can be used, that is, as related to corruption cases, money laundering, drug and human trafficking, organized crime, Internet crimes, and cross-border crimes. These conditions are a substantial restriction on the use of informants as contrasted to their use under the Communist regime and during the several years following the downfall of Ceausescu. New laws also require that the police ensure the safety of witnesses, informants, victims of crime, and magistrates and their families.

Policies on the use of deadly force have been developed within the Romanian police system that restrict the use of lethal force to only those who threaten life or serious bodily injury. Even a warning shot is no longer permitted. Reports are now required for any use of force with weapons of any kind, and if someone is injured or killed by the police, an investigation is conducted and the necessary reports are completed.

Private detectives and security officers are no longer permitted to operate without police oversight. Contract security companies, detective businesses, and personal bodyguard companies are now authorized and controlled by the police. Finally, a new law created a National Police Officer organization, a professional nonprofit association that will protect police officers' rights. The organization has to be consulted when any new mandatory regulations are drafted that affect the police.

One change in education for the police and other justice officials has been established as a result of cooperation between Tiffin University (TU), the University of Bucharest, and the United States Agency for International Development. TU helped the University of Bucharest start a Master of Community Justice Administration (MCJA) degree program that has seen approximately sixty Romanian police, court, and corrections professionals from all hierarchical levels complete the program over the past four years. Included in the list of graduates is one of Romania's nine Supreme Court justices. Your authors were major contributors to this project and taught many classes at the University of Bucharest. In referring to TU's help in setting up the MCJA program, the United States ambassador to Romania Michael Guest said, "You can be proud that the program they developed is training up the next generation of leaders in Romania to promote greater appreciation for the rule of law."

With all of the colossal structural changes and far-reaching mandates to improve the police, some mundane but nevertheless important changes have also transpired that affect the work life and effectiveness of the police. While some Romanian citizens criticized the introduction of a roomier, more expensive Volkswagen police cruiser to replace the Romanian-made, but smaller, Dacia automobile, the fact is that the officers now have a faster, more maneuverable, and larger police cruiser to spend their tour of duty in. The traffic police in Bucharest have recently received nine Piaggio motor scooters worth about $2,400 each. Even better, more gasoline is available, and the police can actually engage in some motor patrol activity. The Romanian police have also received some modest pay increases.

With their work shift almost over, the officers in the police cruiser at Piazza Universitatii may just have to do a little peacekeeping as they notice some children outside the McDonald's restaurant becoming a little too aggressive in asking citizens for money. The children are street beggars and seldom are they any real problem or are there many of them, but today they are pushing their luck. Late or not, the officers just may give them a talking to.

CHAPTER 5

A structure of ranks from police officer to sergeant, through lieutenant and captain and up to chief indicates the authority and responsibility with which each position in the organization is charged. As with other bureaucratic institutions, police organizations designate hierarchical relationships in order to establish chains of command, communication sequences, control, and accountability . . . Owing to methodical record-keeping, formalized rules and regulations, specialized division of labor, and both internal and external checks and balances, the structure of police agencies ensures that laws are enforced but, theoretically, not at the expense of Americans' civil liberties. (Berg, 1992: 82–83)

Uniform police officers, foreground, watch as plainclothes police officers demonstrate in front of the Versailles prefecture, west of Paris, in this Oct. 18, 2006 file photo. French police unions say authorities are compromising public security by being soft on crime-ridden neighborhoods, but police are also under pressure amid renewed bouts of violence around the first anniversary of the three weeks of riots. (Credit: © AP Photo/Remy de la Mauviniere, Files)

POLICE BUREAUCRACY

OBJECTIVES:

1. The student will understand the concept and features of bureaucracy as a form of organization.
2. The student will understand the advantages and disadvantages involved in the delivery of police services bureaucratically.
3. The student will learn alternatives and improvements to police bureaucracy.
4. The student will understand the functionalist, conflict theory, and interactionist views of policing and bureaucracy.
5. The student will learn about police bureaucracy on an international level.

If you were to visit any police agency (anywhere in the world) you would likely observe that all police personnel within the agency are not exactly alike. For example, you are likely to note that while their uniforms may initially look similar, individual officers bear insignia that differentiate between those of higher or lower rank. You will notice that some officers give orders and appear to be in charge, while others obey them and carry those orders out. You will see that the particular agency appears to be further divided into smaller units (sections, squads, or divisions) that appear to specialize in particular areas of police responsibility, for example, an investigations unit, a patrol unit, a communications unit, etc. As a further example, if you were to visit the national police in Kenya you would learn that they include several specialized units, some of which may look unfamiliar to an outsider: the Anti-Stock Theft Unit, the Anti-Motor Vehicle Theft Unit, the Tourism Police Unit, the Anti-Corruption Police Unit, the Presidential Escort Unit, Diplomatic Unit, and the Anti-Terrorism Police Unit (http://www.kenyapolice.go.ke/history.asp).

In a given police agency, you might overhear a couple of lower-level officers talking about preparations to take a competitive examination that is required to "make sergeant," that is, to gain promotion to a higher rank. Further, it will become clear to you that much of the agency's day-to-day functions (despite what you may have assumed as a result of watching police dramas on television) involve extensive record keeping and paperwork, for example, files on cases, forms recording crime reports, police statistics, etc., although some of the information is likely nowadays to be maintained electronically. If you were eventually to talk to one of the higher-ups in the agency and asked how the agency was doing, he or she may mention something about the agency's clearance rate (generally, the ratio of cases cleared by arrest to cases known or reported to the agency). What you are seeing and hearing is the delivery of policing services to the public using one type of formal organization (see Tosi, 2008) that sociologists have come to call a **bureaucracy**.

A few words about the development of **formal organizations**, which are generally defined as larger groups whose short-term and long-term activities are planned to achieve certain objectives. In our daily lives we interact with other human beings in a number of settings and locations, for example, at home with our family; at work with colleagues, supervisors, clients, or customers; at play with friends; and at the grocery store with other shoppers and store personnel. Many of these relationships have strength, emotional investment, and relative permanence (e.g., that with family members) attached to them. The participants involved in them form a **primary group**. Others (e.g., that with the sales clerk who serves us at the grocery store) are generally impersonal, transitory, and merely temporary. These **secondary group** interactions often take place within formal organizations. Note also how the concepts of primary and secondary groups parallel the concepts of informal and formal control over behavior that we became familiar with in Chapter 2. This is to say primary groups (those we feel close to and whose judgments about us we value) exercise informal control over our behavior, while formal control over our behavior is the province of secondary groups (official agencies, including the police, who are given the task of making sure people behave properly). Increasingly, modern societies have tended to rely on

bureaucracy

Goal-oriented organizations specifically designed to abide by rational principles so that the effective attainment of their goals is achieved as efficiently as possible.

formal organizations

Larger groups whose short-term and long-term activities are planned to achieve certain objectives.

primary group

A group in which relationships among members have strength, emotional investment, and relative permanence (e.g., with family members) attached to them.

secondary group

A group in which the interactions and relationships are generally impersonal, transitory and merely temporary (e.g., our relationship with the sales clerk who serves us at the grocery store). These secondary group interactions often take place within formal organizations.

and emphasize these large specialized secondary groups or formal organizations (e.g., police departments, welfare agencies, mental hospitals, etc.) to ensure proper behavior among its members. Simultaneously, primary groups (such as the family, relatives, and friendship groups) are less likely to be relied upon. As an example, police officers will often report being called in to intervene in a family dispute, often one as simple as children disrespecting or mouthing off to their parents.

CHARACTERISTICS OF FORMAL ORGANIZATIONS

Almost all formal organizations, such as the police, courts, and corrections, that deal with the crime problem operate as bureaucracies (i.e., the Federal Bureau of Investigation [FBI], INTERPOL or the International Criminal Police Organization, your local municipal police department or the county sheriff's agency). This particular form of social group became widespread when the Industrial Revolution began to alter the social structures and cultures of various countries in Europe. In many ways, other countries of the world have also followed the path to forming bureaucracies as they have become industrialized. Previously, the Roman Catholic Church and the military were the prime examples of bureaucracy. We owe many of the original insights regarding the structure and functioning of bureaucracies to the work of the famous sociologist Max Weber (1864–1920). He focused on the trend toward increasing **rationalization**, that is, the increasing trend toward explicitly orienting goals and procedures for achieving them without regard to emotional involvement or consequences. "In the place of the old type ruler who is moved by sympathy, grace and gratitude, modern culture requires . . . the emotionally detached, and hence rigorously 'professional' expert" (Gerth and Mills, 1946, quoting Weber). Weber saw bureaucracies as goal-oriented organizations specifically designed to abide by rational principles so that the effective attainment of their goals was achieved as efficiently as possible. However, he was also arguably apprehensive about a future dominated by these organizational forms and by extension, the individuals who ran them. "Once such bureaucratic structures are established, they are practically indestructible, Weber believed, because a bureaucracy is a power instrument of the first order for those who occupy its command posts" (Zeitlin, 1987: 159).

These observations led Weber to examine how large-scale hyperrational social groups were taking over and administering various sectors of the emerging industrialized societies. Bureaucracy results from the application of the principles derived from rationalization to human social groups who are wrestling with a variety of issues and conditions requiring concerted social action. Coordinating societal responses to these problems in the form of various organizational activities, Weber believed, is the distinctive hallmark of industrialized (and, we may extend this to, postindustrialized) countries. Thus, industrialized societies have to face the problem of educating their young to participate in economic and civil life. As a solution they created the practice of mass schooling and an accompanying educational bureaucracy (in the contemporary United States, all the way from the Federal Department of Education to local school districts and schools) to deal with this important issue.

rationalization

The increasing trend toward explicitly orienting goals and procedures for achieving them without regard to emotional involvement or consequences.

According to Weber the characteristics of a typical bureaucracy (see Scott, 1998) include the following (which we will apply to police organizations):

1. Hierarchy of authority: Positions in a bureaucracy are ranked in a hierarchical order (often having the shape of a pyramid), with information moving up the chain of command, while policy decisions and orders flow downward. In a police agency, as we know, the chief or director is at the top of the organizational chart, and may have below him or her, commanders, captains, lieutenants, sergeants, corporals, and line officers. The lower levels of this hierarchy are likely to pass on information regarding cases upward, while overall directions on how to handle these cases are communicated to them by the upper echelons.

2. Impersonality: Bureaucracies carry out their operations and activities on the basis of impersonal rules that clearly state the duties and responsibilities of various office holders, standardized procedures applicable to all cases, and the conduct of office holders with regard to issues that come before the organization. Police academies teach new recruits the agency's rules regarding everything from when and how to write traffic tickets to situations that call for the use of deadly force. Officers are instructed to carry these out without regard or concern as to who the offender may be and the latter's position in society, for example, a ticket has to be given to the person caught speeding even if he or she happens to be a personal friend of the police officer or the mayor of the city where the officer is working.

3. Written rules of conduct: All the duties, obligations, and responsibilities of police officers are specified rather exhaustively, and generally, in writing. Officers are expected to learn these rules and to abide by them (as laid down by the agency) in dealing with all cases that come to their attention. This is one of the reasons why academy training typically pays a great deal of attention to interpreting agency policies and procedures for new recruits and to applying them to a variety of situations the rookie officer is likely to encounter when he or she begins to work on the street. Given varying police bureaucratic traditions (e.g., in Britain, police officers typically do not carry firearms; American police officers always carry them), it is likely that the rules and the means for carrying them out will emphasize the agency's own procedures and the imputed justifications for them. In addition, detailed job descriptions educate officers on the range of their specific duties.

4. Promotion based on achievement: Selection and appointments to bureaucratic offices are made according to specialized (often technical) qualifications rather than other, more personal, criteria. As you may know, police departments use many different tests and occupational qualifications (background checks, educational requirements, written tests, physical tests, psychological examinations, oral interviews, and other criteria) in deciding whom to hire as police officers. These more or less objective and technical requirements intensify and become more stringent when an officer wishes to move up the rank hierarchy.

5. Specialized division of labor: Areas of responsibility are clearly specified and officers are highly specialized in what they deal with. For example, in police

departments, clear distinctions are made with regard to those who are defined as patrol officers and those who are deemed to be investigators. The latter are often subdivided into units that deal with crimes against persons and those who investigate property crimes. It would be virtually unheard of for the lieutenant in charge of property crimes to interfere in the operations of the crimes-against-persons unit and vice versa. Thus the overall goal of the police agency in terms of crime fighting is achieved through the efforts of smaller specialized units. In a sense, the smaller units have divided the goal up into manageable areas of expertise and activity.

6. Separation of the personal from the official: A clear separation is made in terms of property, tools, and rights that adhere to a particular bureaucratic position from the person who happens to occupy that position. Thus, a police officer has to give up the uniform, police vehicle, and the right to write traffic tickets once he or she has left the employment of a police department. A police chief who has retired cannot give orders to subordinates regarding departmental matters anymore. The property, tools, and rights belong to the position and not to the particular individual. It is important to note this because, before the rise of the bureaucracy, such accoutrements were invested in particular individuals, for example, a prince always enjoyed certain rights and privileges, even if he were no more in charge of a certain area of activity that had earlier been deemed his responsibility.

When taken together, the characteristics outlined above have one overriding goal, and that is to expend the organization's resources (time, personnel, money, etc.) in ways that help achieve the organization's goals as speedily and efficiently as possible. We have also seen that these characteristics define police agencies accurately (including the highly fragmented police bureaucracy in the United States that we are familiar with; the highly centralized French police bureaucracy described below; and police systems of countries in between—see Hunter, 1990). They also appear to describe the activities, personnel, and routines of these agencies with a great degree of correctness. Given the historical origins of policing in the military, perhaps their adoption of bureaucratic functioning is understandable. Having established that police agencies indeed are, and operate as, bureaucracies, let us turn our attention to the issue of what is gained and what may be lost through their adherence to this particular organizational form.

POLICE BUREAUCRACY: ADVANTAGES, DISADVANTAGES, AND ALTERNATIVES

When we say some particular secondary group is a "bureaucracy" or that someone is behaving like a "bureaucrat," we typically do not mean these as compliments. On the contrary, it is meant to be an insult and a put down of that group, its activity, or that person. As Stillman (1987: 3) makes clear, both this organizational form and those who work within it evoke strong negative feelings:

Few things are more disliked in our modern society than bureaucracy; hardly any occupation is held in lower esteem than that of a bureaucrat. Both bureaucracy and bureaucrats are subject to contempt and criticism in both the public and private conversation. "Inefficient," "full of red tape," "big," "unresponsive," "unproductive," "inhumane," and "inept" are frequently among the emotionally charged criticisms regularly leveled at bureaucracy and bureaucrats.

In addition to complaining about their dealings with customers and clients, "police bureaucracies are accused by these critics of limiting the spontaneity and self-realization of their employees" (Dantzker, 2002: 146).

How then do we reconcile the fact that large and significant portions of contemporary society (including, as we have seen, police services) are thoroughly controlled by an organizational form for which we appear to have very little affection? This is because bureaucracies have certain underappreciated inherent strengths in addition to their widely known limitations. Further, and on balance, it is difficult (although perhaps, not impossible) to design alternative organizational forms (a few of which we will discuss later in this chapter) that can accomplish the same goals with a higher degree of competence or a greater amount of efficiency.

Advantages of Police Bureaucracy

If we were to consider the six defining elements of bureaucracy that we learned above and examine each of them in a police context, we will find that there are certain advantages to organizing them in this way. First, the presence of a hierarchy makes it clear who is in charge and designates individuals at the higher levels (who presumably have proven themselves fit to lead) who will think about and plan for the long term, while those at lower levels can work on the day-to-day processing of cases that come to the attention of the agency. This also solves the issues of leadership, coordination, and evaluation. Second, with regard to impersonality, when dealing with members of the public who show up in the police department as offenders, victims, and witnesses, it is a good idea to expect officers to treat them professionally, correctly, and as equally as possible, without fear or favor. Would we want serious cases involving perpetrators who happen to be friends with police officers to be dismissed offhand without proper investigation? Third, written rules of conduct allow both officers and members of the public to know what is acceptable and unacceptable in terms of police behavior, thus increasing accountability. Again, would we prefer that cases that come before the police department be handled according to the idiosyncrasies of whoever happens to be on duty that day or would we prefer streamlined, uniform policies and procedures to be followed? Fourth, having technical qualifications and achievements as the basis for evaluating recruits and personnel is better than having vague qualifications and nepotism as the method by which jobs and promotions are handed out to individuals. In a case that involves us, do we want the best-qualified officer on the job, or one with the right connections regardless of how unqualified they may be? Fifth, the clearly designated areas of specialization that result from a complex division of labor allows for all aspects of an agency's mission to be covered and completed. Should we ignore traffic accidents and focus only on burglaries or is it important that both be responded to? Finally, it is appropriate that there be compartmentalization of the personal and the professional in that mixing the two makes the particular individual seem larger than the position. If the latter were to happen, we would be unable to get rid of people who are incompetent or inefficient in carrying out their police duties.

Disadvantages of Police Bureaucracy

Obviously, while the above are plausible defenses of police bureaucracy and its practices, the presence of many criticisms of the same (enough perhaps to fill several books) cannot be ignored. Even Weber, the sociological chronicler of bureaucracy is quoted (Bendix, 1962) as saying, "It is horrible to think that the world would one day be filled with nothing but those little cogs, little men clinging to little jobs and striving toward bigger ones." Let us consider some common criticisms of police bureaucracies.

First, the most widespread criticism of bureaucracies is the plethora of rules and regulations that they create and then insist on being followed. The rigidity of these complex systems of rules stifles creativity and flexibility while speedier and more efficient responses are sacrificed. Imagine if a police department is criticized for its aloofness from the public it serves. To combat this, a new departmental policy is instituted that requires every police contact with a citizen (good and bad) to be documented. The idea is that these contacts would be tallied and summed up in the form of a point total that will be used for merit evaluations of individual officers and for departmental annual reports to the public (i.e., "We run a very approachable and citizen-oriented department: last year our officers made 50,554 individual contacts with members of the public"). While officers will no doubt attempt to follow these reporting requirements, is the time spent on this activity a wise use of the department's resources? Here is another amusing example of a typical police bureaucratic rule found in many departments taken from Dantzker (2002: 164) that has little to do with efficiency but continues to be adhered to:

> The wearing of hats on patrol has been a traditional policy of most police departments for many years. Many of today's police officers cannot understand the need for a policy that requires the officer before exiting the patrol car to put on the uniform hat or face disciplinary action. Granted a hat keeps the weather off the head, but what other value does it have? What is the reason for requiring uniform hats to be worn? That it makes an officer look professional may be a satisfactory reason for this policy among supervisors, however, many patrol officers find it difficult to accept such reasoning.

Another way of thinking about the negative impact of bureaucratic rules and requirements on policing is to consider them as serving to curtail the discretion that police officers have typically enjoyed as they go about their daily work. While discretion is discussed in more detail in Chapter 8, rigid bureaucratic rules can clearly impinge on an individual officer's ability to deal with events and situations according to his or her autonomous judgment. Black (1983) suggests that discretion in the application of rules is needed for three reasons. First, because the law as it is written typically "overreaches." For example, people may exceed the posted speed limit for a number of valid reasons, for example, to take someone who is injured to hospital quickly. Second, we may make a point about the law even by not always enforcing it. If we have an apologetic driver who understands the gravity of the speeding violation but is perhaps under stress or pressure (e.g., returning home after his or her mother's funeral) what greater purpose is achieved by giving that individual a ticket? Third, allowing officers to "interpret" the rules using their own judgment enables them to decide if the person confronted is telling the truth or is lying rather than having to mechanically hand tickets out. In each of these three situations, if we rigidly adhered to the rules that the department has framed to enforce speed limits without discretion, the concerned officer would not be able to make any exceptions at all.

A second problem that has been identified commonly with bureaucracy has come to be known as the **Peter Principle** (Peter and Hull, 1969). This formulation states (paraphrased), "In every hierarchy, every employee tends to rise to his or her level of incompetence." As we have seen, bureaucracies are structured and function as hierarchies. The problem here stems from the bureaucracy's mechanism for promoting employees (which we would think of as a positive). A lower-level employee who performs well will be promoted to a higher position and if he or she does well there, is likely to get promoted to an even higher one. At some point, the employee reaches his or her "level of incompetence" and is not promoted anymore. The end result is that incompetent individuals essentially fill positions in the bureaucratic hierarchy. Take, for example, a patrol officer who does his or her job extremely well and has mastered all the requisite skills allowing him or her to excel at that position, for example, good spatial awareness, driving skills, tactful public interaction, and communication ability. He or she is, as a result of superior performance, promoted to police sergeant. Most of the earlier skills he or she had developed are now less important and the individual officer has to develop a whole new set of skills. The latter skill set is likely to include active participation in meetings, conveying management decisions to squad officers and helping apply them, interacting and coordinating with higher- and lower-ranking colleagues, etc. You will notice that there is very little overlap between the two sets of needed skills and that the promoted sergeant may probably be not likely do as well and may even be incompetent in the new position. The argument made by following the Peter Principle is that this individual, similar to many others in a bureaucracy has found his or her level of incompetence and is therefore likely to stay there. Of course, if he or she proves competent in the sergeant's position, promotion to lieutenant will require further retooling and relearning what is needed to be successful. However, at some point in the ladder of hierarchy, learning and competence peter out. As a result, the individual is stuck and the organization ends up with people who are essentially deadwood. While this problem is widely alluded to in the organizational literature and anecdotal evidence is often mentioned, the frequency and nature of its occurrence in police bureaucracies is not clear.

The third commonly mentioned problem that afflicts bureaucratic organizations is also named after its originator: **Parkinson's Law**. Parkinson (1957) is credited with the finding that, in organizations, "work expands to fill the time allotted for its

....

peter principle

The idea that in every hierarchy, every employee tends to rise to his or her level of incompetence.

....

parkinson's law

The idea that work expands to fill the time allotted for its completion.

completion." It is argued that the inherent and inevitable tendency of bureaucracy is to keep on growing. In order to appear busy, important, and in control of matters within their purview, bureaucrats spend their time having meetings, talking (perhaps nowadays, e-mailing) about various issues to death, creating forms that have to be filled out, hiring and listening to outside consultants, and writing memoranda about what they have planned (individually and together) and decided to do. As a result of all this activity something that may take relatively little time to complete (in the sense of carrying out the actual work) becomes stretched and made more complicated to fill out the time available for its completion. Further, after all these bureaucratic exertions, the staff and administrators will agree that they are all overworked and justified in hiring more help. As a consequence, new employees are hired and the agency itself expands. Of course, this means a bigger budget, a larger building to house the expanded number of employees, and more administrators to watch over them. Parkinson thought that bureaucracies therefore tend to grow (in all ways) at the rate of 6 percent or more per year. Indeed, administrators when touting their successful leadership of particular organizations, invariably mention by how much they have increased the size of the agency's budget and the number of its employees over a given period of time. While the evidence regarding the invariability and inevitability of organizational growth is somewhat mixed (see Scott, 1998) there is some truth to Parkinson's Law as a description of possible bureaucratic tendencies, if left unchecked. Police agencies, since they deal with issues of safety and security, are inevitably drawn into the vortex of arguments for needing to grow under any and all circumstances. It would be virtually impossible to find an example of a police department that has voluntarily decided to cut its staff because either the population of its jurisdiction or its crime rates have fallen or both. On the other hand, it would not be that difficult to find examples of police departments and administrators that have insisted that they do not have enough personnel, that they are overworked, and that their budget allocations are inadequate regardless of the nature of its population base (increasing or decreasing) and its crime rates (increasing and decreasing). Here is one example of a police department more or less "gaming the system" in asking for more personnel despite being told not to (quoted in Swanson, Territo, and Taylor, 1988: 463):

> In San Jose, California, the police department's budget requested no new personnel in accordance with the city administrator's restrictions. However, when presenting the budget request to the council, police officials included a frank description of conditions, using simple and carefully selected graphics. Immediately subsequent to this presentation, the San Jose City Council added ninety new positions to the police department's budget. This incident also gives rise to considering how a police administrator can be effective in obtaining funds from appropriators.

Alternative Police Organizational Forms

As a result of the dissatisfactions often expressed regarding bureaucracies and their manner of functioning, several attempts have been made over the years to come up with alternate ways of carrying out organizational work. In this section, we will look into several alternative police organizational forms. In considering these, however, you should remember that these arrangements have been, for the most part, temporary, supplemental, and fielded with highly specific purposes in mind. In other words, these alternative arrangements have come nowhere near to changing or even replacing the dominant military-based bureaucracy as the preferred way of providing police services to the public.

team policing

Organizing groups of police officers (each with its own supervisor) to serve specified geographic areas of a police department's jurisdiction.

1. **Team Policing**: The idea behind this alternative approach to policing the community is twofold: to reduce the distance between the police and the public they serve and to take away the impersonality that many citizens encounter in the traditional police bureaucracy. Team policing has been hailed as "one of the most dynamic experiments that has altered the organizational design of police departments in both the United States and Great Britain" (Swanson, Territo, and Taylor, 1988: 118). Team policing involves organizing groups of police officers (each with its own supervisor) to serve specified geographic areas of a police department's jurisdiction. Within departmental guidelines, each local "team" is free to decide how they will organize and deliver police services (e.g., the specific allocations of personnel, time, beat routes, etc.) to the residents of their area. Local residents gain familiarity and feel comfortable with their local team police officers. You will notice how this organizational alternative consciously breaks up the management control and uniformity that is usually exercised in a traditional bureaucracy and decentralizes it at the level where the actual services are delivered.

2. Intra- and Inter-Agency Task Forces: A task force is a specialized unit or squad established for the purpose of solving a serious problem or a series of related problems. In many cases, these units are disbanded after the issue that resulted in their establishment is no longer of concern or has been solved. If there have been a number of residential burglaries in an area, a temporary task force of detectives may be assigned to deal with that problem. Their duties will include keeping track of cases, sharing information, investigating leads, identifying patterns, fingerprinting suspects, and ultimately arresting those responsible jointly.

Task forces that involve a number of different agencies may also be established. Crime and criminals do not respect the boundaries of police jurisdictions, particularly in a highly mobile American society with a fragmented system of policing. Kidnappers often cross state lines with impunity. Upper-level drug dealers may operate in a number of urban and suburban areas at the same time. To reduce a lot of the problems that arise when dealing with multiple bureaucracies, personnel from various agencies often team up to form interagency task forces. These task forces will work together to deal with a specific problem (e.g., the case of the 2002 Washington, D.C., area sniper killings, where two serial killers operated in a metropolitan or multistate area that encompassed a number of jurisdictions). Oakland, California, used a task force called SMART (Specialized Multi-Agency Response Team) that coordinated police, other government and nongovernment agencies, including housing, the utility company, and the fire department to combat the use of rental units as locations for drug-related activity (Green, 1995).

Again, you will notice that the problem orientation of these units allowed them to focus organizational resources on particular topics (often, high-profile crimes). This means that they are somewhat more nimble in responding to cases than in a typical bureaucracy where the standing rules and regulations requiring all cases to go through "proper channels" renders it less flexible.

3. Quality Circles: In a typical police bureaucracy, lower-level officers have very little say in the policies and procedures that affect their work. Ironically, they are likely to be the group that is most familiar with the implications of new policies in everyday practice. For example, is there a better way to test the skills that are needed when hiring new police officers? A group consisting of police officers who have recently been hired and higher-ranking officers who were involved in personnel selection might be able to provide suggestions for improving the quality of the hiring process. Quality circles were first conceived and utilized in the business sector (based on Japanese participatory management practices) and have more recently moved into the public organizations. "A quality circle consists of a group of employees who meet on a regular basis for the purpose of identifying and solving common work problems" (Roberg, Crank, and Kuykenadall, 2000: 162). The idea here is to allow line officers to participate in how policies and budget decisions are shaped and to harness their intimate knowledge (of working on the street or in other police situations) to infuse such decisions with pragmatism and relevant efficiency.

Overall, the three alternatives to traditional police bureaucracies represent attempts that seek to flatten existing hierarchies (e.g., quality circles), introduce personal relationships with clients into the bureaucracy (e.g., team policing), and break down the traditional division of labor (e.g., task forces). All of these are ways of breaking out of the rigidity of traditional bureaucratic structure and functioning.

POLICE BUREAUCRACY: THREE SOCIOLOGICAL PERSPECTIVES

In Chapter 1, we learned about the three common sociological perspectives useful in analyzing society and its components. Having learned in this chapter about a specific type of social group, the police bureaucracy, let us examine it using the perspectives of functionalism, conflict, and interactionism, as we have done so for different issues in every chapter.

As we have learned, functionalists are interested in how and what a given social group contributes to the overall stability and functioning of society. Thus, the police bureaucracy is seen as an efficient way for society to carry out the three functions that are typically associated with policing: crime fighting, order maintenance, and service. Thus, the police bureaucracy exists to coordinate available resources and to direct them toward the achievement of these objectives. Let us take each one of these functions in turn (we will be examining them in greater detail in later chapters). The crime-fighting function incorporates both crime prevention (creating conditions and helping members of a community to make sure that crime does not occur, or at least occurs infrequently) and crime detection (dealing with crime after it occurs such that the culprits are arrested and subsequently punished). The crime-fighting function (particularly the crime detection aspect of it; police departments often asked to be judged by their clearance rate, that is, the ratio of crimes cleared by arrest over the known number of crimes) is the one that is most often identified with police bureaucracy. The order-maintenance function is to make sure that everyday life in the community flows smoothly and without hindrance. Thus, we would want that on any given day, members of the community be able to go about their business, to work or to school, and for traffic to flow as smoothly as possible. While this function of the police is not often understood or publicized, think about how much city life would be disrupted if we did not have police officers directing traffic flow after a major accident at a busy thoroughfare during the morning rush hour. Finally, police bureaucracy exists to provide a service to the public. Again, this is a police function that is not well understood. In the case of the accident just discussed, police officers, often being the first on the scene, provide first aid to those injured. Further, they serve as school resource officers, provide directions to lost motorists, and sometimes rescue trapped animals. All of these disparate activities that the police bureaucracy coordinates and delivers help maintain predictability and social order.

Conflict theorists, as we have seen, view society and its components as competitive battlegrounds wherein individuals and groups attempt to gain access to scarce resources, and winning is generally accomplished at the expense of other individuals and groups. Bureaucracy (including police bureaucracy) represents one more social arena where this ongoing battle is played out, both internally and externally. For conflict theorists, the question that has to be asked is who benefits from the existence of bureaucracy in the form that we have described earlier? Internally, given the inherent inequality that is built into bureaucratic hierarchies, one group (the administrators) has greater power and influence than others (the line staff and officers). There is very little that the subordinate groups within the bureaucracy can do to change this. The higher administration enjoys greater pay, better benefits, and other perks and also gets to tell those below them what to do. Obedience is expected (sometimes, even when unethical conduct is asked for) and lower-level officers can be fired for insubordination. Obviously, the opposite cannot happen in a bureaucratic set up. External to the police organization, those who are well-off and their political lackeys use it to do their bidding. Generally police agencies are used to oppress and suppress those who might threaten elite domination. The police enforce property laws, but these laws only make sense if you already own property: if you have nothing, you have nothing to lose. Thus the police protect property owners against those who are poor (lack property) and the dispossessed. Think also about the use of police officers in the south to break up civil rights protestors during the civil rights marches of the 1960s and of the misuse of the FBI by President Richard Nixon to cover up details of the 1972 break in to the Watergate headquarters of the Democratic Party by members of his re-election team. Conflict theorists see police bureaucracy as involved in the ongoing competition for scarce resources and a means by which superior groups control and punish those who may threaten their position.

Interactionists focus less on the macro-level issues that interest functionalists and conflict theorists and more on the internal workings of bureaucracies. For them the issues surrounding workplace interaction and the internal work cultures that develop within police bureaucracies are more relevant. Beyond the formal organizational hierarchies and resulting charts, how do members of the police bureaucracy work together and interact on a daily basis (e.g., jargon, slang, humor, gossip, informal networks, friendships, cliques, political factions, etc.) to create a shared understanding of their work and their own interrelationships? For example, it is often suspected by the public that police officers have to write a certain number of traffic tickets per day (per week, per month), that is, they have to meet a quota. At the same time, you will never find in the formal policies and procedure documents of any police department a statement that indicates that officers have to write X number of tickets. However, interactionists are likely to observe that there is probably some informal understanding among traffic and patrol officers and their supervisors that to be doing a good day's (or week's or month's) work, one ought to be writing X number of tickets on average. Write many more tickets than X, and the officer is likely to be considered a rate buster. If the officer writes tickets that are substantially lower, he or she will be considered to be shirking work. Notice that this number is the product of the informal work culture of the department. A rookie officer is unlikely to learn this information during academy training, but is likely to learn of it while interacting with his or her colleagues on a daily basis. Similar is the case with interpretations of laws such as those governing speed limits. A highway patrol officer is unlikely to stop and ticket everyone going one mile over the speed limit. He or she is definitely going to ticket those who are observed going twenty or twenty-five miles over the speed limit. The tipping point for whether a speeding ticket will be issued or not, therefore, lies somewhere between one and twenty. However, the ticketing circumstances more or less likely depend on the learning experienced by the officer within the informal work culture of the particular highway patrol bureaucracy.

Let us now turn our attention to, as we have done in every chapter, and examine how the police are organized in France, which does not follow Anglo-American models of policing and criminal justice.

POLICE BUREAUCRACY INTERNATIONALLY: FRANCE

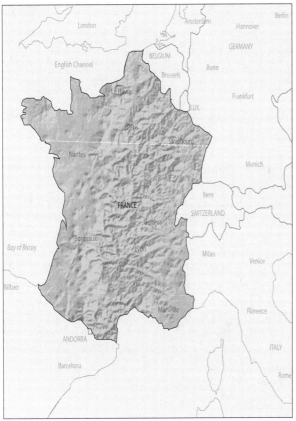

France is often described as having a centralized system of policing, especially when compared to the highly fragmented American police bureaucracy (Hunter, 1990). This will allow us to compare issues of hierarchy and control (especially the tensions between the local and national control) and how they play out in another country. "France has a single system of codified law and a single system for the administration of justice, both of which can be traced to Napoleon Bonaparte" (Hunter, 1880: 120–121). Fairchild (1993: 67) tracks the current organization of the police in France back to the elaborate "Napoleonic system of internal spying and policing that consolidated the power of the

dictator." Historically, the French police have broader mandates in regulating their society that are above and beyond typical police functions of crime fighting, order maintenance, and service. Fairchild (1993: 67) notes that their duties also include "public health regulation, housing regulations, population registration, and other regulatory activities."

The work of policing France is divided between two major police organizations: the Police Nationale, under the Ministry of the Interior and the Gendarmarie Nationale, which is controlled by the Ministry of Defense. Thus, French policing involves a combination of civilian and military personnel. The Police Nationale is the larger entity and is responsible for policing urban areas (including Paris) while the Gendarmarie Nationale deals with smaller towns and the rural parts of France with populations below 10,000, according to Terrill (1992). France is divided administratively into ninety-five departments (or administrative subdivisions). A commissioner who coordinates with and reports to the director general (overall head and a senior civil servant) of the organization is in charge of each departmental branch of the Police Nationale. The Gendarmarie Nationale consists of ten regional units that parallel the division of France into ten military areas. The leadership of the Gendarmarie Nationale under the Minister of Defense consists of the director general and an inspector general (there is an equivalent official in the Police Nationale as well). While the director general is legally trained, the inspector general is an army general in rank. According to Terrill (1992: 193), members of the Gendarmarie Nationale exhibit "a tendency to view themselves as an elite law enforcement corps," perhaps superior to those in the Police Nationale. In addition to these two national police forces, beginning in 1983 in an apparent effort at decentralization, the Police Municipal (or municipal police), under the control of the mayor were formed, though not in all cities (Kania, 1989). Therefore, the Police Municipale consists of only a "few forces . . . limited in numbers and authority" (Hunter, 1990: 121). Along with the geographical division of responsibility mentioned above each of these organizations consist of specialized functional units (e.g., civil order, criminal investigations, etc.) as well.

The first feature of French policing that will strike an American observer is the unquestioned mixture of the civilian and military organizations in the work of law enforcement. In the United States, this would provoke suspicion, if not outright opposition, given American sensitivities regarding the involvement of the federal armed forces (army, navy, air force) in matters other than national defense against external threats. However, given historical tradition and France's centralized national government, as opposed to the United States that has a federal form of government, this is understandable. Second, notice the expanded span of control that the French police bureaucracy enjoys in French society: it is involved in a large number of regulatory activities, most of which are generally within the purview of other (local, state, and federal) agencies in the United States. Again, American traditions of divided government and suspicion of overzealous federal involvement can be contrasted with the lack of these characteristics and the acceptance of centralized governmental authority in French society. Finally, given the concentration of the police bureaucracy at the central government level, coordination and control over the allocation of police personnel and resources is generally much quicker than in the United States. If, for example, there was industrial unrest and violence taking place in the Lyons region, the interior minister can simply move the forces needed to quell the disturbances from elsewhere in France. Think about how difficult it would be for the president or the attorney general (since the United States does not have a cabinet-level position equivalent to the French interior minister) to accomplish the same action quickly and efficiently in the American context. It would also be instructive to note that such a concentration of the police bureaucracy and its authority renders the French system somewhat less responsive to local conditions, concerns, and citizens. Kania (1989) suggests, therefore, that local dissatisfaction played a part in the creation of the Police Municipale in various French cities.

France, as we have seen, has a different way of structuring its police bureaucracy. In the accompanying box, we learn about the conflicts between traditional bureaucratic policing and what is referred to as "purpose-led policing" that has been attempted in Canada.

SUMMARY

We began by learning about the place of primary groups, secondary groups, and formal organizations in society. One particular type of formal organization, the bureaucracy, permeates social life and almost all police agencies are structured in this way. We learned about the six common characteristics of a bureaucracy and found them to be applicable to police agencies. While bureaucracies generally have a bad reputation, we learned that there are advantages and disadvantages to structuring police services in this manner. We became familiar with some emerging alternatives to police bureaucracy. Next, we utilized the perspectives of functionalism, conflict, and interactionism to police bureaucracy and considered the unique insights that develop as a result. Finally, we looked at how police services are organized and delivered in France, a country where these activities are highly centralized.

KEY TERMS

Bureaucracy: Goal-oriented organizations specifically designed to abide by rational principles so that the effective attainment of their goals is achieved as efficiently as possible.

Formal organizations: Larger groups whose short-term and long-term activities are planned to achieve certain objectives.

Parkinson's Law: The idea that work expands to fill the time allotted for its completion.

Peter Principle: The idea that in every hierarchy, every employee tends to rise to his or her level of incompetence.

Primary group: A group in which relationships among members have strength, emotional investment, and relative permanence (e.g., with family members) attached to them.

Rationalization: The increasing trend toward explicitly orienting goals and procedures for achieving them without regard to emotional involvement or consequences.

Secondary group: A group in which the interactions and relationships are generally impersonal, transitory, and merely temporary (e.g., our relationship with the sales clerk who serves us at the grocery store). These secondary group interactions often take place within formal organizations.

Team policing: Organizing groups of police officers (each with its own supervisor) to serve specified geographic areas of a police department's jurisdiction.

 REVIEW QUESTIONS

1. What are the major features of bureaucracy as identified by the sociologist Max Weber?

2. What are the advantages and disadvantages to carrying out policing by utilizing bureaucratic organizations?

3. Describe the major similarities and differences between the police bureaucracy in France as compared to that of the United States.

 DISCUSSION QUESTIONS

1. Is it possible to carry out policing without resorting to bureaucratic organizations? Discuss how this would or would not be possible.

2. Do you think the bureaucratic structure of policing is relevant for a globalized society the twenty-first century?

3. Which of the three sociological perspectives on police bureaucracy make the most sense to you? Discuss why?

REFERENCES

Bendix, Reinhard (1962) *Max Weber: An Intellectual Portrait.* Garden City, NY: Anchor Books.

Berg, Bruce L. (1992) *Law Enforcement: An Introduction to Police in Society.* Boston, MA: Allyn and Bacon.

Black, Donald L. (1983) "Police Discretion: Selective Enforcement" In Carl B. Klockars (eds.) *Thinking about Police: Contemporary Readings.* New York: McGraw-Hill.

Dantzker, Mark L. (2002) *Understanding Today's Police.* Third Edition. Upper Saddle River, NJ: Prentice Hall.

Fairchild, Erika S. (1993) *Comparative Criminal Justice Systems.* Belmont, CA: Wadsworth.

Green, L. (1995) "Cleaning Up Drug Hot Spots in Oakland, California: The Displacement and Diffusion Effects." *Justice Quarterly* 12: 737–754.

Gerth, Hans H., and C. Wright Mills (1946) *From Max Weber: Essays in Sociology.* New York: Oxford University Press.

Hunter, Ronald D. (1990) "Three Models of Policing." *Police Studies* 13: 118–124. http://www.kenyapolice.go.ke/history.asp. "History of the Kenya Police." Retrieved on July3, 2007.

Kania, Richard R. E. (1989) "The French Municipal Police Experiment." *Police Studies* 12: 125–131.

Parkinson, C. Northcote (1957) *Parkinson's Law and Other Studies in Administration.* Boston: Houghton Miflin.

Peter, Laurence J., and Raymond Hull (1969) *The Peter Principle; Why Things Always go Wrong.* New York: William Morrow.

Roberg, Roy, John Crank, and Jack Kuykendall (2000) *Police and Society.* Second Edition. Los Angeles: Roxbury Publishing Company.

Scott, Richard W. (1998) *Organizations: Rational, Natural and Open Systems.* Upper Saddle River, NJ: Prentice Hall.

Swanson, Charles R., Leonard Territo, and Robert W. Taylor (1988) *Police Administration: Structures, Processes and Behavior.* Second Edition. New York: Macmillan.

Stillman, Richard J. (1987) *The American Bureaucracy.* Chicago: Nelson-Hall.

Terrill, Richard J. (1992) *World Criminal Justice Systems: A Survey.* Second Edition. Cincinnati, OH: Anderson Publishing Company.

Tosi, Henry L. (2008) *Theories of Organization.* Thousand Oaks, CA: Sage.

Zeitlin, Irving M. (1987) *Ideology and the Development of Sociological Theory.* Englewood Cliffs, NJ: Prentice Hall.

BUREAUCRACY-LED VERSUS PURPOSE-LED POLICING IN CANADA

Chris Braiden

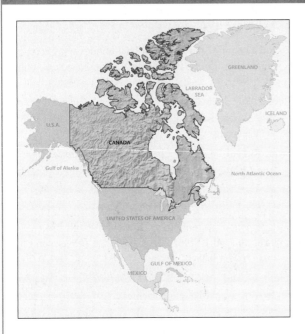

Bureaucracy is a relatively new word in the English language, a product of the industrial revolution as it evolved from the feudal system. At the time, the masses were illiterate and had lived off the land for centuries. The Oxford dictionary defines bureaucracy as "government by central administration." Bureaucracy was founded on the military model of command of the 1800s. Industrial bureaucracy was designed to coordinate workers in performing simple functions in isolation from each other. The automobile production line of the early 1900s is a classic example of this. Bureaucracy has a central hierarchical chain of command that's function-driven. It's driven by generic rules of behavior. Workers are not expected to coordinate their work or to know what the big picture is. That's the boss' job. Workers are mere functionaries. The bosses do the coordination and the workers do what they are told. Bureaucracy presumes you can't give ordinary people choices in the workplace because they will all make bad decisions. Bureaucracies govern by rules and policies created by the central bureaucrats. Criticism from the bottom is not tolerated. Bureaucracy, by design, is past-based and repetitious. Max Weber who wrote extensively on the subject described it as, "The authority of the eternal yesterday. The concept of the *official secret* is bureaucracy's special invention."

The police began adopting the bureaucratic model of management in the early 1900s when policing was chaotic, political, and corrupt. Almost a century later it still is the dominant management model and it is obstructing badly needed change in police organization, structure, and culture.

Police bureaucracies are still in the pyramid hierarchy with the boss on top and everyone else positioned below. The result is that today the fundamentals of policing are the same as they were in the 1970s; Random Patrol, Follow-Up Investigation, and Rapid Response, were all proven through research years ago to be very ineffective. This inner fixation-on-function leads to what I call "Management by Stomping Around." Each rank is so busy placating the rank above it that they spend most of their time stomping on the heads of the rank below whom they are supposed to be leading.

There are many leadership *ranks* in policing, but very little leadership *behavior*. In fact, bureaucracy and leadership are the opposite of each other. Police bureaucracy is afraid of leadership and it certainly doesn't reward it; it stultifies it. Conformity suffocates creation. The price of all this is that there is a need for truth and honesty and the necessity to face reality. The reality of the street doesn't get to the top until it is exposed in the media. Frank Serpico and the New York Police Department, Rodney King and the Los Angeles Police Department, Waco and the Bureau of Alcohol, Tobacco, and Firearms (BATF), and Ruby Ridge and the Federal Bureau of Investigation are riveting examples. Certainly, police agencies need a system of governance, but that governance must be leader-driven, and not follower-driven. The primary duty of the top bureaucrat is to impregnate the agency with leadership *behavior* at all levels. For this to happen, the chief must be at the bottom and the community at the top. The heads must be turned around so that each layer is looking up at those they are leading to make sure they have what they need to get the job done. And so, as we are in the new millennium, police management must reinvent itself. It must move from bureaucracy to leadership. It must move from function to purpose.

In 1990, my new police chief with the Edmonton Police Service (EPS), Doug McNally, asked me to deliver on a promise he made to our police commission when they appointed him a couple of weeks before. Doug was one of our own and he knew me well. His promise was to expand the ideas of community policing across one of our divisions (we had four). I accepted, on two conditions. We include the entire organization, and we follow my plan.

I wrote "A Process for Change" plan. The plan had very little to do with bureaucracy but much to do with leadership and purpose. It was constructed upon the logic of garage sales. Logic is transferable from one discipline to another. Garage sales are logical. They force us to do things we have been avoiding. They force us to reexamine everything in the context of the present. They force us to decide what to keep and what to get rid of.

The plan had two fundamental foundations. Generalize where possible; specialize where necessary. Decentralize where possible; centralize where necessary. Specialization has been the aspirin for everything in policing since the 1960s. The answer to everything has been to create a specialized unit to deal with it.

I'm not a fan of mission statements but I believe in core values. Core means central, something to aim at. The purpose of a core value is to unite all parts of the whole in pursuit of a common purpose. The first thing we did was answer what is Consent Policing Core Purpose. We agreed upon a core value that epitomized that purpose; "Committed to Community Needs." Every decision made on organizational change was driven by that core value. Community *needs* versus organization *wants!*

In 1974 the EPS had forty boxes on its organization chart. In 1990 it had 121. Our plan was to evaluate every one of those boxes against our core value by asking and answering five questions. What was *it* created to do? What was *it* doing now? Should *it* be doing what *it is* doing now? If not, what should *it* be doing now? How should *it* do what it should be doing now? Through this simple logical process we made many revealing discoveries that could never have been discovered using conventional bureaucracy. One of our primary aims was to get more officers on the road and to use those people more wisely based on our core value.

We started with a work-load analysis of 204,000 calls-for-service (CFS) to determine where the hotspots were and who was doing the work. What follows are some of our discoveries. In 1990, 34 percent of all sworn officers handled all 171,880-dispatched CFS. But those ordinary coppers initiated 85 percent of all *criminal* charges for that year. What was the other 66 percent doing? Not very much of anything! For examples, in 1990 there were 5,700 reported stolen autos; the Stolen Auto Unit with eight detectives recovered thirty-eight of them. Our specialized Vice Squad made 2 percent of all vice arrests. Our specialized Drug Squad made 7 percent of all drug arrests—and most of them *were not* big cases. Some detectives didn't make a single arrest that year!

Like most agencies, the EPS had gone to Differential Response, which really means handling the call over the phone rather than dispatching a car. Remember; action/reaction. In 1990 there were 112,000 reported crimes. Of that total, 55,000 were "investigated" over the phone mainly by civilian staff who would *legitimize* the complaint by giving a file number to the caller. This led to what we called the Second Call; *honest* people who would call back to report extra stuff stolen after they got their file number.

We stopped giving file numbers over the phone. Instead, people were directed to the twelve community police stations that we opened up in the neighborhoods identified by our hotspots, mainly in strip malls where there was parking. These stations, open 12/7, always with at least one police officer present along with volunteers, were in addition to our four divisional stations that are open 24/7. In the space of three years, 625,000 walked into those sixteen stations to report their complaints that didn't require police attendance at the scene. During that period the number of dispatched calls dropped significantly so that the patrol officers could focus more on problem solving, and far more citizens had their complaints handled face-to-face with a police officer rather than over the phone, and the number of reported thefts dropped dramatically. It's harder to lie eyeball-to-eyeball to a copper than it is to a faceless voice over the phone.

What did this all amount to? Well, our Process for Change team presented 132 recommendations for change to our management team of which I was a member. We accepted 112 of those recommendations. When I left the EPS, all of those 112 recommendations had been implemented, we had sixteen decentralized police stations versus four, there were ninety-two more coppers on the street, no one lost a rank or a job, but lots of fiefdoms disappeared because there were sixty-five fewer boxes on the organization chart. And all of this work was achieved with no increase in budget. I felt good.

Change is the only constant. Everything is in a perpetual flux of being and becoming. That is the constant lesson of life. So it is with policing. We have needed to change for decades—but the events of the last dozen years scream out at us to change. That change in policing must first come from the people who have been most resistant to change in the past, the bureaucrats. And they can change. We could not have done our thing in Edmonton without the full cooperation of our bureaucrats. Within policing, we must be totally honest with ourselves first, then to each other, and then to those we serve. We must go back and rediscover our purpose and then rebuild our police services around that purpose, but in the context of society of today. That is my wish for the future, and that is what keeps me going in my consulting work.

CHAPTER 6

Crime fighting is associated with a model of traditional policing that contemporary advocates of community policing consider a failure. But I believe that the founders of the crime-fighting philosophy deserve credit for bringing the police closer to professionalism. Traditional policing is not a failure, because it has provided successful services to the public—services that people have learned to expect from their local police department. (Palmiotto, 2000: 13–14)

Police officers escort Miguel Angel Mejia, center, an alleged Colombian paramilitary drug lord, in Mariquita, west of Bogota, Friday, May 2, 2008. Mejia, the second of two drug-trafficking twins, who were among the country's main cocaine shippers, was captured early Friday in Honda, 95 kms (60 miles) west of Bogota, authorities said. (Credit: © AP Photo/Fernando Vergara)

POLICE AND CRIME FIGHTING

OBJECTIVES:

1. Students will become familiar with the historical development of the crime-fighting model as a major function and mission of policing.

2. Students will become familiar with the War on Crime and the War on Drugs as major forms of police crime fighting.

3. Students will become familiar with the functionalist, conflict theory, and interactionist perspectives on police and crime fighting.

4. Students will become familiar with the international approach to police and crime fighting.

The American police system can historically be traced to the police system that originated in England in the latter part of the ninth century, under the rule of King Alfred the Great. In this English system, the people of the hamlets were responsible for peace keeping (Inciardi, 2007: 160).

Policing grew slowly in the English realm. Laws preceded the need for policing. Without laws holding some act or behavior of a person in violation against the government or against the citizens of the government, there can be no violations. Only when laws were passed by a recognized government were citizens held accountable for their offenses. A significant component of law violations is people. In unpopulated rural areas there usually exist little violations of law or crime. The densely populated, urban areas are more associated with crime and lawbreakers. When people moved from the rural to urban areas, those areas showed increases in crime. Another component of criminal activity is the presence of material goods. Without material goods, for example, a horse, jewelry, or clothes, property crimes would be almost nonexistent. The other form of crime, referred to as crimes against people, usually has been substantially less than property crimes.

Police Model

As discussed in Chapter 4, the movement from the rural farming areas to urban industrialized communities led to the creation of the London Metropolitan Police Department in 1829. This department became the model for the United States police system. In 1845 New York combined its day watch and night watch into one police department, thereby creating the first police department in the United States.

As also mentioned in Chapter 4, the major issues confronted the early police departments were the adoption of uniforms, arming of the police, and the amount of appropriate force to be used by police officers in making an arrest. The police were eventually forced to wear uniforms and, due to the violence of this period, they had to be armed. American society has accepted the norm of police officers wearing uniforms and being armed. However, the police's use of force is still an issue of contention in the first decade of the twenty-first century.

The decentralized, politically influenced neighborhood-oriented approach to policing dominated the nineteenth century. The police methods under the political influence were criticized. City populations in the latter half of the nineteenth century grew substantially with city politicians having a difficult time governing them. Governmental agencies, including the police, were ineffective and inefficient in providing services to the growing urban population. Decentralized power within city neighborhoods encouraged waste, duplications of efforts, and corruption. This along with immigration, housing shortages, crime, diseases, and overcrowding led to the initiation of a reform movement. The reformers supporting middle-class values stressed standards of honesty in political leaders and advocated that policies and procedures to remove politics from the police recruitment process be established in governmental operations.

Kelling and Moore (1988) divided policing into three eras: the political, reform, and community eras. As mentioned in the previous section, policing in America was decentralized. The first era discussed is the political era. Under the political era, political machines recruited and controlled the police department and the police officers working the streets. During this period the police provided social services to citizens in their neighborhood. For example, they provided housing for immigrants, ran soup kitchens, and assisted immigrants in finding work. In addition, they encouraged citizens to vote for specific candidates and helped to rig elections (3).

The second era was the reform era. The reform era worked to break the hold politicians had on police departments and police officers. This era saw conflict between reformers and city ward leaders. The reforms confronted the relationship between politicians and the police. They were also concerned with police misconduct such as corruption and laws regulating morality (4).

The third era was the community problem-solving era, on which additional information is presented in Chapter 10. During the 1970s and 1980s, foot patrols regained their popularity. Foot patrols reduced the fear of crime, increased citizen satisfaction toward the police, improved police attitudes toward citizens, and improved moral and job satisfaction of the police (10).

Simultaneously, Herman Goldstein's concept of problem-oriented policing (see Chapter 10 for additional information on problem-oriented policing) was being initiated in several cities. Problem-oriented policing emphasizes that the police are charged with resolving a repetitive crime or disorder problem.

The re-emphasis on foot patrols and the adoption of problem-oriented policing along with storefront mini police stations played a significant part in the evolution of community policing. The concept of community policing involves a close relationship between the police and citizens (11,12).

Fighting Crime

After the New York City Police Department was established in 1845, the goal of "fighting crime" became the mainstay of the American police. This "fighting image" included requiring police officers to wear uniforms and to be armed. Although it was decades before all police forces in America would adopt the role of "crime fighters," it should be recognized that this was the initial sign of what was to come.

Most of what a police officer does during his or her tour of duty does not involve crime fighting activity. Probably anywhere from 80 to 90 percent of police activity involves providing noncriminal services to the community (Palmiotto, 2005: 37). From the latter part of the nineteenth century up to the first decade of the twenty-first century, the primary mission of the police has been related to arresting criminal offenders, solving crime, and preventing and deterring crime. The police mission is a crime fighting one, and the police in modern times readily accept this role and want to follow the precepts of "crime fighters."

In the first decades of the twentieth century, **August Vollmer,** the police chief of Berkeley, California, became a key figure of American policing. Vollmer's model of

....

august vollmer

Often considered an early professional police administrator who advocated training and a college education for police officers. He advocated the use of technology in solving crime. Vollmer is recognized as an early police innovator and leader and a strong proponent of the police as crime fighters.

policing centered on a police officer who was a skilled and dedicated "crime fighter" and who was trained to perform a complex job. His concept further held that science and technology were an important element of policing along with the police being involved with the community they served (Peek 2009: 27–28).

National Crime Commission

Beginning with the establishment of the Chicago Crime Commission in 1919 and continuing through the 1930s, crime commissions were established in twenty-four states. The federal government established two national surveys: The National Crime Commission in 1925 and the **National Commission on Law Observance and Enforcement**, often referred to as the **Wickersham Commission**, in 1929. The concept of a "War on Crime" emerged as a major element of the National Crime Commission report. The members of the National Crime Commission, the Chicago Crime Commission, and the Committee on Law Enforcement of the American Bars Association of 1922 all accepted the concept of a War on Crime (Douthit, 1975; 319).

In 1925 President Calvin Coolidge appointed a National Crime Commission to study the crime problem. This meant that the "crime problem" had been recognized as a problem for the federal government. Traditionally, the federal government had narrow law enforcement concerns, consisting of enforcing custom laws, counterfeiting, and mail fraud. With the passage of the thirteenth amendment and the Volstead Act, which outlawed liquor, along with the Harrison Act, designed to regulate the import, manufacture, and dispensing of drugs, and the White Slave Act, making it a crime to transport girls and women across state lines for illicit purposes, the federal government had a substantial role to play in law enforcement.

The National Commission on Law Observance and Enforcement (Wickersham Commission) in their *Report on Lawlessness in Law Enforcement* included a major attack against the War on Crime. One of the major concerns of the Wickersham Commission was the use of brutality known as the "Third Degree." The Wickersham Commission stated, "The third degree is a secret and illegal practice. Those who employ it either will not talk, or else will make formal denial of its existence. The victims are likely to exaggerate or even fabricate accounts to further their ends or to decline to talk because of fear of police retaliation. Police reporters know a great deal, but they are dependent upon the police for their information, and are often likewise reticent" (1931: 21).

The Wickersham Commission found a variety of third degree methods used against suspects, such as, "A sharp, but not heavy, regular blow of a club on the skull, repeated at regular intervals, so that the regularity of the blows arouses anticipation which increases the torture; assuring suspects that they would not be hurt, then suddenly felling them unconscious by a blow from behind with a club or a slab of wood, followed by further sympathy and reassurance when the man revives, only to have the same thing suddenly happen again, the man never seeing who strikes him" (No. 11: 92). Third degree torture included physical violence against a suspect, which often left them with swollen faces, all sorts of bruises and cuts, and blood splattered all over them. One New York magistrate noted, during the 1920s, that when several Italians

....

national commission on law observance and enforcement (wickersham commission)

Established in 1929 by President Herbert Hoover who appointed the attorney general George W. Wickersham as chair of the commission. The commission promoted the concept of the War on Crime and was critical of "third degree" methods, the use of excessive force, by the police.

were brought before him for alleged violence, he found that their backs did not have a spot that was not raw from a beating they had received at the hands of the police.

The early decades of the twentieth century saw the third degree employed as a common and recognized practice among the police in the United States (No. 11: 90–91). Those who supported the third degree methods as an important tool in crime fighting made several arguments to support it. Those who considered third degree an abomination outlined their objections. Arguments in support of the third degree are as follows: (1) its use is necessary to get all the facts; (2) it is used only against the guilty; (3) obstacles in the way of the police make it almost impossible to obtain convictions except by third-degree methods; (4) police brutality is an inevitable, and therefore an excusable, reaction to the brutality of criminals; (5) restrictions on the third degree may impair the morale of the police; (6) the existence of organized gangs in large cities renders traditional legal limitations outworn (Wickersham, 1931, No. 11: 174–180).

Some of these arguments supporting the third degree may have been acceptable to some group in the first decade of the twenty-first century. A close review of several of the reasons shows how foolish the supporters of the third degree were with their arguments. For example, why is brutality necessary to get the facts about a case? If a suspect has not been convicted of a crime, which is the courts responsibility, then how can the police know for certain that the people who they use third-degree tactics against are guilty? How can brutality be condoned against another human being? It would seem that a rational and logical person would realize that brutality is not the answer for solving crimes and is a poor tool in the so-called fight on crime. The points made here are very strong arguments against the third degree. This is particularly true in the first decade of the twenty-first century, when members of society are less tolerant of police misconduct and know their rights.

New Deal

The New Deal considered social order as important to economical order and prosperity. The War on Crime was one approach of taking the public's attention away from the Great Depression. The anticrime campaigns were used to muster a rallying cry in support of the government.

In the 1940s, the rank and file of law enforcement was seriously depleted as police officers went to war. The 1940s were a period in which America concentrated on winning the war. Following World War II, police veterans returned to their police agencies or war veterans entered the field of policing for the first time. Not much emphasis was placed on the War on Crime during the 1940s. The 1950s were a period in which America was recovering from the war and the Great Depression. During that period, goods were produced for the war effort and not for consumer consumption. Americans became consumers in the 1950s and this consumer mentality of Americans is still going strong. With an emphasis on consumerism and an improved economy, crime began to increase, or at least gained the attention of the authorities. Youth gangs became a concern in large cities such as New York. Organized crime received national attention, along with police corruption.

The Challenge of Crime in a Free Society

As mentioned in Chapter 4, the 1960s were a decade of turmoil, violence, and chaos that resulted in changes in society and reemphasized the War on Crime. Violent crime was increasing at a rate that concerned law enforcement. Aggravated assault, forcible rape, and robbery doubled. The increase in crime, beginning in the 1960s, continued to climb until the mid-1990s. In addition to the crime rate increase, the decade had numerous assassinations, including those of President John Kennedy, Robert Kennedy, and Martin Luther King, Jr. Mass murder seemed to have been discovered in the 1960s, with Charles Speck murdering eight student nurses in Chicago and Charles Manson's family going on a killing rampage, not to mention Charles Whitman, who climbed a tower at the University of Texas in August 1966 and shot forty-four people, thirteen fatally. The Civil Rights Movement escalated during the 1960s, leading to violence against those marching and supporting civil rights for black Americans. Civil rights radicals who did not believe in the peaceful approach of Martin Luther King, Jr., advocated violence against white American society. Urban riots occurred in Watts, Los Angeles; Harlem, New York; Miami; Detroit; Chicago; Newark; and Atlanta. In addition, riots occurred in many smaller communities. To add to the high crime rate, assassinations, mass murders, violence against civil rights supporters, and urban riots, America was involved in a war. The Vietnam War was an unpopular war, which led to student unrest on university campuses from Columbia in New York City to Berkeley in California. The war became unpopular with each passing year in the 1960s. The police, as the defenders of the status quo, became the enemy of many groups. The peace movement confronted the police, and often resulted in violence. Civil Rights supporters had problems with the police, especially in the south, because they supported Jim Crow laws and segregation. The more militant groups disliked the police because they felt that the police were defending a corrupt and aggressive government.

Many groups held the police in the 1960s in disdain, sometimes calling them "pigs." Appeals for law and order began early in the 1960s. "Law and Order" became a campaign issue for the first time in American history between President Lyndon Johnson and his Republican opponent, Barry Goldwater. The law and order appeal was a call to get back to the grassroot values of America. Law and order advocates wanted to return to the perceived morality of earlier decades. The turmoil, chaos, and violence had to be curbed.

In response President Lyndon Johnson launched his War on Crime when he announced the formation of the **President's Commission on Law Enforcement and Administration of Justice.** In 1968, President Johnson was able to pass his first piece of law and order legislation. This legislation, known as the Omnibus Crime Control and Safe Streets Act, was meant to allay the fears about crime and calm agitation over inner-city riots and anger over United State Supreme Court decisions that supposedly overruled the police (Inciardi, 2007: 8). The primary provision of the Omnibus Crime Control and Safe Street Act was Title I, which established the Law Enforcement Assistance Administration (LEAA). The LEAA was to develop new techniques, devices, and approaches in law enforcement, and award grants to policing programs (Inciardi, 2007: 10). The emphasis of the LEAA was to fight the War on Crime.

president's commission on law enforcement and administration of justice

President Lyndon Johnson established this commission in 1965. In 1967 the commission released its general report in *The Challenge of Crime in a Free Society.* Additional task force reports on the police, courts, corrections, juvenile delinquency, youth crime, organized crime, and science and technology were published.

War on Crime

The 1960s were a decade in which the federal government dealt with domestic social problems and foreign wars. Following the passage of the Safe Streets Act of 1968, the federal presence in crime, the criminal justice process, and policing increased substantially. Federal grants were provided to the local police for equipment, training, and for the appointment of additional police officers. To this day the national government plays a significant effort in state and local crime-fighting efforts. In the early 1970s, James Vorenberg, the executive director of President Johnson's Commission on Law Enforcement and Administration of Justice, reported, "The Principal gains by the police in the past five years have been in lowering the level of hostility of the police and young people, particularly blacks" (1972: 3). Vorenberg further comments that the changes that have improved police-citizen relations did not produce a significant impact on crime. He concludes that he finds "it hard to point to anything that is being done that is likely to reduce crime even to the level of five years ago" (p. 15).

In a democracy, such as in the United States, the War on Crime can never be won; crime can only be controlled. Democracies guarantee their citizens civil and human rights; individual civil rights come at the expense of controlling government actions against citizens. When governments go to war, there are usually losers and winners. When do our governments, federal, state or local, expect to win their war against crime? The War on Crime has become propaganda for politicians to help them win elections and for police administrators to gain the support of the public.

The Regan and Bush administrations of the 1980s and early 1990s had a conservative view in approaching the War on Crime. Emphasis was on enhancing penalties for firearm violations and encouraging prison construction, and federal grants provided law enforcement agencies with technology to fight crime. The Clinton administration continued the same approach on the War on Crime. In August 1994, Congress passed the Crime Control Bill, which was signed by President Clinton. The **Violent Crime Control and Law Enforcement Act of 1994** emphasized the crime-fighting approach to crime. The War on Crime in the mid- to late 1990s under the Clinton administration was not defunct, even though its emphasis was on community policing.

WAR ON DRUGS

The **Controlled Substance Act (CSA)**, Title II of the federal Comprehensive Drug Abuse Prevention Act of 1970, requires law enforcement agencies to control the abuse of drugs and other chemical substances. A consolidation of numerous laws that regulate the manufacture and distribution of narcotics, depressants, and hallucinogens, the CSA places chemical substances under five schedules. A drug's placement is based on its medical use, potential for abuse, and dependence liability. The Department of Health and Human Services and the Drug Enforcement Agency (DEA) may add, delete, or change the schedule of a drug. When the DEA receives a petition, it initiates its own investigation of the drug (Palmiotto, 1997, 426).

---

violent crime control and law enforcement act of 1994

Emphasized the crime-fighting approach to crime. One of the main goals of the act, to put more "cops on the beat," is present in Title I, "Public Safety and Policing." The federal government would provide matching funds for those communities who are willing to hire additional police officers. Money was also available for the construction and expansion of correctional facilities.

---

controlled substance act (CSA)

Title II of the Federal Comprehensive Drug Abuse Prevention Act of 1970, requires law enforcement agencies to control the abuse of drugs and other chemical substances.

For most of its history, the United States has had a "drug problem." After the Civil War, veterans were given morphine to numb the pain of their injuries and became addicted to drug. In fact, so many veterans became addicted to morphine that it was called the "war disease." American women also have a long history of consuming both legal and illegal drugs. Prior to the passage of the first narcotics law in the United States in 1914, the Harrison Act, women were associated with a variety of drugs, especially opiates, which could be purchased as over-the-counter remedies. Drugs such as sedatives and tranquilizers were also prescribed more often for women than for men. Women constitute a higher number of emergency-room treatment cases for prescription-drug overdoses than men (Bush-Baskette, 2000: 920).

Drugs continued to be used illegally even after the passage of the Harrison Act of 1914. During the 1960s, Americans rebelled against the status quo of drugs being harmful. Marijuana, cocaine, and designer drugs became popular among the youth of middle class America. Cocaine became the choice of the professional—doctors, and lawyers, and celebrities. A drug culture had developed in America. A large portion of Americans found using drugs to be an acceptable lifestyle choice. They did not consider it wrong or a crime. However, others in society became concerned about the use of drugs, especially with so many people accepting it and arrogantly using it in public. Many Americans wanted something to be done and action was taken when President Nixon assumed office in 1971.

In a message to Congress on June 17, 1971, President Richard Milhous Nixon initiated America's first "War on Drugs." He portrayed drug abuse as "a national emergency," labeled it "public enemy number one," and called for "a total offensive" (Wisotsky, 1986: 3). President Nixon's War on Drugs included doubling the manpower of the Bureau of Narcotics and Dangerous Drugs and eventually consolidating the various agencies with drug authority into the DEA (Wisotsky, 1986: 3). Under Nixon, drugs were linked to crime, an important plank in President Nixon's reelection campaign. The assumption behind the War on Drugs was that by decreasing drug use, crime would also decrease.

In 1982 President Ronald Reagan became the second president to declare a War on Drugs. In advancement of this war, the Reagan administration hired an additional 500 DEA agents and founded thirteen regional antidrug task forces that compiled a record number of drug seizures and convictions (Elwood, 1994: 39). During the Reagan administration, the military was brought into the drug war and by executive order, the Central Intelligence Agency (CIA) was formally brought in as well. President Reagan established the South Florida Task Force on Crime to control massive illegal immigration and drug smuggling. The Internal Revenue Service (IRS) intensified its Special Enforcement Program aimed at drug offenders. The attorney general of the United States ordered the director of the Federal Bureau of Investigation (FBI) to assume authority over the DEA (Holden-Rhodes, 1997; 56).

The election of President George H. W. Bush in 1988 continued the War on Drugs.

National policies have not really changed since the initial **National Drug Control Strategy (NDCS)** was adopted in 1989 under President George H. W. Bush.

national drug control strategy (NDCS)

Established by President George H. W. Bush in 1989 under the requirements of the Anti-Drug Abuse Act of 1988. This strategy was a continuation of the War on Drugs.

Regardless of the political party or the president in power, all administrations use similar strategies as revisions of the NDCS.

President William J. Clinton also continued the War on Drugs during his administration. This took on an added international dimension (see next section) for example, the secretary of defense, William Cohen, and Colombia's President Andres Pastrana agreed to United States military cooperation in the war on drug trafficking, including a pledge by the secretary of defense to increase military training of Colombia's armed forces and increase sharing of aerial and satellite intelligence data (Myers, 1998: 14).

With the election of George W. Bush in 2000 there were few significant changes to the ongoing War on Drugs. The biggest change in America that occurred under the presidency of President George W. Bush came after the incident of September 11, 2001.

POLICE AND CRIME FIGHTING: THREE SOCIOLOGICAL PERSPECTIVES

The first sociological perspective of functionalism would consider the development and specification of the crime-fighting function of the police as an attempt by an important social organization to be responsive to that of society's needs. Thus, as society changed from an agricultural to an industrial one, the nature of law enforcement and crime fighting changed along with it. That crime fighting became the central mission of police departments was a reflection of the needs perceived by citizens and the changed circumstances—they were afraid of crime, and the earlier system of kin policing was not viable anymore. Police agencies attempted to carry out their enforcement functions in the most effective ways possible by declaring war on crime and drugs, which led the police into a national effort to fight the two. Of course, there were certain dysfunctions that crept into these wars—inefficiency, and loss of privacy—that would later be corrected by the police themselves.

Those who follow the conflict sociological perspective are suspicious of efforts by formal organizations in society to achieve certain ends, in this case, crime fighting by declaring twin wars on crime and drugs. Who are the targets and victims of these wars? Conflict theorists will point to people in the United States who do not believe in the War on Drugs. One such group consists of African Americans who have often interpreted the War on Drugs as a war on African Americans and their families. Minorities are disproportionately represented among those arrested for drug-related crimes and are disproportionately incarcerated. African Americans and other minorities comprise approximated 75 percent of inmate populations in state correction institutions (Hall, 1997: 611). One supporter of this concept wrote the following about a war on the African family (Hall, 1995: 618):

> Americans may have become acculturated to the overrepresentation of African American males in the criminal justice system. Most view it as normal and justified, given what is taken for granted to be an enormous potential for violence in this population.

Members of the dominant culture have become desensitized to the social injustice inherent in this pattern, a vicious cycle of root causes which include lack of employment, opportunity and reduced motivation to obtain skills, poverty, racism, increased family instability, and diminishing positive role models. These root causes are far more significant as causal factors than any "alleged" genetic predisposition toward violence among African men. In discussing the "war on drugs" it would be remiss to not at least make students aware that there exists a segment of the American population that believes the "war on drugs" is in reality a war on the African Americans.

The third sociological perspective, that of interactionism, will focus on the rhetoric underlying and the image presented by the declaration of wars on crime and drugs. What or who were the individuals who decided that dealing with these problems required preparation as though the country was going to war. Think, for example, if instead of declaring a War on Drugs, this was declared to be an educational and public health problem that was to be characterized by counseling users to stop using drugs and teaching them how to do so. If you think this is a strange way of approaching the problem, remember that we chose to deal with the issue of high tobacco use in this country (and rather successfully) using exactly such a strategy, and not by declaring a "War on Tobacco." Given the predominant war image, the police are also likely to see themselves as soldiers who should be able to wipe out the enemy with means that are fair or foul. How are such views and messages propagated and sustained among the police?

Let us turn our attention to how the crime-fighting mentality has led to what is literally a war in Colombia.

 # POLICE AND CRIME FIGHTING INTERNATIONALLY: COLOMBIA

With a population of 43 million, Columbia in South America has declared a similar War on Drugs. It was drawn into this war after it became a major producer of coca leaves, from which cocaine is ultimately obtained. Victims of the United States sponsored War on Drugs on Colombian soil have included judges who have been assassinated by drug traffickers. Federal buildings, including police buildings, have been bombed. One complaint the Colombians have against the United States is that the latter was instrumental in destroying the coffee cartel. Coffee was once the mainstay of Colombia's economy. It appears that the United States government was upset about Colombia bartering coffee for industrial goods with Communist countries. Colombians also ask why the United States does not stop the drug trade at its source: the consumer (Fricker, 1990: 54–58). Colombia, throughout the 1990s and in the first decade of the twenty-first century, has been continuously involved in the United States sponsored War on Drugs. President Clinton vowed that the $1.3 billion antidrug package he signed into a law would not lead to "Yankee imperialism." The antidrug package allowed United States troops to serve as advisors and to train two Colombian army battalions in the War on Drugs. The goal was for the Colombian battalions to destroy drug plantations and laboratories in guerrilla-controlled areas of South Colombia (Clinton Steps up U.S. War on Drugs, August 21: 1). Colombian presidents have supported the War

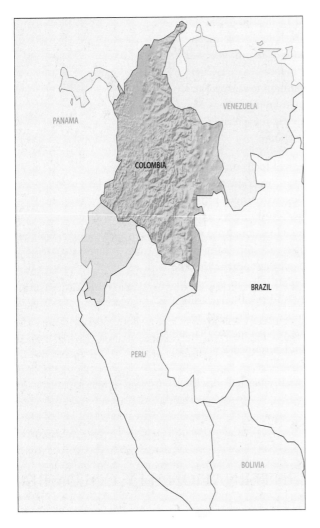

on Drugs, but the war does not seem winnable, nor does it seem that much progress has been made.

In a *St. Petersburg Times* editorial, the following was stated, "The idea of going into this drug-producing country [Colombia], wiping out the drug crops and replacing them with alternative crops is ridiculous. Guess what happens after the United States spends $1.3 billion to rid Colombia of drug crops? That's right, the drug crops will once again be planted" (2000: 15A). In addition, the author of this chapter has spoken to numerous drug investigators who have freely told this author that the drug war is being lost.

Perhaps seemingly comprehensive crime-fighting efforts such as the War on Drugs may never be won, since to win it would require the eradication of all drugs and drug use. Older Americans remember that America did not lose the Vietnam War; America withdrew its armed forces. The American people either did not support or got tired of supporting a war thousands of miles from their shores. Will the War on Drugs involving Colombia have a similar outcome so as to constitute another Vietnam?

The crime-fighting activities of the police are important, but can lead to real wars. Another concern is how the concept of the police as professional crime fighters, which is drilled into recruits through socialization and training, has consequences in terms of their own later ethical behavior on the job. We will learn about this in the accompanying box describing the situation in Kosovo.

 # SUMMARY

The American police view themselves and are perceived as crime fighters. This concept of the American police can be traced to the late eighteenth and nineteenth centuries. August Vollmer, an early advocate for the professionalism of policing established this "crime fighting" image of the police. Vollmer, as police administrator of the Berkley Police Department, created several techniques for the police's "fight on crime." Vollmer's model of policing centered upon a police officer who was a

skilled and dedicated crime fighter, trained to perform a complex job. The 1930s had a profound effect on American policing. The early 1930s were associated with a crime wave, which became a major concern of the national government. It was in the 1930s that the FBI emerged as a major factor in policing. This era also marked the acceptance of the American police in their crime-fighting role and image. The 1940s were the decade of the "World War," and the 1950s were the decade of America "getting back to normal." It was not until 1965 that President Lyndon Johnson reemphasized the War on Crime. Federal legislation was passed that provided equipment and training for local law enforcement. The War on Crime initiated by President Johnson has not been a complete success even though there are those in American society and law enforcement who still believe in it. The second war that law enforcement is fighting is the War on Drugs. President Richard Nixon initiated this in 1971. The War on Drugs was taken up again by President Ronald Reagan in 1982 and every president since Ronald Regan has promoted the War on Drugs. The War on Drugs has still not been won in the first decades of the twenty-first century. This war will probably never be won if there are consumers and producers of drugs. The best we can hope for in the War on Drugs is to control the trafficking of drugs.

KEY TERMS

August Vollmer: Often considered an early professional police administrator who advocated training and a college education for police officers. He advocated the use of technology in solving crime. Vollmer is recognized as an early police innovator and leader and a strong proponent of the police as crime fighters.

Controlled Substance Act (CSA): Title II of the Federal Comprehensive Drug Abuse Prevention Act of 1970 requires law enforcement agencies to control the abuse of drugs and other chemical substances.

National Commission on Law Observance and Enforcement (Wickersham Commission): Established in 1929 by President Herbert Hoover who appointed the attorney general George W. Wickersham as chair of the commission. The commission promoted the concept of the War on Crime and was critical of "third degree" methods, the use of excessive force, by the police.

National Drug Control Strategy (NDCS): Established by President George H. W. Bush in 1989 under the require-ments of the Anti-Drug Abuse Act of 1988. This strategy was a continuation of the War on Drugs.

President's Commission on Law Enforcement and Administration of Justice: President Lyndon Johnson established this commission in 1965. In 1967 the commission released its general report in *The Challenge of Crime in a Free Society.* Additional task force reports on the police, courts, corrections, juvenile delinquency, youth crime, organized crime, and science and technology were published.

Violent Crime Control and Law Enforcement Act of 1994: Emphasized the crime-fighting approach to crime. One of the main goals of the act, to put more "cops on the beat," is present in Title I, "Public Safety and Policing." The federal government would provide matching funds for those communities who are willing to hire additional police officers. Money was also available for the construction and expansion of correctional facilities.

REVIEW QUESTIONS

1. Explain the goals and objectives of the War on Crime.

2. Write an essay on why the War on Drugs was implemented.

3. Write an essay either supporting the War on Crime or the War on Drugs.

DISCUSSION QUESTIONS

1. Is it important to have an understanding of police history? Justify your answer.
2. Has the War on Crime been a success?
3. Has the War on Drugs been a success?

REFERENCES

Bush-Baskette, Stephanie (2000) "The War on Drugs And The Incarceration of Mothers," *Journal of Drug Issues,* Volume 30, No. 4.

Douthit, Nathan (1975) "Police Professionalism and the War Against Crime in the United States, 1920-1930" in George L. Mosse, ed., *Police Forces in History,* Beverly Hills: CA: Sage Publications.

Elwood, William N. (1994) *Rhetoric in the War on Drugs: The Triumphs and Tragedies of Public Relations,* Westport, CT: Praeger.

Fricker, Richard L. (1990) "A Judiciary Under Fire," *ABA Journal,* February.

Hall, Mary F. (1997) "The 'War on Drugs': A Continuation of the War on the African American Family." *Smith College Studies in Social Work,* 67, 3: 237–249.

Holden-Rhodes, J. F.(1997) *Sharing the Secrets,* Westport, CT: Praeger.

Inciardi, James A. (2007) *Criminal Justice,* Seventh Edition, New York, NY: Harcourt.

Kelling, George L. and Mark H. Moore (1988) *The Evolving Strategy of Policing,* U.S Department of Justice: National Institute of Justice.

Myers, Stephen A. (1998) "U.S. Pledges Military Cooperation to Colombia in Drug War," *The New York Times,* Section A, page 14, column 3.

Palmiotto, Michael J. (2000) *Community Policing: A Strategy for the 21ˢᵗ Century,* Gaithersburg, MD: Aspen Publishers.

Palmiotto, Michael J. (2005) *Policing: Concepts, Strategies and Current Issues in American Police Forces,* Second Edition, Durham, NC: Carolina Academic Press.

Palmiotto, Michael J. (1997) *Policing: Concepts, Strategies, and Current Issues in Policing,* Durham: NC: Carolina Press.

Peek, Kenneth J. (2009) *Policing in America,* Belmont, CA: Wadsworth.

President's Commission on Law Enforcement and Administration of Justice (1967) *Task Force Report: The Police,* Washington, DC: Government Printing Office.

St. Petersburg Times (2000) "Winning the War on Drugs starts in United States," *St. Petersburg Times,* September 22.

Vorenberg, James (1972) The War on Crime: First Five Years, The Atlantic Monthly (May).

Wisotsky, Steven (1986) *Breaking the Impasse in the War on Drugs,* New York, NY: Greenwood Press.

POLICE AND CRIME FIGHTING IN KOSOVO

Aleksandra Snowden and Arvind Verma

Kosovo is the newest nation-in-making, as its recognition as an independent country is still under negotiation. The former province of Serbia, Kosovo is today inhabited mainly by ethnic Albanians, who, according to a 2008 census, make up 92 percent of the population out of 2.13 million inhabitants. The Kosovo Serbians had earlier comprised roughly one-fourth of the population, but their numbers have drastically come down after the Balkan conflict. The ethnic tensions between Kosovo Albanians and Kosovo Serbs can be dated back to as early as the late fourteenth century. Nevertheless, under the Communist regime of Marshall Tito, the region enjoyed peace for almost three decades after the end of World War II. But by the late 1980s, ethnic conflict broke out all over the Balkans, splitting up the region and leading to horrible bloodletting on every side. The intervention of the NATO forces and the United Nations (UN) finally brought peace with the establishment of the independent nations of Croatia and Bosnia, but the situation in Kosovo lingered on. Finally, on February 13,

2008, Kosovo proclaimed independence from the Republic of Serbia after a decade-long struggle for independence. These events from the more recent past have shaped the criminal justice system that is still under formation in the country.

The journey to Kosovo's independence began in earnest in 1996 when the Kosovo Liberation Army (KLA) was formed. The KLA claimed responsibility for attacks on police outposts, and the Serbian police swiftly responded in action against suspected Albanian separatists. The clash between the KLA, on the one hand, and the Serbian police, on the other, attracted the attention of the wider international community, which stepped in during the spring of 1999 when Serbian security apparatus was withdrawn from Kosovo. By mid-1999, NATO and the Federal Republic of Yugoslavia signed a military technical agreement that led to the immediate withdrawal of the Yugoslav army and police force from Kosovo (Wilson, 2006). The complete withdrawal of Serbian police from Kosovo left a vacuum with no local institutions to take care of the public security functions (Eide and Holm, 1999). A competition began between the Kosovo Force-UN coalition and the KLA to assume authority that created considerable chaos (Eide and Holm, 1999). Finally, the United Nations Mission in Kosovo (UNMIK) intervened and divided the provision of public security in Kosovo between the KFOR, UNMIK international civilian police (CIVPOL), and the Kosovo Police Service (KPS) (Wilson, 2006).

Specifically, the UN secretary general proposed a three-stage process for UNMIK in the field of police and security (Decker, 2006) for the successful implementation of both short- and long-term tasks. The first stage included establishment of KFOR supremacy in maintaining law and order, which operated with advice from the CIVPOL officers. The second stage included transferring policing duties to CIVPOL officers, who gained executive policing powers and took the responsibility for the establishment of an indigenous police force, the KPS. The last stage included transferring executive policing to the KPS, while CIVPOL continued to maintain the advisory and monitoring role (Decker, 2006). It took the UN several months to deploy and organize enough civil police, and make the UNMIK police an operational force. Thus, the gradual transfer of the policing authority to the regional commands of CIVPOL (Brand, 2003) took time. This resulted in KFOR being held responsible for a variety of tasks, including transportation, mine clearance, border security, and fire services (Bernabeu, 2007).

The need for an indigenous criminal justice system and the serious law and order challenges of this postconflict society made the development of local police forces and their monitoring by international police observers critical for sustaining peace (Baskin, 2004; Vaccaro, 2000). In addition, police reforms of the war-torn and socially divided society required immediate attention from international authorities. Moreover, in Kosovo, the local police institution had to be built up from scratch. The task facing the UNMIK was incredible: in the ethnically polarized Kosovo conflict, the police were the primary players in the "ethnic cleansing" and were forced to leave the province. Moreover, practically all police officers during the last decade were Serbs who had left the province after the NATO involvement, while most of the Kosovo Albanian officers left the service or were dismissed during the Serbian purges of Albanians in public offices in the early 1990s (Eide and Holm, 1999). The most important challenge was that new cadres had to be identified, recruited, and trained before an authentic Kosovo Police Service could be introduced (Eide and Holm, 1999).

The United Nations Mission in Kosovo was responsible for developing a new indigenous police force (Vaccaro, 2000). In June 1999, UNMIK began recruiting Kosovo Police Service (KPS) officers, and a few months later the Organization for Security and Co-operation in Europe (OSCE) established the Kosovo Police Service School in Vushitrri, a town in western Kosovo (Wilson, 2006). The OSCE set the training period for the KPS officers initially for four weeks but over time it was increased to twenty weeks (Decker, 2006). The only way that police can be effective in controlling crime and maintaining order is ensuring policing practices that are respectful of the rights of all citizens and is responsive to their needs (Neild, 2001). Thus, the KPS officers were taught basic policing methods, human rights training, and the practical application of human rights to on-the-job situations (Decker, 2006). The training in Kosovo

Police School is setting high standards and a variety of subjects such as Police Ethics, applicable legislation in Kosovo, Crime investigation, Collecting evidence, Conducting interviews, Democratic policing norms, use of fire arms, forensics, and traffic control are being imparted (KPS, n.d.). Although the initial aim of inducting 3,000 local police recruits per year was not achieved, by the year 2000 there were about twenty-five hundred KPS officers on the job in Kosovo, and by 2004 there were almost six thousand KPS officers on the job in Kosovo (Wilson, 2006).

UNMIK police commanders initially supervised and controlled the activities of the new police force in order to transfer increasing responsibility to the indigenous police force. Additionally, the UNMIK police commanders gradually shifted the role of the international police from law enforcement duties to a supervisory and cadre role, and, then, to traditional CIVPOL monitoring and mentoring functions (Vaccaro, 2000). Subsequently, the number of CIVPOL officers had decreased in order to provide for the gradual transfer of executive policing to the local KPS institution. There were 6,500 CIVPOL officers and over 5,000 KPS officers serving at the high-point in the mission's staffing (Decker, 2006). In late 2006, there were roughly 8,000 KPS officers and 1,800 CIVPOL officers in Kosovo (Decker, 2006). As of late 2006, KPS officers have executive authority in nearly every unit and station in Kosovo (Decker, 2006). The relatively new police force is based on the ideal of democratic policing and professionalism. Slowly, Kosovo police is gaining the confidence of the citizens to establish peace and security and give a sense of democratic community to the local people.

References

Baskin, M. (2004) *Building Local Democracy under conditions of Uncertainty in Kosovo*. Meeting Report 291.

Bernabeu, I. (2007) Laying the foundations of democracy? Reconsidering Police reform under UN Auspices in Kosovo. *Security Dialogue*, 38, 71–92.

Brand, M. (2003) *The Development of Kosovo Institutions and the Transition of Authority from UNMIK to Local Self-Government*. Centre for Applied Studies in International Negotiations, Geneva.

Decker, D. C. (2006) Enforcing human rights: The role of the UN civilian police in Kosovo. *International Peacekeeping,* 13, 502–516.

Eide, E. B. & Holm, T. T. (1999) Postscript: Towards executive authority policing? The lessons of Kosovo. *International Peacekeeping,* 6, 210–219.

Kosovo Police Service (n.d.) Kosovo Police History. Retrieved October 15, 2009 from http://www.kosovopolice.com/?page=2,2.

Neild, R. (2001) Democratic police reforms in war-torn societies. *Conflict, Security & Development,* 1, 21–43.

Vaccaro (2000) *Evolution of police monitoring in peace operations.* Verification Yearbook 2000.

Wilson, J. M. (2006) Law and Order in an Emerging Democracy: Lessons from the Reconstruction of Kosovo's Police and Justice Systems. *The Annals of the American Academy of Political and Social Science,* 605, 152–177.

CHAPTER 7

Despite the importance of maintaining order, it is also controversial—for at least two reasons. First, there is no clear and consistent definition of disorder. Unlike criminal laws that define acts, public disorder is a condition. (Kelling, 1995: 163)

A police officer orders Muslims to stand behind a barricade outside the Hameediya Mosque, the scene of bomb explosions in Malegaon, about 300 kilometers (188 miles) northeast of Mumbai, India, Saturday, Sept. 9, 2006. A pair of bombs rigged to bicycles ripped through the crowded streets of a western Indian city Friday as Muslim worshippers were leaving afternoon prayers, killing at least 31 people and injuring more than 100, a top official said, calling the violence "a terrorist act." Authorities quickly clamped a curfew over the city of Malegaon, where the blasts occurred, which has a long history of violence between Muslims and Hindus. (Credit: © AP Photo/Gautam Singh)

POLICE, ORDER MAINTENANCE, AND SERVICE

OBJECTIVES:

1. The student will have an understanding of order maintenance and service as functions of policing.

2. The student will be able to explain the concepts of order and disorder and how they relate to order maintenance.

3. The student will be able to explain why some police scholars consider order maintenance the primary role of the police.

4. The student will be able to explain the public safety function of the police.

5. The student will understand the functionalist, conflict theory, and interactionist approaches to police involvement in order maintenance and service.

6. The student will learn about police, order maintenance, and service on an international level.

The primary reason for establishing policing in society is to maintain order or social control. Chapter 6 discusses crime fighting, a mandate created by officials in the 1930s and deemed central to policing; most police agencies are not involved in crime fighting most of the time. If you look again at the list of major functions associated with the police discussed in Chapter 2, you will find that most of them have to do with order maintenance and service. Further, studies of how most police officers (Wilson, 1968) actually use their time indicate that crime fighting is not their major activity. Most police officers, it turns out, are involved in order maintenance. From ancient times to the twenty-first century, social order in the tribe, village, community, city, state, and country had to be maintained. Without social order, societies have difficulty operating in an efficient manner. Throughout history, the people of the tribe or village, the military, or police officers were given the duty and responsibility to maintain order so that farmers could farm, ranchers could ranch, and factory workers could produce goods for consumption. When social order is absent and chaos exists, society cannot move forward; it will not even be able to maintain the status quo.

Generally, the police problem of maintaining order takes priority over law enforcement. There are several reasons for this. First, police officers encounter more order maintenance problems than law enforcement problems. Second, order maintenance exposes the police officer to physical danger (Wilson, 1968: 17–19). Skolnick considers the police officer's focus on danger an important aspect of the police officer's "working personality." James Q. Wilson continues, "I would add that the risk of danger in order maintenance patrol work, though statistically less than the danger involved in enforcing traffic laws or apprehending felons, has a disproportionate effect on the officer partly because its unexpected nature makes him more apprehensive and partly because he tends to communicate his apprehension to the citizen" (Wilson, 1968: 20).

Several scholars consider order maintenance or peacekeeping the primary role of the police (Wilson, 1968; Bittner, 1990; Wilson and Kelling, 1982). In 1982, order maintenance by the police received attention when James Q. Wilson and George L. Kelling published their article **Broken Windows** in *The Atlantic Monthly*. This article discussed studies dealing with maintaining order in a neighborhood. The authors found that while officers walking a beat did not necessarily reduce crime, residents in foot patrol areas felt safer and had a higher opinion of the police than residents in other areas.

Disorderly people are one factor that causes annoyance and fear. Such individuals may not necessarily be violent. They are panhandlers, rowdy teenagers, the mentally disturbed, prostitutes, vagrants, and drug addicts. The Broken Windows study found that residents in Newark, New Jersey, placed a high value on social order and felt

....

Broken Windows

An article on order maintenance that first appeared in *The Atlantic Monthly* in 1982. This article dealt with maintaining order in a neighborhood. The article indicated that while officers walking a beat did not necessarily reduce crime, residents in foot patrol areas felt safer and had a higher opinion of the police than residents in other areas.

reassured when the police were involved in maintaining order (29–31). Wilson and Kelling argue that at the community level, disorder and crime are linked together. They use the example of the Broken Windows. If one window is broken and goes unrepaired, then this sends the message that no one cares and it is okay to break more windows. Wilson and Kelling discuss how such untended behavior can lead to a breakdown of community controls and disorder. When property becomes abandoned, windows are broken, children are not corrected for rudeness, families begin to move out, and the area loses its stability and becomes disorderly. When the neighborhood becomes disorderly as the norm, crime generally will flourish and violence will become a common occurrence (32).

Kelling and Coles (1996: 86–87) explain several reasons for the erosion of traditional policing. First, the gruff behavior of police officers was offensive to citizens. Next, aggressive patrol strategies, whose goal is to arrest offenders in the act of committing a crime, were not successful. Third, the Kansas City Preventive Patrol Experiment invalidated the long-held idea that routine police vehicle patrols prevented crime in 1974. Fourth, research in the 1960s and 1970s revealed that police officers exercised discretion and that their activities were not routines like those of factory workers. Fifth, a police "culture" existed that often viewed the public as the "enemy." The police developed a "thin blue line" mentality. The police considered themselves warriors, the protectors, and guardians of society. With police secluded in their police vehicles, they never got to know the people in the communities they patrolled (Kelling and Coles, 1996: 86–88).

In 1994, the newly elected Mayor of New York City, Rudolph Giuliani, and William Bratton, the Police Commissioner, implemented an order maintenance policing strategy that emphasized aggressive and proactive enforcing of misdemeanor violations, quality-of-life offenses such as graffiti, loitering, public urination, public drinking, panhandling, turnstile jumping, and prostitution. The New York City Police Department (NYPD), with the support of Mayor Giuliani and Commissioners William Bratton and later Howard Safir, adopted the Broken Windows concept and required police officers to enforce laws and city ordinances that affected the "quality-of-life" in neighborhoods. The **Quality-of-Life Initiative** of the NYPD is given credit for the phenomenal decrease in crime in New York City (Silverman, 1999).

The NYPD enforced public order statutes to achieve civility and stability within neighborhoods. The crime reduction efforts of the NYPD are based on goal-oriented policing. Aggressive policing was applied on a citywide basis and police officers, supervisors, and commanders were held responsible for crime reduction in their spheres of authority. In addition to the Broken Windows concept adopted by the NYPD, several other strategies were adopted. First, Strategic Crime Analysis, known as **CompStat**, a computer system for compiling crime statistics, was utilized to target police efforts at crime reduction. *CompStat* has four steps in reducing crime: accurate and timely intelligence, rapid officer deployment, effective tactics, and relentless follow-up assessment. Crime statistics from every city precinct are compiled weekly, and a computer report is generated. Pin maps would be produced indicating arrests, crime complaints, and shooting incidents.

Quality-of-Life Initiatives

An order maintenance policing strategy that emphasized aggressive and proactive enforcing of misdemeanor violations, quality-of-life offenses such as graffiti, loitering, public urination, public drinking, panhandling, turnstile jumping, and prostitution.

CompStat

A computer system for compiling crime statistics was utilized to target police efforts at crime reduction.

The crime statistic maps are displayed during crime strategy meetings in order to develop tactics and strategies at crime reduction. *CompStat* is given credit in playing a major role in reducing crime in New York City. The following crime statistics decreases have been credited to *CompStat*: from 1993 to 1997, there was 60% decrease in murder and non-negligent manslaughter, 48% decrease in robbery, and a 45% drop in burglaries (Local Initiatives, 2002: 1–2).

The **Model Block program** was the second approach the NYPD used to reduce crime. Pin mapping was used to target high-crime neighborhood city blocks. Residents were trained in crime reduction strategies to reduce crime on their block. Several neighborhood residents were selected to attend various workshops and were instructed on problem solving. City blocks that were successful in crime reduction were awarded "model block" status. One such block achieved an almost 83% decrease in index crimes between 1996 and 1998 (Local Initiatives, 2002: 2).

A third approach used by the NYPD is known as the "**After School Program for Interactive Recreation and Education (ASPIRE)**." The After School Program was a cooperative relationship between the NYPD, the Housing Bureau, and the New York City Housing Authority. This program served youngsters between the ages of nine and nineteen years who lived adjacent to public housing. A ten-week program was offered that taught leadership, diversity, and decision-making consequences. The objectives of ASPIRE are to foster and maintain a positive police–youth relationship (Local Initiatives, 2002: 2–3).

PUBLIC SAFETY

Closely aligned with the idea of maintaining order is the implication that the police will enhance perceptions of public safety. Traditionally, the police maintain order by patrolling city streets, and investigating criminal acts and undercover operations. The maintaining of order by police includes being involved in traffic safety and traffic accidents, and controlling public disorders and/or collective violence. The first public safety area to be reviewed will be the patrol function of the police.

Patrol

The primary unit of the police department that has the responsibility of maintaining order is the patrol unit. Approximately 50% of police personnel are assigned to patrol. The patrol officer functions as a generalist whose time has generally been assigned to respond to service calls and to patrol a specific geographical area, known as a beat or sector. The functions of the patrol force are reactive that react to 911 or service calls responding to a citizen's complaints. Even in the first decade of the twenty-first century, with many police departments claiming to have implemented community policing, the public, politicians, and police agencies consider service calls a primary task of patrol. It seems unlikely that service call will go away any time in the near future. The public considers it the job of the patrol force to handle domestic calls, barking dogs, rowdy neighbors, and similar nuisances. Patrol officers in many cities during their tour of duty go from one service call to another service call. Often, service calls are backed up and the relief shift continues responding to the service calls.

Only by becoming familiar with their beat can the patrol officer recognize disorderly or suspicious situations. In the first decade of the twenty-first century, the patrol officer has probably the most difficult job within the police department. The patrol officer has the primary order maintenance function and he is the first to come into contact with disorderly or criminal conduct. Yet, the patrol officer neither seems to receive recognition nor is held in great esteem for the job he does.

Traffic Safety

Since the automobile was introduced in America, the police have been given the responsibility for the safe movement of automobiles and pedestrians. Overseeing roadways, motor vehicles, and pedestrians has been one of the primary order maintenance functions of the police. With an increase in the number of automobile drivers, young and elderly, and with approximately 40,000 fatalities yearly, in addition to millions injured, traffic safety has to be considered one of the major public safety functions of the police. Traffic safety, as an important order maintenance function of the police, often gets overlooked. The police are responsible for efficient traffic flow, traffic management, and enforcement of traffic laws and strategies to keep fatalities and accidents to a minimum. There are many approaches to traffic safety that police agencies can adopt. In the twenty-first century, new trends and new technology will become important for traffic safety. For example, technology is either in place or is being developed that will aid in high-speed pursuits, enforce speed laws, and fight traffic light violations, for example, camera radar and red light enforcement camera. Automobiles and highway systems are going to be more automated as artificial intelligence becomes applied to them (Sweeney, 2001: 1).

One problem created in cities by the increased number of automobiles has been parking (or the difficulty of making it available as and when needed). Most cities have parking problems with the enforcement of parking laws under the jurisdiction of the police. Parking in cities is a major problem because of the limitations of parking spaces. Business owners and residents must hunt for parking spaces either in parking garages or where on-street parking may be available. Parking areas provide opportunities for specific types of crimes such as muggings and *car-jackings*. These crimes create problems for the police. Deterrence to muggings and *car-jackings* consists of increased police bicycle and foot patrols along with video camera surveillance (Sweeney, 2001: 6).

In the last few decades, interstate highway rest areas have been the scenes of serious crimes. In the early 1990s, the famous basketball player Michael Jordan's father was murdered at a rest stop in North Carolina. Rest stops in California and Florida have received national attention for violent criminal activity. At one point, Florida assigned state troopers to the rest areas when tourists from Germany were murdered there. As most Americans who travel interstate highways and use the rest areas know, there are no attendants to staff them. Thus, rest areas have become locations for crimes such as illicit drug dealing, assaults, and car-jacking, further increasing fear among travelers.

TERRORISM AND ORDER MAINTENANCE

Terrorism is not a new phenomenon and has been used as an ideological strategy for centuries in many parts of the world (see Reich and Lacquer, 1998). However, since the 1960s, acts of terrorism have grown significantly. During this period, terrorist acts have increased in their sophistication and have become a means for obtaining the political and religious objectives of numerous groups throughout the world. While there are crime-fighting aspects to respond to terrorism, given the goal of terrorists to spread fear and panic through the general population, local police often deal with it as an order maintenance issue. The Federal Bureau of Investigation (FBI) has authority over terrorism taking place in the United States. The FBI has defined terrorism as follows:

> Terrorism is the unlawful use of force or violence against persons or property to intimidate or coerce a government, the civilian population, or any segment thereof, in furtherance of political or social objectives. (U.S. Department of Justice, 1993: 20)

Terrorist acts taking placing in the United States during the 1980s and early 1990s were all homegrown (Revell, 1989: 16). However, this changed in 1993 when a radical Islamic sect bombed the World Trade Center on February 23, 1993. For Americans, this act of terrorism hit home. This was the worst act of terrorism committed by foreign nationals on American soil until that time. It caused the death of 6 individuals and an estimated 1,000 injuries. Major media coverage was given to this act and resulted in the realization by the United States of its vulnerability and the harm a few terrorists could do.

Two years after that, in 1995, a terrorist attack on the Murrah Federal Building in Oklahoma City by Timothy McVeigh resulted in the worst act of domestic terrorism in the United States, in which 168 individuals were killed. Acts of terrorism continued to occur sporadically during the 1990s. During the 1996 Summer Olympic Games in Atlanta, Georgia, a pipe bomb placed there by Eric Rudolph exploded in Centennial Olympic Park (Morrison, 2005: 1). The perpetrators of these actions in the 1990s were both radical right-wing domestic terrorists. The FBI reported preventing five acts of terrorism in 1996, and twenty in 1997. It is unknown how many acts of terrorism have been prevented by other policing agencies. For example, the so-called Millennium Bomber, Ahmed Ressa, who planned to blow up Los Angeles International Airport, was stopped at the Canada–U.S. border by an alert Customs agent, on the eve of the twenty-first century (Williams, 2008: 1).

Recent threats to the order maintenance function of the police include the acts of terrorism that occurred on the morning of Tuesday, September 11, 2001. Two commercial jet airliners from Boston's Logan Air Terminal were hijacked and used as missiles when they crashed into the World Trade Center in New York City. The twin towers collapsed, leading to the death and injury of thousands of people. Hijackers took over a third plane that embarked from Washington's Dulles Airport. The hijackers crashed this plane into the Pentagon. A fourth jetliner was hijacked from Newark, New Jersey Air Terminal, and the passengers forced the plane to be landed in an open field near Pittsburgh, PA.

The terrorist attack on September 11, 2001 made clear that the United States had international enemies who wanted to destroy American property and kill or injure civilians. The U.S. government traced the September 11 attack to Osama bin Laden, head of the al-Qaeda movement whose goal is to destroy the United States. Bin Laden and his terrorist organization were protected by the Taliban, a radical Muslim religious group who ruled Afghanistan. In 2002, the U.S. military drove out the Taliban from Afghanistan and replaced the government. Osama bin Laden and his followers escaped to other countries and were not allowed to operate openly in Afghanistan. Today, while Osama bin Laden and his radical Muslim group both are wanted by the U.S. government and are a major threat to the United States, they remain at large. This episode has shown that Americans and their cities and government buildings are vulnerable to terrorist attacks.

Shortly after September 11, 2001, President George Walker Bush declared war on terrorism. The United States is still fighting this war and this war may be expected to continue for several decades. Because of the September 11 attacks, Americans are more security conscious. Airport security has increased tremendously. As a matter of fact, no longer is airport security a private business with private security personnel employed. Airport security and personnel are government employees. Also, major landmarks and buildings that appear to be more vulnerable to terrorists' actions are given higher security protection than in the past. With the heightened concern with security in America, the role of local policing must increase. Most of us who will read this book still have September 11 fresh in our minds. We realize that the New York City Police, firefighters, and other emergency personnel responded under tremendous pressure. Now, emergency personnel in other cities, towns, and hamlets must be ready to provide security. It should be recognized that local police play major roles in actively working to prevent terrorist attacks, both international and domestic.

Previously, even political officials and police administrators felt relatively safe from terrorism. They did not believe that there existed any possibility of their cities being a target for terrorism. This has changed. Political officials, police administrators, and citizens of midsize and small cities do not feel as safe and secure today as they did prior to 9/11. The United States has become vulnerable to those who want to commit the violent act of terrorism. However, since 9/11, officials of our federal, state, and local governments are taking actions to prevent and to apprehend potential terrorists. In a vast country such as the United States that has open borders and freedom of movement for its citizens, noncitizens, and illegal persons, it seems almost impossible to prevent a hideous act of terrorism by a misguided or evil individual or groups of individuals who are convinced that their cause is just.

Several large police departments such as New York City and Los Angeles, California, have created Anti-terrorists Units. These police departments are not only cooperating by sharing information with each other, but also sending officers assigned to their Anti-Terrorist Units to foreign countries to collect intelligence information on potential terrorists and terrorist organizations. The Los Angeles Police Department (LAPD) established its Anti-terrorist Division (ATD) in 1983. Police departments need an intelligence unit that can collect, analyze, and cooperate with other units and agents of government by sharing information.

The NYPD preceded LAPD in working with federal agents to combat terrorism. In 1979, The Joint Terrorism Task Force was initiated with the FBI. Eventually other law enforcement agencies were brought into the Task Force, such as the New York State Police, the New York/New Jersey Port Authority Police Department along with the U.S. Marshals, Alcoholic, Tobacco, and Firearms, Immigrations and Naturalization Service, and the Diplomatic Security Service of the Department of State. The primary goal of the Task Force was to become a close-knit, cohesive intelligence unit that would deal with terrorism investigations. All the law enforcement agencies of the Task Force signed a formal memorandum agreeing to the Task Force's objectives (Martin, 1999: 24).

The idea behind the Joint Terrorism Task Force is that all personnel, regardless of their parent organization, work as a team. They must think and perform as a team. This uses the individual's talents and skills for the benefit of the Task Force. Investigators may labor for months on leads of potential terrorists or acts and investigating terrorism. Since quick results are rare, the Task Force may not always get the acknowledgment it rightly deserves. In 1999, there were sixteen Joint Task Forces in the country to fight terrorism. Since 9/11, every state has at least one Joint Terrorism Task Force.

The city of Wichita, Kansas, is one such city that has become involved in the Joint Terrorism Task Force for Kansas. In its course of action, the Wichita Police Department assigns a detective to the Task Force. All information obtained by the police department on terrorism is forwarded to the Task Force. The only information the Task Force shares with the police department is through the police chief. Wichita, a midsize city, has a population of approximately 330,000. When smaller cities and unincorporated areas of the county are included, the metropolitan population increases to about 500,000. In order to respond to terrorism, the Public Safety Departments came into an agreement to cooperate and work together. These agencies include the Wichita Police Department, County Sheriff's Department, city and county Fire Departments, Emergency Medical Service (EMS), and the Environmental and Health Emergency Disaster Unit. The Public Safety Task Force developed a list of approximately 200 sites in the county that could be potential targets. These included, but were not limited to, churches, synagogues, mosques, the Federal Court House, hotels, and malls. The Public Safety Task Force provided the list to police officers who could increase patrolling of these buildings on their beats. In addition, the Public Safety Task Force applied for a Department of Justice grant for personnel protection equipment. The equipment purchased included gloves, trek suites, masks, gloves, and booths as protection against biological and chemical agents. This protective equipment is kept in the vehicle trunks of every Wichita Police officer and Sheriff's Deputy. The Fire Department personnel are the hazardous material specialists and air-quality specialists. With federal funding, the Wichita Police Department hopes to purchase a second helicopter that can be used for surveillance of vulnerable buildings and sites, which are often not close to one another (Lee, 2003).

ORDER MAINTENANCE, SERVICE, AND THE POLICE: THREE SOCIOLOGICAL PERSPECTIVES

In the previous chapter, we considered how the three sociological perspectives, functionalism, conflict, and interactionism, might be used to understand the crime-fighting functions of the police. Let us do the same for the other important functions of the police: order maintenance and service. Functionalism, the perspective that focuses on the structure and functions of various elements in a society, would consider order maintenance (including making the public feel safe) as a relevant and important function for the police. In a sense, the police in a given community serve as an agency that can be depended on to take care of certain residual functions that others are incapable or unwilling to perform. For example, when there is a traffic accident, we cannot expect the roads department of the local municipality to deal with it in an immediate way; this responsibility often goes to the police. Similarly, in recent times we see police officers serving as school resource officers (SROs) and help the schools with teaching certain classes and chaperoning high-school dances. These are order maintenance and service functions. The functionalist would look at these examples and argue that police took on jobs because they were necessary in society and if at some point in the future, these were deemed to be unneeded, then these particular expectations would disappear.

A conflict theorist would examine the order maintenance and service functions of the police more skeptically. Whose interests are the police representing when they carry out the maintenance of order and which masters do they actually serve? For example, it could be argued that SROs are in schools not to "help the kids," but to gather information and intelligence on the activities and pursuits of the young. In doing so, they represent the interests of those who are older (parents, businesses, and community members) who want to make sure that the "kids don't cause trouble" in the community by having parties with illegal drinking (of those below the age) and using drugs. So in this case, the SRO program represents the interests of one group that has power and control against another that has neither.

An interactionist is likely to notice the variations in how police mission-related terms such as "order maintenance" and "service" are interpreted by different police departments and groups within them (fresh recruits and veterans). For example, one of the norms of policing in general is that police officers serve the public and the community at all times. Is this true of all departments and police officers? An officer may drive past an accident (perhaps he or she is off duty or just getting back from his or her shift). The way these norms are interpreted in a large city (formally, he or she is expected to call for someone else or informally, to respond himself or herself, or to just drive on) may differ from that in a small town or rural county. How are these ambiguous expectations communicated to new officers and where does such socialization take place? When an officer moves from one department to another, what meanings does he or she rely on under such circumstances?

We have learned that order maintenance and service are two major functions that the police traditionally carry out. In order to further our understanding of these functions in other countries, let us take a look at the police forces of two different nations, New Zealand and Finland.

POLICE, ORDER MAINTENANCE, AND SERVICE INTERNATIONALLY: NEW ZEALAND

As we have seen, the primary function of the police in any country is order maintenance. One national police agency that has the support of the country's people is New Zealand. The roots of New Zealand and specifically its policing can be traced to its colonization by the British in the first half of the nineteenth century. In 1840, New Zealand became a crown colony of Great Britain. Following this declaration of New Zealand being a crown colony, the colonization of New Zealand began in earnest. For the most part, New Zealand, as a colony of Great Britain, left policy decisions to Britain. Prior to 1875, New Zealand was a decentralized colony. In 1875, New Zealand became a politically unified country, without a written constitution, and with laws adopted similar to England. Slums in New Zealand are almost nonexistent and the seeds of the welfare state reside deep in the cultural history of the country. The people of New Zealand have developed a classless society that can be possibly developed anywhere. The culture reinforces conformity and discourages extremism and radicalism.

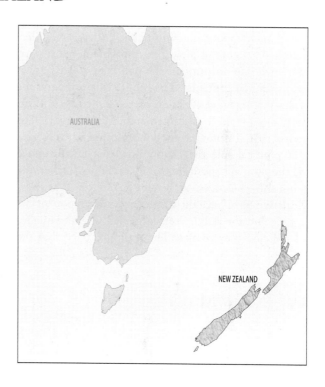

The police in New Zealand were founded in 1867 as a national force. Colonial administrators organized the structure like the British system (Swanton, Hanigan, and Psila, 1985). In 1868, New Zealand passed the "Police Force Act" that brought the police even closer to the political philosophy of the British police. However, unlike other countries, New Zealand police seem to be independent of political influence. For example, the Chief Commissioner of Police, head of the country's National Police, is selected by the national government from among candidates nominated by the outgoing incumbent. This process allows the police to maintain some control of their future head.

According to the 2000 Census, New Zealand had a population of 3.8 million people with police personnel numbering 8,613. This includes 6,808 sworn officers and 1,805 nonsworn officers (Miller, 1996). Historically, the New Zealand police have been regarded as a valuable national institution and they have carefully exploited this through public relations positions. In 1898, New Zealand adopted a policy of being unarmed. New Zealanders respect and support the police and the latter have maintained a positive public image. The police of New Zealand are considered to be nonpolitical and to have a professional bureaucracy. The police in New Zealand for decades have been allowed to conduct searches without search warrants in cases involving drugs, firearms, and weapons like knives. Under the "Police Act," police officers are permitted to hold suspected offenders and to take their pictures, fingerprints, palm prints, and footprints. In addition, police officers can "use reasonable force" as necessary to hold a suspect. The "Arms Act of 1983" made every police officer an armed officer, and any one applying for a handgun needs a police recommendation (Das and Palmiotto, 2005).

The police of New Zealand are considered to be respected public servants and to have political influence (Glynn, 1975; Palmer, 1986). The police are considered to be the custodians of the order maintenance function. New Zealand politicians strongly defend the order maintenance function of the police. The police reflect the values of New Zealand. For the most part, those who do not support the police are looked down upon as malcontents. The politicians support the order maintenance function of the police as a means to maintain social order and stability. Palmer (1986) writes that, "Although the police do not actively seek this political role they know how to take advantage of the strategic position … in order to further the aims and objectives of the police service." The New Zealand police have the confidence and support of the people and the public seems satisfied with the quality of policing they receive. The positive image that the

police have from the public has resulted in the police becoming more cautious and zealous in maintaining their positive image of integrity and public support (Bayley, 1976). In summary, the New Zealand police may have an easier job in maintaining order than police agencies in other countries that do not have the public's trust and support.

The maintenance of order requires that the police should be involved in traffic safety and traffic accident behavior, the control of public disorders or potential disorders, and violence that threatens individuals or groups.

Finally, maintaining order and providing service are important challenges to all police departments. Imagine these challenges in a huge country such as India with its population of more than 1 billion (see accompanying box) and a form of policing that adapts a Western model to a South Asian setting.

 # SUMMARY

The primary reason for establishing policing in society is to maintain order. From ancient times to the twenty-first century, social order in the tribe, village, community, and state had to be maintained. Without social order, societies cannot be civilized and advancements cannot be made. Throughout history, the people of the tribe or village, military, or the modern police officer were given the duty and responsibility to maintain order so that farmers could farm, ranchers could ranch, and factory workers could produce goods for consumption. When social order is absent and chaos exists, society cannot move forward; it will not even be able to maintain the status quo.

Scholars consider order maintenance the primary role of the police. Wilson and Kelling in their article on Broken Windows Policing argue that at the community level, disorder and crime are linked together. Further they claim that disorderly neighborhoods are vulnerable for criminality. Order maintenance goes hand-in-hand with crime prevention. This concept must not be forgotten if crime has to come under control and be reduced. The

combining of order maintenance and crime prevention was the approach Mayor Rudolph Giuliani implemented in New York City on his election as Mayor in 1994.

This chapter emphasized that order maintenance plays a major role in policing. One of the major factors for having a formalized police department is order maintenance. When Mayor Rudolph Giuliani came into office in New York City, he implemented an order maintenance policing strategy, which emphasized aggressive and proactive enforcing of misdemeanor violations, quality-of-life offenses such as graffiti, loitering, public urination, public drinking, panhandling, turnstile jumping, and prostitution. The by-product of New York City's order maintenance strategy was that crime decreased.

Order maintenance is the major mission of not just the American police. It is the formal mission of all formal police departments throughout the world. Of course, it is hoped that when police are working toward their goal of maintaining order, they do so within the guidelines of respecting the human rights of the citizens. One such country that has the respect, trust, and support of politicians and the people is New Zealand. Unlike America, New Zealand has a national police force. The reputation of the New Zealand police can rarely be matched by any other police agency in the world. The New Zealand police have a history free from political influence and corruption. For the most part, the order maintenance function has been performed free from controversy and confrontation. Finland, on the other side of the world, has the trust and confidence of the people of their country. The Finnish police are considered to be well trained and organized and do a good job in maintaining order in Finland.

The police are expected to maintain public safety, which falls under the realm of order maintenance. Several operational areas of public safety for the police include patrol, criminal investigations, and traffic safety. The police maintain order by foot patrol, auto patrol, horse patrol, bicycle patrol, and air patrol. Citizens expect the police to provide patrol service to respond to emergency service calls when needed. Criminal investigation allows the police to arrest and prosecute those who violate the law thereby creating disorder. Criminal investigators work to create order by putting away those who commit crimes. Finally, traffic safety plays an important role in order maintenance and public safety in our modern days.

Since the inception of the automobile, the police have been given the responsibility for the safe movement of automobiles and pedestrians. Overseeing roadways, motor vehicles, and pedestrians has become one of the primary responsibilities of the police in maintaining order. Police involvement in traffic safety can involve traffic investigations and reconstruction of an accident scene, usually when a fatality occurs. Additional order maintenance functions related to traffic safety include protecting property, having motor vehicles towed from an accident scene, and transporting injured to hospital. Traffic safety includes patrol officers directing traffic, providing escort services, and impounding abandoned vehicles. Law enforcement actions performed as traffic safety measures by the police officers often include issuing citations for traffic infractions, making arrests for motor vehicle law violations, preparing case for court, and appearing as a witness for the prosecution. As a function of order maintenance responsibility, police officers provide assistance to motorists, conduct road checks for driver's licenses and for other violations such as drinking while driving, and conduct safety checks for motor vehicles.

With international terrorists striking the United States on September 11, 2001, the role of American police changed. On that day, four commercial airline planes were hijacked. Two of those airplanes were flown into the World Trade Center in New York City, one plane crashed into the Pentagon, and the fourth landed into an open field in Western Pennsylvania, after passengers began attacking the hijackers. Because of 9/11, local law enforcement agencies have to be concerned about terrorism. Order maintenance for the local law enforcement agencies now includes prevention, investigations, cooperation with federal agencies, and passing on intelligence information to the FBI, the lead agency dealing with terrorism. Finally, we considered in this chapter how the police maintain order in New Zealand.

 KEY TERMS

After School Program for Interactive Recreation and Education (ASPIRE): A cooperative relationship between the NYPD, the Housing Bureau, and the New York City Housing Authority. This program served youngsters between the ages of nine and nineteen years who lived adjacent to public housing. A ten-week program was offered that taught leadership, diversity, and decision-making consequences. The objectives of ASPIRE are to foster and maintain a positive police–youth relationship.

Broken Windows: An article on order maintenance that first appeared in *The Atlantic Monthly* in 1982. This article dealt with maintaining order in a neighborhood. The article indicated that while officers walking a beat did not necessarily reduce crime, residents in foot patrol areas felt safer and had a higher opinion of the police than residents in other areas.

CompStat: A computer system for compiling crime statistics was utilized to target police efforts at crime reduction.

Model Block program: It is used by NYPD to reduce crime. Pin mapping was used to target high-crime neighborhood city blocks. Residents were trained in crime reduction strategies to reduce crime on their block.

Quality-of-life initiatives: An order maintenance policing strategy that emphasized aggressive and proactive enforcing of misdemeanor violations, quality-of-life offenses such as graffiti, loitering, public urination, public drinking, panhandling, turnstile jumping, and prostitution.

REVIEW QUESTIONS

1. What are the reasons for the erosion of traditional policing?
2. Explain the strategies implemented by the New York Police Department that led to a decrease in crime.
3. Explain the public safety functions of the police.

DISCUSSION QUESTIONS

1. Which police strategy is more effective in decreasing the crime rate: *CompStat* or "Broken Windows?" Give an explanation for your answer.
2. Do you consider that one of the functions of local police is to fight terrorism? Provide an explanation for your answer.
3. Are there any differences in the order maintenance responsibilities between the New Zealand and Finnish police?

REFERENCES

Bayley, David H. (1976) *Forces of Order: Police Behavior in Japan and the U.S.* Berkeley, CA: University of California Press.

Bittner, Egon (1990) *Aspects of Police Work.* Boston, MA: Northeastern University Press.

Das, Dilip and Michael J. Palmiotto (2005) *Policing in Canada, India, Germany, Australia, Finland and New Zealand: A Comparative Research Study.* Lewiston, NY: Mellon Publication.

F2 Newwork (2002) *Staying a Beat ahead of Crime,* http://www.smh.com.au/articles/2002/11/02/103602709056.html.

Finnish Police (2002) http://www.poliisi.fi/home.nsf.pages.

Glynn, James Francis (1975) *The New Zealand Policeman.* Wellington: Institute of Public Administration.

Kelling, George L. (1995) "Acquiring a Taste for Order." In V. E. Kappeler (ed.) *The Police & Society.* Prospect Heights, IL: Waveland Press.

Kelling, George L. and Catherine M. Coles (1996) *Fixing Broken Windows.* New York, NY: Free Press.

Laitinen, Ahti (1994) "Police in Finland." In D. Das (ed.) *Police Practices: An International Review.* Metuchen, NJ: The Scarecrow Press.

Lee, Robert (2003) Interview with Deputy Chief on February 13, 2002.

Local Initiatives (2002) *How New York, NY, Reduced Crime and Strengthened Community*, http://www.ncpc.org/nyc.htm.

Martin, Robert A. (1999) "The Joint terrorism Task Force."In *FBI Law Enforcement Bulletin*, March.

Miller, Iran (1996) *Demography and Attrition in the New Zealand Police 1985–1995*. Wellington, New Zealand: New Zealand National Police Headquarters.

Morrison, Blake (2005) "Special Report: Eric Roberts Writes Home."In *USA Today*, http://www.usatoday.com/news/nation.

Palmer, Geoffrey (1986) "The Legislative Process and the Police." In N. Cameron and W. Young (eds.) *Policing at Crossroads*. Wellington: Allen & Unwin.

Reich, Walter and Walter Lacquer (1998) *Origins of Terrorism*. Washington, DC: Woodrow Wilson Center Press.

Revell, Oliver B. (1989) "International Terrorism in the U. S." In *The Police Chief*, March.

Silverman, Eli B. (1999) NYPD *Battles Crime*. Boston, MA: Northeastern University Press.

Swanton, Bruce; Carry Hannigan and Trish Psila (1985) *Police Source Book, Edited*. Phillip Act. Melbourne, Australia: Australian Institute of Technology.

Sweeney, Earl (2001) *Traffic Safety in the New Millennium Strategies for Law Enforcement*. Washington, DC: U.S. Department of Transportation.

U.S. Department of Justice, Federal Bureau of Investigation (1993) *Terrorism in the U. S. 1982–1992*. U.S. Government Printing Office.

Williams, Carol J. (2008) "Millennium Bomber Sentenced Tossed Out of Court." In *Los Angeles Times*, August 16, http://www.latimes.com/news/nationworld/nation/la-me-bomber.

Wilson, James Q. (1968) *Varieties of Police Behavior: The Management of Law and Order in Eight Communities*. Cambridge, MA: Harvard University Press.

Wilson, James Q. and George L. Kelling (1982) "Broken Windows." In *The Atlanta Monthly*, March.

POLICE AND ORDER MAINTENANCE IN INDIA

Arvind Verma and T.K. Vinod Kumar

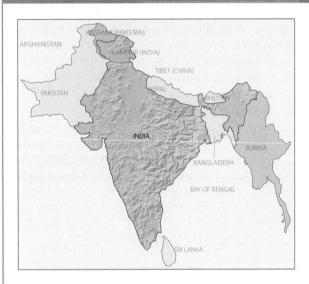

India is a country with a population of over a billion and area of 3,287,590 km². It is a multilingual, multireligious, and multiethnic society which is perhaps the most diverse nation in the world. After becoming independent in 1947, the country adopted a constitution, which envisaged a federal structure for the country with one central government and various state governments to administer the regions. The federal structure in India is characterized by strong unitary features and bias toward the center.

Chapter XI of the Constitution deals with the relations between the Union and the State. The VII schedule of the Constitution enumerates the Union, State, and Concurrent lists that delineate the subject matters on which laws can be legislated by the Parliament and the State legislatures. Powers of legislation and administration of matters regarding the criminal justice system are shared between the state and central governments. List I of the Schedule VII (Union list) places with the central government responsibilities with regard to Central Bureau of Investigation, recruitment and management of the Indian Police Service (IPS), Institutions of Police training, forensic science, and police research. Center also has a role in other fields of police administration such as operating Central Police Organizations, and enacting laws to ensure a uniform criminal justice system. List II (State

List) of the scheduled VII vests the state governments with powers regarding public order, police, High Court, and prisons. List III or the Concurrent list details the areas in which both the central and the state governments can legislate such as criminal law, criminal procedures, and preventive detention for reasons of security of state.

Though police is a state subject, order maintenance and crime prevention cannot be totally considered a state problem since there are problems that have interstate ramifications, and call for a coordinating role by the center. This is all the more accentuated by the quasi-federal, unitary nature of the constitution. However, the major share of the task of order maintenance, and prevention and detection of crime is vested with the state government.

There is a similarity in organizational, procedural, and legal aspects of the criminal justice system in different states. The state police organization is under the Home Department of the state government whose minister is the political head and is assisted by a senior civilian bureaucrat. The state police department is headed by a Director General of Police (DGP) or an Inspector General of Police. The DGP is a career police officer belonging to the IPS. The police hierarchy under him consists of Additional DGPs, IGPs, SPs, ASPs/DySPs, Inspectors of Police, Sub-Inspectors of Police, Assistant Sub-Inspectors, Head Constables, and Constables. The central government recruits officers to the IPS and allots them to the states. Officers recruited to the IPS begin their service at the senior rank of Assistant Superintendent of Police in the state. IPS officers are recruited, trained, and groomed to provide overall leadership in the police forces in the states and the center.

Order maintenance, law enforcement, and prevention and detection of crime are the basic functions of the police. The effectiveness and efficiency of the police force is largely determined by its capacity to maintain order, enforce laws fairly, and prevent and detect crime—against both person and properties. The methods adopted depend on the situation, social conflict, and the nature of crime. However, the police primarily depend on willingness of the citizens to cooperate with the police, obey the laws, and accept the legitimacy of the system. For dealing with law violations, the police undertake crime records analysis, liaison with community, application of preventive laws, and finally registration and investigation of cases.

There is a well-developed system of recording and studying reported crime against property and criminals involved in such cases. These records help in the crime prevention efforts made by the police. Though the systems of records vary across states, there is an underlying commonality. At the police station level, crime records are of great help to local officers and supervising officers, as they assist them to undertake a proper study of crime and criminals in their jurisdiction. These records are of great use to the new officers coming to the post and having no previous experience in the area. They assist the investigating officer in the process of narrowing down on possible criminals who could have committed the crime.

Records of all cases registered by the police are kept at the station level. This assists in obtaining a correct picture of the types of crimes and modus operandi, crime-prone areas, crime rates, tendencies of crime rates, etc. Police stations also maintain crime maps on which locations of all crimes occurring in the station limits are marked. The map is intended to give a graphic representation of the geographical distribution of crimes within the station limits. Besides this, detailed records are maintained of conviction of criminals operating within the station limits. Records are also maintained of important events, disputes, organizations, etc., within the station limits.

Besides maintaining records of criminals and bad characters, the police also take measures to keep ex-convicts and bad characters under surveillance to prevent and control crimes. Regular checks of ex-convicts are done to assess as to whether they are still involved in criminal activities. The police also check their movements and determine discreetly if they are leading a lawful life. The police also keep a close watch on known depredators and suspects. The arrival of suspicious strangers in the police station limits is monitored and their antecedents generally verified. The police are empowered by the Habitual Offenders (Restriction) Acts and Rules, and Courts and Executive Magistrates are empowered by section 565 of the Criminal Procedure Code (CrPC) in these tasks.

While crime records and monitoring criminals assist in crime prevention, police beats and patrols are also conducted for the purpose of preventing and detecting crimes and maintaining law and order on a day-to-day basis. These measures ensure the presence of police in the community to elicit cooperation of the residents in the task of maintaining order and crime prevention. The pattern of beats and patrols varies, depending on whether the area is urban or rural. In rural areas, generally a cluster of villages is treated as a beat. The police officer in charge of the beat works closely with the community and works to obtain the trust and cooperation of the local people. He develops an intimate knowledge of the area and the people, which stands him in good stead in maintaining order, and preventing and detecting crime. He upholds liaison with important citizens living in the area and tries to secure their support for the preservation of peace and maintenance of law and order. The beat officer on his visits to the villages collects information about movement of strangers in the area, movement of bad characters, presence of any person wanted in any specific crime, occurrence of any unreported crimes, and any undetected offences with a view to obtain clues for their detection, and also keeps a watch on dangerous criminals requiring surveillance. He also does night patrol in selected areas where there is a tendency for offences to occur and bad characters to operate. In some states, an elaborate "village notebook" is maintained where the visiting police officer records major activities and population characteristics.

In urban areas, police station jurisdictions are divided into "police beats" having compact similar areas bound by well-defined roads. These beat areas are served round the clock. A constable on town patrol is generally responsible for preserving order, preventing offences, apprehending offenders, and ensuring the protection and safety of the residents and their property within the patrol area. He deals with all fights, affrays, or assaults, and may take into custody any person who may be drunk or disorderly or otherwise incapable of looking after himself. He also takes note of any crime committed and directs the complainant to proceed to or himself informs the nearest police station, and takes action as is necessary to arrest the offender and guard the scene of crime. In the case of traffic accidents, he clears the scene of onlookers and maintains the scene intact and at the same time sends word to the police station. He takes measures to prevent the commission of mischief, nuisance, or other crime in his beat. He also reports the occurrence of such hazards as fires and electric hazards, and renders help as necessary. Night patrol is a part of preventive efforts that are carried out routinely in both rural and urban areas. In a large measure, these are intended to prevent property crimes at night by habitual criminals. Most areas are also covered by wireless-fitted patrol vehicles that are available to react promptly to occurrences of crime or other incidents that require the attention of police.

One of the important duties of police is to be aware of situations that may lead to breach of peace. When a breach of peace is anticipated, police can take action under Chapters VIII, XI, and XII of the CrPC of India and under provisions of the Indian Police Act. If the breach of peace apprehended relates to land and water disputes, action is taken under sections 145–148 CrPC. Under section 106 CrPC, a person convicted of any offence such as assault, breach of peace, criminal intimidation, etc., can be bound over by a designated court to keep peace. Action can be taken under section 107 CrPC for preventing breach of peace or disturbance to public tranquility. Sections 109 and 110 CrPC are useful instruments at the disposal of the police for checking and controlling activities by criminals and bad characters. Crime prevention efforts reduce instances of crime in the society. However, if a crime involving a cognizable offence occurs, and information regarding it has been intimated to an officer in charge of a police station, he is bound to register a case and commence investigation. The Indian police have a reasonable reputation in detecting serious crimes and apprehending dangerous offenders that helps in deterring people from committing crimes. Indian crime rates are generally low in comparison to developed countries.

At present, the police are also using a variety of situational prevention techniques in order to handle the threat of crime in rapidly growing urban areas. They are seeking the cooperation of builders, architects, and resident associations in developing designs to prevent crimes. For instances, in the National Capital Region (NCR) around the capital city of New Delhi, the police routinely hold meetings with these groups to develop preventive strategies. There is a particular emphasis on security at entry and exit, where gates are manned by security guards and personal identities are verified by modern technological means. Mumbai police have implemented a special traffic control system that monitors movement of traffic and keeps a watchful eye over the area. Video cameras are now being installed in greater numbers, particularly in crowded market places and transport hubs.

Due to the growth of IT industry, the police have established special cyber crime units that specialize in working with the industry to prevent e-crimes. Special laws have been enacted that require cyber cafes to keep a record of people using the internet from their locations. This has helped in tracking extremists who send threatening messages or hatch plans to carry out terrorist attacks.

The police have also developed a large number of preventive methods to handle order maintenance problems in the country. In view of the fact that the number of people assembling for protests, public demonstrations, and even religious celebrations runs into thousands, the police have to deal carefully in handling such large crowds. They deploy personnel in carefully selected locations to monitor trouble makers and work with local leaders to ensure peaceful conduct of public events. These strategies have been very useful in the policing of elections which are gigantic affairs in the country. For example, in the 2004 national elections, an estimated 360 million people actually stood in queues to cast their vote. In India, elections have always been competitive and require major administrative and police arrangements. The police have utilized situational preventive methods to monitor polling booths, in order to ensure the safety of electronic voting machines and millions of voters. Despite the threat of violence by secessionists and left-wing extremists, India has been able to hold regular elections for the past sixty years. In this, the police have played a major role in preventing violence and ensuring free and fair election.

The Indian police have achieved a measure of success in order maintenance and crime prevention efforts. In view of the large population, developing economy, and incredible diversity, these achievements cannot be discounted. India presents a unique case of a large country, with colonial history and extreme differences still functioning as a robust democracy where people choose their governments and system of governance. The contribution of the police to the strength, integrity, and vibrancy of Indian society needs appreciation. However, it must be acknowledged that these efforts are hampered by constraints such as lack of sufficient manpower to meet the demands of a large population, overloaded courts, and lack of modern physical infrastructure.

CHAPTER 8

Police discretion refers to the exercise of choice by law enforcement officers in the decision to investigate or apprehend the disposition of a suspect, by carrying out of official duties, and the application of sanctions .... Decisions to stop and questions someone, arrest a suspect, and perform many other police tasks are made solely by individual officers and must often be made quickly and in the absence of any close supervision. (Schmalleger, 2006: 221)

Police are confronted by protesters in Copenhagen, Denmark, Monday, May 14, 2007. Police fired tear gas in clashes with rock-throwing rioters protesting the demolition of a decrepit building Monday in Copenhagen's hippie enclave. At least 16 people were arrested, police said, while one police officer and one protester were injured. The protesters set fire to a barricade on the main road outside the Christiania district of the Danish capital, sending thick, black smoke into the sky. (Credit: © AP Photo / John McConnico)

POLICE DISCRETION

OBJECTIVES:

1. The student will be able to define the concept of police discretion.
2. The student will know the different forms of police discretion.
3. The student will be able to define full enforcement.
4. The student will be able to explain the practicality of police discretion.
5. The student will learn about the functionalist, conflict theory, and interactionist approaches to analyzing police discretion.
6. The student will learn about how police discretion is exercised on an international level.

here are numerous issues relating to policing that are major concerns in the first decades of the twenty-first century. One of the major issues facing policing today is the use of police discretion. This issue can be traced to the ninth century when King Alfred the Great created the mutual pledge system to maintain order in his kingdom. From the ninth century to our modern day, the concept of discretion has existed with those individuals who have the legal authority to enforce the laws of the centralized government. The constables of the middle ages in England, along with thief-takers, used discretion not to arrest specific individuals because of their station in society or simply because they were friends. Discretion still exists in modern policing. The big awakening occurred when police administrators admitted that police discretion existed. This was not always the case (see Davis, 1975; Walker, 1993).

In the 1950s, it was common for police administrators to claim that police officers investigated every crime that occurred and that every single law was equally enforced. Police chiefs made public announcements that all offenses committed, regardless of the seriousness of the offense, were investigated with equal effort and that all laws were enforced with the same priority. Those practitioners and scholars who understood policing recognized that it would be impossible for the police to give equal weight to every crime reported or to enforce every law. More practically, the police often will not have sufficient information to conduct an investigation, or there may be insufficient police personnel to investigate a crime thoroughly. Given their inability to investigate every crime, the police have established a set of priorities in criminal investigations. Investigative priorities hold that more serious crimes are ranked higher. For example, to investigate a murder, more time, effort, and resources will be required than, say, the theft of a car stereo. Realistically, it is impossible for the police to enforce all the state and federal laws. No police department has sufficient police personnel to enforce all the laws and criminal violations. Since the police cannot investigate all crimes or enforce all laws, we should expect that the police will exercise a certain amount of discretion in deciding which laws to enforce and which crimes to investigate. Without the "use of discretion," the police would have a difficult time functioning.

Pound (1940: 925–926) defines discretion as "an authority conferred by law to act in certain conditions or situations in accordance with an official's or an official agency's own considered judgment and conscience. It is an idea of morals, belongs, to the twilight zone between laws and morals."

There appears to be no doubt that the police, simply by the position they hold in society, intentionally or unintentionally, may be involved in coercion. The police have been given the responsibility to "enforce the law." Enforcing the law does have a connotation of coercion. However, the police must guard against allowing their discretion to be abusive or to become the common practice of police misconduct.

Police authority is awesome. The police in a free society, such as the United States, may be viewed as an anomaly. The government has given the police a great deal of authority, under a government system that reluctantly grants authority and when granted, attempts to curtail the authority granted. Police authority specifically deals with the power to arrest, to search and seize, and to use force when needed. The primary reason that police authority should be considered awesome has to be

....

police authority

It specifically deals with the power to arrest, to search and seize, and to use force when needed. Police authority allows the police to take away one's freedom, invade an individual's privacy, and place citizens under surveillance.

the power of the police to take away one's freedom, invade an individual's privacy, and place citizens under surveillance (Goldstein, 1977: 1). Studies on policing since the early nineteenth century indicate that persons who have the most contact with the police are, for all practical purposes, without political clout. These are the poor, the immigrant, and the minorities.

AMERICAN BAR FOUNDATION SURVEYS

It was not until the 1950s that surveys of the criminal justice field and policing were based on governmental reports and statistics. Criminal justice surveys were conduced on the local level. These studies never revealed what the police actually did in their daily activities. In 1953, Supreme Court Justice Robert H. Jackson called for a national study of criminal justice agencies since he believed the criminal justice field was in shambles. With funding received from the Ford Foundation, the research arm of the American Bar Foundation conducted studies for the purpose of determining to what extent criminal justice agencies were following prescribed standards (Kelling, 1999: 21).

Conversely, the exercise of discretion implies that the police must consider a variety of factors before taking legal action. Police officers may choose not to make an arrest, even if probable cause exists. For example, there are situations where the police officers did not arrest college students since they knew the students wanted to become attorneys and an arrest for drug possession may have affected their chances of becoming an attorney.

The American Bar Foundation study found that the police in their daily work activities take drunks into custody, chase prostitutes from the streets, solve disputes, direct traffic, and investigate automobile accidents, to mention just a few. The study further discovered that the police were expected by the public to solve a wide range of problems. When the public gets upset with the police, administrative control and legislation is often passed to appease the public. The American Bar Foundation found that often the police would take persons into custody to conduct further investigations and harassment was frequently used as a method of controlling a crime problem. Further, the American Bar Foundation found that police officers regularly made decisions whether to stop and search someone, whether to initiate an investigation, whether to make an arrest, and even whether the arrestee should be physically detained. Prior to the American Bar's study, it was assumed that the police were mandated to make an arrest when evidence of a crime existed. It seems state statutes, municipal ordinances, police manuals, and the professional model of policing reinforced this belief. The police were influenced by other components of the criminal justice field such as the knowledge about the personal biases of judges (Goldstein, 1993: 31–39).

FULL ENFORCEMENT

If the police were to be denied the opportunity to use discretion, then a **full enforcement** policy of enforcing all laws would be in effect. The police would not have the authority to ignore or overlook certain violations or even provide an offender with a

full enforcement

The policy of enforcing all laws would be in effect. The police would not have the authority to ignore or to overlook certain violations or even provide an offender with a warning to avoid illegal actions.

warning to avoid illegal actions. Police functions would become rather mechanical and would not take into account the actions behind a specific act being committed.

The exercise of discretion implies that the police must consider a variety of factors before taking legal action. In the 1970s, the *National Advisory Commission on Criminal Justice Standards and Goals: Police* recommended that every police agency recognize that discretion exists at both the administrative and operational levels. The Commission recommended that police agencies establish policy statements limiting discretion and that they provide guidelines for the exercise of discretion within department policies. According to the Commission, the police have considerable discretion. The *Commission* further reported that the discretion was paradoxical. Police discretion flouts legal decisions, criminal statutes, and often the expectations of the legislature. Often, police administrators have denied police discretion but the *Commission* reported that it could not be ignored. Police are decision makers who, as a routine exercise, use discretion to resolve conflict that may threaten public order (1973: 22–23).

The National Advisory *Commission on Criminal Justice Standards and Goals: Police* reported that many police administrators do not want to acknowledge that all laws are not fully enforced. If the administrators admitted that discretion existed, then it may appear that the police are shirking their duty and intentionally ignoring the law. The Commission further claims that police agencies have received little direction from either the legislative or judiciary branch on discretion. Law is defined as being mandatory, such as to arrest, rather then providing the police with discretionary guidelines. Judiciary decisions deal with specific cases and, for the most part, ignore police policy decisions. The Commission recommended that police agencies analyze court decision and translate the decisions of the court into policy statements that provide guidelines on exercising police discretion. When police officers are left to make their own decisions in the exercise of discretion without guidance, an inherent risk occurs. Errors by police officers in the exercise of discretion can be minimized when the police department has established policies to guide police personnel (1973: 22–23). Goldstein (1963: 144) believes that if police officers are to be granted discretion, then the need for criteria in the use of discretion becomes essential.

Any criterion established by the police administrator places him in a precarious position. How can the police chief develop discretionary guidelines that will be clearly understood and followed by all police officers? Often in the past it was much easier for the police chief to avoid the issue by taking no action at all.

TYPES OF POLICE DISCRETION

Administrators are decision makers and this truism holds true for police administrators. Those who hold administrative positions can often make decisions concerning those who may benefit and those who may lose from those decisions. Administrators have to implement polices based on the laws passed by the legislative branch. It has been left to the government administrator to clarify ambiguities created by the statutes passed in the legislation. The administrative choices of administrators are either procedural or substantial. A procedural decision structures the administrative context of the discretion. Examples of procedural decisions include decisions to create specialize units, budgetary decisions, and training decisions. Procedural decisions influence substantive decision making. Substantial decision making will be categorized as either allocative or regulatory. Allocative decisions have distributive consequences and determine the level of services among groups, classes, and geographical areas. A regulatory decision refers to the enforcement of a rule or law and consists of two broad choices. These choices include the decision to intervene in specific circumstances and the action to be taken in those situations. Can the action that has been taken solve the problem? Police administrators make regulatory decisions (Brown, 1988: 21–23).

Administrative discretion includes decision making, which incorporates the beliefs or operational style of the administrator. There are two types of judgments that are characteristics of operational styles. They are value judgments, which contain a belief system, and reality judgments, which establish a casual connection among events. Operation styles are important determinants in how administrators respond to events and in explaining discretionary decisions. Personal attributes could shape the operational style or the operational style could be shaped by the organization (Brown, 1988: 26–28). Police discretion cannot always be structured by proscribing specific actions or by issuing policy statements. However, police administrators must not fail in developing policy guidelines about complex issues. These concerns are about cutting moral, legal, and constitutional corners, which create and perpetuate the ambiguous nature of police work. One of the primary consequences of such moral ambiguity is an isolated police culture and its "blue curtain."

When the police take short cuts, this sends improper messages to citizens about how problems should be solved. When police agencies fail to wrestle with the moral and legal issues of social policies, police departments risk litigation. This can jeopardize departmental efforts to deal with serious problems. Most problems can usually be managed, once they are properly understood and alternative solutions explored (Kelling, 1999: 15).

The chief administrator of any organization has the responsibility to establish policies that will assist in maintaining the credibility of the organization. Managing a police department should be no different as far as establishing policies and guidelines for the members of the organization is concerned. Most of us realize that the police mission, goals, and objectives are different from other organizations, but basic managerial principles emphasize that policies and guidelines must be established to guide the members of the police department. This includes the command staff, supervisors, and line and staff personnel.

In the late 1960s and 1970s, police departments were more or less forced to recognize that police discretion existed or at least give lip service to its existence. During this period of time, police discretion meant flexibility in which police officers used discretion not to bring embarrassment to the officer or the police agency. Some police agencies considered police discretion to mean the judgment police officers used in deciding whether to arrest or not. Also, there were police departments that considered police discretion to be **selective enforcement**.

Selective enforcement of laws can be examined by flexibility and the legality of police discretion. Examining selective enforcement involves controversial police discretional issues such as when to use force, appropriate uses for surveillance and undercover techniques, or stopping-and-questioning practices. An examination of selective enforcement does not cover the various methods to dispose of social or legal issues by means other than prosecution (Goldstein, 1977: 94–95). Davis (1969: 4) in the following statement considers the total picture of police discretion:

> A public officer has discretion whenever the effective limits on his power leave him free to make a choice among possible courses of action or inaction.

Some elements of this definition need special emphasis. Especially important is the proposition that discretion is not limited to what is authorized or what is legal but includes all that is within the effective limits of the officer's power. This phraseology is necessary because a good deal of discretion is illegal or has questionable legality. Another facet of the definition is that a choice to do nothing—or to do nothing now—is definitely included; perhaps inaction decisions are ten or twenty times as frequent as action decisions. Discretion is exercised not merely in the final disposition of cases or problems but in each interim step, and interim choices are far more numerous than the final ones. Discretion is not limited to substantive choices but extends to procedures, methods, forms, timing, degree of emphasis, and many other subsidiary factors.

Many police administrators recognize that they need to be truthful as far as the issue of police discretion is concerned. Today, the police administrator knows that the public recognizes that the police do not enforce all laws as it would be impossible to do so. Modern American society is much too sophisticated to believe police propaganda that the police enforce all laws equally, regardless of how trivial or serious the offense. The police need to recognize that they come out ahead when they are upfront with the public. The credibility of the police becomes tarnished when the police claim to be performing a function that they cannot do or have not attempted to accomplish.

PRACTICALITY OF POLICE DISCRETION

Why do the police have discretion? Can society expect the police to enforce all the laws passed by the legislative branch? And ordinances passed by city councils? Would it be realistic to expect the police to have full enforcement of the law? Is it not realistic for the police to selectively enforce the laws that the majority of the public would want enforced? If the police practiced full enforcement, would this not create a logjam in the legal process? Is there sufficient jail space if full enforcement is practiced?

Are there sufficient prosecutors, judges, and courtrooms for the full enforcement of laws? The legal system must practice discretion if it has to function in an efficient and effective manner. The following statement by Delattre (2006: 49) provides a realistic and logical explanation as to why the police are granted discretion: "Police are granted discretion because no set of laws and regulations can prescribe what to do in every possible circumstance. The possibilities are too numerous for us to have rules for everything that may happen." Delattre considers any attempt to make rules for every possible situation demeaning to an officer's intelligence. Also, when the police bureaucracy becomes rule-bound, flexibility is lost and the organization loses its productivity (50).

Being practical, discretion allows the police administrator to make decisions on policies and practices. Generally, administrators, supervisors, or patrol personnel are all involved in practicing police discretion. The discretion that the police have also allows them to decide which means they will use to maintain order and what approaches they will use in helping those in need of assistance (Delattre, 2006: 495). "Discretion is a special kind of liberty—the freedoms to make decisions that affect the lives of others, which other citizens are empowered to make. Special liberties entail special duties."

As mentioned previously in this chapter, the police enjoy discretionary autonomy to perform their police functions. Several researchers (Brown, 1988) emphasize that police officers often consider following legal restrictions in enforcing the laws, such as due process, causing a hindrance to crime control.

The need to control police discretion may have been a major reason for the **U.S. Supreme Court** decisions that provided judicial guidelines for the police. With police administrators, state legislatures, and the appellate courts of the various states failing to curb police abuses or perceived abuses of citizens' constitutional rights, the U.S. Supreme Court stepped in to provide guidance. The 1960s and 1970s were decades that emphasized the constitutional rights of citizens at the expense of police discretion. Prior to the U.S. Supreme Court curtailing police actions deemed unconstitutional, the police maintained order as they pleased. Most states had vagrancy, loitering, and disorderly conduct laws, which gave the police a great deal of authority. The state statutes on these laws were so vague that the police could virtually arrest anyone. For an extended period of time, the police were able to get away with discretion when enforcing laws such as disorderly conduct since they generally did not arrest anyone or used to arrest everyone. They arrested those citizens that lacked political clout to do something about police discretion in making arrests in these areas.

During the 1960s and 1970s, the U.S. Supreme Court under Chief Justice Earl Warren rendered many landmark decisions that required the police to follow guidelines established by the U.S. Supreme Court. These guidelines were established using the Bill of Rights as a means to control police actions. The Supreme Court has the authority to interpret the U.S. Constitution and the Amendments to the Constitution. In 1803, the U.S. Supreme Court, under Chief Justice John Marshall in the *Marbury v. Madison* case, decided that the Supreme Court of the United States has the power of judicial review to determine the legality of the laws and the actions of

U.S. Supreme Court

The Court's decisions provide judicial guidelines for the police.

the legislative and executive branches of government. The *Marbury v. Madison* case determined that the judges were responsible for protecting the rights of individuals. It has been taken for granted that the U.S. Supreme Court has the right to review actions performed by the executive branch of government. The police fall under the executive branch of government and the Court has been reviewing police actions for decades.

One of the major cases of the 1960s, which still holds sway, is *Miranda v. Arizona* (384 U.S. 436, 1966), which requires that the police must inform a suspect of his constitutional rights against self-incrimination and his right to an attorney. These rights include that a suspect does not have to speak to the police if asked any questions about a crime and if he decides to speak, then he has the right to have an attorney present. Also, the suspect is warned that anything he says can and will be used against him in a court of law. Finally, *Miranda* requires that the police inform the suspect that if he cannot afford an attorney, then one would be appointed prior to questioning. The *Miranda* case falls under the Fifth Amendment, which requires the police to inform a suspect of his constitutional rights. The police represent the government; therefore, the Bill of Rights has been interpreted in conjunction with the Fourteenth Amendment to protect citizens from illegal and inappropriate police actions. The Fifth Amendment states: "… nor shall [he] be compelled in any criminal case to be a witness against himself, nor be deprived of life, liberty, or property, without due process of law …."

The Fourth Amendment is an important Amendment that protects citizen rights and provides guidelines on police discretion. This Amendments deals with police activities such as arrest, due process, probable cause, search and seizure, warrants, line-ups, and hot pursuit. The Fourth Amendment states:

> The right of the people to be secure in their persons, houses, papers, and effects, against unreasonable searches and seizures, shall not be violated, and no Warrants shall issue, but upon probable cause, supported by Oath or affirmation, and particularly describing the place to be searched, and the persons or things to be seized.

In the 1914 Supreme Court case, *Weeks v. United States* (232 U.S. 383, 1914), the court decided that illegally obtained evidence seized by federal law enforcement officers cannot be admissible as evidence in a federal court. This decision became known as the "exclusionary rule." However, it was not until 1961 that the "exclusionary rule" became applicable to the states. In *Mapp v. Ohio* (367 U.S. 643, 1961) case, the Supreme Court applied the exclusionary rule to state law enforcement officers. *Mapp* decided that the use of illegally obtained evidence could not be used in state courts. In *Terry v. Ohio* (392 U.S. 1, 1968) case, the Supreme Court ruled that the police could detain an individual without probable cause for questioning. The stopping of a person is permitted and does not constitute an arrest when unusual behavior has been observed leading to the reasonable suspicion that a criminal act may be likely. It should be noted that reasonable suspicion has not been defined as strictly being a probable cause. The police officer can select specific facts to justify his suspicion. Therefore, a police officer may frisk a person if he believes the suspect may be dangerous, but he may search only for weapons and not for evidence.

In addition to the Fourth and Fifth Amendments, the Supreme Court has also used the Sixth Amendment to control police discretion. One of the most important issues pertaining to the Sixth Amendment, as it applies to criminal investigations, is the lineup. The lineup is one technique the police use to identify the potential suspect of a crime. The police place several suspects in a line for the express purpose of having either the victim or a witness identify the suspect as being the criminal. Once the suspect has been formally charged with a crime, the Supreme Court considers a lineup to be a "critical stage of the proceedings" which requires counsel to be present. In *United States v. Wade* case decided in 1967 (388 U.S. 218), the courts ruled that the police use of a lineup must be conducted in a fair manner free from bias. For example, the individuals in the lineup should be of the same sex, approximately the same age and height, with similar skin texture and hair color, and should be wearing similar clothes.

The previous mentioned cases are only a few examples of how the U.S. Supreme Court has provided guidelines regarding police discretion. The police must follow court guidelines or lose public credibility. When a police officer loses credibility to the court, he can no longer function as a police officer. Not only the U.S. Supreme Court can dampen police discretion, but also the appellate and trial courts of an officer's respected state are constantly making decisions that provide guidelines for police discretion.

State legislation can also control police discretion. The best example of this is domestic violence law, which requires the police to make an arrest when they have probable cause that a crime has been committed or is about to be committed. Most states, such as Kansas, have domestic violence laws in which police officers who fail to make an arrest during a domestic violence call, in which bruises and marks appear on one of the parties, can be charged with a crime. This action completely takes away police discretion. The domestic violence law may be paving the way for further such laws, which further eliminates police discretion. Driving-while-Intoxicated (DWI) may be another violation, which may in the future require that police officers arrest all DWI under penalty that they have committed an illegal act by not making an arrest.

GUIDELINES FOR POLICE DISCRETION

As this chapter has emphasized, the police have discretion, but that discretion at times has been severely criticized as either unethical, abusive, or a reflection of deviant behavior. Walker (2001: 152), a well-respected police scholar, had the following to say about police discretion:

> Courts and legislatures may rule, but the implementation of the law is left to officers on the street. Discretion is a basic and inescapable part of policing, and while the exercise

of discretion often reflects sound judgment, it also often represents an unacceptable deviation from the law. The effective implementation of policy—whether a statute, court decision, or department policy arising from an oversight recommendations that a department make serious effort to see that it is in fact implemented.

As earlier brought to the attention of the reader, there are various methods used to control police discretion but the most effective means of observing, reviewing, and keeping police discretion focused on legitimate avenues is the police agency itself. Police administrators, commanders, supervisors, and the individual officer must be held accountable for discretionary acts that lead to a violation of civil, constitutional, and human rights of all people.

One model that could be used to establish guidelines for police discretion would be the one recommended by George Kelling, who served as an advisor to the New York City Transit Police. The New York City Transit Police used problem solving to solve problems. A policy-study group was organized that consisted of line officers, supervisors, managers of the transit police, along with civilian employees of the New York Transit Police. To obtain information about transit problems, surveys of patrons were conducted and focus groups formed to clarify the subway's problems and obtain the public view of suggested police tactics (33).

Kelling reports that line officers wanted guidance from police administrators but were skeptical about what would be obtained. Line officers felt that police administrators simply dumped problems onto them. The Transit Police recognized that civil libertarians, who were more concerned about individual rights than public disorder, would sue once order maintenance strategies were implemented. This included controlling panhandling that could be considered a violation of the First Amendment free speech clause by civil libertarians (Kelling, 1999: 33).

All police departments must police themselves. They have a responsibility to oversee police discretions and also that police officers are performing ethically, morally, and in a fair, impartial, and just manner to all people they come in contact with. When all police officers learn to protect the civil rights, constitutional rights, and human rights of all people, regardless of their attitudes, believes, appearance, or group association (which seems an impossible goal), then and only then may it be possible for the police to win the trust of society.

The major reason police discretion comes under fire is that some groups in American society do not play by the rules fairly. Often the citizen and the police are not on the same page. If trust is to be gained, somehow the police and the citizen must develop some understanding of where the other fellow is coming from. It appears that police discretion cannot be completely removed from policing; otherwise policing will become extremely mechanical. However, a trust and confidence must be developed between the people and the police. The police administrators, commanders, and supervisors are the key to building the trust in the people. The courts and legislative and executive branch will always be there and will in all probability make policies for police agencies. The police need leadership, especially in the handling of police discretion.

POLICE DISCRETION: THREE SOCIOLOGICAL PERSPECTIVES

We have used the three sociological perspectives, functionalism, conflict, and inter-actionism, to analyze and understand a variety of police issues in various chapters of this book. Let us use these perspectives to examine the issue of police discretion. Func-tionalists often discuss the manifest and latent functions of various institutions and practices in society. Using those terms, the discussion of full enforcement vs. selective enforcement becomes understandable from this perspective. You will recall that mani-fest functions are those that everyone agrees on and relates to. For example, a college has the manifest function of educating young people. Latent functions are those that, while understood to exist, are rarely acknowledged by members of society. In the above example, the college also serves as a marriage market where individuals may find suit-able partners, with the right amount of education, to marry. Similarly, for functional-ists, the idea of full enforcement, for example, all laws are enforced without fear or favor by the police, helps them maintain confidence in police capabilities. At the same time, the latent function of selective enforcement allows police to concentrate scarce time and resources on areas of policing that they believe are important.

Conflict theorists are likely to see police discretion with some amount of suspicion and distrust. They are likely to ask who benefits from the use of discretion by police since it inevitably means that some people are going to be subjected to the full weight of police powers while others are likely to be ignored or let go lightly. Again, this is more than likely to mean that the rich and the powerful are given the benefit of the doubt by police while the poor and the powerless are going to be targeted and victimized. For example, while crime on the streets (often carried out by lower socioeconomic class members) is targeted and dealt with seriously, crime in the suites (e.g., environmental pollution by corporations and Medicaid fraud by doctors) is ignored and dismissed lightly even if perpetrators are arrested and prosecuted. So class biases are built into the exercise of discretion. Similarly, conflict theorists would argue that biases against minority groups are also built into police decisions, such as who to detain on traffic stops and who to arrest among suspects of a crime.

Finally, interactionists would focus their attention on the variations in the imple-mentation of police discretion by departments and by groups, even though they are all applying the same law. If a juvenile were stopped for disobeying a citywide curfew ordinance, would every police department treat him or her the same way? How are meanings and cues about who to let go and who to take into custody or give a warning to communicated and implemented? An interactionist would be interested in the con-struction of various meanings associated with the use of discretion (e.g., doing some-thing, ignoring, treating as trivial, and treating as serious) among particular groups of police officers. The interactionist would also be interested in how these meanings are communicated to new recruits and accepted as understood by those who have served in particular departments for longer periods of time.

Discretion in carrying out our duties is inevitable for the police; it would be important to learn how police forces in other countries deal with the same issue. Let us take a look at how police in the nation of Denmark handle discretion.

POLICE DISCRETION INTERNATIONALLY: DENMARK

Unlike the U.S. police, discretion has not become a major concern for the Danish police. In Denmark, the police benefit from wide discretionary powers with little control over police practices. The Danish police, unlike their American counterparts, have not been the subject of extensive research. The Danes appear to have greater trust with government officials than do Americans. The Danish people place the police in the upper layers of trust, with the medical field. How many Americans would put the police at the upper levels of trust?

Generally, police discretion consists of two types of powers: the power of suspicion and the power of prosecution. In both types of power, discrimination and abuses can occur because of police actions (Homberg, 2000: 179–180). In any study of police discretion, we have to understand that there are actions taken that, in all probability, are only known to the officers involved. Only when a police officer makes an arrest does his action usually become known. For the most part, only visible actions taken by police officers can be observed. A study of Danish police officers on police discretion found that discretion did not necessarily lead to discrimination. The investigator in the Danish study argues that since offenders are rarely caught in the commission of a crime, discrimination is inevitable. The police use their experiences to determine a potential crime or criminal (Homberg, 2000: 186–187). "This proactive approach use of power of suspicion must be discriminatory in nature" (Homberg, 2000: 187). Police that are proactive rely on police officers' ability to discriminate between persons who are suspicious and those who are not suspicious. Obviously, some individuals will be considered suspicious and prime targets for police surveillance and interrogation. The police cannot avoid the use of discretion and of making individual judgments. They will question an innocent person who lives in the wrong neighborhood or who belongs to the wrong segment of society rather than an

individual who happens to be a member of an acceptable group. The researcher of this study believes it not practical for the police to equally divide their surveillance activities to all citizens. The Danish police practice police discretion to the same extent that American police do (Homberg, 2000: 186–187). However, they appear not to be as scrutinized, examined, studied, or criticized to the same extent to operate as much under the microscope when compared to their American counterparts.

Among the negative effects of police discretion are opportunities for police misconduct involving corruption and abuse. For an example of this widespread phenomenon, see the accompanying box on Britain and its police force.

SUMMARY

During the 1950s, it was common practice for police administrators to claim that police officers investigated every crime that occurred and that every single law was always equally enforced. Police chiefs made public announcements that all crimes committed, regardless of the seriousness of the offense, were investigated with equal effort and that all laws were enforced with the same priority. Of course, this did not occur. Even if the police wanted to give equal time to investigate all crimes, regardless of their seriousness, this would be impossible, because they lacked sufficient manpower or because often there were insufficient clues for an investigation.

The initial recognition of police discretion was made public by the American Bar Foundation study on policing. The American Bar Foundation study found that police officers were making decisions that were discretionary in nature. Further impetus occurred during the 1960s and 1970s when the police began to recognize publicly that police discretion existed. President Johnson's 1967 Crime Commission and the 1970s National Advisory Commission on Criminal Justice Standards and Goals acknowledged that police discretion existed. The National Advisory Commission further recommended that police agencies establish policies that limit police discretion.

Certain segments of American society are not pleased with police discretion. Issues pertaining to police discretion include racial profiling, discrimination, and police abuses. Of course, society approves of removing individuals who fail to follow the rules laid down by society. Do not the police fall into the same category? Are they not the caretakers of society? Are not the police the maintainers of the status quo? If the police lose their discretionary authority, then will not police work become mechanical? Do we want robots for police? Or do we want intelligent, thinking people who, based on experiences, will discriminate in an impartial and fair manner when using police discretionary authority?

Since the 1970s, there have been many studies on policing and their discretionary powers. Police literature is inundated with such topics. Some of the literature paints a negative picture of police discretion, while there exists other literature that paints a positive picture of discretion. Regardless of the negative or positive connotation about police discretion, it will always be with us. The police must be held accountable every time they use discretion. The police agency that employs police officers must put in place policies that provide guidelines on the use of discretion. Of course, the courts, and legislative and executive branches of government along with citizen organizations can monitor police abuses of discretion. Finally, we considered the exercise of discretion by police in another country, Denmark. While the police will always use discretion, we remain hopeful that there will be a system of checks and balances to deal with those officers who abuse their discretionary powers.

KEY TERMS

Full enforcement: The policy of enforcing all laws would be in effect. The police would not have the authority to ignore or to overlook certain violations or even provide an offender with a warning to avoid illegal actions.

Police authority: It specifically deals with the power to arrest, to search and seize, and to use force when needed. Police authority allows the police to take away one's freedom, invade an individual's privacy, and place citizens under surveillance.

Selective enforcement: Generally, the police ignored many violations and often enforced laws under specific conditions. Selective enforcement of laws can be examined by flexibility and the legality of police discretion. The police never practiced full enforcement.

U.S. Supreme Court: The Court's decisions provide judicial guidelines for the police.

REVIEW QUESTIONS

1. Compare the view of police discretion in the 1950s with the first decades of the twenty-first century.
2. Discuss the guidelines of police discretion.
3. Discuss police discretion in Denmark.

 DISCUSSION QUESTIONS

1. Should American police have discretion similar to the police of Denmark?
2. Do guidelines on police discretion hamper the ability to do their job?
3. Of the three sociological perspectives discussed in this chapter, does conflict theory best support police discretion?

 REFERENCES

Brown, Michael K. (1988) *Working the Street: Police Discretion and the Dilemmas of Reform*. New York, NY: Sage Publication.

Davis, Kenneth (1969) *Discretionary Justice: A Preliminary Inquiry*. Baton Rouge, LA: Louisiana State University.

Davis, Kenneth (1975) *Police Discretion*. St. Paul, MN: West Publishing.

Delattre, Edwin J. (2006) *Character and Cops: Ethics in Policing*. Washington, DC: The AEI Press.

Goldstein, Herman (1963) "Police Discretion versus the Real," *Public Administration Review* 3, 3p: 140–148.

Goldstein, Herman (1977) *Policing a Free Society*. Cambridge, MA: Ballinger Publishing Company.

Goldstein, Herman (1993) "Confronting the Complexity of the Police Function." In L. E. Ohlin and F. J. Remington (eds.) *Discretion in Criminal Justice*. Albany, NY: SUNY Press.

Homberg, Lars (2000) "Discretionary Leniency and Typological Guilt: Results from a Danish Study of Police Discretion." *Journal of Scandinavian Studies in Criminology and Crime Prevention* 1: 179–194.

Kelling, George L. (1999) *Broken Windows and Police Discretion*. Washington, DC: Office of Justice Program, U.S. Department of Justice.

National Advisory Commission on Criminal Justice Standards and Goals (1973) *Police*. Washington, DC: U.S. Government Printing.

Pound, Roscoe (1940) "Discretion, Dispensation, and Mitigation: The Problem of the Individual Special Case." *New York University Law Review* 35.

Schmalleger, Frank (2006) *Criminal Justice Today: An Introductory Text for the 21st Century*. Ninth Edition, Upper Saddle River, NJ: Prentice-Hall.

Walker, Samuel (1993) *Taming the System: The Control of Discretion in Criminal Justice*. New York: Oxford University Press.

Walker, Samuel (2001) *Police Accountability*. Belmont, CA: Wadsworth Press.

POLICE DISCRETION: A BRITISH PERSPECTIVE

Stephen Tong

Police discretion in Britain has been influenced by history, legislation, police powers, occupational culture, politics of crime fighting, performance measurement, police hierarchies, and a diverse population (Dixon, 1997; Newburn and Reiner, 2007). This account will aim to define police discretion in its broadest sense before detailing the nature of the practice of discretion. Although there are similarities across Britain, as a whole it should be noted that there are and have been significant differences in the history and model of policing in Northern Ireland and criminal justice practices in Scotland.

The Metropolitan Police Service (London) was founded in 1829 by Sir Robert Peel in an attempt to create a nonmilitary, professional police service (Emsley, 1996). Although Peel wanted to ensure that there were significant differences to the military, particularly in appearance, there were similarities including the requirement for drill, discipline, and a rank structure (Emsley, 1996; Rawlings, 2002; Jones, 2008). Although the rank structure was similar to the military, the autonomy enjoyed by police constables marks a clear distinction between British police services and more military models

of policing (Bowling and Foster, 2002; Jones, 2008). It is this autonomy that Jones (2008: 82) describes as the "freedom" for officers to make decisions according to their own "judgment." This view of discretion accepts that a broad range of decisions can be made by officers and that there is an element of freedom to action/inaction in police practice. It is this level of freedom that will be dependent on the characteristics of the jurisdiction concerned. The wording of legislation, local and national policing policies, political governance, systems of accountability, training, supervision of officers, and the nature of crime within different countries are just some of the influences that may impact on the way police discretion is exercised (Dixon, 1997; Newburn and Reiner, 2007).

In Britain, the doctrine of constabulary independence as determined by common law allows a certain freedom for the police to make decisions without undue influence (Newburn and Reiner, 2007). Lord Denning states a police constable "… is not the servant of anyone, save the law itself" (Denning, 1968 cited in Newburn and Reiner, 2007: 921). Lord Denning's statement could be interpreted as a constable having total freedom when making decisions with the exception of the law but this does not prevent influence of other kinds. It was during this decade of Lord Denning's statement that the "discovery of discretion" revealed more about the decision making of constables (Waddington, 1999: 31). Up until this time, there was little research revealing how police constables performed their role and it was widely assumed that the police enforced the law rigidly (Banton, 1964). In truth, officers were engaged in routine under enforcement, deciding if they should or should not arrest on the basis of individual judgments of events (Banton, 1964; Neyroud and Beckley, 2001). However, it has been clearly acknowledged that the police did not have the resources to enforce the law as society believed they did and it would certainly not be desirable for full enforcement now, particularly as the police rely on the cooperation and "consent" of citizens to fulfill their duty (Banton, 1964; Jefferson and Grimshaw, 1987; Reiner, 2000). So in many respects, the practice of discretion can provide a more "amicable" approach to policing a community from which consent is required to achieve police objectives (Waddington, 1999).

The operation of police discretion has attracted considerable controversy in Britain (Neyroud and Beckley, 2001; Newburn and Reiner, 2007). Police constables enjoy minimal supervision but the basis of their decision making can be influenced by police culture (Young, 1991). "Cop" culture has been held responsible for influencing and nurturing sexism and racism, resulting in stereotyping of particular groups (Bowling and Foster, 2002; Sanders and Young, 2007). Heavy-handed policing and intensive stop and search tactics by police officers sparked off the Brixton Riots in London in 1981, resulting in widespread damage and casualties (Reiner, 2000; Bowling, 1998). The following Scarman Enquiry reported on the events in Brixton and pointed to poor police tactics, lack of community consultation, and the importance of public tranquility over law enforcement as areas that needed to be addressed (Reiner, 2000). Despite some improvements to the adversarial nature of stop and search tactics and treatment of particular groups, some discretionary police practices remain problematic particularly for marginalized groups (Newburn and Reiner, 2007; Jones, 2008).

Waddington (1999: 63) argues that discretion is inevitable as the "police do not enforce the law because they cannot." Attempts to control discretion have included race relation training, additional guidance for procedures in the Police and Criminal Evidence Act 1984, attempts to enhance the objectivity of complaint process, and improvements to probationary training (Macpherson, 1999; HMIC, 2002; Police Reform Act, 2002). However, as Waddington (1999: 32–33) argues, "decisions taken on the street" are "unreviewable" and supervision is "virtually nonexistent." Police learning has reflected a "craft" rather than a "profession" and the importance of the development and practice of "professional discretion" has been raised in the recent review of policing in the United Kingdom (Flanagan, 2008; Tong & Bowling, 2006; Tong, 2009a). There have been increasing calls to review police training in the United Kingdom to address these and other shortcomings in police practice (Wood and Tong, 2009; Tong, 2009b). Foster (1999) argues that police officers require a broader knowledge of the environment they police within and this will inevitably lead to better use of discretion. If higher education for police officers is required to provide greater "contextual knowledge" and more effective use of discretion, then more substantial partnerships between the police and universities will be required.

References

Banton, M. (1964) *The Policeman in the Community*, London: Tavistock Publications.

Bowling, B. (1998) *Violent Racism: Victimization, Policing and Social Context*, Oxford: Oxford University Press.

Bowling, B. & Foster, J. (2002) 'Policing and the Police', in M. Maguire, R. Morgan & R. Reiner (eds.), *The Oxford Handbook of Criminology*, 3rd Edition, Oxford: Oxford University Press, pp. 980–1033.

Dixon, D. (1997) *Law in Policing: Legal Regulation and Police Practices*, Oxford: Oxford University Press.

Emsley, C. (1996) *The English Police*, 2nd Edition, Harlow: Longman Publishing.

Flanagan, Sir R. (2008) *The Review of Policing. Final Report*, London: Home Office.

Foster, J. (1999) 'Appendix 22: Memorandum by Dr Janet Foster, Institute of Criminology, University of Cambridge', in *Home Affairs Committee, Police Training and Recruitment: Volume Two*, London: The Stationery Office, pp. 239–261.

HMIC (2002) *Training Matters*, London: HMIC.

Jefferson, T. & Grimshaw, R. (1987) *Interpreting Policework: Policy and Practice in Forms of Beat Policing*, London: Allen & Unwin.

Jones, T. (2008) 'Discretion', in T. Newburn & P. Neyroud (eds.), *Dictionary of Policing*, Cullompton: Willan Publishing, pp. 82–83.

Macpherson, Sir W. (1999) *The Stephen Lawrence Inquiry*, London: TSO.

Newburn, T. & Reiner, R. (2007) 'Policing and the Police', in M. Maguire, R. Morgan & R. Reiner (eds.), *The Oxford Handbook of Criminology*, Oxford: Oxford University Press, pp. 910–952.

Neyroud, P. & Beckley, A. (2001) *Policing, Ethics and Human Rights*, Cullompton, Devon: Willan Publishing.

Police Reform Act (2002) London: The Stationary Office.

Rawlings, P. (2002) *Policing: A Short History*, Cullompton, Devon: Willan Publishing.

Reiner, R. (2000) *Politics of the Police*, 3rd Edition, Oxford: Oxford University Press.

Sanders, A. & Young, R. (2007) 'From Suspects to Trial', in M. Maguire, R. Morgan & R. Reiner (eds.), *The Oxford*

Handbook of Criminology, Oxford: Oxford University Press, pp. 953–989.

Tong, S. (2009a) 'Introduction: A Brief History of Criminal Investigation', in S. Tong, R. Bryant & M. Hovarth (eds.), *Understanding Criminal Investigation*, Chichester: Wiley & Sons Publication, pp. 1–13.

Tong, S. (2009b) 'Professionalising Investigation', in S. Tong, R. Bryant & M. Hovarth (eds.), *Understanding Criminal Investigation*, Chichester: Wiley & Sons Publication, pp. 197–216.

Tong, S. & Bowling, B. (2006) Art, craft and science of detective work. *Police Journal* 79, 323–329.

Waddington, P. A. J. (1999) *Policing Citizens*, London: London University Press.

Wood, D. & Tong, S. (2009) The future of initial police training: A university perspective. *International Journal of Police Science and Management* 11(3), 294–305.

Young, M. (1991) *An Inside Job: Policing and Police Culture in Britain*, Oxford: Clarendon Press.

CHAPTER 9

All occupational groups share a measure of inclusiveness and identification. People are brought together simply by doing the same work and having similar career and salary problems. As several writers have noted, police show an unusually high degree of occupational solidarity. It is true that the police have a common employer and wear a uniform to work, but so do doctors, mail carriers, and bus drivers. Yet it is doubtful that these workers have so close-knit an occupation or so similar an outlook on the world as do the police. Set apart from the conventional world, the police officer experiences an exceptionally strong tendency to find a social identity within the social milieu. (Skolnick, 1996: 96)

Newly-promoted Philippine National Police officers take their oaths during mass oath-taking and pinning of ranks ceremony at police headquarters at Camp Crame, Quezon city north of Manila Monday January 21, 2008. More than 20,000 police officers nationwide, representing 17-percent of the total police force, were promoted to various ranks in the biggest promotion ever accorded the entire police force. (Credit: © AP Photo/Bullit Marquez)

THE POLICE SUBCULTURE

OBJECTIVES:

1. The student will understand the concepts of culture and subculture.
2. The student will understand the concept and features of police subculture.
3. The student will learn about features that the police subculture shares with and those different from the parent culture.
4. The student will understand the functionalist, conflict theory, and interactionist approaches to analyzing police subculture.
5. The student will learn about police subculture on an international level.

Human beings, unlike other species that inhabit the earth, do not possess particular genetic predispositions that program them to behave in certain ways (e.g., some species of birds are genetically equipped and instructed at certain points in their lives to build nests). This introduces a great deal of variability and plasticity to human behavior in response to the common questions of existence. Think, for example, about the range of possibilities that human beings bring to the common questions of what to wear (kilt, kimono, shirt, and saree), what to eat (haggis, baklava, sushi, and curry), and how to shelter themselves in order to survive (igloo, thatched hut, stucco, and ranch house). **Culture** is the guidance that a given society provides to these common questions of existence. Well-known anthropologist Geertz (1970: 64) comments that to be human:

> "is not just to talk; it is to utter the appropriate words and phrases in the appropriate social situations on the appropriate tome of voice .... It is not just to eat; it is to prefer certain foods cooked in certain ways and to follow a rigid table etiquette in consuming them; it is not even just to feel certain quite distinctive emotions—patience, detachment, resignation, respect."

Culture consists of the total way of life of a society or large group of people. There is clearly a close and binding relationship between a society and its culture. As Ackoff and Rovin (2003: 8) point out, "A society is a social system whose parts are communities that have a common culture, and by a culture we mean a common view of reality and the same habitual ways of carrying out the community's functions." It is therefore impossible to think of a society without an attendant culture and similarly impossible to think of a culture without an accompanying society. The two are so closely connected that one is often indistinguishable from the other.

Culture is further subdivided into **material culture** and **nonmaterial culture**. Material culture is made up of all the tangible objects and inventions that are devised, used, and understood by those who share a given culture. Thus, artifacts such as homes, plates, automobiles, socks, blackboards, the cross as a religious symbol, telephones, the Stars and Stripes, computers, football stadiums, etc., are all part of the material culture of American society. Nonmaterial culture is made up of intangibles such as language, customs, values, norms, principles, scientific formulae, etc., that is, it exists at the level of ideas, beliefs, and mental imagery. While these ideas and thoughts may be written down and also have practical implications, they are generally not concrete. However, these ideas are as equally important as tangible objects in any given culture. The relationship between material and nonmaterial culture can be illustrated by taking the example of a cooking recipe. The recipe itself (let us say it is for making delicious apple pie) exists in a cookbook and at that point represents little more than an idea for a dish, that is, it is nonmaterial culture. When you assemble the ingredients, mix them together, and bake the apple pie, it turns into a tangible item for your consumption, that is, it becomes a beloved part of the food available in and associated with American material culture.

Not all items included in the nonmaterial culture of a society have a direct and practical relationship with material culture. For example, the idea of democracy (rule

culture

Consists of the total way of life of a society or large group of people.

material culture

Is made up of all the tangible objects and inventions that are devised, used, and understood by those who share in a given culture, for example, artifacts such as homes, plates, automobiles, socks, blackboards, the cross as a religious symbol, telephones, the Stars and Stripes, computers, and football stadiums are all part of the material culture of American society.

nonmaterial culture

Is made up of the intangibles of a culture such as language, customs, values, norms, principles, scientific formulae, etc., that is, it exists at the level of ideas, beliefs, and mental imagery.

of the people or masses) may be a part of the culture of a society. However, a given society may choose to implement that political idea or may prefer an alternative type of government such as a monarchy (e.g., Brunei and Nepal). In that society then, democracy remains only in the nonmaterial culture. Further, whether we choose to implement democracy in the form of a parliamentary government involving a Prime Minister as its head (e.g., the United Kingdom and India) or a presidential government that is led by a President (e.g., the United States and the Philippines) will also vary. Similarly, material culture can lead to nonmaterial cultural changes. For example, think about the first introduction of the automobile to the routines of policing. This led inexorably to the idea that the police should react very quickly to reports of crime (i.e., the norm of quick or rapid reaction became associated with the police) using the police car. For a time after the widespread incorporation of automobiles into their everyday work, as we learned in studying police history, the police began to emphasize and wished to be judged most of all by their reaction time. As a result, minor changes that they were able to implement that shaved a few seconds or minutes from their overall reaction time came to be hailed as major achievements. Overall, the material and nonmaterial aspects of a culture are linked together intimately.

Two final points need to be made regarding the culture of any given society. First, cultures are never static; they change and continue to evolve, as societies exist over time. Think about the changes that have taken place in American culture as a result of moving from a primarily agricultural to an industrial and then to an information-based society. Just in terms of living quarters, American residents moved from residing in farmhouses and rural shacks to urban tenements and row houses to suburban subdivisions and high-rise apartments. Similarly, American culture moved from justifying the virtual exclusion of women from voting and participating in the public arena to one in which women not only were given the right to vote, but also were then later able to aspire to, run for, and eventually, hold political office. Second, despite our emphasis on the close connections between a society and its culture, the latter is never monolithic. Thus, Swidler (1992), for example, defines culture as a "tool kit" that includes a set of stories, rituals, and world views. Human beings in that culture access and use these tools as they see the need in varying ways and under different circumstances. From this perspective, cultures are never completely and totally cohesive. They do not dominate the behavior of individual members exclusively and rigidly. Individuals have some amount of latitude in picking and choosing their own repertoire of beliefs and behaviors from within a culturally approved range. Variation and diversity, therefore, always exist within a single culture, giving rise among other things, to **subcultures**.

DEFINING THE POLICE SUBCULTURE

Now that we have understood the concept of culture, let us turn our attention to the related concepts of **parent (or dominant) culture** and subculture, the latter being one where we will locate policing (not just as an occupation or a particular type of bureaucracy) as a particularly distinct way of life for its members (see Wyer, 2009). The parent culture of any given collection of people is that which is identified with the

---

subculture

Consists of certain material and nonmaterial aspects of a way of life associated with a group in society that is different from the parent (or dominant) culture.

parent (or dominant) culture

The features of a given culture that are identified with the most powerful group or groups in that society.

most powerful group or groups in that society. In the United States, despite their early presence in parts of the Southwestern United States and currently growing numbers of people who speak Spanish as their native language, the dominant language of this country is not Spanish. Again, the presence of Native Americans, who populated this country before all others, has not meant that one of the Native American languages became the national language of the United States. English, one of the languages that were brought over by immigrants to this country who landed on the East Coast in the seventeenth and eighteenth centuries, has achieved that status. Thus, the language associated with the most powerful group of people in this country is the dominant language.

A subculture consists of certain material and nonmaterial aspects of a way of life associated with a group in society that is different from the parent (or dominant) culture. Any subculture while possessing many important differences with the parent culture will also simultaneously share a number of elements with it. For example, while the subculture of motorcycle gangs such as the Hell's Angels will have clear differences (focus of interests and activity, clothes, etc.) with the parent culture, they will also share similarities in terms of language and food (i.e., they are more than likely to speak English when conversing and will most probably not be vegetarian teetotalers, similar to other Americans).

Subcultures arise due to a number of reasons:

1. People who migrate to a new country may adopt certain cultural practices and, at the same time, retain others from the old country, for example, Polish immigrants to Chicago may become interested in baseball and American football, and yet keep dancing the polka.

2. Other subcultures can be associated with activities, some of which may be related to sports and recreation, for example, the subculture of chili enthusiasts who know about and consume the dish in its many regional forms (should it be cooked with beans or without beans), and the subculture of body builders, enthusiasts of professional wrestling, or NASCAR racing fans.

3. Subcultures may be regional or local in terms of their origin. The religious subculture of Mormons in Utah may not share many similarities with that of the Catholics in neighboring New Mexico. At the same time, when those from the northeastern parts of the United States visit or move to the Old South, they begin to notice differences in food habits (grits, anyone) and language use ("Y'all"). This obviously works in the other direction as well.

4. Subcultures could develop around carrying out criminal activities. For example, juvenile gangs or groups of street kids (and those associated with them) may engage in providing illegal services such as prostitution and illegal goods such as cocaine or marijuana to customers.

5. Subcultures may also be related to occupations or professions. Thus, electricians, neurosurgeons, and professors (to name three professions) form groups with particular interests and specialized language to describe their work and to deal with common problems or issues that they may confront. It should not surprise us then that the police also form a subculture.

Cox (1996: 164) contends that the police subculture tells officers "how to go about their tasks, how hard to work, what kinds of relationships to have with their fellow officers and other categories of people with whom they interact, and how they should feel about police administrators, judges, the law, and the requirements and restrictions they impose." Others (e.g., Crank, 1998) prefer to use the term police culture, rather than police subculture, to describe the same phenomenon.

To illustrate, let us take two issues. First, there is the socially unpleasant yet biologically and chronologically inescapable matter of human mortality and death. Henry (1995: 93) observes that the police are one of the few occupations other than those in the medical/health field who are likely to face "frequent and intense exposure to death." As a result, the folklore of the police subculture he studied contains pervasive death-related themes, symbols, and images. Henry (1995) believes that frequent exposure to this grim topic socializes young officers and teaches them how to maintain professional distance from deaths that occur during work and also to confront the very real likelihood of their own mortality. In other words, the police subculture both informs and educates its members regarding their occupation and how to "really" go about doing it in terms of becoming, acting, and being a police officer. Thus, when Herbert (1998: 356), who was a researcher (and not a police officer), refused to accompany officers to scenes of death, he was "subtly reminded that (he) did not possess the requisite moxie for police work."

Second, let us look at the issue of language. Subcultures often tend to produce their own jargon and shorthand references to common matters that are only understandable to "insiders." For example, the military bureaucracy refers to large-scale terminations of personnel as a reduction in force (RIF) and U.S. federal agencies that sponsor research issue requests for proposals (RFPs) to fulfill their research needs. Berg (1992: 173) quotes the following regarding the police subculture:

> "When the police are searching for a child rapist, they may speak about hunting a *skinner* or a *short-eyes*. The New York City's transit police use the term *lushworker* to describe people who rob drunks and sleeping passengers on the subway trains."

The specialized language used in these situations serves to keep relevant individuals in the know (i.e., police officers) together and to separate them from those who are not aware of the meanings of the words (i.e., the public).

CHARACTERISTICS OF THE POLICE SUBCULTURE

Most authors who have studied the police subculture describe it as being shaped by a profound sense of **self-differentiation** from the public and, to a lesser extent, from their own administrators. Westley (1970) finds that the police subculture informs the public that it is supposed to be protecting and serving in a largely unfriendly and unflattering manner. Like many other subcultures, the parent culture is viewed in terms of us (the police) vs. them (the public or everyone else). Using the terms we learned above, we can say that despite sharing some aspects of a common culture with

self-differentiation

How the police subculture defines itself as distinct from the public that it is supposed to be protecting and serving.

the public, the police occupational subculture defines itself by its differences with the former. The public is viewed as hostile, untrustworthy, and capable of doing violence. As a result, it is important for police officers to be secretive, always supportive of each other, and remain united. The basis for this differentiation, it has been argued, lies in the unique legal power that police alone possess: their everyday ability to use force and (as and when needed) deadly force, to achieve their goals. No other organization, public or private, possesses such power to compel obedience in everyday life. Even the military can use force only during situations of war or extreme domestic emergencies, and only when specifically asked to do so. The police, therefore, view themselves as being different, and in turn, the public views the police as different (although, in general, opinion polls show that the public has a positive image of the police). The theme of us vs. them is, therefore, reinforced on both sides of the police–public divide.

A second characteristic of the police subculture is the overall emphasis on internal **solidarity** or social cohesiveness. Police officers are expected to stick together and help each other out as members of the same "team" under all sorts of circumstances, minor and major. The common experiences that police officers share, that of going through an academy, wearing the same uniforms, enforcing the same laws, sharing in a common departmental regimen and bureaucratic hierarchy, and needing to back each other up (sometimes in dangerous situations), lead to bonding with fellow officers (and with officers in other police departments). Manning (1989: 163) observes that "The police officer is dependent on other police officers for assistance, advice, training, working knowledge, protection in case of threats from internal or external sources, and insulation against the public, and periodic dangers." Waddington (1999: 287), for example, mentions the importance of British police officers talking to each other ("an audience of their peers") within the confines of the departmental canteen (cafeteria) in attempting to work out and provide "purpose and meaning to inherently problematic occupational experience." McNulty (1994) shows that much of what passes for "common sense" among police officers is generated as a result of collective responses to work situations that they encounter. Hale (1989) suggests that subcultural solidarity is at the bottom of the so-called blue wall of silence that is thrown up when allegations of misconduct by fellow officers are made or investigated.

A third characteristic associated with the police subculture is its emphasis on **isolation**. We have noted previously the sense of self-differentiation that pervades policing. Taken to its extreme and without the balance provided by countervailing experiences, police officers feel that they are separate and isolated from every other group in society. Police officers typically socialize with other police officers, and most likely, so do their spouses and families. Partly, this is similar to members of other occupations (professors partying with other professors and doctors meeting with other doctors on the golf course), but is also a response to the particular nature of police jobs (shifts, perceived public hostility, etc.). Some of this isolation is, to be sure, self-imposed. Police officers may feel that to get too close to those who are not fellow police officers may affect their autonomy and discretion to act, in case that individual ever gets into trouble (e.g., if you are the best of friends with Joe Public, would you give Joe a ticket the next time you stop him for speeding?).

solidarity

The social cohesiveness of the police subculture that expects police officers to stick together and help each other out as members of the same "team" under all sorts of circumstances, minor and major.

isolation

The sense of self-differentiation that pervades policing, which if taken to its extreme and without the balance provided by countervailing experiences, results in police officers feeling that they are separate from every other group in society.

Finally consider the following set of six "truths" that Sparrow, Moore, and Kennedy (1990) report is characteristic of the police subculture:

1. Police are the only real crime fighters.
2. No one understands the nature of police work except fellow officers.
3. Loyalty to colleagues counts more than anything else.
4. It is impossible to win the war on crime without bending the rules.
5. Other citizens are unsupportive and make unreasonable demands.
6. Patrol work is only for those who are not smart enough to get out of it.

Do these "truths" serve to reduce police solidarity and isolation or are they likely to have the opposite effect? Even the last one, which may be considered an expression of the relative lack of prestige that patrol divisions suffer from, has another subcultural message. Patrol officers regularly interact with the public; officers in other divisions may not (detectives do so, but on their own terms, not the public's). Hence, getting away from patrol work indirectly increases the officer's isolation and his or her greater identification with other police.

ASPECTS SHARED WITH PARENT CULTURE

Herbert (1998) makes the important point that one should not think of the police subculture as existing in complete opposition to the public and to the formal bureaucracy that we discussed in Chapter 5. In other words, there are significant areas where the police subculture shares ideas, values, and norms that are similar to the formal bureaucracy within which it exists. Based on observations of the Los Angeles Police Department (LAPD), Herbert (1998) identifies these commonalities as including the following areas:

- Law: Police officers may base their actions and behavior on subcultural socialization about how to use their discretion. However, they are still bound by the basic responsibilities and powers as defined by the law and act in concrete situations that they encounter based on these definitions.
- Bureaucratic control: Many researchers underscore how the informal norms of the police subculture often serve to skirt and subvert bureaucratic rules; Herbert (1998: 354) suggests that these descriptions do not recognize that "Bureaucratic stipulations principally define the social and spatial world of concern for officers—they determine the type and location of incidents for which officers will assume responsibility." Thus, the overlap between the subculture and the larger bureaucratic culture determines the officer's actions.
- Adventure/machismo: While there has been increased emphasis on community policing, both the formal culture and informal subculture of policing continue to emphasize the importance of aggressiveness and bravery.

- Safety: Both the police administration and fellow officers encourage officers to be safe and to value their own personal security in the process of policing communities, particularly those known to be unfriendly to them.

- Competence: The police subculture emphasizes the importance of being able to take control over areas of responsibility, that is, each officer should be able to pull his or her own weight. The formal bureaucracy similarly looks for and rewards officers who are competent, for example, are able to make a number of felony arrests or traffic citations.

- Morality: Police officers see themselves as involved in a battle between good and evil in which they are unequivocally warriors on the side of good. The formal bureaucracy encourages these attributions as well.

So the point is that in many ways the police subculture is based on and draws strength from the formal bureaucratic culture. Extending this further, we can see that the above characteristics are also themes that the larger parent (or dominant) culture emphasizes regarding what is expected of the police. The larger culture wants its police officers in going about their daily work to follow the law and organizational rules, to be brave and competent, to stay safe, and finally to be morally good, upstanding individuals. One cannot fail to see in the above how the normative expectations of the culture are transmitted to individual officers through formal bureaucratic structures (such as academy training) and through informal subculture-based socialization. While there are differences (sometimes starkly so), the police subculture shares, in a number of ways, many values and norms with the parent culture.

The process of teaching qualified police recruits about the organization and its culture begins immediately after their applications have been accepted and they undergo basic training in the **police academy**, defined by Grant and Terry (2005: 368) as "a school where officers learn on the job techniques prior to receiving full police powers." Sociologists use the term *socialization* to refer to the process of learning to become members of any social group. More accurately, it is professional or occupational socialization when the intent is to integrate members into a job and the context in which that job is located, such as being a police officer in a particular police department. It continues formally and informally through **field training** and in-service training (or retraining). While much of the learning encountered during these stages is knowledge- and skill-related (e.g., how to write a report; how to patrol or purse eluding offenders), a larger (and perhaps, more important) portion will deal with what it means to become and be a police officer, sociologically and psychologically. The socialization process is obviously at its most intense during the academy training and field training stages. Let us turn our attention to the impact of these periods in shaping the identity and interactions of police officers in their chosen occupation. Interspersed with the following discussion is the work of John Van Maanen whose 1973 description of the police socialization process is considered a classic one.

police academy

School where officers learn on-the-job techniques prior to receiving full police powers.

field training

A probationary phase that is a period in which a more experienced police officer (referred to as an FTO, who is generally not an academy instructor) guides the trainee on day-to-day routines and practical procedures that members of the department are expected to follow and carry out.

BEFORE AND DURING ACADEMY TRAINING

Van Maanen (1973) divides up the process of police socialization into four stages: choice, introduction, encounter, and metamorphosis. The first two phases occur before and during academy training and will be described here, while the next two will be taken up in the following section. During the choice stage, two intersecting decisions are involved. A particular individual (among many others) has to make a decision about becoming a police officer, considering its advantages and disadvantages, and then applying for that job by meeting various related requirements (e.g., age, education, lack of prior felony convictions, and various examinations including physical agility and interviews). At the same time, a police department has to decide whether that individual (among many others who may have applied) satisfies the various requirements and to pick him or her for the job (based on the minimum entry criteria, background investigations, performance on written and oral interviews, etc.).

The second stage that Van Maanen (1973) names introduction refers to the recruit's police academy experience. Formal requirements for learning curricular content (report-writing skills, knowledge of the law, tactical driving, local ordinances, etc.) are often state-mandated in terms of the number of hours spent on various topics. In addition, departmental policies and procedures (patrol procedures, shift operations, processing arrestees, deadly force policies, etc.) will be dealt with. The department-specific policies and procedures will, of course, vary depending on the size and jurisdiction of the police agency. More importantly, informal learning regarding particulars of the department's own internal climate, environment, social processes, and interactions also occurs. This is accomplished through hearing examples and anecdotes ("war stories") as well as in comparisons to other departments and police organizations, for example, exhortations about "This is how we do it here (and why it is better than how other departments may do it)."

Police academy training can be stressful (Violanti, 1992) and in the view of trainees may or may not be preparing them for important job tasks they may face as police officers (Talley, 1986). Britz (1997) shows that the level of socialization that the police academy can inculcate in police recruits is affected by the latter's individual characteristics such as gender. Although the study findings are inconclusive, Mahoney (1997) raises an important question regarding the authoritarian nature of police academy training. Does such an authoritarian training environment affect the perceptions of police officers regarding community policing (which is often identified with a less authoritarian approach to dealing with the public)? Of course, it should be recognized that in recent times, with the emphasis on community policing, some police academies have become relatively less authoritarian.

DURING AND AFTER FIELD TRAINING

After a recruit has completed police academy training, he or she moves into a probationary phase known as field training. This is a period in which a more experienced police officer (referred to as a Field Training Officer or FTO, who is generally not an academy instructor) guides the trainee on day-to-day routines and practical procedures that members of the department are expected to follow and carry out. Van Maanen (1973) uses the term encounter to describe much of this early period. Since most police officers begin as patrol officers, procedures associated with patrol are likely to be emphasized. As a result, the rookie officer learns (again, formally and informally) the practical applications of many of the concepts and policies that may have been touched upon in the academy. Field training represents for many new officers a "reality check" that brings together for the first time their own ideals and values that led them to policing, the pressures of everyday job demands, and the judgment of individual FTOs (and in a sense, the rest of the department) about how well or how badly they are doing.

After the field training period (generally lasting around six months), and if the new officer has performed tolerably well during this probationary period, he or she enters what Van Maanen calls the metamorphosis stage. He or she begins to look at policing more as a job, and less from the point of view of someone from the outside looking to get into it. Balances are struck between work and other pursuits (family, recreation, etc.) and relationships with other officers (colleagues and superiors) entered into with the idea that the officer is going to be a member of the department for a long time to come.

One important point regarding the transmission of police subculture needs to be made here. It has always been assumed that relevant information regarding the police subculture was passed on from one group to another (usually from veterans to recruits) orally. That is, the veterans told the rookies about "how things are done" and "what this means" as opposed to writing them down and possibly distributing those materials (as is done in the official bureaucracy). Meehan (2000) produces evidence that shows the relevance of newer technologies in the socialization of the police. Instead of story telling, "amusing or sensational audio and videotapes, often remarkable for the startling character of the images they portray than for the relationship to a tradition of shared values" are passed on (Meehan, 2000: 107). One can speculate based on this that even newer technologies such as Internet-based discussion boards and chat rooms may be having an impact on the police subculture as well. Another important variable that affects a new officer's knowledge of the department's structure and friendship patterns is the size of the department (Britz, 1997). Of course, the larger the department, the more of a challenge it becomes to learn about its formal and informal networks.

In all of the four stages mentioned above, it should be noted that the individual police officer is not a passive vessel that the department, through its instructors, FTOs, and others, fills up and shapes as needed. Chan (2001) notes that recruits and trainees participate, reflect, and respond to what they are being told or taught in complex ways. Some may assimilate and imitate departmental advice wholeheartedly, while others may do so partially, while yet others may reject it. As a result, individual policing styles even within a department may vary. It would be safe to say, however, that after socialization into a particular department's subculture, officers within it are likely to be not that much different in terms of policing, but that they are going to be quite different from officers in other departments and from members of the public that they once were.

THE POLICE SUBCULTURE: THREE SOCIOLOGICAL PERSPECTIVES

Let us now use the three sociological perspectives that we have learned and consider how they would view the police subculture. From a functionalist point of view, the police subculture performs some extremely important functions within a police department and among police officers in general. Rules and regulations that govern police behavior in a variety of situations are often nebulous and unclear. The police subculture interprets these rules in a practical and understandable manner to its members. It also serves to socialize new recruits during their police academy experience and during field training into guidelines about "how we do things" and how the wide discretion that all police officers have is to be exercised. Now, given that some aspects of society may also be dysfunctional, it is possible for the subculture to give its members guidelines and informal understandings that serve to subvert the police department's larger goals and functions. For example, merchants may provide officers with free food and drink (a mild form of corruption) and the police subculture will encourage officers to accept these "gifts." You can see how this would be officially unacceptable. Functionalists would expect these practices to disappear over time; otherwise they would serve to undermine the organization's existence.

Conflict theorists, given their view of society and its institutions as a competitive arena, would interpret police subculture differently. They are likely to focus on the pernicious and negative aspects of police subculture and how it affects its members in ways that either (a) result in them siding with powerful groups against others in society or (b) separate them from the people in society that they are supposedly sworn to serve in a manner that makes policing an "us vs. them" endeavor. When police subculture informs new recruits about cues regarding stopping people who look a certain way or drive particular vehicles, this may serve to support racial profiling or other discriminatory law enforcement. Further, just because someone has been arrested and that individual and others strenuously argue his or her innocence, members of the police subculture may automatically assume that he or she is guilty, because they have learned that "there is no smoke without fire." Thus, the police (we) are assumed to be always right as opposed to (them) members of the public who may disagree with them.

In addition to the content of subcultural norms and socialization, the third sociological perspective, interactionism, is likely to be interested in the mechanisms by which these are transmitted and learned by individual members. For example, where do lessons on what is acceptable and unacceptable in terms of the use of force take place? While some of them occur during police academy training and during field training, probably the most influential is what a new officer learns just by watching others and then possibly talking to them informally later. Similarly, interactionists would definitely be interested in what recruits and others learn in both formal and informal settings. For example, a police department we are familiar with describes certain cases and matters as being of acute political emergency (APE). This usually means that the case or issue is of high priority (perhaps, the media are paying attention and it is highly publicized) or high-profile individuals (celebrities and locally or nationally important people) are involved. Now, a new recruit (or an officer from another police department or an ordinary citizen) will have no idea what APE means. What is learned and where it is learned thus becomes a matter of importance to the interactionist.

Now that we are familiar with the idea of a police subculture and how it operates, let us take a look at the same phenomenon in another country, the Philippines. This should help us to also figure out how police subcultures are related to the larger cultures that they are encompassed by.

CULTURE AND POLICE SUBCULTURE INTERNATIONALLY: THE PHILIPPINES

The Philippines is an archipelago (a collection of more than 7,000 islands, large and small) located in Southeast Asia. In terms of culture and society, it has been heavily influenced by its colonial heritage that includes both Spain (earlier) and the United States (from 1899 to 1946) as occupying powers during different historical eras. For example, it is the only major country in Asia that has Christianity (followed by 80% of the population) as its dominant religious tradition (there is also an Islamic population that constitutes 15%). Although it is underdeveloped, the Philippines has always been seen as possessing enormous potential to grow into a regional Asian power (see Kunio, 1994). Despite setbacks, it is in the process of transforming itself into a regional Asian power. After a period of dictatorship, the country reverted to democratic politics in the late 1980s. Among major norms associated with the parent Philippine culture that are transmitted to all its members are concepts such as "hiya" (the shame associated with losing face), "utang na loob" (a debt that can never be repaid), and "kamag anakan" (as a result of which an individual has to do anything and everything possible for a relative).

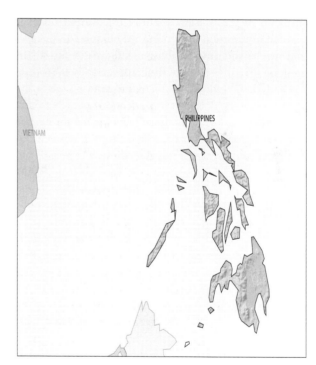

It should, therefore, come as no surprise that its national police organization and structure have taken on features derived from its colonial experiences with Spain (a strong tendency toward centralization) and the United States (working within a democratic ethos, dealing with criticism from a free press, etc.). However, in local "barangays" (communities), the police departments and personnel operate within a subculture that reflects traditions and nuances that adapt the larger

administrative culture. It is this local cultural context that we will explore in trying to understand how the police subculture operates and its personnel have to cope with in order to survive and carry out the essential functions of policing.

Since 1991 the Philippine National Police (PNP) is the federal agency responsible for law enforcement throughout the country. The PNP is the result of the amalgamation (a process that began in 1975) of two antecedent police forces: the national Philippine Constabulary created in 1901 as part of the armed services and the Integrated National Police that consisted of local police agencies. The PNP, numbering around 110,000 officers, is headed by a Director General and is part of the Department of the Interior and Local Government although its structure continues to be hierarchical and militarized.

While describing the presence of extensive corruption within the Philippine police, Kunio (1994: 192) derides it as "rotten to the core." The police "were involved in criminal syndicates undertaking kidnapping, robbery, and car theft (called 'carnapping') in the Philippines." In addition, the PNP has been implicated in harassing and ill treating members of the Muslim minority (there is an ongoing Muslim insurrection in parts of the Philippines), the rape, and mental and physical abuse of children in custody in addition to beating and harassing suspects as well as torturing and killing individuals in confinement. So low is the reputation of the PNP that Morgan and Lopez (1997: 35) provide an example of morbid Philippine humor on this matter: "Question: What is the difference between the PNP and your average criminal syndicate? Answer: There isn't any!" One can easily see how the militaristic traditions of the Philippine police when combined with the stresses of dealing with ongoing organized crime and militant insurgency lead to the subcultural patterns of police behavior that are abusive of human rights and rife with corruption. Recent efforts have been made to demilitarize the police, improve the salary of its poorly paid line officers, enhance their educational qualifications, and get them out on the street interacting with the public.

Stern (2002: 5) notes that while posted as a U.S. Foreign Service officer in the Philippines, he criticized (in a private conversation with one of his assistants) a newly appointed Commissioner of Customs (who had hired members of his family as employees) for nepotism. The point, of course, is that in Filipino society where little is expected of (and even less given by) government, the first responsibility is to family and not to any theoretical construct of "greater good." In the Philippines, the expression is "utang na loob." Add to this the expectation (mentioned above) that individuals have to do their utmost to enhance the welfare of their relatives and the pervasive "unhinged political cynicism" (Somjee and Somjee, 1995) seen in the Philippines. It is possible again to see the expression of important norms from the larger culture in the hiring practices of a Philippine law enforcement organization.

The police occupational subculture in the Philippines can be seen to tolerate or even encourage practices (nepotism, collusion with criminal syndicates, corruption, and human rights violations) that may or may not be supported by the larger polity. The challenge for any police organization is to make sure that the development of its own culture and the inculcation of its own traditions and practices to members do not at the same time result in feelings of apartness from (or superiority over) the public and society it serves. Practices that enhance the police mission (derived from the larger culture or internally cultivated) need to be encouraged while practices that detract from this (again whether originating from the parent culture or from within) need to be questioned and modified or discarded. The PNP appears to be engaged in a similar process of self-examination.

Finally, we learn about the culture of another country (in the accompanying box), Serbia, as it struggles to change the existing police subculture by training its officers in the newer ideas associated with community policing.

 # SUMMARY

An important aspect of understanding the police is to learn about the nature and content of the culture or way of life that they participate in. In this chapter, we learned that culture has both material and nonmaterial aspects, that it is constantly undergoing change, and that there are many commonalities; it is not monolithic. Applying cultural analysis to the police, we learned that they may be considered a part of a subculture, one that is somewhat (though not completely) distinct from the parent or dominant culture. We learned several important characteristics of the police subculture, specifically in the nonmaterial realm such as ideas of separateness from the public as well as solidarity within. The police are socialized into this culture through a variety of mechanisms before and during police academy training and during and after field training. Finally, we learned about the interaction between dominant culture and the police subculture and the consequences of this by looking at another country: the Philippines.

 ## KEY TERMS

Culture: Consists of the total way of life of a society or large group of people.

Field training: A probationary phase that is a period in which a more experienced police officer (referred to as an FTO, who is generally not an academy instructor) guides the trainee on day-to-day routines and practical procedures that members of the department are expected to follow and carry out.

Isolation: The sense of self-differentiation that pervades policing, which if taken to its extreme and without the balance provided by countervailing experiences, results in police officers feeling that they are separate from every other group in society.

Material culture: Is made up of all the tangible objects and inventions that are devised, used, and understood by those who share in a given culture, for example, artifacts such as homes, plates, automobiles, socks, blackboards, the cross as a religious symbol, telephones, the Stars and Stripes, computers, and football stadiums are all part of the material culture of American society.

Nonmaterial culture: Is made up of the intangibles of a culture such as language, customs, values, norms, principles, scientific formulae, etc., that is, it exists at the level of ideas, beliefs, and mental imagery.

Parent (or dominant) culture: The features of a given culture that are identified with the most powerful group or groups in that society.

Police academy: School where officers learn on-the-job techniques prior to receiving full police powers.

Self-differentiation: How the police subculture defines itself as distinct from the public that it is supposed to be protecting and serving.

Solidarity: The social cohesiveness of the police subculture that expects police officers to stick together and help each other out as members of the same "team" under all sorts of circumstances, minor and major.

Subculture: Consists of certain material and nonmaterial aspects of a way of life associated with a group in society that is different from the parent (or dominant) culture.

 ## REVIEW QUESTIONS

1. What does an understanding of the concepts of culture and subculture contribute to the study of policing?

2. Describe the process of socialization into the police subculture during police academy training and subsequently.

3. How does Filipino culture influence the police subculture of the Philippines? Is this a negative or positive influence?

DISCUSSION QUESTIONS

1. Which sociological perspective on police subculture discussed in this chapter do you most agree with? Please explain.

2. How does the police subculture make it difficult for them to interact with the members of the public? How can these barriers be overcome?

3. Do you agree with the idea that the police subculture leads to the isolation of its members from the rest of society? Why or why not?

REFERENCES

Ackoff, Russell L. and Sheldon Rovin (2003) *Redesigning Society.* Stanford, CA: Stanford University Press.

Berg, Bruce L. (1992) *Law Enforcement: An Introduction to Police in Society.* Boston: Allyn and Bacon.

Britz, Marjie T. (1997) "The Police Subculture and Occupational Socialization: Exploring Individual and Demographic Characteristics." *American Journal of Criminal Justice* 21: 127–146.

Chan, Janet (2001) "Negotiating the Field: New Observations on the Making of Police Officers." *Australia and New Zealand Journal of Criminology* 34: 114–133.

Cox, Steven M. (1996) *Police: Practices, Perspectives, Problems.* Boston: Allyn and Bacon.

Crank, John M. (1998) *Understanding Police Culture.* Cincinnati, OH: Anderson Publishing.

Geertz, Clifford (1970) "The Impact of the Concept of Culture on the Concept of Man." Pp. 47–65 In Hammel, Eugene A. and William S. Simmons (eds.) *Man Makes Sense.* Boston: Little, Brown.

Grant, Heath and Karen J. Terry (2005) *Law Enforcement in the 21st Century.* Boston, MA: Pearson Allyn & Bacon.

Hale, Donna C. (1989) "Ideology of Police Misbehavior." *Quarterly Journal of Ideology* 13: 59–95.

Henry, V. E. (1995) "The Police Officer as Survivor: Death Confrontations and the Police Subculture." *Behavioral Sciences and the Law* 13: 93–112.

Herbert, Steve (1998) "Police Subculture Reconsidered." *Criminology* 36: 343–369.

Kunio, Yoshihara (1994) *The Nation and Economic Growth: The Philippines and Thailand.* New York: Oxford University Press.

Mahoney, Thomas E. (1997) *Organizational Socialization and Police Cadet Attitudes in Authoritarian-based Police Academy Environments.* Ann Arbor, MI: University Microfilms International.

Manning, Peter K. (1989) "Occupational Culture." Pp. 360–364 In Bailey, William (ed.) *Encyclopedia of Police Science.* New York: Garland.

McNulty, E. W. (1994) "Generating Common-Sense Knowledge Among Police Officers." *Symbolic Interaction* 17: 281–284.

Meehan, Albert J. (2000) "Transformation of the Oral Tradition of the Police Subculture through the Introduction of Information Technology." *Sociology of Crime, Law and Deviance* 2: 107–132.

Morgan, Peter and Antonio Lopez (1997) "Cleaning Up the Good Guys: Can Manila Rein in Corrupt and Inept Cops?" *Asiaweek* November 11: 35.

Skolnick, Jerome (1996) "A Sketch of the Police Officer's 'Working Personality'." Pp. 89–113 In *Criminal Justice in America: Theory, Practice, and Policy.* Upper Saddle River, NJ: Prentice-Hall.

Somjee, A. H. and Geeta Somjee (1995) *Development Success in the Asia Pacific: An Exercise in Normative–Pragmatic Balance.* New York: St. Martin's Press.

Sparrow, Malcolm; Mark H. Moore and David M. Kennedy (1990) *Beyond 911: A New Era for Policing.* New York: Basic Books.

Stern, Robert H. (2002) "Cross-cultural Communication." *Crime & Justice International* 19 (December): 30.

Swidler, Ann (1992) "Culture in Action: Symbols and Strategies." *American Sociological Review* 51: 273–286.

Talley, Richard A. (1986) "A New Methodology for Evaluating the Curricular Relevancy of Police Academy Training." *Journal of Police Science and Administration* 14: 112–120.

Van Maanen, John (1973) "Observations on the Making of Policemen." *Human Organization* 32: 407–418.

Violanti, John M. (1992) "Coping Strategies Among Police Recruits in a High Stress Training Environment." *Journal of Social Psychology* 132: 717–729.

Waddington, P. A. J. (1999) "Police (Canteen) Sub-culture: An Appreciation." *British Journal of Criminology* 39: 287–309.

Westley, William (1970) *Violence and the Police*. New York: New York University Press.

Wyer, Robert S. (2009) *Understanding Culture: Theory, Research, and Application*. Boca Raton, FL: CRC Press.

CHANGING POLICE SUBCULTURE THROUGH COMMUNITY POLICING TRAINING IN SERBIA

Branislav Simonovic

A pilot project of community policing is at its very beginning in Serbia. This project is a part of police reform in Serbia with the assistance of OSCE and international police cooperation with the police and other state institutions in a great number of developed countries. Police reform in Serbia is being carried out in the following segments: (a) training in contemporary standards of police work; (b) introduction of new methods of external and internal police control; (c) upgrading of methods and techniques of organized crime repression; (d) forensics; (e) introduction of border police; and (f) implementation of community policing.

A working group was established in 2002 with the aim to define the mission, vision, and values to be implemented in the police work in Serbia at the local community level. This working group is a part of macroproject supported and financed by the Danish Center for Human Rights with the aim of developing the missions and visions of strategic reforms of the most important segments of police work in Serbia.

The Commission for development and implementation of the community policing pilot project was established in the Ministry of Internal Affairs of Serbia in July 2000 and it includes, besides national experts, the experts from OSCE. An outline of the future activities on this pilot project has been drawn up. The British government expressed their wish to be included via OSCE into the community policing pilot project in Serbia, and some of their experts had already been engaged with DFID (Department for International Development).

The community policing pilot project in Serbia has started in seven towns with the population ranging from 10,000 to 200,000 people. All the towns have different geographic locations. Some are in the central, well-developed, and urban regions. Some are located in rural and provincial areas. The population in some towns is of different national and religious structure. In some towns with a large number of national minorities, the situation is stable, but in some towns it is tense.

In most of these towns, the preparatory activities on this pilot project have been completed and the local police departments and municipality officials were informed about the project. The commission for the implementation of this pilot project initiated that a Safety Council should be established in each of these towns represented by the police and all relevant subjects of the local community. They have already been established in some of these towns; the preparations are underway in the others. Also the teams to be included in this project have been selected, tasks and duties assigned to the local police, and contacts made with the aim to establish joint working groups with the experts from the police and local community. A specialized independent agency is assessing the public opinion in order to precisely determine the present degree of citizens' trust in police, safety problems, the needs of local citizenry, their expectations in relation to the police and this project, etc.

The next steps will include training of the entire police force (at all levels) in the pilot towns on basic postulates, policy, and global experiences of the community policing, as well as on the planned implementation of the national pilot project. So far the police have been informed about the community policing project through the articles published in the Serbian police journal *Bezbednost*. Fewer policemen were included in seminars and workshops conducted by foreign experts from various countries. This pilot project foresees training and informing of local municipality officials' participation in the realization of this project, media, and public in general.

After a thorough scanning of local needs and assessment of the safety problems to be solved, the individual projects with defined solutions will be drawn up. These projects will be realized by joint efforts of the police and local community experts (multiagency approach). When the training of local policemen is completed, several other community policing schemes and activities will start to be implemented, such as appointment of the beat officers in each area with the aim to implement the neighborhood watch programs and establish close contacts between beat officers and citizens, opening of the citizens' counseling offices, regular contacts with media, and intensification of the programs aimed at the prevention of drug dealing, juvenile delinquency, family violence, threat to vulnerable citizens, and car accidents. The preparations for the implementation of these activities are underway and some of them have already started.

CHAPTER 10

The term community has a variety of meanings. Generally, a community is conceived of a group of people occupying the same geographical areas by which they can identify themselves, and in which a degree of solidarity and social relationships.
(McNall and McNall, 1992: 179)

A Chinese police officer stands on duty near men gathered under a lamp post fitted with security cameras at Tiananmen Square in Beijing, Thursday, Jan. 3, 2008. Beijing has launched a campaign to remove beggars and unlicensed peddlers from Tiananmen Square and a major street running through the city center in the run-up to the Olympic Games, state media reported Thursday. (Credit: © AP Photo/Ng Han Guan)

POLICE AND THE COMMUNITY

OBJECTIVES:

1. The student will learn the major innovations of policing in the nineteenth and twentieth centuries and how it affected the communities served.
2. The student will understand the concept of community as it relates to policing.
3. The student will understand police–community relations and police–race relations.
4. The student will understand community policing and problem-oriented policing.

5. The student will learn about functionalist, conflict theory, and interactionist approaches to analyzing the police–community interaction.

6. The student will learn about police and community on an international level.

The police and the community they serve have a dynamic and interlocking relationship. This relationship may be positive or negative. The idea that the police and community are interconnected may be traced to the concept of order maintenance and the protection of people that we explored in earlier chapters. During ancient times, the family, tribe, or clan assumed the responsibility of protecting its members. In this informal simple process of policing, the people were the police. The Praetorian Guard, a formal form of policing, was established by the Romans to protect the life and property of the emperor. The Romans also established *urban cohorts*, units of 500–600, men to keep the peace of Rome (Palmiotto, 1997: 7–8).

For nearly 200 years, the English police system was structured with citizens being responsible for peacekeeping. This structure of policing known as *mutual pledge* was created by Alfred the Great in the ninth century and is recognized as the first phase in the process leading to modern policing. The mutual pledge system enrolled every male over the age of twelve years for maintaining peace and enforcing the principle that all citizens were held accountable for their neighbors. Under this system, order was maintained through the mutual responsibility of its male citizens since a formalized police structure did not exist.

The **constable** police system evolved as a rural form of policing by the end of the thirteenth century. The parish, a population center of worship, to maintain social order, elected the constable annually. The constable had the responsibility of maintaining the King's peace by the "hue and cry." As a police system, the constable enlisted the entire community and fines were imposed for lack of cooperation and support. In the populated city areas, the *watch and ward* system was established and constables were given the responsibilities of patrolling the streets for fires, guarding the gates of the town between sunset and sunrise, arresting strangers during darkness, and preventing the burglarizing of homes and businesses. The *Statute of Winchester* and the *Justice of Peace Act of 1361* defined the constable and watch and ward police system. This form of policing replaced the mutual pledge systems and its remnants and was in effect until the eighteenth century (Crichley, 1967: 4–9). With the development of the constable and watch and ward systems, we see changes in the previous policing system. Still, this system keeps the constables and watch and ward close to the people. The formal policing system in use today has eliminated the constable and watch and ward systems.

In eighteenth-century Britain, it was literally true that every citizen was a member of the police and every member of the police was a citizen. The only policing system officially recognized was the constable system (Pringle, 1955: 41). According to Patrick Pringle in his book on the **Bow Street Runners**, "The British police was brought into being by reformers, humanitarians, progressives, and radicals; it was formed in defiance

constable

Constable police system evolved as the rural form of policing by the end of the thirteenth century. The parish, a population center of worship, to maintain social order, elected the constable annually. The constable had the responsibility of maintaining the king's peace by the "hue and cry." As a police system, the constable enlisted the entire community and fines were imposed for lack of cooperation and support.

Bow Street Runners

Worked directly for the Bow Street Magistrate who paid their salary. Under the authority of the magistrate, they arrested offenders and apprehended offenders nationwide.

Henry Fielding

Could be credited with initiating modern policing. The policing system he advocated was a strong belief in the police and community partnership. His major goals were to eliminate crime and prevent it in the future.

John Fielding

Used his police budget from the government to increase crime-preventive activities. He increased the number of patrols, and took actions against pickpockets when large crowds existed. He was responsible for tightening up the law against cheats who preyed on tradesmen and established rules for pawnbrokers and required them to obtain a license and to maintain proper records.

of the property-owned capitalists" (12). Contributors in the eighteenth century to British policing were **Henry Fielding** and **John Fielding**. In fact, Henry Fielding could be credited with initiating modern policing. The policing system advocated by Henry and John Fielding and the progressives that followed them were strong believers in the police and community partnership. In 1748, Henry Fielding became the Magistrate of Bow Street. In this position, he also functioned as the Chief-of-Police by maintaining order in his district. Fielding took his position as magistrate during a crime wave. Immediately on assuming his position, Henry Fielding had two goals: eliminate crime and prevent it in the future. In order to achieve these goals, he felt three objectives had to be obtained: "the active co-operation of the public, a stronger police, and the removal of the causes of crime and the conditions in which it flourished" (Pringle, 1955: 81). All three objectives that Fielding hoped to achieve include a positive relationship between the police and community. As a police administrator, Fielding was wise in recognizing that for crime to be controlled, the police need the cooperation of the public. Fielding solicited for the first time something taken for granted in our modern era, that crimes be reported to the police. He placed announcements in the newspapers soliciting the victims of crime to report to him the crime, the description of the offender, and the place, date, time, and circumstances of the offense. By advertising that victims of crime report their offense, Fielding was working toward a police and community partnership. It should be noted that this was an act of originality on the part of Henry Fielding. No one taught of this before Fielding or at least it was not done before Fielding put it into practice.

Being ahead of his time, Henry Fielding introduced preventive policing into England and showed that it was possible to have an efficient police organization without becoming a police state. Henry Fielding turned over his Bow Streets magistrate's position to his half-brother John in 1754. John Fielding remained in this position until 1780 (Pringle, 1955: 114). He used his police budget from the government to increase crime-preventive activities. He increased the number of patrols, and he took actions against pickpockets when large crowds existed. Fielding also used his influence with the government to bring about new legislation to improve policing. He was able to expand the patrol area of the eighty constables under his command. In addition, he was responsible for tightening up the law against cheats who preyed on tradesmen and established rules for pawnbrokers that required them to obtain a license and to maintain proper records. The idea of educating the public on police matters was initiated by Henry Fielding, and continued under John Fielding. He was the first magistrate to allow the press into his court. Also, John Fielding began printing posters with descriptions of those suspected of crimes. These posters were distributed among workers at turnpikes, stables, and public houses (Pringle, 1955: 132–133). John Fielding continued the philosophy of his brother that the police and community must work together to prevent and control crime. Examples of police and community cooperation include increasing preventive police patrols, establishing rules and requiring pawnbrokers to keep records, developing wanted posters, and allowing the news media into courtrooms. Like his brother, John Fielding was ahead of his time, for he developed concepts still in use today to support a good police and community relationship.

Patrick Colquhoun, a disciple of Henry and John Fielding, has been described as the first major writer of public order and the first person to use the term police as it is used in our modern day. Colquhoun was a strong advocate of a centralized, uniform, and paid police system for London. He believed that crime could never be eliminated but that it could be prevented and controlled to minimize its impact (Reynolds, 1998: 90–91). He wrote *A Treatise on the Police of the Metropolis* in 1806, which dealt with London's crime problem and made recommendations to get it under control. Colquhoun's *Treatise* broke new ground in using statistics related to crime and criminals and made a strong point by declaring that the police should be involved in preventing crime. He further believed that the judiciary and police powers should be separated (Crichley, 1967: 38–39). Colquhoun further supported three ideas of Fieldings which stated that a "central police board should organize an intelligence service; it should maintain a register of known offenders, with classified information about particular groups; and it should publish a *Police Gazette*, not only for the purpose of aiding in the detection of crime, but also as a vehicle of moral education" (Crichley, 1967: 39).

Coloquhoun made recommendations on preventing crime and on the establishment of a police department for London. With an increase in crime, Colquhoun believed that the City of London, dependent on commerce, could not survive if excessive criminal activity existed. Colquhoun's *Treatise* led to the passing of the Thames Police Act in 1800. This law established the River Police to safeguard the Thames River and adjacent land from thieves. Establishing the River Police paved the way for police reform and promoted the reforms of Sir **Robert Peel** (Lyman, 2002: 36). Patrick Colquhoun and his reforms took into consideration the police and community. He believed that a community could not survive with a high crime rate, and therefore he believed in preventing and detecting crime.

In 1829, the British Parliament, because of the political acumen of Sir Robert Peel, passed the Metropolitan Police Act to police the City of London. The contribution of Peel consisted of synthesizing decades of thought-about police organization to secure the passage of legislation creating the London Police. He insisted that political patronage be excluded from appointments and promotions. Subsequently, two police Commissioners, Charles Rowan and Richard Mayne, helped to structure the London Police. They established the semimilitary police disciplinary mechanism, the system of officers patrolling fixed beats, the blue uniform, and various other details (Miller, 1973: 2). The new London Police structure rested on the idea that their role was "preventive" and that this approach could reduce crime by preventing it from taking place. Successful crime prevention was dependent on coordinating police activity from a central administration. Of equal importance was having a full-time day and night patrol with sufficient resources to cover the city. It was expected that police officers patrolling a fixed beat would become familiar with the people of their neighborhood. Another important feature of the patrols was visibility, the idea that the police were readily available to assist the public (Miller, 1973: ix–x). The concept of preventive patrol, police visibility, and fixed patrol beats supports the idea of the police and community being involved in interaction and cooperation. The idea of the police being

Patrick Colquhoun

Made recommendations on preventing crime and on the establishment of a police department for London. With an increase in crime, Colquhoun believed that the City of London, dependent on commerce, could not survive if excessive criminal activity was tolerated. Colquhoun's *Treatise* led to the passing of the Thames Police Act in 1800. This law established the River Police to safeguard the Thames River and adjacent land from thieves. Establishing the River Police paved the way for police reform and promoted the reforms. He believed in the prevention of crime, the detection of crime, and the fact that a community could not survive with a high crime rate. His thinking has influenced modern police thinking.

Robert Peel

Passed the Metropolitan Police Act to police the City of London. The contribution of Sir Robert Peel consisted of synthesizing decades of thought-about police organization to secure the passage of the Police Act, creating the London Police. His major contribution to the London Police was his insistence that political patronage be excluded from appointments and promotions.

readily available to assist the public is the cornerstone of modern day policing and the foundation for their partnership.

Modern municipal policing came to the United States when the New York State legislature in 1844 passed legislation to provide funds to combine the city's day and night watches into one police unit. The London Police were the model for the New York City Police Department (NYPD), but since both police departments were implemented under different cultures and political philosophies their developmental paths varied. New York's police authority was personal, rested on the closeness of their relationship with citizens, and was much less bureaucratic or legal than the London Police. However, the New York police were more informal and politically influenced than their London counterparts (Miller, 1973: 16–17). Initially, the New York City Police were not armed and did not wear uniforms. In the 1850s, the New York police became armed and accepted the uniform requirement. This was opposite to the London Police who have never been armed and wore a blue uniform from day one of their existence. Another major distinction between the New York Police and the London Police was what was considered the appropriate use of force to make arrests. Other American cities followed the New York model for their police. Typically, the American police officer came from the neighborhood he patrolled and was to be personal and civil in their dealings with their areas.

Policing in the United States in the nineteenth century grew as the population increased, but for most of the century the police came under political control. As mentioned in Chapter 4, the states made attempts to control the influence of politicians on police departments. To combat political influence, police reformers came to the forefront.

Community

Since this chapter covers police and community, it might be a good idea to discuss what we mean by community. The term community has a number of different meanings. Usually, the term community is applied to a group of people occupying the same geographical area by which they can identify themselves, and in which a degree of solidarity exists (McNall and McNall, 1992: 179). Thus, it is a population residing in a geographical area that embraces all aspects of social life—a local area over which people more often than not are using the same language, conforming to the same mores, feeling more or less the same sentiments, and acting upon the same attitudes. Community is about territoriality, settlement, and social relationships. The term community is generally used to identify local, small geographical groups with communal relationships, such as villages, towns, or neighborhoods (Gusfield, 1975: 32–33), but it may be used to describe a large population in a large geographical area or even a city. Robert MacIver (1936) considers community to mean "an area of common life, village or town, or district, or country or even a wider area" (22). He states that, "to deserve the name community, the area must be somehow distinguished from other areas, and the common life may have some characteristics of its own such that frontiers have some meaning" (23). Robert Nisbet's (1966: 47) writing about community in the nineteenth and twentieth centuries can be applied in the initial decade of the twenty-first century.

> The word, as we find it in much nineteenth and twentieth century thought, encompasses all forms of relationship which are characterized by a high degree of personal intimacy, emotional debt, moral commitment, social cohesion, and continuality of time. Community is founded on man conceived in his wholeness rather than in one or another of the roles, taken separately, that he may hold in social order.

Communities are often described as rural or urban. Population size usually distinguishes rural and urban communities, but this distinction has been criticized as arbitrary and devoid of significance. Other distinguishing criteria used have been density of population and legal status of the locality as rural or urban.

A rural community consists of a group of families on contiguous land who generally think of themselves as living in the same locality. The rural community gives itself a name and interacts with each other through visiting, borrowing, and lending tools, exchanging services, or participating in social activities. Often, a community will have a center for common activities that includes institutions such as a church or school. Community members know one another and their relationships appear to be intimate.

Urban communities generally consist of a large group of people living in a small geographical area who have their own government and engage in various economic enterprises. Urban communities are often a loose structure in the social sense. They are more often than rural communities to be characterized by anonymity. For example, an individual may travel one block from his home and not be known by anyone. Generally, urban communities are more heterogeneous. People living in urban areas are likely to associate with each other chiefly on the basis of interest rather than locality. There is less general association among people than occurs in rural communities. Generally, until recently, it was accepted that urban communities had a higher rate of crime, violence, drugs, divorce, desertion, prostitution, and other forms of deviance. However, rural communities have also seen an increase in violence, crime, drugs, and other forms of deviant behavior that have been associated with the urban community.

Social Service Approach to Policing

The "political era" of policing in the United States lasted from its initiation until about the second decade of the nineteenth century. During this period, there was a close relationship between the police and politicians. Policing was under the control of local government. In urban areas, local politicians oversaw police operations. The police worked closely with the community's politicians to control the neighborhood. Police tasks included crime prevention and order maintenance and a range of social service activities. For example, the police in New York City helped recently arriving immigrants with finding jobs. They distributed supplies to the poor in Baltimore and assisted the homeless in Philadelphia. They were expected to respond to complaints or for requests for assistance. They were not expected to curtail crime (Fogelson, 1977: 16–17).

Although police departments had a centralized hierarchical organizational structure, they did not function along these lines. Usually, the community or neighborhood ward leader had a great say about policing in that area. Police officers reflected the ethnic makeup of the community in which they lived and worked. Kelling and Moore (1988: 4) had the following to say about policing during this era:

> First, police were integrated into neighborhoods and enjoyed the support of citizens—at least the support of the dominant economic and political interests of an area.
>
> Second, and probably as a result of the first, the strategy provided useful services to communities. There is evidence that it helped contain riots. Many citizens believed that police prevented crimes or solve crimes when they occurred. And the police assisted immigrants in establishing themselves in communities and finding jobs.

Initially, women in policing provided social services and were primarily educated and worked as social workers. They supervised dance halls, skating rings, penny arcades, movie theaters, and places of recreation. Women also searched for missing persons. During the early era of women entering the police, it was recognized that the police provided the first line of social defense. In other words, the police had the opportunity to intervene before the social service agencies or the courts could (Higgins, 1951: 824). Women's role in policing was primarily "preventive." Although women police officers had the same authority to make arrests and to enforce criminal laws, neither male nor female officers thought their tasks were similar. The belief, during this period, was that female officers could provide counseling and guidance while the male officers would make arrests (Appier, 1992: 3). Around the 1910s, women began to be involved in policing when the "crime prevention model" was emphasized. The crime prevention model had three major elements (Appier, 1992:5):

1. It was thought that females would be more successful in performing crime prevention activities than the males. The highest form of policing is social work.
2. Crime prevention is the most important function of the police.
3. Women are inherently better than men at preventing crime.

The evolution of women in policing had its roots in the protection movement, initiated by organizations to look after women and children (Appier, 1992: 6–7). From the 1910s to the 1940s, the role of women in policing involved exclusively interpersonal work, for example, tasks that required a high level of empathy, attention to detail, and cooperation with others such as comforting lost children, responding to letters about missing persons, and interviewing female and juvenile offenders and victims of crime. Policewomen made referrals to social service agencies, and gave advice to parents about mischievous children and to married couples on domestic relations cases (Appier, 1992: 17). The social service aspect of policing eventually gave way to the crime-fighting model of policing as discussed in Chapter 6.

An early nineteenth-century police administrator who believed in the police and community cooperation was Arthur Woods, the New York City Police Commissioner from 1914 to 1919. **Commissioner Arthur Woods** was an innovator who broke new

Commissioner Arthur Woods

Police Commissioner of New York City Police Department who believed in police–community relations. An innovator who worked to get the police to interact with the community.

grounds in police and community communication. Woods' vision was to give the rank and file police officer a sense that police officers were important, that the police officers' job had public value. He believed the public would benefit from the police in several ways: "the public would gain an increased respect for police work if citizens came to understand the complexities, difficulties, and significance of the policeman's duties; and through this understanding, the public would be willing to develop rewards for conscientious and effective police performance" (Skolnick and Bayley, 1988: 37). Woods believed deeply in police and community interaction and he directed police Captains to organize junior leagues in their precincts. The youngsters were presented with junior police badges, drilled, and asked to help the police by reporting violations in their neighborhoods. Police Sergeants were assigned to visit schools and students learned that police work was more than making arrests. Police work meant improving the neighborhood, making it safe and a good place to live. To put his philosophy of the police and community working together into practice, Woods established "play streets." The police would place barriers in impoverished neighborhoods for several hours during the day at either end of a tenement street closing it to traffic. Thus, youngsters could play outdoors without danger from traffic. In addition, Commissioner Woods made contact with Greek, Italian, and Yiddish language newspaper publishers and was able to persuade them to print circulars in the language of their paper about city ordinances on such issues as pushcart vendors (Skolnick and Bayley, 1988: 37–38).

Woods was ahead of his time when he held police officers responsible for the social conditions of a street or neighborhood. He believed unemployment a key cause of crime, and police precincts were used for distributing industrial and social information. Unemployed residents could ask the police to assist them in finding employment. Boys who were considered delinquency risks were referred to social agencies such as the YMCA and Big Brothers (Skolnick and Bayley, 1988: 38). The Woods' policing philosophy was appreciated and recognized in New York City. One noted journalist, Cambell McCulloch, wrote the following in *The Outlook*, on February 10, 1915:

> Too many persons and particular the foreign-born population … the law stands for a vast machine of menace. The new police idea is wholly different. It aims to do something that in America seems never to have been tried as an angle of police duty—to strive for the inculcation of the thought that the law is an engine of mutuality, of good will, of positive influence; that it is constructive. The new police idea is to present the police as a protector.

Woods' philosophy was one of respecting people of the community. He saw them as equal partners and felt that police and community relations could only be successful with open dialog that reflected mutual trust and respect. Woods' philosophy gave the police officer a sense of importance and a feeling that the job was vital. It also gave the community a sense of participation and mutual respect when they cooperated with the police. The Woods' policing philosophy continues to be relevant. Police still have difficulties in obtaining the cooperation and respect from the community. This may be more so in impoverished communities than in affluent communities. With the advent of the community policing philosophy, the police are making attempts to put the Woods' philosophy into practice. Later in this chapter, community policing will be discussed.

POLICE–RACE RELATIONS

America's experience with police–race relations can be traced back to 1619 when the first slaves from Africa landed in Jamestown, Virginia. Slaves from Africa did not come willingly to America and resisted the institution of slavery in various ways. Many captured Africans committed suicide while traveling from inland to the coast of Africa. There were insurrections by the Africans traveling from the coast of Africa across the Atlantic to America to be sold into slavery. Slaves in America would steal from their owners, lie, neglect the work they were forced to endure, and run away from their owners (Websdale, 2001: 15–17).

Slave patrols played an important role in controlling slavery. Most counties in the South had slave patrols. Slave patrols checked the passes of slaves when they left plantations. They conducted periodic checks of slave quarters, searching for stolen property and contraband. Slave patrols received compensation for searching plantations for guns and contraband. They also administered whippings for various infractions. Slave patrols would also hunt down runaway slaves (Websdale, 2001: 20–21). It was not unusual for slaves to leave the plantation, to avoid either punishment or work. Communities employed slave patrollers to be on duty during the evenings and generally worked in their own counties. Slave patrols were organized on a legal bureaucratic basis with a Captain as a supervisor (Hadden, 2001: 76–90). Slave patrollers were farmers and businessmen who worked in this capacity to supplement their income. Slave patrols provided security for White residents in Southern communities. Men in slave patrols were responsible for areas closest to their homes. With the ending of the Civil War and the passage of the Thirteenth Amendment, slave patrolling ended (Hadden, 2001: 198).

The federal government passed constitutional amendments to protect the rights of Blacks from abuses, for example, by the police. During the Reconstruction period, 1865–1877, Amendments were added to the U.S. Constitution giving Blacks equality along with the passage of federal legislation that protected the civil rights of Blacks. The Thirteen, Fourteenth, and Fifteenth Amendments (or Civil War Amendments) did the following: the Thirteenth Amendment outlawed slavery, the Fourteenth Amendment gave citizenship to former slaves, and the Fifteenth Amendment gave voting rights to Black males.

Immediately after the Civil War, several Southern states passed legislation designed to separate Whites and Blacks in public places. The Reconstruction period was short-lived and Southern Whites eventually regained political power that they lost during the Reconstruction period. In the 1880s, segregationist laws began to be passed to give Whites supremacy over Blacks. In 1881, Tennessee passed the South's first Jim Crow law, segregating the races on railroad cars. In 1887, the U.S. Supreme Court declared the Civil Rights Act of 1875 (which made it illegal to discriminate against Blacks in public facilities) unconstitutional (Websdale, 2001: 23). The Supreme Court decision that sealed Jim Crowism was the 1896 *Plessy v. Ferguson* case that spelled out the separate-but-equal doctrine. The Supreme Court thus approved segregation and Jim Crow was the law of the South until the 1954 U.S. Supreme Courts decision in **Brown v. Board of Education** *of Topeka* overturned *Plessy v. Ferguson.*

The police maintain the status quo of society and with the implementation of Jim Crow laws, police in the Southern states were given the responsibility of enforcing these laws. Although Blacks have been discriminated against, other groups have also borne the brunt of discrimination and of physical and verbal abuse. Mexican Americans, primarily in the Southwest, have for decades been victims of discrimination and prejudice. The Japanese in the West, the Jews, and to some extent the Italians suffered racial discrimination and prejudice. During the development of the United States, various minorities have suffered discrimination and been the victim of mob violence. Members of minority groups were often not allowed to be police officers and if they were, could not get promoted or obtain choice assignments.

Throughout America's history, collaboration between the police and minority communities was nonexistent and poor at best. The 1960s were a low point. In surveys conducted for the *Task Force Report: The Police* (1967), a substudy of The President's Commission, the following was found: "nonwhites, particularly Negroes, are significantly more negative than whites in evaluating police effectiveness in law enforcement; Negroes show greater attitude differences from whites with regard to police discourtesy" (146). *The Task Force Report* further indicated that the police did not provide adequate police protection to Blacks, that they were often cause of the riots that occurred in Black neighborhoods in the 1960s, and that often the police did not treat them as human beings (148). According to *The Task Force Report*, the following occur when the police and the community lack cooperation and mutual respect (1967: 144):

1. Hostility, or even lack of confidence of a significant portion of the public, has extremely serious implications for the police. The attitude interferes with recruiting, since able young men generally seek occupations that are not inordinately dangerous and that have the respect and support of their relatives and friends.

2. Public hostility affects morale, and makes police officers less enthusiastic about doing their jobs well. It may lead some officers to leave the force, to accept more prestigious or less demanding jobs.

3. Many police officers now view their relations with the public as poor. This has been reflected in surveys of patrolmen as well as in their statements.

Without question minorities had a negative attitude toward the police in the 1960s. This negative attitude toward the police had to be addressed. It could not continue and the reform approach consisted of police–community relations programs.

Brown v. Board of Education

The 1954 U.S. Supreme Court decision that found segregation in education was unconstitutional.

POLICE–COMMUNITY RELATIONS

With the police having a major problem with the ethnic and racial minority communities, something had to be done to bridge the gap that existed. Not only did the police have a problem of lost trust with minority communities, but they also had problem with middle and upper class communities. A large segment of the population was against the Vietnam War and a portion of White society demonstrated against it. The police were placed in a position of maintaining order against an unpopular war. They were forced to enforce laws that were not popular. In addition, they had to handle problems of society that were not their doing and for which they lacked control over.

During the 1960s and the 1970s, "police–community relations" became an important issue. Police departments created police–community relations programs; colleges and universities began courses in police–community relations. A number of books were published on this topic. The President's Commission on Law Enforcement and Administration of Justice in *The Challenge of Crime in a Free Society* defined police–community relations as (1967: 100):

> It is not a public-relations program to "sell the police image" to the people. It is not a set of expedients whose purpose is to tranquilize for a time an angry neighborhood by, for example, suddenly promoting a few Negro officers in the wake of a racial disturbance. It is a long-range, full-scale effort to acquaint the police and the community with each other's problems and to stimulate action aimed at solving those problems.

The President's Crime Commission (as the President's Commission on Law Enforcement and Justice is referred to) emphasized that police–community relations is not the business only of a specialized unit but of every member of the department. It further recommended that police–community relations involve not only instituting programs and the changing of procedures and practices, but also re-examining police officers' attitudes. The President's Commission suggested that the police learn to listen to people and to understand why people are critical of them. People who are critical of the police will have a difficult time respecting them and cooperating with them. Police officers will find it difficult to maintain their poise and equanimity when they are denounced and sneered at, or even threatened. Further, the police must adapt themselves to the rapid changes in patterns of behavior that were taking place in the United States (100). The Commission recommended (100–101):

> Police departments in all large communities should have community-relations machinery consisting of a headquarters unit that plans and supervises the department's programs. It should also have precinct units, responsible to the precinct commander, that carry out the programs. Community relations must be both a staff and line function. Such machinery is a matter of greatest importance in any community that has a substantial minority population.

During the period the President's Crime Commission was in operation, American police officers were being accused of police brutality against minorities. The McCone Commission, which investigated riots in Los Angeles, observed (1965: 28):

> An examination of seven riots in northern cities of the U. S. in 1964 reveals that each one was started over a police incident, just as the Los Angeles riot started with the arrest of Marquette Frye. In each of the 1964 riots "police brutality" was an issue, as it was here, and indeed, as it has been in riots and insurrections elsewhere in the world. The fact that this charge is repeatedly made must not go unnoticed, for there is a real danger that persistent criticism will reduce and perhaps destroy the effectiveness of law enforcement.

The image of the police during the mid-1960s to early 1970s was low. Police–community relations programs sought to regain trust and respect for the police. Earle (1980: 37) outlined eight police–community crises areas during this time: (1) loss of faith in the police; (2) attention to community groups; (3) verbal abuse; (4) police–citizen contacts; (5) professional attitude, training, and appearance; (6) police brutality; (7) police isolation; (8) confusing laws. Some of these crises exist today. Alvin Cohen and Emilio Viano (1976: 502–503) observed the following: "Loss of faith in the law enforcement establishment is increasingly manifested among the citizenry, especially minority group members, by increases in crime rates and riots; community indifference; charges of police prejudice, brutality, and disrespect for citizens; and complaints of lack of police protection."

Community residents play a major role in crime control and prevention. Without citizens' willingness to report, the police often would not know that a crime has occurred. The police would also have a difficult time in solving crimes if victims and witnesses would not step forward. Thus, the concept of police–community relations was advocated to solve the crises that existed between the police and the community. This implies that the interaction between the two is an important element in successful policing. A police–community relationship serves several purposes (Pace and Curl, 1985: 8):

1. It allows agents of the system to more fully understand the importance of human behavior.

2. It lets the different components of the system know what kind of services the public desires.

3. It is a vehicle to let the public know what they are getting in services, thus serving as an information and public relations media.

4. It allows the agents of the system and the public to interact on common problems and to develop positive attitudes about one another.

5. It allows the public and the system to work in a mutual endeavor to curb community problems. These problems are often not of a criminal nature, and the agency acts merely as a catalyst to resolve a social problem. For example, a court may collect payments for child support even though no criminal or civil tort has ever been taken.

In the 1970s, departments emphasized team policing, directed patrol, and crime prevention. These strategies along with police–community relations became incorporated into community policing. In the late 1970s, the United States entered a period of relative calm. The 1980s were referred to as the "decade of greed" and the 1990s, the decade of prosperity. In the 1980s, community policing philosophy came to the fore.

COMMUNITY POLICING

We come to a consideration of community-oriented policing, the latest philosophical trend in this area. The concept of community-oriented policing has a variety of meanings. Some police administrators believe that community policing has always taken place in smaller police departments, where the police officers know most residents on a first-name basis. Some police administrators consider problem-oriented policing (see next section) to be community policing. Others believe that community policing consists of specialized units who often are assigned to high-crime areas. Probably, some police administrators give lip service to community policing, since they consider it to be the latest buzzword or police fad, and often claim they are committed to community policing and have implemented it in their departments. Community policing "is one of those terms that simultaneously suggests so much that is general and so little that is specific that it risks being a barrier rather than a bridge to discourse about development in policing" (Wycoff, 1988: 104). Community policing can be a confusing term but several researchers have provided several useful definitions. Stipak (1994) offers a good definition: "Community policing is a management strategy that promotes the joint responsibility of citizens and police for community safety, through working partnerships and interpersonal contacts" (115). Robert Trojanowicz provided an expanded definition that is as valid today as when he first gave it (Trojanowicz and Bucqueroux, 1994: 2–3):

> Community policing is a philosophy and an organizational strategy that promotes a new partnership between people and their police. It is based on the premise that both the police and the community must work together to identify, prioritize and solve contemporary problems such as crime, drugs, fear of crime social and physical disorder, and overall neighborhood decay, with the goal of improving the overall quality of life in the area.

Unlike traditional policing which holds that the community has no role to play in policing, the concept of community policing focuses on a partnership with both the police and community as equals. Community problems must be solved with the involvement of both entities. Thus, the beat officer functions as a "mini" police chief who is a problem-solver. This beat officer works closely with the community with the common goal of maintaining a quality of life that is safe to live and work in. Two scholars Skolnick and Bayley (1988), who have studied community policing in departments throughout the world, concluded that common elements to all the community policing approaches exist. These are:

1. a growing reliance on "community-based crime prevention" through the use of citizen education, neighborhood watches, and similar techniques, as opposed to relying entirely on police patrols to prevent crime;

2. the reorientation of patrol from being primarily an emergency-response force (chasing calls) to using "proactive" techniques such as foot patrol;

3. increased police accountability to the citizens they serve;

4. decentralization of command and police authority, with more discretion allowed to lower ranking "generalist" officers, and more initiative expected of them.

Bayley (1994: 104) further describes community policing as "the most serious and sustained attempt to reformulate the purpose of and practice of policing since the development of the 'professional' model in the early twentieth century." He notes that community policing rests on three points. First, the police cannot solve society's crime problems alone. Second, the resources of the police have to be deployed proactively against crime and criminals. Third, routine police patrol is too passive; it does not deter crime. Police patrol should create a moral order with a respectable public appearance, and behavior should reflect the standards of the local community (102–104).

In a study of community policing in Chicago, DuBois and Hartnett (2002) found four key lessons about community involvement in community policing. First, community support must be won; it should not be assumed that the community would support the police. Second, to obtain community involvement, the community must be organized. Third, training in community policing is as important for the community as it is for the police. Fourth, there is a risk that not all members of the community will buy into the police and community partnership (5).

For community policing to be successful, organizational change of the police structure must occur. Traditionally, the police organization has had a paramilitary, bureaucratic structure. Historically, police administrators ruled in an autocratic manner with the supervisor or person with the highest rank never being questioned by a subordinate. The management philosophy of policing has been a "do as I tell you" approach. For community policing to work, a more democratic approach to management is needed. Here, employees of all ranks and at all levels should be involved in the decision-making process. Changes in training and recruitment, leadership style, and promotion criteria are needed. A flattening of the police hierarchical structure also seems beneficial to the community policing philosophy. Changes in the police structure require that clarification and articulation of the department's values be clearly spelled out and that these values serve as guidelines for department personnel (Birzer, 2000: 244–245).

Community policing requires internal and external support. External support is needed from elected officials, business owners, community activists, residents, and public and nonprofit agencies. Internal support for community policing should come from all those employed by the police department such as sworn police officers and civilians, line and staff personnel, supervisors, command staff, and rank and file. Police executives should support decentralization and a close police and community partnership. Supervisors and police personnel working in the community should be involved in decision making in their community (Birzer, 2000: 245). Finally, as mentioned, the sector that the beat police officer is responsible should be considered a "mini-police department" with the beat officers solving community problems with the community.

PROBLEM-ORIENTED POLICING

The concept of "problem-oriented policing" has been infused as an important element of community policing. "Problem-oriented policing is an approach to policing that encourages and assists all members of a police agency to engage in proactive problem solving. For all practical purposes, the philosophy of community policing has as its foundation the problem-oriented police design" (Palmiotto, 2000: 194). This approach, expounded by Goldstein (1979, 1990) and Eck and Spelmen (1988), attempts to go beyond the limitations of traditional policing by focusing on the ends of policing rather than the means. It encourages police initiatives to address community problems, attempting to solve them by analyzing their causes, assessing the appropriateness of current strategies, developing new solutions and monitoring their effectiveness, and engaging community resources and input. Goldstein (1990) describes problem-oriented policing as based on the following:

1. Policing consists of dealing with a wide range of quite different problems, not just crime.

2. These problems are interrelated, and the priority given to them must be reassessed rather than ranked in traditional ways.

3. Each problem requires a different response, not a generic response that is applied equally to all problems.

4. Use of the criminal law is but one means of responding to a problem; it is not the only means.

5. Police can accomplish much in working to prevent problems rather than simply responding efficiently to an endless number of incidents that are merely the manifestation of problems.

6. Developing an effective response to a problem requires prior analysis rather than simply invoking traditional practices.

7. The capacity of the police is extremely limited, despite the impression of omnipotence that the police cultivate and others believe.

8. The police role is more akin to that of facilitators, enabling and encouraging the community to maintain its norms governing behavior, rather than the agency that assumes total responsibility for doing so (179).

Problem-oriented projects can range from fighting fear of crime, as Baltimore County did in the 1980s, to controlling prostitution as Wichita, Kansas, did, to holding a community safety fair, as Sedgwick County Sheriff's Department in Kansas did. They can focus on minor community problems to very serious ones, e.g., gangs, curfew violations, drug dealing, crack houses, graffiti on buildings, burglaries, robberies, or malicious mischief. (Palmiotto, 2000: 187–188)

POLICING AND THE COMMUNITY: THREE SOCIOLOGICAL PERSPECTIVES

Let us use the three sociological perspectives that we have identified to understand how they would see the relationship between the police and the community. From a functionalist perspective, police relationships with the community can be either functional (positive) or dysfunctional (negative). Obviously, every department would like to be in a functional relationship with the community it serves. Here, the public would have confidence in the police department's ability to deal with crime and related problems and would exhibit their trust in the police department by reporting crime to them and interacting with them in a friendly way. Thus, the partnership that is so important to the philosophy of community policing would be nurtured. The other and opposite reality may be, however, that the community may have lost confidence in the department and is suspicious of it. Over time, members of the police department would also reciprocate with anger at, and with suspicion and harassment of, citizens they see as noncooperative or not helpful. As you can see, this sets up a vicious cycle of problems generating greater problems between the police and their community. The challenge for all police departments then, from a functionalist perspective, is not fall into this vicious dysfunctional cycle that would serve to tear apart the two entities.

Given their view of the police as representing the powers that be and those who control what is permissible in a given community, conflict theorists are likely to be suspicious of efforts by the police to connect with the community. These efforts are not as innocuous as they may seem. Whose interests are the police serving when they ingratiate themselves in this way with the public? conflict theorists would ask. They would see it as a mechanism for controlling lower classes and minority groups for the upper classes and majority group. This is done so that those oppressed by the system are lulled into believing that the police are impartial and even-handed and care about subordinate groups. For the conflict theorist, this is, of course, far from the truth.

From an interactionist standpoint, there would be two interests. The first is in understanding what the police "mean" when they say that they are doing "community policing." What activities come under this title and what do not and who decides this? For example, an officer who is on bicycle patrol in a public park chats with people gathered there. Is the officer now engaging in community policing or merely carrying out the traditional policing function of patrolling? How does this get defined and by whom? The second interest that interactionists would have is to identify from the public's point of view what their understanding of community policing is. In the above example, when the bicycle officer stops to talk to a group of people in a part, what are the cognitive, emotional, and behavioral meanings that people in that group attach to the interaction? Do they see it as threatening, an invasion of privacy, an enjoyable conversation, or something else? The use of various cues on the part of the officer (e.g., smiling or not smiling, tone of voice, and body positioning) would be of interest to an interactionist.

As mentioned earlier in this chapter, community policing appears to be a universally acceptable philosophy for many police forces throughout the world. One such country is China, which given its history, size, and vastness possesses major challenges. Next, we take a brief look at how community policing is accomplished there.

POLICING AND THE COMMUNITY INTERNATIONALLY: CHINA

Traditionally, China has left social control or the more familiar term, law and order, to local communities. Social life was regulated first by the family, then the community, and as a last resort, the state would step in. Continuing this tradition of maintaining social order, the People's Republic of China has empowered local people to take control of their own communities by involving them in community policing as indicated by community solidarity, community activism, and a low crime rate (Wong, 2001: 128–129). The following traditions on social regulations and crime control seem to fit into the community policing philosophy. "First, crime control is a local, indigenous and above all, family affair; second, crime control starts with prevention; third, to be effective, crime prevention must be multifaceted, comprehensive, and integrated enterprise, involving the individual, family, clan, neighborhood, community, and state; and fourth, to be effective, crime control and prevention measures should be variegated" (Wong, 2001: 131). The Chinese tradition of order maintenance fits well into the community policing philosophy. For example, the community policing philosophy holds that the people are stakeholders in controlling crime and that they should be involved in crime prevention and control. In addition, the Chinese approach to community policing that holds the family and community as the first lines of defense of social order is in tune with the community policing philosophy (see also Jiao, 1995, 2001).

Although community policing appears to be an innovative policing approach, in preindustrialized

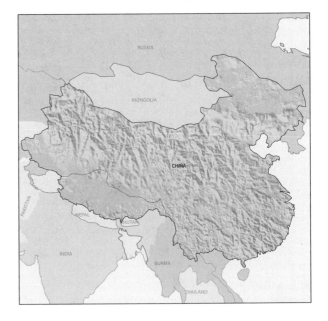

societies this has not always been the case. China provides an excellent example of holding social control at the local level on an informal basis. The idea that order maintenance was a local concern has a long historical tradition in Chinese philosophy (Wong, 2001: 142–143) of government and individual societal relationships.

Finally, we learn about the challenges of policing far-flung urban and rural communities in a country that is less populated than China but is still vast geographically, that is, Australia (see accompanying box).

SUMMARY

The concept of police and community can be found as far back as ancient times when the people and the police were one. During ancient times, the family, tribe, or clan assumed the responsibility of protecting its members. The evolution of policing was a slow process and is continuing to this day.

The U.S. police system has its roots in England where it was held that citizens were responsible for peacekeeping. Every male over the age of twelve years was responsible for maintaining peace. Eventually, the constable system arose with that individual responsible for maintaining the "king's peace." It was not until 1829 that modern policing was initiated in London. The concept of the London Police was one of crime prevention with the police organized under a centralized administration.

Modern municipal policing came to the United States when the New York State legislature in 1844 passed legislation to provide funds to combine New York City's day and night watch into one police unit. The NYPD was modeled on the London Police. New York City became the model for the rest of the country. Initially, the police took a social approach to policing but during the 1930s a crime-fighting approach was adopted. The crime-fighting model continues to be

vogue. However, during the 1980s, community policing became popular and more recently, has adopted or claimed to have been adopted by a large number of police departments.

Community policing may be considered an outgrowth of race relations and police–community relations. Police scholars and officials recognized that the police, to be successful, need the cooperation and support of the people who reside in their communities. The police will be unable to maintain order if the people lack respect and trust of the police and refuse to cooperate in assisting the police in maintaining order. Community policing as a concept requires the police to work jointly with citizens of the community who will be given input in issues affecting the community. The police following the community policing philosophy will be "problem-solvers." They will identify the problem, analyze the problem, develop solutions, and evaluate the solution to determine if was successful. Under the community policing philosophy, the police and community are working together as a team to be problem-solvers of mutual problems to both the police and community. Finally, we considered community policing in a country that is dissimilar to the United States in terms of its social structure and culture: China.

KEY TERMS

Bow Street Runners: Worked directly for the Bow Street Magistrate who paid their salary. Under the authority of the magistrate, they arrested offenders and apprehended offenders nationwide.

Brown v. Board of Education: The 1954 U.S. Supreme Court decision that found segregation in education was unconstitutional.

Commissioner Arthur Woods: Police Commissioner of New York City Police Department who believed in police–community relations. An innovator

who worked to get the police to interact with the community.

Constable: Constable police system evolved as the rural form of policing by the end of the thirteenth century. The parish, a population center of worship, to maintain social order, elected the constable annually. The constable had the responsibility of maintaining the king's peace by the "hue and cry." As a police system, the constable enlisted the entire community and fines were imposed for lack of cooperation and support.

Henry Fielding: Could be credited with initiating modern policing. The policing system he advocated was a strong belief in the police and community partnership. His major goals were to eliminate crime and prevent it in the future.

John Fielding: Used his police budget from the government to increase crime-preventive activities. He increased the number of patrols, and took actions against pickpockets when large crowds existed. He was responsible for tightening up the law against cheats who preyed on tradesmen and established rules for pawnbrokers and required them to obtain a license and to maintain proper records.

Patrick Colquhoun: Made recommendations on preventing crime and on the establishment of a police department for London. With an increase in crime, Colquhoun believed that the City of London, dependent on commerce, could not survive if excessive criminal activity was tolerated. Colquhoun's *Treatise* led to the passing of the Thames Police Act in 1800. This law established the River Police to safeguard the Thames River and adjacent land from thieves. Establishing the River Police paved the way for police reform and promoted the reforms. He believed in the prevention of crime, the detection of crime, and the fact that a community could not survive with a high crime rate. His thinking has influenced modern police thinking.

Robert Peel: Passed the Metropolitan Police Act to police the City of London. The contribution of Sir Robert Peel consisted of synthesizing decades of thought-about police organization to secure the passage of the Police Act, creating the London Police. His major contribution to the London Police was his insistence that political patronage be excluded from appointments and promotions.

REVIEW QUESTIONS

1. Explain police–community relations to a citizens' group.
2. Explain the history of police–race relations.
3. Sell community policing to your colleagues.

DISCUSSION QUESTIONS

1. Police should be familiar with key policing innovators and thinkers. Discuss.
2. There is a similarity between police–community relations and community policing. Discuss.
3. Community policing should be the model for all police departments. Discuss.

REFERENCES

Appier, Janis (1992) "Preventive Justice: The Campaign for Women Police, 1910–1940." *Women and Criminal Justice* 4, 1: 3-36.

Bayley, David H. (1988 or 1994) *Police for the Future*. New York, NY: Oxford University Press.

Birzer, Michael (2000) "Organizational Change and Community Policing." In M. J. Palmiotto (ed.) *Community Policing: A Policing Strategy for the 21st Century*. Gaithersburg, MD: Aspen Publishers.

Cohen, Alvin and Emilio C. Viano (1976) *Police Community Relations: Images, Roles, Realities*. Philadelphia, PA: J.B. Lippincott Co.

Crichley, T. A. (1967) *A History of England and Wales 900–1966*. London: Constable.

DuBois, Jill and Susan M. Harnett (2002) "Making the Community Side of Community Policing Work: What Needs to be Done?" In D. J. Dennis (ed.) *Policing and Community Partnerships*. Upper Saddle River, NJ: Prentice-Hall.

Earle, Howard H. (1980) *Police–Community Relations: Crisis in Our Time*. Third Edition. Springfield, IL: Charles C. Thomas Publisher.

Eck, John E. and William Spelman (1988) *Problem-solving: Problem-oriented Policing in Newport New*. Washington, DC: National Institute of Justice.

Fogelson, R. M. (1977) *Big City Police*. Cambridge, MA: Harvard University Press.

Goldstein, Herman (1979) "Improving Policing: A Problem-oriented Approach." *Crime and Delinquency* 25, 2.

Goldstein, Herman (1990) *Problem-oriented Policing*. New York, NY: McGraw-Hall.

Gusfield, J. (1975) *Community: A Critical Response*. New York, NY: Harper and Row.

Hadden, Sally E. (2001) *Slave Patrols: Law and Violence in Virginia and Carolinas*. Cambridge, MA: Harvard University Press.

Higgins, Lois (1951) "Historical Background of Policewomen's Service." *Journal of Criminal Law, Criminology, and Police Science* 41, March/April.

Jiao, Allen Y. (1995) "Community Policing and Community Mutuality: A Comparative Analysis of American and Chinese Police Reforms." *Police Studies* 18, 1: 69–91.

Jiao, Allen Y. (2001) "Police and Culture: A Comparison between China and the U. S." *Police Quarterly* 4: 156–185.

Kelling, George and Mark Moore (1988) "The Evolving Strategy of Policing." *Perspective on Policing*, No. 4. Washington, DC: US Justice Department.

Lyman, Michael D. (2002) *The Police: An Introduction*. Second Edition. Upper Saddle River, NJ: Prentice-Hall.

MacIver, R. M. (1936) *Community: A Sociological Study*. London: Macmillan.

McCone, John (1965) McCone Commission Report, New York, NY: Macmillan.

McCulloch, Cambell (1915) *The Outlook*.

McNall, Scott and Sally McNall (1992) *Sociology*. Englewood Cliffs, NJ: Prentice-Hall.

Miller, Wilbur R. (1973) *Cops and Bobbies*. Chicago, IL: University of Chicago.

Nisbet, R. (1966) *The Sociological Tradition*. New York, NY: Basic Books.

Pace, Denny F. and Beverly A. Curl (1985) *Community Policing Concepts*. Sacramento, CA: Custom Books.

Palmiotto, Michael J. (1997, 2000) *Policing: Concepts, Strategies, and Current Issues in American Police Forces*. Durham, NC: Carolina Academic Press.

Pringle, Patrick (1955) *Hue and Cry*. London: William Morrow and Company.

Reynolds, Elaine A. (1998) *Before the Bobbies*. Stanford, CA: Stanford California Press.

Skolnick, Jerome H. and David H. Bayley (1988) *Community Policing: Issues and Practices Around the World*. Washington, DC: National Institute of Justice.

Stipak, B. (1994) "Are You Really Doing Community Policing?" *Police Chief*, October.

The President's Commission on Law Enforcement and Administration of Justice (1967) *Task Force Report: The Police*. Washington, DC: U.S. Government Printing Office.

Trojanowicz, Robert and Bonnie Bucqueroux (1994) *Community Policing: A Contemporary Perspective*. Cincinnati, OH: Anderson.

Websdale, Neil (2001) *Policing the Poor: From Slave Plantation to Public Housing*. Boston, MA: Northwestern University Press.

Wong, Kam C. (2001) "Community Policing in China: Philosophy, Law and Practice." *International Journal of the Sociology of Law* 29.

Wycoff, Mary Ann (1988) "The Benefits of Community Policing: Evidence and Conjecture." In J. R. Green and S. D. Mastrosfski (eds.) *Community Policing: Rhetoric or Reality*. New York, NY: Praeger.

COMMUNITY AND POLICING IN AUSTRALIA: STYLES OF POLICING IN RURAL AND URBAN COMMUNITIES

John Scott and Patrick C. Jobes

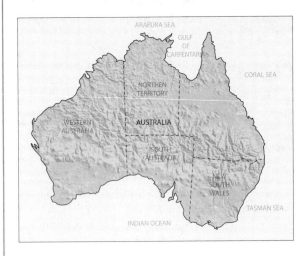

Our premise is that the strategies and techniques that police officers employ are adaptations to the types of communities they serve and the law enforcement system of which they are part. A characteristic of Australian policing is that law enforcement occurs through a single state police service. Observations of policing in rural and urban areas of New South Wales (NSW), Australia, indicate that, despite being part of a single state police service, officers develop working philosophies that are systematically adapted to the locations they serve.

Community is among the most diverse and contentious concepts in the social sciences (Dewey, 1960). Tönnies' (1957) distinction between *Gemeinschaft* and *Gesellschaft* guides our discussion. The ideal type *Gemeinschaft* is a village which has a long-standing, small, self-sufficient, stable population who know each other informally and share common beliefs, values, and behaviors. The ideal type *Gesellschaft* is a city with fluid, large, heterogeneous population who use secondary interaction to accommodate to a diverse normative system. Although not technically a continuum, we describe rural and urban as ranging between these idealized extremes of social organization.

Rural communities and urban cities are much more complex and diverse than these definitions. While it is possible to simplistically compare rural and urban, more accurate analyses require examining how different types of rural communities generate different amounts and types of crime. In NSW, rural towns range from tiny homogenous primary industry villages to rapidly expanding small cities with mixed demographic composition. Although similar differentiation exists between cities, the differences between locations in cities provide more information for understanding types of crime and styles of policing (Pennings, 1999).

Structural conditions, such as characteristics of the local population, the quality of the community, and established systems of social support, influence crime rates. Levels of crime in New South Wales are associated with residential instability, income inequality, levels of education, higher proportions of youth, and unemployment in both rural and urban areas (Weatherburn and Lind, 1998). The range of criminal activities in rural areas is similar to those in cities, though rural communities have more of specific offenses such as stock theft, large-scale drug importation and cultivation, illegal fishing and shooting, and environmental crimes (Pennings, 1999). Crime in rural Australia has recently attracted attention amid concern over youth suicide, Indigenous crime, hate crime, and domestic abuse. Increases in crime in rural communities have been interpreted as a response to a struggling rural economy. Law enforcement is one function among many in rural settings. In most rural communities, officers are as likely to administer to tragedies and accidents as they are to serious crime.

Rural areas on average have lower rates of indexed crimes than do urban areas (Mukherjee, Walker, Scandia, and Dagger, 1987). Sydney and Perth, respectively, had victimization rates of 10.4% and 14.6%, compared to 7.8% and 9.7% for New South Wales and Western Australia (Australian Bureau of Statistics, 1999, 2000a, 2000b). However, rural averages emphasize the low crime rates of modal small homogenous primary industry towns and mask the extremely high crime rates of a few, largely racially polarized towns. Indeed, some statistics indicate that rates for select offenses may be higher than the Sydney metropolitan area, clearly cautioning against a romanticized reading of "the bush" as a law and order Arcadia. A broad distinction can be drawn between low- and high-crime rural communities. Similar differences are also found in cities, where inner city and socially disorganized suburbs exhibit disproportionately higher crime rates than other suburbs.

Social fragmentation has been closely associated with highly urbanized environments where there is greater anonymity, population transience, and a general weakening of social control institutions. In communities characterized by fragmentation and conflict, police are likely to develop strong ties of mutual dependence. Police may adopt a "closed shop," avoiding criticism and harassment by isolating and insulating themselves from the communities they serve (Jobes, 2002). As a result, police develop distinctive police-centered cultures with unique normative structures. In the extreme, interaction with the public may be reduced to confrontational associations, typified by an "us and them" mentality, which defines community as "outsiders" and locates officers on "the inside." Consultation between community and police is viewed as interference and interactions are based on a client–server relationship in which the public are passively dependent on the police.

The small size and relative isolation of most rural towns in NSW provide increased opportunity for intimate and informal interaction between police and local communities. Police typically reside within such communities, their private lives being closely intertwined with their public role. Local officers are often known to the community and connected to the community through informal social networks. Accomplished officers are integrated into a local community and make effective use of established local social networks, adopting a "peacekeeping" role commensurate with community expectations regarding the proper duties of a police officer. Successful integration into a community can indirectly reduce crime and accelerate law enforcement responses as an officer becomes increasingly sensitive to and familiar with the vagaries of a local environment, local population, and local social organization. As a consequence, clearance rates in rural areas are typically higher than in cities. The more integrated an officer is within a community, the more likely residents are to confide information that leads to apprehending a suspect. What develops is a "localistic," as opposed to "legalistic," approach to policing. Greater importance is accorded to establishing and maintaining public tranquility or "the peace," as opposed to imposing law and order at any cost. Most police have no difficulty in adapting to this role. Police in rural towns tend to view their communities as having little crime and see their role as that of providing a community service (Jobes, 2002).

As indicated, with a localistic model of policing, the public influences how police work is done. The community has more input defining important aspects of the role of the police, including police discretion. Police discretion is not solely influenced by the organizational structure of a department but is likely to be influenced by the way in which the community is organized. Immersion into the community can exacerbate the problematic aspects of police work, as local officers are expected to become part of the community, even if it compromises objectivity. This may produce strain between roles of an officer as law enforcer and local resident. Yet, the reward is community support, which can improve quality of life and allow police to carry out their work more effectively (Jobes, 2002).

The localistic model does not necessarily translate to an idealized form of community policing. A localistic approach may be helpful in *Gemeinschaft* communities, but is likely to present problems in less integrated communities where officers may be compelled to privilege particular social groups and sectional interests. Powerful groups in the community may significantly influence how police determine who is and is not subject to surveillance. The outcome may lead to over- or under-policing of specific interest communities. While policing is a partnership for some members of the community, for others it is experienced as something imposed.

While rural communities tend to have a strong sense of geographic and social identity, the problem remains: who is defined as belonging to the community in terms of residing in it and contributing to its prosperity? For example, racial and ethnic discrimination have been reported to be common in many rural areas (Coorey, 1990; Cunneen, 1992). Much research into rural policing has focused on towns with extreme law enforcement problems, often the legacy of colonial dispossession and alienation. Aboriginals have been characterized by some rural community leaders as law breakers and have been targets of law and order rhetoric. Consequently, a disproportionate share of police resources has been allocated to racially segmented towns such as Burke, Brewarrina, Dubbo, Walgett, and Wilcannia in the same way that they have been in urban racial and ethnic enclaves. In such places, police often develop a distinction between "good" and "bad" Aboriginals. The good Aboriginal is usually well behaved, recognizing and adapting to a subordinate role in the local social hierarchy. A bad Aborigine may be regarded as defiant or disrespectful, refusing to adapt to the dominant normative culture (O'Connor and Gray, 1989).

Over-policing, whether in rural or urban communities, has resulted in Indigenous persons feeling harassed and resentful about police intrusion into their daily lives. Some have developed an oppositional subculture hostile to the dominant culture, and to police as instruments of White policies of control and subjugation. Aborigines come to view police with fear and contempt, stereotyping them as oppressive. Police respond in a similar fashion, stereotyping Aborigines as violent, uncooperative, and disorderly. Each group sees themselves as victims, the police casting themselves as having a difficult job with little support. Extreme polarization is the result. Some officers in racially antagonistic communities have experienced strain in being a member of White institutional society in juxtaposition to the Indigenous social system. A response has been to avoid disrupting the dominant normative system and adopting a reactive law enforcement style of policing, which may involve the prejudice, abuse of powers, and cultural insensitivity.

Criminology has only recently recognized the diversity of communities and the complexity of the relationship community structure to crime and policing. Graycar (1999) has emphasized the need for incorporating this recognition into research on crime and programs for law enforcement. A fragmented community implies an integrated police culture, while an integrated community implies a more fragmentary police culture. Officers in polarized communities do not really have a choice of becoming part of an integrated community. To be a successful police officer in a homogeneous community often requires immersion, even if it compromises objectivity and creates tensions and strains for officers.

The experience of policing in rural NSW demonstrates that we should be cautious in valorizing specific models of policing as appropriate and functional in all social contexts. While police-centered approaches have recently been discredited in favor of community policing models, support for such models of policing seems to be grounded in city-centric understandings of police work. Difficulties may be apparent in a localistic approach to policing if community verges toward the ideal type of *Gesellschaft*. The result may be an abuse of police discretionary powers. If the ideals of community policing appear limited, it is because few environments are likely to conform to the *Gemeinschaft* ideal of a community. There are degrees of divergence from this ideal, since many rural towns are composed of multiple communities whose borders are dynamic and constantly in flux.

When law and order problems have arisen in ethnically and racially polarized places, whether urban or rural, throughout NSW, the response from the political right has been to define particular social groups as the cause of troubles, while the political left has tended to focus on police and police culture. Each response fails to acknowledge the subtle ways in which social organization influences crime and the response to crime.

References

Australian Bureau of Statistics. (1999) *Crime and Safety Western Australia 1999*, Canberra.

Australian Bureau of Statistics. (2000a) *Crime and Safety New South Wales 2000*, Canberra.

Australian Bureau of Statistics. (2000b) *Recorded Crime 2000*, Canberra.

Cain, M. E. (1973) *Society and the Policeman's Role*, London: Routledge & Kegan Paul.

Carcach, C. (2001) *Economic Transformation and Regional Crime*, Canberra: Australian Institute of Criminology.

Coorey, L. (1990) 'Policing of violence in rural areas', in T. Cullen, P. Dunn & G. Lawrence (eds.), *Rural Health and Welfare in Australia*, Wagga: Centre for Rural Welfare Research, Charles Sturt University pp. 80–101.

Cunneen, C. (1992) 'Policing and Aboriginal communities', in *Aboriginal Perspectives on Criminal Justice*, Monograph Series No. 1, Canberra: Institute of Criminal Justice, pp. 76–92.

Devery, C. (1993) *Disadvantage and Crime in New South Wales*, Sydney: New South Wales Bureau of Crime Statistics and Research.

Dewey, R. (1960) The rural–urban continuum: Real but relatively unimportant. *American Journal of Sociology* 66(1), 60–66.

Graycar, A. (1999) Strategic directions: Planning for safer communities. *Conference on Crime in Rural Communities: The Impact, the Causes, The Prevention*, Canberra: Australian Institute of Criminology.

Hogg, R. & Carrington, K. (1998) Crime, rurality and community. *The Australian and New Zealand Journal of Criminology* 31(2), 160–181.

Jobes, P. C. (2002) Effective officer and good neighbour: Problems and perceptions among police in rural Australia. *Policing: An International Journal of Police Strategies and Management* 25(2), 256–273.

Jobes, P. C., Crosby, E., Weinand, H. & Donnermeyer, J. (1999) Crime mapping in rural Australia. *Mapping the Boundaries of Australia's Criminal Justice System*, Canberra: Australian Institute of Criminology.

Mukherjee, S. K., Walker, J. R., Scandia, A. & Dagger, D. (1987) *The Size of the Crime Problem in Australia*, Canberra: Australian Institute of Criminology.

O'Connor, M. & Gray, D. (1989) *Crime in a Rural Community*, Annandale, NSW: The Federation Press.

Pennings, J. (1999) Crime in rural NSW: A police perspective. *Conference on Crime in Rural Communities: The Impacts, the Causes, the Prevention*, Sydney: NSWPS.

Tönnies, F. (1957) In C. P. Loomis (ed. and Translator), *Community and Society*, East Lansing, MI: Michigan State University Press.

Weatherburn, D. & Lind, B. (1998) Poverty, parenting, peers and crime-prone neighbourhoods. *Trends and Issues in Criminal Justice*, 85, Canberra: Australian Institute of Criminology.

CHAPTER 11

While this report has concentrated on recommendations for action by governments, the Commission is convinced that governmental actions will not be enough. Crime is a social problem that is interwoven with almost every aspect of American life. Controlling it involves improving the quality of family life, the way schools are run, the way cities are planned, and the way workers are hired. Controlling crime is the business of every American. (President's Commission on Law Enforcement and Administration of Justice, 1967: xi)

Police and ambulance personnel at the site were a man had opened fire with an automatic weapon, wounding a woman in the leg in Taby, north of Stockholm, Sweden early Sunday July 2, 2006. Police mounted a huge operation and later found the gunman shot dead in an elevator in a nearby apartment building. (Credit: © AP Photo/Pontus Altin)

POLICE AND CRIME PREVENTION

OBJECTIVES:

1. The student will learn about the concept and assumptions regarding crime prevention.
2. The student will learn about the community's role in police crime prevention efforts.
3. The student will learn specific crime prevention strategies, including defensible space and crime prevention through environmental design.
4. The student will learn about the role of crime prevention in community policing.

5. The student will become familiar with the functionalist, conflict theory, and interactionist approaches to analyzing police and community crime prevention.

6. The student will learn about the police and crime prevention on an international level.

The idea of crime prevention as an important function of policing can be traced to the first half of the nineteenth century. Sir Robert Peel established crime prevention as one of the London Metropolitan Police's original goals. Since the President's Commission on Law Enforcement and Administration of Justice (1967), the American police have recognized crime prevention as one of their important functions. Police departments have established crime prevention units to assist homeowners, apartment dwellers, and business owners to avoid being a victim of a crime. For the last several decades, the police have recognized that the cooperation of the citizenry is essential to crime prevention. The citizens must also understand that they have a major role in crime prevention by taking preventive measures to avoid becoming a victim of a crime.

As we enter the first decades of the twenty-first century, the American legal system has formalized what constitutes crimes. The legislative branch of our federal and state governments has passed laws outlawing specific behavior as criminal. Crime can be defined as "a positive or negative act in violation of the penal law; an offense against the state" (Black, 1968: 444). Criminal acts are further divided into crimes against people and crimes against property. Crimes against people include: homicide, assault, robberies, and rape. Crimes against property include: burglary, theft, and auto theft.

ASPECTS OF CRIME PREVENTION

There are numerous views as to who has the responsibility for crime prevention. The first approach is that each individual person has the responsibility of avoiding becoming a crime victim, thereby shouldering responsibility for crime prevention. The second approach holds that the neighborhood or community has the responsibility for crime prevention. The third approach suggests that the police have a major responsibility for preventing crime. When these three aspects are closely examined, it seems logical that the individual, the community, and the police all have to share responsibility for preventing crime. Successful crime prevention involves the participation of all formal and informal structures, as well as the willingness and cooperation of individuals to be made aware of the dangers that may place them in harm's way.

The concept of crime prevention involves education, training, public relations, and the development of strategies to prevent criminal activities. For the last several decades, there have been a variety of crime prevention studies, programs, and strategies advocated for protecting individuals, neighborhoods, government, and private organizations from being victims of crime. The *National Crime Prevention Institute,* housed in the Criminal Justice Department of the University of Louisville, describes "crime prevention as any kind of effort aimed at controlling criminal behavior." The *Institute* further divides crime prevention into: "Direct controls of crime includes only those which reduce environmental opportunities for crime, and Indirect controls all other measures, such as job training, remedial education, police surveillance, police apprehension, court action, imprisonment, probation and parole" (National Crime Prevention Institute, 1986: 2).

The goal of crime prevention is to prevent people from being a victim of crime and to protect property. The concept of crime prevention holds that measures can be taken where people can prevent becoming victims. A crime prevention program has several distinct characteristics: (1) the program must be in place before the crime has been committed; (2) the program will focus on direct controls over behavior; (3) the program will focus on the environment where crimes are committed; (4) the program will have an interdisciplinary effort based on human behavior; and (5) the program will be less costly and more effective than punishment or treatment (Jeffery, 1977: 37). Both the government and the private sector have been involved in crime prevention efforts to decrease the chance of individuals and businesses from being crime victims. Crime prevention programs can involve attempts to reduce crime and the fear of crime, and to eliminate annoying offenses such as drunkenness and urinating in public places.

No other component of the criminal justice system has the advantage that the police possess in working with the community to prevent crime. They investigate crimes, solve crimes, arrest offenders, and recover stolen property. By the nature of their positions, the police are aware of the offender's method of committing a crime. With a criminal's method of operation known, the next step is to take preventive measures.

When the **crime prevention model** was constructed in the 1910s, it emphasized that crime prevention was an important function of policing. The "crime prevention model" preceded the **crime control model** that was developed in the 1930s and that emphasized the arrest process. While the crime prevention model was considered a female-generated model, the crime control model was considered a male-generated model. The belief, during this period, was that women police officers would be more successful at performing crime prevention activities than male police officers (Appier, 1992: 3). In the 1930s, the crime prevention model began to lose ground to the crime control model. The crime control model emphasized managerial efficiency, technological sophistication, and crime fighting. The crime prevention–social work approach of policing fell into disfavor by police administrators. With the emphasis on the crime control model, the role of women officers, the crime prevention specialist, decreased.

It was not until the late 1960s that crime prevention was rediscovered. The President's Commission on Law Enforcement and Administration of Justice in 1967 once again recognized that the police had a role to play in crime prevention. With the re-emphasis on crime prevention, police departments began to develop crime prevention programs and strategies. Today, many police departments have crime prevention units or minimally, an officer who does security checks for residents and businesses.

---

crime prevention model

Goal of crime prevention is to prevent people from being crime victims and the protection of property. The concept of crime prevention holds that measures can be taken to prevent people from becoming victims.

---

crime control model

Emphasizes managerial efficiency, technological sophistication, and crime fighting.

The police attempt to obtain the cooperation of the neighborhood and business associations in order to convince them to put in place crime prevention strategies. The primary role of crime prevention is educating and providing consulting services to the neighborhood and community. A few crime prevention programs include preventing rape, mugging, shoplifting, and juvenile delinquency. Students are recommended to take a crime prevention course to learn about crime prevention programs if one is available at their college or university.

The *Neighborhood Watch*, because of its impact on crime prevention and its wide acceptance by both the community and the police, should be reviewed. The Neighborhood Watch has received a great deal of national media attention and police practitioners and students studying crime prevention should have an understanding of how it operates. Neighborhood Watch programs are instituted to reduce crime as well as the fear of crime. The concept requires citizens of a neighborhood to play a role in controlling crime in their neighborhood. Residents of a specific neighborhood can either be homeowners or apartment dwellers who band together to establish a sense of security and safety. The Neighborhood Watch Association meets regularly in order to provide information on crime prevention techniques. The police crime prevention specialist functions as an advisor to the Neighborhood Watch Association. The success of Neighborhood Watch depends on neighborhood residents being actively involved in making their own neighborhood secure and safe.

THE COMMUNITY'S ROLE IN CRIME PREVENTION

The community has a role to play in crime prevention. In 1967, the President's Commission on Law Enforcement and Administration of Justice in their *Task Force Report: The Police* recognized that the police needed the people in order to solve crime. Without community support, police officers would be unsuccessful in solving and preventing crimes. The *Task Force Report* found that "The police need help from citizens, from private organizations, from other municipal agencies, and from crime prevention legislation" (221). The Report advocated that businesses have a responsibility to work toward decreasing thievery, robberies, and burglaries. They recommended educational programs in crime prevention and crime prevention campaigns, and promoted the idea that professional and social organizations should provide crime prevention strategies to their members, and to the larger public.

The President's *Task Force Report: The Police* recommended numerous crime prevention strategies that could be built into community planning. For example, the *Task Force* considered that police input was an important tool in community planning. Community planning should consider crime prevention strategies and tactics recommended by the police. The President's *Task Force* further suggested that "To reduce crime in their communities citizens must be prepared to back up the police force with more than slogans. They need to keep in mind, but in perspective, the possibilities of crime in their daily lives and take responsible steps to limit criminal opportunities" (228). The *Task Force* further recommended that municipal governments have to become more involved in crime prevention by providing "the mechanism for coordination of all the local agencies whose activities and police can have an effect on crime prevention and on opportunities for the detection and apprehension of criminals after crimes have been committed" (228). Additional support for crime prevention came from the National Advisory Commission on Standard and Goals in the 1970s.

The establishment of **Community Crime Prevention Programs (CCPPs)** in the 1970s indicated that community organizations and local institutions had an important role in crime prevention efforts. The goal was for the police and community organizations to provide the impetus in neighborhood crime prevention efforts (Rosenbaum, Lurigio, and Davis, 1998: 20).

In the final decades of the twentieth century, the police came to the realization, with a push from federal government studies, that they cannot solve crime when left to their own devises. To be successful as crime solvers, they need the cooperation and assistance of the community. Of extreme importance, the police need the community to put into place successful crime prevention strategies. Effective crime prevention can only be obtained with community involvement. Only when citizen participation exists in crime prevention can we expect that crime will be reduced. Even when crime has decreased, crime prevention participation by citizens should be maintained to make sure that crime will not take an upward turn. One of the major problems of citizen's involvement in crime prevention is their lack of long-term staying power. Most citizens can muster enough energy for the short term only, although long-term involvement is needed to keep crime under control.

Obtaining the involvement of residents of a specific neighborhood may require a great deal of effort. It has been estimated that approximately 10–20% of neighborhood residents will, at any one time, be involved in crime prevention activities. The goal of neighborhood crime prevention programs is to reduce the opportunity for crime in order to reduce crime. A wide variety of programs that can be implemented to ensure this include improved housing, education, and employment opportunities, to name a few. Not only do neighborhoods need to reduce crime, but they also have to correct the underlying causes of their crime problem (1989: 488).

CRIME PREVENTION STRATEGIES

Defensible Space

Defensible space as a crime prevention approach to reduce crime is an approach that is workable and to a great extent successful. The term defensible space can be traced to a conference held in 1964 at Washington University in St. Louis, Missouri. Two sociologists and two architects, along with police officers from the St. Louis Police Academy, discussed physical features that produced security in public housing (Newman, 1973a: 1). "Defensible space is a surrogate term for the range of mechanisms—real and symbolic barriers, improved opportunities for surveillance" (Newman, 1973b: 3).

Community Crime Prevention Programs (CCPPs)

Were established in the 1970s and are an indication that community organizations and local institutions have an important role in crime prevention efforts. The goal for the police and community organizations is to provide the impetus in neighborhood crime prevention efforts and CCPPs.

---

defensible space

Is a model for residential environments, which inhibits crime by creating the physical expression of social fabric that defends itself.

The defensible space concept provides residents of public housing a milieu of security from crime. Areas of defensible space include lobbies, hallways, playgrounds, and adjacent streets. The four elements of defensible space—territoriality, natural surveillance, positive picture of locality, and environment—are all perceived to influence disorder and crime in the area. Defensible space concepts hold that the inhabitants of public housing can control disorder and crime in their public housing complex. The theory claims that residents can assert territoriality for their public housing complex while natural surveillance allows the inhabitants to observe legitimate residents along with potential offenders. The last two elements of the concept—positive picture of locality and environment—should project a feeling of safety from disorder and crime for residents of public housing. To a great extent, public housing in the late 1980s and 1990s, with grants from the Department of Housing and Urban Development, put into operations all, or segments of, the four elements of defensible space. Residents of public housing complexes in a joint effort with their local police departments reclaimed their living environment from drug dealers, drug users, and other criminal offenders. The criminal element was chased away with police cooperation. The residents reclaimed their territory, the housing complex. Natural surveillance helped them to identify the legitimate residents from law violators. Playgrounds were reclaimed so that children could play safely. This led to a positive feeling about the locality where they resided. The environment was cleaned and graffiti removed from walls; grass was planted where none existed. Defensible space is a practical approach to crime prevention not only in public housing, but also in neighborhoods that have a high crime rate.

Crime Prevention through Environmental Design

Oscar Newman initially made environmental techniques to the prevention of crime popular in his study of *defensible space*. These methods have been used for residential areas, commercial businesses, schools, and parking garages. Clarence Ray Jeffery, the theorist who developed the concept of **crime prevention through environmental design (CPTED)**, believed that crime prevention involved the physical design of buildings along with citizen involvement and the effective use of police agencies. According to Jefferies, the physical environment in terms of buildings, each floor of a building, and each room in a building should be examined. Jefferies correctly claims that usually a mall area of the city is responsible for the majority of crime. However, he maintains that analysis of crime ignores house-by-house or block-by-block variations in crime rates. He advocates that for the purpose of crime prevention, crime data be utilized to determine in what areas of a community crime generally occurs (National Crime Prevention Institute, 1986: 120).

The trust of the CPTED model implies that the physical environment can be orchestrated to prevent potential offenders from committing incidents of crime and to improve the quality of life. Tho individuals prone to criminal activity can have this inclination removed by a physical environment that places stumbling blocks in the way of the potential offender. CPTED involves creating a physical environment

Crime Prevention Through Environmental Design (CPTED)

This model holds that crime prevention involves the physical design of buildings along with citizen involvement and the effective use of police agencies. The physical environment, in terms of buildings, each floor of a building, and each room in a building, should be examined.

in which people can be free from the fear of crime and have a feeling of safety. The CPTED model includes not only information from the architectural field, but also information from the sociological, psychological, and law enforcement fields. It is a cooperative effort to reduce crime and to meet the needs of individuals and the community. Planning is extremely important to the CPTED model and strategies are needed if CPTED is to be put into operations.

Timothy D. Crowe (1991: 30) indicates that there are three overlapping strategies in CPTED: "natural access control, natural surveillance, and territorial reinforcement." The purpose of access control is to reduce the opportunity to commit a crime. Methods used to control access to an area can include gates, guards, locks, and shrubbery. The aim of this strategy should be to create an allusion that the risk involved in attempting a criminal act is greater than the opportunity. The purpose of surveillance is to observe outsiders or intruders into the neighborhood. When strangers are under surveillance, the risk of committing an offense increases. Strategies of surveillance include police and security guard patrols, lights, and windows. The third strategy, territoriality, implies that physical design contributes to a perception of ownership or influence; potential offenders can recognize the resident's ownership or influence over a geographical area. Also, natural access control and surveillance contribute to a feeling of territoriality (Crowe, 1991: 30–32). To be successful, CPTED must be practical and be understood. Residents, storeowners, school officials, and parking garage owners must visualize the benefits of CPTED before implementing the model.

CPTED can be successful when carefully planned and thought out. In a study conducted by Casteel and Peek-Asa (2000) on the effectiveness of CPTED in reducing robberies, it was found, after reviewing sixteen CPTED evaluations from all sources over the past thirty years, that most interventions were in convenience stores. The results of the Casteel and Peek-Asa study reveal that the CPTED approach appears to be effective in reducing robberies. The study does show clear trends regarding which components of the CPTED approach are the most effective. The authors conclude that the devastating effects of robberies on employees, high costs to doing business, and the threat of lawsuits are compelling reasons to incorporate CPTED as a crime prevention and reduction strategy (114). Another study in support of CPTED playing a role in decreasing of crime within convenience stores was done in Wichita, Kansas (Carver, 1995). The study found that CPTED techniques were effective in preventing crime within the stores when properly applied. The author of the convenience store crime problem recommended that the Wichita Police Department train several police officers in the CPTED concept. He further found that the CPTED techniques were used effectively by the English in home security and the South Africans in preventing bank robberies.

In addition to preventing crime in housing, convenience stores, and banks, CPTED can play an important role in decreasing crime in schools, specifically elementary and secondary schools.

The concept of "defensible space" developed by Oscar Newman and the concept of "CPTED" developed by Jefferies both preceded ideas pertaining to *situational crime prevention.*

CRIME PREVENTION AND COMMUNITY POLICING

The concept of neighborhoods and communities being involved in crime prevention fits into the concept of community policing. "Community policing is a conveniently elastic term which is often used loosely to accommodate virtually any policing activity of which its proponents approve" (Weatheritt, 1987: 7). These days it seems that a majority of police departments in America and throughout the world are claiming that they are involved in community policing. However, it does seem that police departments are to a certain extent being influenced by the community policing philosophy.

Community-oriented policing emphasizes listening rather than talking to people. A key component of community-oriented policing is problem solving that encourages all police personnel to be involved in any situation they consider to be an ongoing problem. The philosophy of community policing has as its foundation the problem-oriented police design. The primary idea behind problem-oriented policing is police accountability to the community and a focus on addressing community concerns. Community-oriented policing draws on this idea but takes it even further by emphasizing full community participation in the problem-solving process (Palmiotto, 2002: 174). Problem-solving policing can range from fighting fear of crime in Baltimore County to controlling prostitution in Wichita, Kansas, or having a community safety fair in Sedgwick County, Kansas. The focus of problem solving can range from minor to very serious community problems. These problems can include gangs, curfew violations, drug dealing, crack houses, graffiti on buildings, burglaries, robberies, or malicious mischief (Palmiotto, 2002: 188).

As a philosophy, community policing takes seriously the concerns and inputs of citizens who live and work in the neighborhoods and communities (Palmiotto, 2002: 130). One important component of community policing is crime prevention.

A number of police agencies have integrated their crime prevention efforts into community policing. Crime prevention contributes information to the community on techniques and strategies to reduce and prevent crime. Both physical and social aspects of the neighborhood are addressing crime prevention. Crime prevention deals with problem solving and can, and should, be incorporated into the community policing operations. The Chicago Police Department (1992: 6) made it one of their principles for change to community policing: "Crime control and prevention must be recognized as dual parts of the fundamental mission of policing. Solving crime is and will continue to be an essential element of police work. But preventing crime is the most effective way to create safer environments our neighborhoods."

The linkage of crime prevention and community policing is designed to strengthen the security and safety of neighborhoods and community as a whole. Crime prevention programs have discovered that neighborhood associations and individuals can play a successful part in their own security and safety. Programs such as block watches, neighborhood watches, business and security surveys, and security training have all proven useful in involving the citizens in crime prevention. These programs, by involving the citizens in problem solving, initiate a police–citizen partnership. They also leave the citizens with a sense of empowerment over their own safety. Community policing delineates problem solving, empowerment, and a community–police partnership to prevent crime, and more importantly, gives the community a sense of security and safety.

Differences do exist between crime prevention and community policing. As a philosophy, community policing administers public safety while crime prevention has to be considered the central goal of policing. Crime prevention provides information and instruction to the community on how to prevent specific types of crime, how to motivate residents in prevention endeavors, and how to create a hostile environment to crime. Community policing is incorporating crime prevention into its operations. (Criminal Justice Management and Training Digest, 1996a: 3), and is now being practiced by both rural and urban police departments. Crime prevention for the last several decades has sold to our individual citizens, neighborhoods, communities businesses, and governmental agencies the concept that it offers a viable means to reduce crime and the fear of crime, and to provide a sense of security and safety to those areas implementing programs. However, crime prevention strategies do not address the concerns of those individuals who by chance, either by being in the wrong place at the wrong time or by being targeted, are victims of criminal offenders.

COMMUNITY CRIME PREVENTION: THREE SOCIOLOGICAL PERSPECTIVES

We turn now to understanding community crime prevention using the three sociological perspectives that we have become familiar with: functionalism, conflict theory, and interactionism. A functionalist will look at the various responsibilities that are included under crime prevention such as Neighborhood Watch and Operation ID and how they contribute to achieving the overall goals of a police department. These activities would be seen as functional to achieving the goals of law enforcement, order maintenance, and service. For example, Neighborhood Watch allows police officers to be informed of suspicious activities in various areas under their jurisdiction that allows them to carry out their goals of preventing and deterring crime better. Thus, the functionalist would focus on what each of these activities contributes to the optimal functioning of the police agency and how society benefits from these. It would also be assumed that inefficient and dysfunctional activities would be trimmed or discarded, as they do not contribute positively to societal and organizational functioning.

The conflict theorist would examine crime prevention activities and try to understand who benefits most from these. While police agencies may be quick to say that they benefit everyone, the conflict theorist will argue that these activities mostly benefit certain powerful elements in the society. By paying attention to the annoying drunk, lying in the gutter by the side of a street, who may be reported to the police by neighborhood watch, their attention is diverted away from the similarly drunk president of the local bank who is sexually harassing his female employees. Since the former individual has little (if any) power and the latter is an elite member of the community, who benefits by the police focusing their attention on only one of these offenders?

Thus, police crime prevention activities become yet another arena where the rich and powerful benefit to the detriment of the less well-to-do and powerful.

An interactionist studying the same set of crime prevention activities would attempt to find answers to a different set of questions. For example, the interactionist would be interested in knowing how members of the police force and the public perceive and understand crime prevention activities. What particular activities would come under this title and what would be excluded? They would also be interested in knowing how these classifications and distinctions are made. For example, Drug Awareness Resistance (DARE) programs involve officers going to elementary schools and talking to kids about the types and dangers associated with various psychoactive substances. Would this be considered as crime prevention or not, given that it may serve to prevent drug offenses among these kids in the near term? Next, would the public perceive this as crime prevention or not?

Next, let us examine community crime prevention efforts in one of the major Scandinavian social democracies, Sweden. Their efforts at crime prevention stand in sharp contrast to those of the United States, particularly in terms of the greater involvement of a variety of government organizations and local groups.

COMMUNITY CRIME PREVENTION INTERNATIONALLY: SWEDEN

To understand the community's involvement in crime prevention in another country, we look at how these issues are handled in Sweden, which is a capitalist Scandinavian country, generally regarded as also having a large welfare state, which is slightly larger than California and shares borders with Finland and Norway. Its population of more than nine million consists mostly of native Swedes. Compared to other countries, although increasing in recent decades, it has a relatively low crime rate. It also has a centralized criminal justice system and police force.

Crime prevention in Sweden is broader than involving just the police or the criminal justice system and is deemed a collective responsibility. The country's crime prevention strategy is national in scope and related policies are based on three premises. First, they argue that attention "must be given to how societal developments, as well as political decisions concerning matters other than crime policy can exert an influence on criminality" (Government of Sweden, 2000: 4).

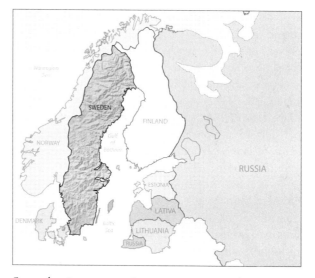

Second, crime prevention must encourage interactions between criminal justice agencies, schools, and social welfare agencies. Third, the involvement of citizens in crime prevention efforts is important and local municipalities are encouraged to create crime prevention councils. The National Council for Crime Prevention provides technical help such as best practice manuals and financial assistance to lower governmental entities to carry out crime prevention.

While Sweden targets opportunities for committing crime (i.e., the situational prevention of crime), it also focuses attention on reducing recruitment of individuals to criminal lifestyles through interventions, and reducing criminal activity among persistent offenders through education, work training, and treatment. Two pertinent observations can be made about Sweden's approach. First, it is a highly comprehensive form of community crime prevention that would be difficult to conceive of in a large, decentralized country such as the United States. Second, it involves a large degree of cooperation and interaction among various community entities that needs to be encouraged if we are to move beyond piecemeal approaches to the problems of crime.

Finally, we consider the crime prevention efforts at the national and local levels in a South American country, Chile (see accompanying box).

 ## SUMMARY

The idea of crime prevention as an important function of policing can be traced to Sir Robert Peel who established crime prevention as one of the Metropolitan London Police goals. Since the President's Commission on Law Enforcement and Administration of Justice Report in the late 1960s, crime prevention has become an acceptable function of policing in America. The concept of crime prevention involves education, training, public relations, and the development of strategies to prevent criminal activities. For the last several decades, there have been a variety of crime prevention studies, programs, and strategies advocated to help prevent the individual, neighborhoods, and government and private organizations from being victims of crime.

The community has a role to play in crime prevention. National commissions such as the President's Commission on Law Enforcement and Administration of Justice and the National Advisory Commission on Criminal Justice and Goals brought to national attention the importance of crime prevention for the community. The goal of CCPPs in the 1970s indicated that community organizations and local institutions had an important role in crime prevention efforts. The goal was for the police and community organizations to provide the impetus in neighborhood crime prevention efforts.

In the final decades of the twentieth century, the police came to the realization, with a push from the federal government studies, that crime cannot be solved when left without the cooperation and assistance of the community. Only when citizen participation exists in crime prevention can we expect that crime can be reduced.

A community crime prevention approach involves the police and the communities working together to not only reduce crime, but also prevent crime. To achieve community crime prevention, several techniques and strategies are put into operation. *Defensible space* as a crime prevention approach is workable and to a great extent successful. It provides residents a secure environment relatively free from crime. Another technique similar to "defensible space" is CPTED. This concept of crime prevention through environmental design holds that crime prevention involves the physical design of buildings along with citizen involvement and the effective use of police agencies. The thrust of the CPTED model implies that the physical environment can be orchestrated to prevent potential offenders from committing incidents of crime along with improving the quality of life. The third strategy to prevent crime is *situational crime prevention*. This approach hopes to reduce the "opportunity for crime." Techniques used in "situational crime prevention" include a wide variety of crime prevention categories. They can include: burglar alarms, fenced yards, graffiti cleaning, street lighting, baggage screening, CCTV systems, identification cards, and credit card photographs.

The concept of neighborhoods and communities being involved in crime prevention fits into the concept of community policing. Crime prevention and community policing are interrelated. Police agencies have integrated their crime prevention efforts into community policing. Crime prevention deals with problem solving and can be incorporated into the community policing operations. The linkage of crime prevention and community policing can only strengthen the security and safety of neighborhoods and community as a whole. The goal should be to integrate crime prevention into community policing operations. Sweden provides an example of how an integrated, comprehensive community crime prevention effort can be mounted.

 KEY TERMS

Community Crime Prevention Programs (CCPPs): Were established in the 1970s and are an indication that community organizations and local institutions have an important role in crime prevention efforts. The goal for the police and community organizations is to provide the impetus in neighborhood crime prevention efforts and CCPPs.

Crime control model: Emphasizes managerial efficiency, technological sophistication, and crime fighting.

Crime prevention model: Goal of crime prevention is to prevent people from being crime victims and the protection of property. The concept of crime prevention holds that measures can be taken to prevent people from becoming victims.

Crime prevention through environmental design (CPTED): This model holds that crime prevention involves the physical design of buildings along with citizen involvement and the effective use of police agencies. The physical environment, in terms of buildings, each floor of a building, and each room in a building, should be examined.

Defensible space: Is a model for residential environments, which inhibits crime by creating the physical expression of social fabric that defends itself.

 REVIEW QUESTIONS

1. What is the community's role in crime prevention?
2. Explain crime prevention strategies.
3. Explain crime prevention through environmental design.
4. Explain the importance of crime prevention to community policing.

 DISCUSSION QUESTIONS

1. Discuss whether there is any difference between defensible space and CPTED.
2. Discuss whether too much emphasis is placed on the community's role in crime prevention.
3. Discuss whether crime prevention has a limited value for community policing.

REFERENCES

Appier, Janis (1992) "Preventive Justice: The Campaign for Women Police, 1919–1940." *Women and Criminal Justice* 4, 1: 3–36.

Black, Henry Cambell (1968) *Black's Law Dictionary*. Fourth Edition. St. Paul, MN: West Publishing.

Carver, Ronald (1995) *Applying Crime Prevention Through Environmental Design Techniques to the Convenience Store Industry*. Wichita State University, unpublished thesis.

Casteel, Carri and Corinne Peek-Asa (2000) "Effectiveness of Crime Prevention Through Environmental Design (CPTED) in Reducing Robberies." *American Journal of Preventive Medicine* 18, 4S.

Chicago Police Department (1992) *Together We Can*. Chicago, IL: Chicago Police Department.

Criminal Justice Management and Training Digest (1996a) "Crime Prevention and Community Policing: A Vital Partnership Part I." In *Washington Crime News Service*. Washington, DC: Washington Crime News Service, 2, 1: January 24.

Criminal Justice Management and Training Digest (1996b) "Crime Prevention and Community Policing: A Vital Partnership Part II," *Washington Crime News Service*, Washington, DC: Washington Crime News Service, 2, 3: February 7.

Criminal Justice Management and Training Digest (1996c) "Crime Prevention and Community Policing: A Vital Partnership Part III," *Washington Crime News Service*, Washington, DC: Washington Crime News Service, 2, 4: February 21.

Crowe, Timothy D. (1991) *Crime Prevention Through Environment Design*. Boston, MA: Butterworth-Heinmann.

Government of Sweden (2000) *Community Involvement in Crime Prevention: A National Report From Sweden*. Stockholm, Sweden: Government of Sweden.

Jeffery, C. Ray (1977) *Crime Prevention Through Environmental Design*. Beverly Hills, CA: Sage Publications.

National Advisory Commission on Criminal Justice Standards and Goals (1973) *Police*. Washington, DC: U.S. Government Printing Office.

National Crime Prevention Institute (1986) *Understanding Crime Prevention*. Boston, MA: Butterworth.

Newman, Oscar (1973a) *Architectural Design for Crime Prevention*. Washington, DC: U.S. Department of Justice.

Newman, Oscar (1973b) *Defensible Space: Crime Prevention Through Environmental Design*. New York, NY: Collier Books.

Palmiotto, Michael J. (2002) "The Influence of Community in Community Policing in the Twenty-first Century." In R. Muraskin and A. R. Roberts (eds.) *Vision For Change*. Third Edition. Upper Saddle River, NJ: Prentice-Hall.

President's Commission on Law Enforcement and Administration of Justice (1967) *The Challenge of Crime in a Free Society*. Washington, DC: U.S. Government Printing Office.

Rosenbaum, Dennis P., Arthur J. Lurigio and Robert C. Davis (1998) Belemont, CA: West/Wadsworth.

The President's Commission on Law Enforcement and Administration of Justice (1967) *Task Force Report: The Police*. Washington, DC: U.S. Government Printing Office.

Weatheritt, Mollie (1987) "Community Policing Now." In P. Wilmot (ed.) *Policing and the Community*. London: Policy Studies Institute.

COMMUNITY CRIME PREVENTION IN CHILE *Lucía Dammert*

In the last decade, crime and fear of crime have increased steadily throughout Latin America. Even in Chile, frequently regarded as the safest country in Latin America (Ward, 2001; Ayres, 1998), public insecurity dominates public discourse. The Chilean case has two unique characteristics that differentiate it from neighboring countries. First, there is a general public trust in police forces (Frühling, 2001). While the police were involved in the previous military government (1973–1990), the public still regards them as well-trained, efficient, and generally not corrupt. The government has made a clear decision to assuage the public's insecurity by fighting crime through policies of community participation in crime prevention (Dammert, 2002), and through alterations of police operational strategies.

The 1990s witnessed important changes in public security policies in Chile, related specifically to the community's role in crime prevention. Chile moved from security policies based on police force to policies that increase the role of citizens in crime prevention. These

prevention-oriented policies were accompanied by an increase in public investment in crime control, particularly in the area of police infrastructure. The government embarked on an effort to control crime through preventive policies that emphasize the importance of community–police relationships and community involvement through situational and social prevention initiatives.

In the last decade, the Carabineros de Chile (National Police Force) developed several programs to strengthen police–community relationship. The latest operational strategy, *Plan Cuadrante*,[1] delineates new patrol sectors and the amount of policing needed in each sector or cuadrante. Thus, this plan with its new police sectors strengthens the police–community relationships by better focusing police resources and by enhancing face-to-face contacts between the community and police officers. These efforts are aimed to diminish the public's fear of crime through community participation, while also lowering the rates of victimization (Ward, 2001; Frühling, 2001).

Several community crime prevention initiatives have been implemented in Chile in the last decade. Most of them were developed by local governments as well as national public institutions with ties to community organizations. Thus, most of these programs had limited scope and sometimes dealt with crime prevention as a secondary issue. Despite the importance of such programs, there was a clear need for a national policy on community crime prevention that could develop initiatives for poor communities (whose local governments lacked funding for such programs) and also design long-term programs involving several community as well as civil society leaders. To address these two issues, in the year 2000 the Ministry of the Interior started a new program "Comuna Segura, Compromiso

---

1. The Plan Cuadrante was first tested in Santiago's South precinct during the year 1999. After an internal review of the process in the year 2000, the National Police Force (Carabineros de Chile) decided to implement it in Metropolitan Santiago.

100" ("Safe Neighborhoods, Full Commitment"). Even though the program's management, design, and budget are under the Ministry of the Interior, local governments play a key role in their implementation.

The design of the program defines a process of incremental participation of neighborhood at the yearly basis. Consequently, during the first two years, twelve comunas (neighborhoods) joined the program (twelve each year) and sixteen neighborhoods were included in 2003. These neighborhoods are selected by an index developed by the Ministry that includes four risk variables: drug consumption, crime rates, domestic violence, and poverty rates. The process of implementation includes two phases: during the first year, a *Local Council of Citizens Security* is created in each neighborhood. Its members are local authorities, police representatives, representatives of other national programs such as drug prevention, and several civil society leaders. The Council has a *Secretario Técnico* (Professional Secretary hired by the Ministry of the Interior who works at the local municipality) who provides technical support for the council, and studies and analyzes the local context, which serves as a basis for the *Local Security Plan*. This person also has the responsibility to enhance community participation in crime prevention by organizing meetings, seminars, and open dialogs among citizens and community leaders.

After the council is created and the *Secretario Técnico* is hired, the second phase of the program starts and relates directly to the development of the *Local Security Plan* in which the main problems (thematic and spatial) are addressed. The plan allows the council to define specific strategies that help diminish crime and/or fear of crime in specific areas. These strategies are based on the community's resources (specifically neighborhood organizations), which are essential for implementation. The third phase of the program starts with a call for projects at the local level that focus on problems highlighted in the Local Security Plan. Projects can be presented by any legal community institution with a presence at the local level. Thus, the Council defines the projects that will be funded for a year in each neighborhood and the *Secretario Técnico* supervises and collaborates with each institution to develop them.

In 2001, 361 projects were funded in 12 neighborhoods around the country. The main topics addressed related to situational prevention (street lighting and remodeling of public spaces) and social prevention (activities for youth at risk, senior citizens, and other vulnerable populations). Many of the projects were managed by nontraditional institutions founded at the local level, such as youth groups. This program has been an excellent opportunity for such institutions to show the effectiveness of nontraditional activities of crime prevention, such as theater groups, youth groups working with high-risk children, and rehabilitation programs for formerly incarcerated women and their children.

The program covered forty neighborhoods (more than one-third of the country's population) by the year 2003. However, since its creation, several challenges have been detected not only in the design of the program, but also in its implementation process. Perhaps the most important issue is the need to redefine community participation as a concept that involves long-term commitment to change attitudes and norms at the local level. Obviously the implementation of the projects is an excellent first step toward the development, and, in some cases, consolidation of community involvement in crime prevention; however, it is not enough.

Second, in most neighborhoods, youth problems have captured the focus of communities. However, the experience of the first year of implementation shows that initiatives focusing on youths yield better results when youth groups are involved. In that sense, there is a need to involve more youth groups in each community to help involve more youth in crime prevention.

Nevertheless, this initiative has had an impact on security policies at the national and local levels. The importance of the Council has been recognized even in communities not engaged with the national program, many of which have organized their own programs. There is a clear recognition that a Local Security Plan is necessary to design sound interventions in specific areas of the neighborhood. Finally, the community initiatives developed during the first year of implementation reflect that in order to be successful, communities must recognize the diverse nature of crime prevention, and the need to incorporate several community groups to implement crime prevention initiatives.

References

Ayres, R. (1998) *Crime and Violence as Development Issues in Latin America and the Caribbean*, Washington, DC: World Bank.

Dammert, L. (2002) *Participación comunitaria en prevención del delito en América Latina. ¿De qué participación hablamos?* Santiago: Cuadernos del CED.

Frühling, H. (2001) 'Las estrategias policiales frente a la inseguridad ciudadana en Chile', in H. Frühling and A. Candina (eds.) *Policía, Sociedad y Estado. Modernización y Reforma Policial en América del Sur*, Santiago: CED.

Ward, H. (2001) *Police Reform in Latin America: Current Efforts in Argentina, Brazil, and Chile*. Washington, DC: Woodrow Wilson International Center for Scholars.

CHAPTER 12

When the story first broke that a cop had viciously attacked Haitian immigrant Abner Louima in a Brooklyn precinct bathroom on a hot August night in 1997, few in the black community doubted the account. In the white community, many were far more skeptical. That gap in perceptions about police and how they might behave has emerged as one of the most vexing social issues of the 1990s—threatening the racial harmony of cities and the integrity of the justice system. (Marks, 1999: 1)

A crowd of Sikhs protest outside Prime Minister Tony Blair's official residence, 10 Downing Street in London Wednesday, July 3, 2002, demanding the right to be recognized as a separate ethnic group when equal opportunity is measured. (Credit: © AP Photo/Steve Holland)

POLICE AND SPECIAL POPULATIONS

OBJECTIVES:

1. The student will understand the relationship between police and various special (or subordinate) populations in society.
2. The student will understand various patterns of interaction between police and subordinate populations.
3. The student will understand various issues concerning police treatment of racial and ethnic minorities and women.
4. The student will learn how functionalism, conflict theory, and interactionism view police interactions with special (or subordinate) populations.
5. The student will learn about police and special populations on an international level.

n the course of carrying out their work involving crime fighting or crime prevention, maintaining order, and providing service, police officers come across a variety of individuals belonging to different groups. For example, the officer may rouse a homeless woman from the park bench that she has been sleeping on; may stop, question, and arrest an individual belonging to a minority ethnic group; may deal with a juvenile who has run away from home by referring him or her to a shelter; may give a traffic ticket to an elderly individual who is going the wrong way on a one-way street and steer that individual in the right direction; and may respond to a domestic violence call involving a gay couple. In each of these cases, the officer is legally and constitutionally bound to consider these people as individuals and to respond to their problematic situations accordingly.

At the same time, it would be preposterous to argue that in each of these situations an individual police officer notices nothing more about these individuals than that a specific individual has attracted that officer's attention and needs to be dealt with in some way. That is to say, each one of the officers involved is likely to react to each of these individuals on the basis of more than just the legal characteristics of the situation. In the case of the homeless woman, the officer may be interested in making sure that she goes to a shelter that can provide a place to sleep for females. Or the officer might think of her as a "woman of easy virtue" and react accordingly. In the case of the juvenile, the home and parental situations of the runaway are sure to be noted and investigated. Or, the member of an ethnic minority may be questioned with a great deal of suspicion and hostility because he happened to have been stopped in a part of town with only a few such people in the resident population.

Thus, the status of the individual involved in each of the above cases as a female, a member of an ethnic or racial minority, someone below the age of adulthood, a senior citizen, or a homosexual intrudes into the delivery of a particular police service and the carrying out of certain police procedures. The common denominator that underlies the interactions between the police and members of these groups is in the way that police officers interpret clues (implicit and explicit) regarding the identities of the individuals involved, and react to them in ways that are different from that of individuals who do not possess these characteristics. It goes without saying that one reason that we are interested in these differential interactions is that they are often based on negative and disagreeable connotations (e.g., a juvenile accused of shoplifting in a store must be definitely guilty because everyone knows juveniles shoplift) on the part of the police. The unequal handling that such individuals may be subjected to at the hands of the police is a definite concern in democratic societies that are based on assumptions about "equal treatment under the law." While there are a variety of possible social characteristics (e.g., intelligence, social class, sight or hearing ability, religion, and language ability) that society and therefore the police may use to differentiate among its members, in this chapter we will consider the impact of differences based on race/ethnicity, gender, age, and sexual orientation on policing and vice versa.

Sociologists use the term **subordinate groups** to describe "one whose members, because of physical or cultural characteristics are disadvantaged and subjected to unequal treatments by the dominant group and who regard themselves as objects

subordinate groups

One whose members, because of physical or cultural characteristics, are disadvantaged and subjected to unequal treatment by the dominant group and who regard themselves as objects of collective discrimination.

of collective discrimination" (Kendall, 2005). In the above examples (and in a U.S. context: females, juveniles, non-Whites, and homosexuals), the individuals mentioned clearly fit the definition of being members of subordinate groups. Of course, subordinate groups will exist only in relation to **dominant groups**. A dominant group is "one that is advantaged and has superior resources and rights in a society" (Feagin and Feagin, 2002). Again in the above examples and in an American context, consider whether the police would deal with males, adults, Whites, or heterosexuals in exactly the same manner as they would with females, juveniles, non-Whites, and homosexuals? Sometimes, the term "minority group" is used instead of subordinate group, and the term "majority group" is used for dominant group. Although the ideas underlying these pairs of terms are similar, often one gets caught up in the quantitative aspects of these terms leading to confusion. For example, it is numerically inaccurate to define women as a minority group in the United States since they now constitute the majority of the population. However, we would definitely not consider them a dominant group because of the lack of power and control that women have in important American institutions such as politics and the economy. As an example that is more relevant to us, let us note that although women constitute a clear majority of the American population, they are only around 10–12% of all police officers (see, e.g., Polisar and Milgram, 1998). Similarly, in South Africa until 1994, although Blacks were about 90% of the population (and thus numerically, a majority), they held no meaningful power and were treated miserably by the Whites, who despite being a minority, ruled the country and controlled all of its institutions. Thus, Blacks in South Africa, until the arrival of a democratically elected government, were the subordinate group and Whites the dominant group.

One of the defining elements of being considered a member of a subordinate group is that the individual is likely to be perceived and treated in a negative and biased way that may involve either **prejudice** or **discrimination** or both. Although often confused, each of these terms represents a different idea. Prejudice refers to an attitude that evaluates an individual member of a subordinate group negatively on the basis of certain negative characteristics that are associated with that group even if the individual does not conform to those expected characteristics. For example, any given African American may be assumed not to be academically talented and in need of remedial education simply by virtue of his or her race/ethnicity. Discrimination, on the other hand, is an act that involves overtly treating members of a subordinate group negatively and unequally. As you can see, while both are negative toward subordinate groups, prejudice is an attitude or frame of mind, while discrimination involves actually behaving or doing something.

The two ideas are connected to each other, although not necessarily in a causal fashion. It is possible to relate the two, the famous sociologist Merton (1949) pointed out, in any one of the following combinations. In a democratic society where we guarantee equal rights and equal protection regardless of a person's background characteristics, we assume that members of the police will be **unprejudiced nondiscriminators**, that is, they do not harbor negative attitudes toward any particular subordinate group and will also never act negatively toward them. Another individual may be a **prejudiced discriminator**, one

dominant groups

A group that is advantaged and has superior resources and rights in a society.

prejudice

Refers to an attitude that evaluates an individual member of a subordinate group negatively on the basis of certain negative characteristics that are associated with that group even if the individual does not conform to those expected characteristics.

discrimination

An act that involves overtly treating members of a subordinate group negatively and unequally.

unprejudiced nondiscriminator

One who does not harbor negative attitudes toward any particular subordinate group and will also never act negatively toward them.

prejudiced discriminator

One who harbors negative attitudes toward any particular subordinate group and will act negatively toward them.

who does harbor negative attitudes toward any particular subordinate group and will act negatively toward them, for example, a police officer believes all Arabs are terrorists and proceeds to harass and intimidate any Arab he or she comes in contact with. A third individual may be a **prejudiced nondiscriminator**, that is, one who does harbor negative attitudes toward any particular subordinate group but does not act negatively toward them, for example, the police officer believes that all women who are out at night alone are "whores" and "sluts" but does not necessarily do anything following this belief when he or she encounters a woman while on patrol at night. Finally, a fourth individual may be an **unprejudiced discriminator**, that is, one who does not harbor negative attitude toward a subordinate group, but does act negatively toward them, for example, a police officer who does not believe that all juveniles are troublemakers, but as a result of how other fellow officers behave toward juveniles, goes along and treats them as such whenever he or she comes in contact with a juvenile.

Finally, in every society there are various forms of prejudice and discrimination (Winterdyk and Antonopoulos, 2007). This is to say that systematic patterns that combine prejudice and discrimination exist that result in beliefs about and actions toward subordinate groups that are unequal. Members of subordinate groups are therefore not believed to be or treated as equal members of a given society. The most common pattern based on perceived biological differences such as skin color, complexion, hair, and/or eye color is referred to as **racism**. In the South African example mentioned above, it is clear that until 1994, the country operated under an official ideology of racism (referred to as **apartheid**). A related version of such prejudice and discrimination that is based on cultural differences is known as **ethnic bias**. For example, even among members of ostensibly the same race, differences based on lifestyle, language, food, or other cultural items are seized upon, resulting in unequal treatment. It would be difficult to distinguish in terms of physical features between native Japanese and Koreans (about 1% of the population of Japan) settled for generations in Japan. However, the latter are subjected to prejudice and discrimination (i.e., ethnic bias) based on their lineage and cultural differences. For example, Korean Japanese are not allowed to become Japanese citizens even after generations of having lived in Japan. Similarly, biased beliefs about and actions toward one of the genders (almost always women) are called **sexism**. The pattern of prejudice and discrimination that we have been commenting about that targets juveniles fits under the title of **ageism** (although it should be pointed out that most of the time, this refers to negativity toward the elderly). Finally, negative attitudes and actions toward homosexuals are generally referred to as being motivated by **heterosexism**.

Regardless of the form of prejudice and discrimination, in every society each of these patterns leads to **stereotyping** and **scapegoating**. Stereotyping is defined as a fairly rigid, oversimplified (positive or negative) view or image of a particular social group that is then applied to individuals who belong to that group. It is possible to have stereotypes that relate to the different social groups that we began our discussion with. For example, racist or ethnic-based stereotypes such as all Asian Americans are academic over-achievers or that all Italian Americans have connections to the Mafia. Ageist stereotypes may focus on juveniles who are all said to drive rashly and

prejudiced nondiscriminator

One who harbors negative attitudes toward any particular subordinate group but does not act negatively toward them.

unprejudiced discriminator

One who does not harbor negative attitudes toward any particular subordinate group, but does discriminate against them.

racism

Unequal treatment of members of certain groups, based on perceived biological differences such as skin color, complexion, and hair and/or eye color.

apartheid

An official ideology of racism.

ethnic bias

Prejudice and discrimination that is based on cultural differences among groups, sometimes even if they are of the same race.

sexism

Biased beliefs about and actions toward one of the genders (almost always targeting women).

ageism

The pattern of prejudice and discrimination that negatively targets either the young or the elderly.

heterosexism

General term for negative attitudes and actions toward homosexuals.

stereotyping

A fairly rigid, oversimplified (positive or negative) view or image of a particular social group that is then applied to individuals who belong to that group.

scapegoating

A process by which members of subordinate groups are blamed for the problems and frustrations experienced by members of the dominant group.

irresponsibly or elderly drivers who are all deemed to be always going too slowly while either not knowing or forgetting where they are headed. Sexist stereotypes may define all women as being too emotional or being concerned only about their appearance. Stereotypes about homosexuals may hold all of them to be sexually unrestrained and promiscuous (while simultaneously denying them the right to marry and settle down with one partner).

Scapegoating is another consequence of the various patterns of prejudice and discrimination described above. In this social phenomenon, members of subordinate groups are blamed for the problems and frustrations experienced by members of the dominant groups. For example, widespread White unemployment may be blamed on immigration (too many Mexican citizens are coming into the country, many of them illegally, and they are taking away our jobs), affirmative action (they had to give whatever jobs are available to African Americans and Hispanics because it is the official policy of the federal government), or foreigners (people in China and India are taking away our jobs by being unfairly willing to work at cheaper rates). After the bombing of the World Trade Center and the Pentagon on September 11, 2001, the problem of terrorism in the United States was blamed on all individuals who looked "Arab" even if they were loyal American citizens and were not even of Arab origin, but had more or less similar physical features.

POLICE FUNCTIONS AND SUBORDINATE POPULATIONS

Among the various functions that we identified with the police are the following:

- crime fighting (or law enforcement) through preventing and detecting offenses;
- order maintenance through making sure that life flowed smoothly in a community;
- service by helping members of a community.

The broad and pervasive mandate (backed up by the right to legally use force) makes it especially important that police functions be carried out with due attention and sensitivity to all groups (not just the dominant ones) in a community. Thus, in carrying out each of these functions, police officers have the difficult task of at once being impartial, while also attempting to be aware of the risks of prejudice and discrimination. It is all the more important for the police since, as we have pointed out elsewhere in this book, they are the most visible representatives of the government. Think of the following possibilities. While engaging in crime fighting through crime detection, police detective cannot assume that a female suspect he or she encounters is going to be either guilty or not guilty based on stereotyping ("Cherchez la femme"—Look for the female vs. A women cannot be so violent). When carrying out crime fighting through crime prevention, a police school resource officer (SRO) must be willing to work with schools and neighborhoods that draw members of diverse racial and ethnic groups. While maintaining order in the form of traffic enforcement, a police patrol officer cannot automatically assume that if a juvenile happens to be driving a sports car, he or she definitely has "the need for speed" and has therefore already flouted traffic laws. This would be scapegoating. In terms of service, a police officer who is a first responder in the case of, for example, a bomb planted in a gay bar by a hate group, should not assume that all patrons of that bar are HIV-positive and therefore hesitate in providing medical assistance that would be available to others if needed.

One of the ways that police forces across the world have dealt with perceived prejudice and discrimination by them against subordinate groups has been to attempt to recruit members of those groups into their ranks. The idea is that with members of these groups also serving as police officers, three results may be achieved. First, subordinate group recruitment acts as a symbol of the police department's commitment to stand against prejudice and discrimination of that given group. Second, it sends a positive message to subordinate group members who see one of their own (who presumably is coming from the same background and therefore may understand issues in a manner sensitive to the concerns of group members) in uniform. Third, subordinate group members who are employed as police officers are likely to provide direction and meaning to police department efforts to reach out to members of the group that he or she represents.

The rest of this chapter will examine two major issues regarding police–subordinate group interaction. First, we will consider how the various characteristics that subject individuals belonging to certain subordinate groups to bias of one kind or the other affect policing and how those individuals are in turn affected by the police (generally, in a negative fashion). Second, we will examine how attempts at inclusiveness (i.e., recruiting and including members of subordinate groups into policing) are faring with regard to these groups. We look at these two questions in relation to three major subordinate groups: those based on race/ethnicity, gender, and sexuality. While this is not an exhaustive list, it will allow us to gain further understanding of how police affect certain subordinate groups (and vice versa) in democratic societies where the highest ideals are associated with equality and equal treatment.

Race/Ethnicity

One of the most serious accusations made against police in almost all **multicultural (or plural) societies** (societies that are made up of more than one ethnic group) is that they treat individuals from subordinate racial and ethnic groups with prejudice and discrimination. In an American context, perhaps the most explosive issues associated with police bias, prejudice, and discrimination center around the treatment of racial and ethnic subordinate groups such as African Americans and Hispanics. They are accused of doing so by targeting visible racial and ethnic subordinate groups for greater harassment, unnecessarily stopping and questioning them, arresting them in greater numbers, and brutalizing them, that is, treating them unequally in an overall manner. Sever (2003: 153) argues that, "The topic of race and crime is one of the most essential

multicultural (or plural) societies

Societies that are made up of more than one ethnic group.

research areas in criminology and criminal justice today. A large percentage of arrests and a majority of offenders in the U.S. prison population are from minority groups, making it imperative that we place a strong emphasis on seeking out the underlying reasons for such a disparity." Consider the following quote from two sociologists (Andersen and Taylor, 2002: 326):

> African Americans and Hispanic people are arrested by the police considerably more often that Whites and Asians. In fact … an African American or Hispanic wrongdoer is more likely to be arrested than is White man who commits the same crime even when the White man shares the same age, socioeconomic environment, and prior arrest record as the Black or Hispanic. Once in custody, an African American or Hispanic is more likely to be detained without bail, more likely to go to trial, and more likely to receive a stiffer sentence at the end of the trial than is a White man of similar social background and criminal record.

It should not be forgotten in this regard that historically, police and law enforcement were often at the forefront of treating subordinate group members unfairly and unequally. During the race riots of the early twentieth century and the Civil Rights Movement of the 1960s, the police were the visible and ferocious defenders of an unequal system of laws that actively segregated and marked African Americans for unequal treatment. Penn (2003) notes (while calling for an African American-centered criminology) that, "The unique history of over 240 years of slavery, live in the antebellum South, migration, Black Codes and Jim Crow laws, migration, segregation, affirmative action and disproportionality in the criminal justice system provides clear evidence for a criminological perspective that encompasses the history and culture of the Black people in the United States." Notice how many of the issues mentioned by him are related to the police and law enforcement. When considering the nature of the interactions between the police and members of subordinate racial or ethnic groups, studies have investigated the following three questions:

1. Does police strength increase along with the numbers of subordinate racial and ethnic group members? If this question is answered affirmatively, it may mean that society (or at least that particular locality) views subordinate groups as threatening and thus fields more police as a way of keeping these socially threatening people at bay. In other words, the members of the dominant group use the police to reduce the actual and perceived threat that the subordinate group poses for them. As a result, the police are also likely to arrest more members of the threatening subordinate groups. If there is a negative or no relationship, it means that society (or that community) may be tending toward equality. A body of literature using various levels of analysis such as suburbs, cities, counties, metropolitan statistical areas, states, and countries (see Sever, 2003 for details) has measured the relationship between subordinate population numbers in these geographical areas and the relevant police strengths represented in them. While there are several limitations in the studied examined, the percentage of minorities in a locality does affect the number of police officers positively.

2. How do police officers interact with and treat members of subordinate racial or ethnic groups? For instance, do American police target African Americans because the latter are involved in crime to a greater degree or because the former behave discriminatorily? Cureton (2000: 68) is equivocal on this particular issue, but his review of the literature shows that, out of the sixteen studies on this topic that he examined, eight "showed that subordinate group status was a stronger predictor (compared to criminal conduct) of higher arrests for blacks than whites." This is in comparison to one study that "indicated that criminal conduct and/or crime seriousness was a stronger determinant (compared to subordinate group status) of higher arrests for blacks than whites." Winkel (1991) showed that the police in the Netherlands treated those perceived as not being Dutch citizens quite differently from those perceived to be citizens. He showed experimentally that this had much to do with nonverbal communication patterns that varied between Blacks and Whites. By considering the percent Black, percent Hispanic (in the Southwest United States), and the income inequality between the dominant group and the subordinate group, Holmes (2000) found that police brutality complaints to the Civil Rights Division of the U.S. Department of Justice tend to go up when "threatening people," that is, members of subordinate group, are present. This distrust and differential treatment is perceived and resented by members of the subordinate group. Browning, Cullen, Cao, Kopacha, and Stevenson (1994) report that African Americans in Cincinnati felt that police officers are more likely to stop and "hassle" them when compared to White residents. All these studies lead to a consideration of what has come to be known as **racial profiling**. Although there can be various forms of profiling (see Johnson, 2000, for a critique of drug courier profiles), this term refers to the tendency of police officers in some jurisdictions to stop, question, and search members of subordinate racial and ethnic groups for minor infractions (e.g., a tail light that is not working on an automobile) in comparison to members of dominant racial and ethnic groups. Their constant experience with this form of harassment has led to jokes among African Americans in the United States that they were stopped and questioned for the offense of "driving while black." There are no comparable jokes about being stopped and questioned for the offense of "driving while white." Russell (2003: 97–111) cited various related corollary phenomena such as "walking while black," "idling while black," "standing while black," "shopping while black," and "numerous other offenses which fall under the while black umbrella." All of these entail targeting and harassing African Americans because of preconceptions about the higher likelihood of their being involved with crime. However, Lynch and Schuck (2003: 94) have argued forcefully that racial profiling is based on invalid assumptions about who criminals are (in a statistical and empirical sense) and that, "Even though racial profiling undoubtedly captures some who are guilty, it comes at an unacceptably high individual and social cost."

3. Given that police departments fight charges of racism by exhibiting inclusiveness in employment, how is the recruitment and retention of subordinate group police officers faring? The number of African Americans applying to become members

racial profiling

This term refers to the tendency of police officers in some jurisdictions to stop, question, and search members of subordinate racial and ethnic groups for minor infractions in comparison to members of dominant racial and ethnic groups.

of police forces has tended to be low. It is heavily influenced by the percentage of the population in a given city that belongs to a subordinate group (O'Brien, 2003). Kuykendall and Burns (1980) found that African Americans served as police officers as early as 1861 in Washington, DC. For much of American police history, however, this was rare. It was the Civil Rights movement of the 1960s and subsequent legislation that gave an added push to hire more subordinate group members, especially African Americans, into police departments across the United States. However, it has been suggested that simmering tensions between African Americans and police departments often were taken by the former to mean that they are not welcome within the latter. When included as employees in police agencies, ironically people of similar racial backgrounds resent African American police officers. These officers are often in the unenviable position of being simultaneously distrusted both by their White colleagues and by members of the African American community they police. This is akin to what has been termed **double marginality**, a situation in which someone while is a member of two groups does not receive full acceptance and trust by both groups. This difficult position of African American police officers is reflected in Hacker's (1992: 189) observation that, "a disproportionately high number of … killings of blacks are by black policemen, which suggests that departments tend to give black officers assignments where they encounter suspects of their own race."

Police officers are, of course, members of the society that they police. As such, it should not surprise us that they may carry within them some of the stereotypes that are culturally associated with various racial and ethnic groups and then proceed to act on the basis of these ingrained mental images. In other words, it is possible for both White and African American police officers to hold certain prejudicial opinions about their own groups, other racial and ethnic groups, and each other. The challenge for both a given police officer and his or her agency is to rise above these assumptions and to treat individuals based on their actual and verified behavior.

Women

According to the last census, there were 145 million women compared to 139.8 million men in the United States. As we noted earlier, it is therefore ironic to describe women, who constitute more than half the population of the United States, as a subordinate group. This is one of the reasons that the term "minority group" was deemed inaccurate for those who do not belong to the dominant groups of a society. However, it would be difficult to argue that women are not a subordinate group in the sense of being treated unequally and because they often regard themselves as being subject to prejudice and discrimination. One need only look at the ranks of American political, business, and military leaders to realize that at least till recently, it has been "a man's world." For example, the Supreme Court of the United States, the highest court in the land, has only one woman on it (and the maximum has been two). Further, the last census noted that for every one dollar that is earned by an American man, his female equivalent earns 76 cents. However, despite women constituting a clear majority in the United States, their contribution in terms of being arrested for crimes is a relatively small 22% (although

---

double marginality

A situation in which someone while he or she is a member of two groups does not receive full acceptance and trust by both groups.

this has been increasing in recent times). In general and historically, women have been arrested for relatively minor crimes such as low-level property and drug-related offenses. They are rarely involved in violent crimes. As such, female crime is often given low priority and accorded less seriousness in police work. One consequence of this fact is that much of our discussion regarding women as a subordinate group in policing will not center on prejudicial attitudes and discriminatory treatment of women as suspects of crime, but more as victims of crime. We focus on three questions:

1. Knowing that males are more likely then females to call the police (Kaukinen, 2003), how responsive are the police to female victims of crime? The answer to this question depends to some extent on the likelihood of female victims seeking help from the police. It also depends on what the victimized women expect from the police after they arrive, ranging from simply warning the offenders to arresting them (Hirschel and Hutchison, 2003). Kaukinen (2004) finds a racial dimension to this issue in that White women who have been victimized by someone they know are more likely to seek such help (including from the police) in comparison to female victims of other races. Research has also found that women are more likely to call the police when the male partners use alcohol and drugs, and when the latter are repeatedly drunk (Hutchison, 2003). Urban areas and those where higher levels of stranger assaults take place are likely to report more instances of sexual victimization (Ruback and Menard, 2001). Interestingly, the police are more likely to make an arrest for domestic violence, "when the suspect is an intimate partner as they are when the suspect is someone else the victim knows" (Felson and Ackerman, 2001: 655). While, in general, female victims of domestic violence found the police very helpful (Apsler, Cummins, and Carl, 2003), perceptual and situational barriers to asking for such assistance do exist (Wolf, Uyen, Hobart, and Kernic, 2003).

Tougher police policies against domestic violence, especially those recommending arrest, have become the norm in a number of Western countries (Stewart, 2001). Police decisions to arrest batterers, Coulter, Kuehnle, Byers, and Alfonso (1999) report, based on a questionnaire survey of 398 battered women in a Florida shelter, are likely to depend on offender–victim interactional characteristics such as physical or sexual abuse and stalking rather than on emotional abuse. While research indicates that the mandatory arrest policies appear to be effective (Tolman and Weisz, 1995), over an eighteen-month period, Belknap (1995) found from a survey of Midwestern police officers, that there is more support for mediation rather than arrest. In addition, Fyfe, Klinger, and Flavin (1997) reported that men who physically abuse their spouses are dealt with less punitively than other violent offenders by the Chester, Pennsylvania, police department. Do more women police officers make a difference in terms of how complaints from women are dealt with? Stalans and Finn (2000) find that with regard to domestic violence, there is no difference regarding arrest decisions, but that experienced women police officers are more likely to suggest female victims to go to battered women's shelters and less likely to suggest marriage counseling.

2. A second (though less important) question that researchers have been interested in is how police treat women who are suspected of, or arrested for, committing crimes.

....
chivalry hypothesis

Women are treated less
harshly (i.e., more leniently)
than male suspects by the
police and the criminal justice
system, given traditional
gender expectations and
notions of them being the
"weaker sex."

There are two seemingly contradictory viewpoints on this question. First is the idea, often referred to as the **chivalry hypothesis**, that women are treated less harshly (i.e., more leniently) than male suspects given traditional gender expectations and notions of them being the "weaker sex." This is coupled with expectations regarding how males are supposed to treat females, that is, with respect and helpfulness. A second viewpoint on the treatment of women offenders suggests the opposite. Consistent with the treatment of other subordinate groups, the second view suggests that female suspects are likely to be dealt with greater harshness and severity. Ironically, this may be due to female criminals also having violated norms about how women are supposed to behave, that is, with modesty and decorum. Obviously, both of these viewpoints cannot be correct. The literature, however, is equivocal. Visher (1983) found that chivalrous treatment by the police existed for those female suspects who showed behaviors and characteristics stereotypically designated as feminine. Welle and Falkin (2000), on the other hand, found that women offenders with "romantic co-defendants" face significant and more severe treatment by the criminal justice system.

3. Third, how do women fare as members of police departments? There is a long history of women being involved as police employees, though not necessarily as sworn police officers. Milton (1972) found that the New York City Police Department (NYPD) employed two police "matrons" (note the term used) as early as 1845. The job of early female police employees who were not accorded the status of police officers was to deal with women and girls arrested for offenses such as prostitution and vagrancy. The first female police officer was sworn into that job in Chicago in 1893 (Higgins, 1951). However, it would be safe to say that policing was and continues to be a male-dominated occupation. Even during the Second World War in the United States when women in large numbers worked in industrial and service jobs, policing was identified almost exclusively with men. For as long as policing has existed, even if officers were referred to as "police" instead of "policemen," the speaker clearly meant someone who was male. However, in the twenty-first century United States, we rarely hear the term "policemen" anymore. Instead, the preferred terms nowadays are "police officers" or "peace officers" (a broader term for a variety of criminal justice personnel). These terms, however, have only recently been widely accepted and used. The source of these changes in language has to do with women entering police departments in significant numbers. This phenomenon can be traced to particular amendments to the Civil Rights Act of 1964 (implemented in the early 1970s) that prohibited gender-based discrimination. Even after more than three decades of female police officers, as noted earlier women are only about 10–12% (depending on how the counting is done) of all sworn police personnel.

Morash (1994: 388) summarizes much of the early research on women's participation in policing as follows:

Men and women often have the same difficulties at work. Many police officers, for example, feel that they have little control over the way policing "gets done" on a day-to-day basis. But women also have special problems with the most persistent being sexual harassment at work. Women reported harassment in many forms including supervisors looking at pornographic material in their presence, making unwanted comments about their being homosexual, and trying to have a romantic (or at least sexual) relationship with them. From co-workers they reported physical touching, unwanted jokes about their attractive appearance, and attempts at intercourse. Agencies with high levels of harassment from co-workers also had high levels from supervisors.

There are some other related issues. What influences more women to be hired in police departments? After pointing out that there are variations in hiring among White, Hispanic, and African American women police officers, Zhao, Herbst, and Lovrich (2001) show that overall female employment is heavily influenced by the presence of a female in the position of a strong city mayor. How about the job performance of women police officers? While there were differences in the approaches that the two genders took toward policing citizens, the hostile reception accorded to females entering a predominantly male occupation did not result in unsatisfactory job performance on the part of the women. For example, while there was little difference in job satisfaction when male and female officers are compared (Dantzker and Kubin, 1998), there is greater public acceptance of them (Leger, 1997), and allegations of misconduct by citizens occur proportionally more against male rather than female officers (Lersch, 1998). An authoritative report by the Bureau of Justice Assistance (2001: 2) concluded that, "Research conducted both in the United States and internationally clearly demonstrates that women police officers use a style of policing that relies less on physical force." They are better at defusing and de-escalating potentially violent confrontations with citizens and are less likely to become involved in incidents of excessive force. Finally, Kakar (2002) found that women officers perceive themselves to be equally qualified as men officers in carrying out all aspects of policing.

Has the reception from their male colleagues changed for the better more recently? It is difficult to say although we certainly cannot claim revolutionary improvements. For example, while the proportion of women in policing has increased, they have not found their way into upper-level administrative positions (Wertsch, 1998). The effects of being a "double minority," in this case a female and an African American, in a large urban police department were explored by Pogrebin, Dodge, and Chatman (2000) and Pogrebin and Dodge (2001). They found that such individuals often feel like they are outsiders within their own departments, experiencing both racial and gender discrimination. Sexual harassment of women officers occurs in other countries as well, for example, the United Kingdom (see Brown, 1998). Interestingly, Luna-Firebaugh (2002), based on a survey of 170 Native American police departments, found that such agencies had five times more women in supervisory and command positions compared to nontribal departments. In addition, women in these agencies do not perceive hostility from their male colleagues.

Homosexuals

Homosexuals, that is, those whose sexual orientation may be gay or lesbian, constitute a subordinate group that is also a numerical minority (e.g., estimates range from 7% to 10% of the male population in the United States). The subordinate status of this

homophobia

A term that generally indicates fear of or aversion to homosexuals and homosexuality.

group has historical roots in religious beliefs, traditional mores, and governmental policies (e.g., with regard to gays openly serving in various branches of the military and whether or not the state should recognize gay marriages) that continue to be debated to this day. One of the enduring controversies in society and the police is the degree to which **homophobia**, a term that generally indicates fear of or aversion to homosexuals and homosexuality, affects both the larger and the smaller group. Arnott (1994) found that many police officers believe homosexuals suffer from a mental abnormality and that their (sexual) behavior is intrinsically illegal. This leads them to homophobic beliefs and attitudes toward gays and lesbians. Further, Olivero and Murataya (2001) examined eighteen major textbooks on law enforcement (of the kind that are likely to be prescribed for students taking a law enforcement course at a college or university) and found that only one mentioned gays in a brief discussion. Looking at another society, Yuzgun (1993) detailed in a chilling article how police in Istanbul, Turkey, terrorize homosexuals based on religious and social biases even though there are no specific laws against homosexual behavior. It was found that homosexuals were "hospitalized" in mental asylums, beaten, medically diagnosed (incorrectly) as suffering from syphilis, kicked out of the city, and tortured by the Istanbul police.

Olivero and Murataya (2001) commented based on research that law enforcement agencies are unwilling to address important problems to homosexuals within their jurisdictions such as the prevalence of homicide and hate crimes directed against gays and lesbians. Among other issues, gay victims of hate crimes are often concerned about police bias against them as well as the consequences of their sexual orientation being publicly disclosed (Herek, Cogan, and Gillis, 2002). As a result of the perceived homophobia, lesbians and gay men are less likely to report violent crime victimization experiences to police agencies. The resulting situation is especially unfortunate in that perceptions on both sides (i.e., on the part of the police and homosexuals) have prevented all citizens of a democratic society from being able to access police services while simultaneously deflecting the police from their mandate of serving everyone in their jurisdiction equally.

Olivero and Murataya (2001: 278) suggest that, "gay rights, gay issues, hate crimes against gays etc should all be added as a necessary feature of law enforcement curriculum." In support of this line of action, Younglove, Kerr, and Vitello (2002) find that when police officers are presented with scenarios of domestic violence, they did not show any differences in terms of perception between same-sex and different-sex couples. This study was conducted following a change to California law that included same-sex couples in its delineation of domestic violence. If interpreted positively, the results of this study present a hopeful sign to those concerned about how prejudice against gays may lead to discrimination against them since it appears to indicate that even homophobia may not deter police officers from carrying out legal mandates regarding domestic violence. At worst, it suggests that police officers can act as prejudiced nondiscriminators to use Robert Merton's terms that we studied earlier. The concerns of homosexuals as a subordinate group and their needs (equal to that of other citizens and taxpayers) for protection and service from the police will be the one that will need attention in the near future.

How do police officers who themselves are homosexual in their sexual orientation fare within police departments where "heterosexual masculinity" (Miller, Forest, and Jurik, 2003) is idealized? Thompson and Nored (2002: 203) stated flatly that law enforcement has been a profession that is "particularly open in its discrimination against homosexual employees." They find cases of employment discrimination against gays and lesbians pervasive. Turning to another country, the United Kingdom, Burke (1994: 192) found that given the macho subculture of police departments, gay, lesbian, and bisexual officers often led "double as opposed to integrated lives," leading to increased stress. Miller, Forest, and Jurik (2003) described the struggles of such officers in dealing with pervasive homophobia and sexism who often saw themselves at the forefront of more humane form of policing, particularly with respect to marginal groups.

POLICE AND SPECIAL POPULATIONS: THREE SOCIOLOGICAL PERSPECTIVES

What would the three sociological perspectives, functionalism, conflict, and interactionism, make of the above issues that we have seen with regard to the interaction between the police and particular subordinate sections of the population? From a functionalist perspective, negative treatment of particular groups and individuals belonging to those groups would be dysfunctional behavior on the part of the police, particularly in a society where everyone is supposed to be treated equally. Functionalists would point to laws and policies that protect the rights of the disadvantaged against discriminatory treatment as expressing what would be expected and functional for a democratic society. Given these normative expectations, when police officers treat members of minority groups or homosexuals negatively, those biased individuals should be punished or expelled from the police agency. The functionalist would argue that such behavior exists because there is a gap between what we as a society say is right and what we (or the police who represent us) do in actual circumstances. The goal should be to narrow this gap and make the police act in ways that are functional to society as a whole.

For the conflict theorist, the prejudiced attitudes and discriminatory behavior of police officers toward individuals from subordinate groups crystallize their own critical views toward society. It confirms for them that society, despite claiming to be for equal treatment and respecting the rights of everyone, consists in reality of those few who possess power, wealth, and position, and others who do not have much of these resources. In this competition and conflict, the police, despite their claims to treat everyone equally, are not exactly neutral. They are paid by and support the few elite members (dominant ethnic or racial groups, males, heterosexuals, etc.) to control and manipulate or suppress those who are not like them. The many instances of police brutality and ill treatment of individuals belonging to subordinate groups lead them to ask why, if everything was equal, these actions occur so frequently.

Finally, interactionists who focus on how rhetoric and meanings are interpreted in society are likely to be interested in other questions. For example, the police use certain cues and assumptions to stop particular individuals on the road. The phenomenon of "driving while black" has already been mentioned above. This involves the police stopping individuals who are African American in numbers greater than their proportion in the population. How are these ideas and the cues to look for transmitted to patrol officers in a police department, particularly since such actions are supposed to be illegal? Similarly, interactionists would be interested in understanding incidents of sexual harassment in terms of the general and particular meanings that are involved in gender interaction, and where actions and meanings collide to produce allegations of sexual harassment.

As we have done in other chapters, we examine how the police in the United Kingdom treat members of minority groups. The United States and the United Kingdom share similarities in police and legal traditions; it should not surprise us that there are similarities in the treatment of minorities too.

POLICE AND SPECIAL POPULATIONS INTERNATIONALLY: UNITED KINGDOM

American law enforcement, as we have observed numerous times in this book, originally modeled itself after the United Kingdom, taking on much of that country's policing form and function. In general, while this earlier historical debt is often mentioned, there is little known about how contemporary British policing deals with issues such as dealing with an increasingly diverse population. According to their 2001 Census, non-Whites constituted close to 8% (or slightly more than 4.6 million) of Britain's population (totaling around 58.8 million). Most of the subordinate ethnic groups were from Britain's former colonies in South Asia (India, Pakistan, and Bangladesh) comprising 4% of the total population and the Caribbean and Africa (i.e., Black or African) comprising another 2%. In addition, the British Census also recognizes individuals of mixed ethnicity who are 1.2% of the population. Further, the rate of growth in numbers of these non-White groups has outstripped the White population, making Britain more of a multicultural or plural society than it has been in the past.

In a book written about the United Kingdom more than three decades ago, author Humphry (1972: 11) noted that, "To many blacks in our inner cities, police harassment has become a way of life," and went on to document how members of this subordinate group

had been victimized by the very employees of the state who were sworn to protect them. A decade later, Brake (1983: 4) commented on how Black youth while facing large-scale unemployment were subjected to organized attacks from extreme right-wing groups as well as "heavy police surveillance." It would be safe to say that those concerns, while perhaps somewhat less blatant, have certainly not abated with Britain's increasingly multicultural population. Smith (1997: 101) found that not only were Caribbean Blacks and South Asians more likely to be victimized by crime, but also the former tend to be targets of "proactive law enforcement." Recently, Holdaway (2003) recounted using data from the British Crime Survey, employment statistics, and interviews with members of subordinate ethnic groups that prejudice and discrimination continue to exist in relation to British policing. He finds that there are three areas of concern. First, and familiar to American readers, was the unequal implementation of police powers to stop and search individuals (in other words, a form of racial profiling). Second, the British police appeared to do a less-than-creditable job in the investigation of hate crime offenses against subordinate groups. Finally, there seemed to be a lack of genuine openness to the hiring of non-Whites into the police force. On this last issue, Cashmore (2002) had found in interviews with Black Caribbean and South Asian officers who had been hired that they continued to see the persistence of racism in the police and did not view their work situations favorably. Their views were directly in contrast to official pronouncements about the "benefits of recruiting more ethnic minority officers and enhancing cultural diversity training for police" (Cashmore, 2002: 327). In an earlier paper, Cashmore (2001: 650) had noted that, "Ethnic minority police officers are subject to racist abuse as a way of testing them" and that protesting against such treatment would be detrimental to their careers.

As you can observe, the litany of complaints and general dissatisfaction parallels those we are more familiar with in American policing. Issues of prejudice, discrimination, unequal treatment, profiling, equal employment opportunity, and openness to diversity and multiculturalism are common themes in terms of the interaction between the police and subordinate groups in both countries.

Finally, we look at policing in Native American areas of the United States (see box). Strictly speaking, Native American tribes are not separate countries. However, for purposes of policing and other internal governmental issues, they are treated as separate entities. Given that they are a minority group within the United States, how does policing in areas that Native American tribes control work?

SUMMARY

In this chapter, we focused on how police departments interact with subordinate groups, those that do not possess power and resources in society. The three such groups we examined in this manner are racial and ethnic groups (especially African Americans), women, and homosexuals. We learned about how prejudice (an attitude) and discrimination (actions) are related and operate together to produce certain forms of behavior, some of which result in the unequal treatment of subordinate groups by the police. We examined in particular research findings that elucidate how the police in terms of three questions deal with certain racial and ethnic groups, women, and homosexuals. The first question is how members of a subordinate group who are victims of crime are treated. The second is how the police deal with members of a subordinate group who are offenders. Finally, we consider how well attempts at including members of subordinate groups in police departments by hiring them as police officers have worked. We then focused on the experience of another country, the United Kingdom, in working out its own police–subordinate group inter-relationships.

KEY TERMS

Ageism: The pattern of prejudice and discrimination that negatively targets either the young or the elderly.

Apartheid: An official ideology of racism.

Chivalry hypothesis: Women are treated less harshly (i.e., more leniently) than male suspects by the police and the criminal justice system, given traditional gender expectations and notions of them being the "weaker sex."

Discrimination: An act that involves overtly treating members of a subordinate group negatively and unequally.

Dominant groups: A group that is advantaged and has superior resources and rights in a society.

Double marginality: A situation in which someone while he or she is a member of two groups does not receive full acceptance and trust by both groups.

Ethnic bias: Prejudice and discrimination that is based on cultural differences among groups, sometimes even if they are of the same race.

Heterosexism: General term for negative attitudes and actions toward homosexuals.

Homophobia: A term that generally indicates fear of or aversion to homosexuals and homosexuality.

Multicultural (or plural) societies: Societies that are made up of more than one ethnic group.

Prejudice: Refers to an attitude that evaluates an individual member of a subordinate group negatively on the basis of certain negative characteristics that are associated with that group even if the individual does not conform to those expected characteristics.

Prejudiced discriminator: One who harbors negative attitudes toward any particular subordinate group and will act negatively toward them.

Prejudiced nondiscriminator: One who harbors negative attitudes toward any particular subordinate group but does not act negatively toward them.

Racial profiling: This term refers to the tendency of police officers in some jurisdictions to stop, question, and search members of subordinate racial and ethnic groups for minor infractions in comparison to members of dominant racial and ethnic groups.

Racism: Unequal treatment of members of certain groups, based on perceived biological differences such as skin color, complexion, and hair and/or eye color.

Scapegoating: A process by which members of subordinate groups are blamed for the problems and frustrations experienced by members of the dominant group.

Sexism: Biased beliefs about and actions toward one of the genders (almost always targeting women).

Stereotyping: A fairly rigid, oversimplified (positive or negative) view or image of a particular social group that is then applied to individuals who belong to that group.

Subordinate groups: One whose members, because of physical or cultural characteristics, are disadvantaged and subjected to unequal treatment by the dominant group and who regard themselves as objects of collective discrimination.

Unprejudiced discriminator: One who does not harbor negative attitudes toward any particular subordinate group, but does discriminate against them.

Unprejudiced nondiscriminator: One who does not harbor negative attitudes toward any particular subordinate group and will also never act negatively toward them.

REVIEW QUESTIONS

1. Describe, using examples from policing, how prejudice and discrimination intersect each other (as identified by Robert Merton).

2. How do the police interact in an unequal manner with individuals who are members of subordinate groups based on race/ethnicity, gender, and sexual orientation?

3. What are the similarities and differences in terms of unequal treatment of subordinate groups between the British police and American police?

DISCUSSION QUESTIONS

1. Which sociological perspective on police and minorities as discussed in this chapter do you most agree with? Please explain why.

2. Discuss whether it would be possible for the police to carry out their major functions without treating members of subordinate groups unequally. Explain why this would or would not be possible.

3. Of the three (racial/ethnic minorities, women, and homosexuals) major forms of unequal treatment by the police discussed in this chapter, which one do you consider the most serious and which one the least serious? Support your choices with reasons.

REFERENCES

Andersen, Margaret L. and Howard F. Taylor (2002) *Sociology: Understanding a Diverse Society*. Belmont, CA: Wadsworth/Thomson Learning.

Apsler, Robert; Michele R. Cummins and Steven Carl (2003) "Perceptions of the Police by Female Victims of Domestic Partner Violence." *Violence against Women* 9, 11: 1318–1335.

Arnott, J. S. (1994) "Gays and Lesbians in the Criminal Justice System." Pp. 211–213 In J. E. Hendricks and B. D. Byers (eds.) *Multicultural Perspectives in Criminal Justice and Criminology*. Springfield, IL: Charles C. Thomas.

Belknap, Joanne (1995) "Law Enforcement Attitudes about the Appropriate Responses to Woman Battering." *International Review of Victimology* 4, 1: 47–52.

Brake, Mike (1983) "Under Heavy Manners: A Consideration of Racism, Black Youth Culture and Crime in Britain." *Crime and Social Justice* 20, 1: 1–15.

Brown, Jennifer M. (1998) "Aspects of Discriminatory Treatment of Women Police Officers Serving in Forces in England and Wales." *British Journal of Criminology* 38, 2: 265–282.

Browning, Sandra L.; Francis T. Cullen; Liqun Cao; Renee Kopacha and Thomas J. Stevenson (1994) "Race and Getting Hassled by the Police: A Research Note." *Police Studies* 17, 1: 1–11.

Bureau of Justice Assistance (2001) *Recruiting and Retaining Women: A Self-Assessment Guide*. Washington, DC: Bureau of Justice Assistance.

Burke, Marc (1994) "Homosexuality as Deviance: The Case of the Gay Police Officer." *British Journal of Criminology* 34, 2: 192–203.

Cashmore, Ellis (2001) "The Experiences of Ethnic Minority Police Officers in Britain: Under-recruitment and Racial Profiling in a Performance Culture." *Ethnic and Racial Studies* 24, 4: 642–659.

Cashmore, Ellis (2002) "Behind the Window Dressing: Ethnic Minority Police Perspectives on Cultural Diversity." *Journal of Ethnic and Migration Studies* 28, 2: 327–341.

Coulter, Martha L.; Kathryn Kuehnle; Robert Byers and Maya Alfonso (1999) "Police Reporting Behavior and Victim–Police Interactions as Described by Women in a Domestic Violence Shelter." *Journal of Interpersonal Violence* 14, 2: 1290–1298.

Cureton, Steven R. (2000) "Determinants of Black-to-White Arrest Differentials: A Review of the Literature." Pp. 65–72 In M. W. Markowitz and D. D. Jones-Brown (eds.) *The System in Black and White: Exploring the Connections between Race, Crime and Justice*. Westport, CT: Praeger.

Dantzker, Mark L. and Betsy Kubin (1998) "Job Satisfaction: The Gender Perspective among Police Officers." *American Journal of Criminal Justice* 23, 1: 19–31.

Feagin, Joe R. and Clariece Boohier Feagin (2002) *Racial and Ethnic Relations*. Seventh Edition. Upper Saddle River, NJ: Prentice Hall.

Felson, Richard B. and Jeff Ackerman (2001) "Arrest for Domestic and Other Assaults." *Criminology* 39, 3: 655–675.

Fyfe, James J.; David A. Klinger and Jeanne M. Flavin (1997) "Differential Police Treatment of Male-on-female Spousal Violence." *Criminology* 35, 3: 455–473.

Hacker, Andrew (1992) *Two Nations: Black and White, Separate, Hostile and Unequal*. New York: Ballantine.

Herek, Gregory M.; Jeanine C. Cogan and J. Roy Gillis (2002) "Victim Experiences in Hate Crimes Based on Sexual Orientation." *Journal of Social Issues* 58, 2: 319–339.

Higgins, Lois L. (1951) "Historical Background of Policewomen's Service." *Journal of Criminal Law and Criminology* 41, 6: 822–835.

Hirschel, David and Ira W. Hutchison (2003) "The Voices of Domestic Violence Victims: Predictors of Victim Preference for Arrest and the Relationship between Preference for Arrest and Revictimization." *Crime and Delinquency* 49, 2: 313–336.

Holdaway, Simon (2003) "Victimization Within Constabularies in England and Wales: The Legacy of Immigration." *International Review of Victimology* 10, 2: 137–156.

Holmes, Malcolm D. (2000) "Minority Threat and Police Brutality: Determinants of Civil Rights Complaints in U.S. Municipalities." *Criminology* 38, 2: 343–368.

Humphry, Derek (1972) *Police Power and Black People*. London: Panther.

Hutchison, Ira W. (2003) "Substance Use and Abused Women's Utilization of the Police." *Journal of Family Violence* 18, 2: 93–106.

Johnson, Scott (2000) "The Self-fulfilling Prophecy of Police Profiles." Pp. 93–108 In M. W. Markowitz and D. D. Jones-Brown (eds.) *The System in Black and White: Exploring the Connections between Race, Crime and Justice*. Westport, CT: Praeger.

Kakar, Suman (2002) "Gender and Police Officers' Perceptions of their Job Performance: An Analysis of the Relationship between Gender and Perceptions of Job Performance." *Criminal Justice Policy Review* 13, 3: 238–256.

Kaukinen, Catherine (2003) "The Help-seeking Decisions of Violent Crime Victims: An Examination of the Direct and Conditional Effects of Gender and the Victim–Offender Relationship." *Journal of Interpersonal Violence* 17, 4: 432–456.

Kaukinen, Catherine (2004) "The Help-seeking Strategies of Female Violent Crime Victims: The Direct and Conditional Effects of Race and the Victim–Offender Relationship." *Journal of Interpersonal Violence* 19, 9: 967–990.

Kendall, Diana (2005) *Sociology in Our Times*. Fifth Edition. Belmont, CA: Thomson Wadsworth.

Kuykendall, J. and D. Burns (1980) "The Black Police Officer: An Historical Perspective." *Journal of Contemporary Criminal Justice* 1, 1: 103–113.

Leger, Kristen (1997) "Public Perceptions of Female Police Officers on Patrol." *American Journal of Criminal Justice* 21, 2: 231–249.

Lersch, Kim M. (1998) "Exploring Gender Differences in Citizen Allegations of Misconduct: An Analysis of a Municipal Police Department." *Women and Criminal Justice* 9, 4: 69–79.

Luna-Firebaugh, Eileen (2002) "Women in Tribal Policing: An Examination of their Status and Experience." *Social Science Journal* 39, 4: 583–592.

Lynch, Michael J. and Annie M. Schuck (2003) "Picasso as a Criminologist: The Abstract Art of Racial Profiling." Pp. 81–96 In M. D. Free, Jr. (ed.) *Racial Issues in Criminal Justice: The Case of African Americans*. Westport, CT: Praeger.

Marks, Alexandra (1999) "Black and White View of Police." *Christian Science Monitor*, June 1.

Merton, Robert K. (1949) "Discrimination and the American Creed." Pp. 22–31 In R. W. MacIver (ed.) *Discrimination and the National Welfare*. New York: Harper and Brothers.

Miller, Susan L.; Kay B. Forest and Nancy C. Jurik (2003) "Diversity in Blue: Lesbian and Gay Police Officers in a Masculine Occupation." *Men and Masculinities* 5, 4: 355–385.

Milton, Catherine (1972) *Women in Policing*. Washington, DC: Police Foundation.

Morash, Merry (1994) "The Work Experiences of Policewomen: Still a Minority." In L. A. Radelet and D. L. Carter (eds.) *The Police and the Community*. Fifth Edition. New York: Macmillan.

O'Brien, Kevin M. (2003) "The Determinants of Minority Employment in Police and Fire Departments." *Journal of Socio-Economics* 32, 2: 183–195.

Olivero, J. Michael and Rodrigo Murataya (2001) "Homophobia and University Law Enforcement Students." *Journal of Criminal Justice Education* 12: 271–281.

Penn, Everette B. (2003) "On Black Criminology: Past, Present and Future." *Criminal Justice Studies* 16, 4: 317–327.

Pogrebin, Mark and Mary Dodge (2001) "African-American Policewomen: An Exploration of Professional Relationships." *Policing* 24, 4: 550–562.

Pogrebin, Mark; Mary Dodge and Harold Chatman (2000) "Reflections of African-American Women on their Careers in Urban Policing: Their Experiences of Racial and Sexual Discrimination." *International Journal of the Sociology of Law* 28, 4: 311–326.

Polisar, Joseph and Donna Milgram (1998) "Recruiting, Integrating and Retaining Women Police Officers: Strategies that Work." *The Police Chief*, October.

Ruback, R. Barry and Kim S. Menard (2001) "Rural–Urban Differences in Sexual Victimization and Reporting: Analyses using UCR and Crisis Center Data." *Criminal Justice and Behavior* 28, 2: 131–155.

Russell, Katheryn K. (2003) "Driving While Black: Corollary Phenomena and Collateral Consequences." Pp. 97–11 In M. D. Free, Jr. (ed.) *Racial Issues in Criminal Justice: The Case of African Americans*. Westport, CT: Praeger.

Sever, Brion (2003) "The Minority Population/Police Strength Relationship: Exploring Past Research." *Criminal Justice Studies* 16, 2: 153–171.

Smith, David J. (1997) "Ethnic Origins, Crime, and Criminal Justice in England and Wales." Pp. 101–182 In M. Tonry (ed.) *Ethnicity, Crime, and Immigration: Comparative and Cross-national Perspectives*. Chicago, IL: University of Chicago Press.

Stalans, Loretta and Mary A. Finn (2000) "Gender Differences in Officers' Perceptions about Domestic Violence Cases." *Women and Criminal Justice* 11, 3: 1–24.

Stewart, Anna (2001) "Policing Domestic Violence: An Overview of Emerging Issues." *Police Practice and Research* 2, 4: 447–459.

Thompson, R. Alan and Lisa S. Nored (2002) "Law Enforcement Employment Discrimination Based on Sexual Orientation: A Selective Review of Case Law." *American Journal of Criminal Justice* 26, 2: 203–217.

Tolman, Richard M. and Arlene Weisz (1995) "Coordinated Community Intervention for Domestic Violence: The Effects of Arrest and Prosecution on Recidivism of Woman Abuse Perpetrators." *Crime and Delinquency* 41, 4: 481–495.

Visher, Christy A. (1983) "Gender, Police Arrest Decisions, and Notions of Chivalry." *Criminology* 21, 1: 5–28.

Welle, Dorinda and Gregory Falkin (2000) "The Everyday Policing of Women with Romantic Codefendants: An Ethnographic Perspective." *Women and Criminal Justice* 11, 2: 45–65.

Wertsch, Teresa L. (1998) "Walking the Thin Blue Line: Policewomen and Tokenism Today." *Women and Criminal Justice* 9, 3: 23–61.

Winkel, Frans Willem (1991) "Interaction between the Police and Minority Group Members: Victimization through the Incorrect Interpretation of Nonverbal Behavior." *International Review of Victimology* 2, 1: 15–27.

Winterdyk, John and Georgios Antonopoulos (2007) *Racist Victimization: International Reflections and Perspectives*. London: Ashgate.

Wolf, Marsha; U. Ly; Margaret A. Hobart and Mary A. Kernic (2003) "Barriers to Seeking Police Help for Intimate Partner Violence." *Journal of Family Violence* 18, 2: 121–129.

Younglove, Jane A.; Marcee G. Kerr and Corey J. Vitello (2002) "Law Enforcement Officers' Perceptions of Domestic Violence: Reason for Cautious Optimism." *Journal of Interpersonal Violence* 17, 7: 760–772.

Yuzgun, Arslan (1993) "Homosexuality and Police Terror in Turkey." Pp 159–169 In DeCecco, John P. and John P. Elia (eds.) *If You Seduce a Straight Person, Can You Make Them Gay?* New York: Routledge.

Zhao, Jihong; Leigh Herbst and Nicholas Lovrich (2001) "Race, Ethnicity and the Female Cop: Differential Patterns of Representation." *Journal of Urban Affairs* 23, 3–4: 243–257.

POLICING IN INDIAN COUNTRY IN THE UNITED STATES

Laurence Armand French

Justice during aboriginal times was often a clan function and was doled out only as needed. Warrior societies were the most likely to be assigned the duties of enforcement. This informal format changed with European contact and the reintroduction of the horse. The horse allowed more rapid migration as native tribes were being forced west. This mobility, coupled with the advent of the firearm, allowed the aboriginal de facto police, the warrior societies, to adapt their policing techniques. Hence, the eighteenth and nineteenth centuries saw increased intratribal conflict as well as the constant battle against U.S. expansionism into what was Indian country. Here, there was often little distinction between tribal police and tribal combatants.

The formation of Euro-American police among Native Americans began with the Five Civilized Tribes, notably the Cherokee. As early as 1795, a tribal police force was created to curb horse theft—a problem that did not exist during aboriginal times due to the absence of horses in the Americas. The first Cherokee police force was known as the Regulating Companies, and

eventually a more permanent police structure, the Light Horse Guard, emerged in 1808. This marked the beginning of Euro-American law enforcement adaptations made in Indian country.

Thomas Lightfoot, the Indian agent for the Iowa, Sac, and Fox tribes in southeastern Nebraska, is credited with the movement to recruit Indians as police in Indian country outside the Five Civilized Tribes (Cherokee, Choctaw, Creek, Chickasaw, and Seminole) in Indian Territory, doing so in 1869. Three years later, in 1872, as part of the conditions of the Treaty of 1868, the military special Indian commissioner for the Navajos organized a horse cavalry of 130 Navajos to guard the newly drawn up reservation from theft, especially livestock. Western tribes continue this tradition today with a special police unit designated "Range Officers." The position of High Sheriff of the Cherokee Nation was created in 1875. The High Sheriff served as warden and treasurer of the National Prison, which served all of the Indian Territory (Oklahoma).

At about the same time, Indian agent John Clum was experimenting with his own Indian police force on the San Carlos (Arizona) Apache Reservation. Clum did this in an attempt to wrest civilian control from the military in Indian country. Although not entirely successful, agents Clum and Lightfoot were successful in establishing parallel Indian police forces in Indian country. In 1878, the U.S. Congress authorized an Indian police force in Indian country. A year later, the Indian police force was more than doubled with 800 Indian law enforcement officers under White supervisors. Indian Territory (Oklahoma) had 43 Indian officers to police a 712-square mile jurisdiction. Here the Indian police had to work with U.S. Deputy Marshals and local non-Indian police forces in bringing law to this vast haven for outlaws.

The Curtis Act of June 28, 1898, effectively destroyed tribal governments in Indian Territory and Oklahoma became a state in 1907, further minimizing the role of Indian police. Elsewhere in Indian country, it was clear that the appointment of Indian police and Indian judges by the Indian agent was a clear attempt to abrogate traditional tribal authority and traditions and to replace these with Euro-American ways.

Moreover, once Indian Territory was dissolved and the state of Oklahoma created, a renewed focus was placed on enforcing prohibition in Indian country. These special agents were White and held considerable authority. They were eventually replaced by yet another powerful federal law enforcement agency in Indian country—the Federal Bureau of Investigation (FBI).

The Indian Reorganization Act of 1934 merely reinforced the concept of U.S.-type laws and law enforcement in Indian country while the termination–relocation era of the early 1950s forced state laws and law enforcement upon certain tribes. Often, this was a bad mix, since there appears to have been considerable prejudice among those non-Indians who resided closest to Indian country. These prejudices have extended to courts and law enforcement as well. Both the Bureau of Indian Affairs (BIA) and FBI resorted to military interventions from the 1970s to the 1990s in Indian country. Wounded Knee II and the Mohawk gambling war quickly reminded tribal leaders that a strong sense of federal paternalism, especially when looking at law enforcement, is still a presence during this current era of so-called tribal self-determination.

More than any other law enforcement force, the FBI is the most contentious element in Indian country today. The animosity between the FBI and traditional Native Americans is best illustrated with the Leonard Peltier conviction in 1977 for the execution-style death of two FBI agents on the Pine Ridge Reservation during the post-Wounded Knee II turmoil played out between the American Indian Movement (AIM) and what many Sioux believed to be an oppressive White-influenced tribal government. AIM came to Pine Ridge in the early 1970s because of concerns over the corrupt government of then tribal chairman, Dick Wilson. The Oglala police, under Wilson, were known as "Wilson's Guardians of the Oglala Nation," or as Wilson's GOONs. AIM came to the Pine Ridge reservation on February 27, 1973 and quickly occupied the town of Wounded Knee—the site of the December 1890 massacre of Chief Big Foot and his followers by the U.S. Army. Wounded Knee II soon joined the infamous history of U.S./tribal confrontations.

BIA police, on the other hand, intensified about this same time following passage of the 1968 Indian Civil Rights Act. The first BIA Indian Police Academy (IPA) was established in Roswell, New Mexico, in 1969. The academy moved to Brigham City, Utah, and was located there from 1973 to 1984. It then moved to Marana, Arizona, and operated there from 1985 to 1992, when it moved to its present location at the Federal Law Enforcement Training Center (FLETC) in Artesia, New Mexico. The current BIA police training is based on the 1990 Indian Law Enforcement Reform Act (Public Law 101-379).

The BIA Office of Law Enforcement Services (OLES) is located within the Office of the Commissioner of Indian Affairs and is under the authority of the Deputy Commissioner of Indian affairs within the U.S. Department of the Interior. The director operates under the authority of Public Law 101-379 and has the Criminal Investigation Division, the Drug Enforcement Division, Internal Affairs Division, the Police and Detention Division, the Special Investigative Divisions, and the Training Division (IPA).

Today, the IPA falls under the authority of the director of the FLETC. The FLETC serves seventy Federal agencies, providing training to state, local, and international police much like the FBI Academy. The FLETC serves the majority of federal officers and agents (FBI excluded). It graduates some 23,000 students annually and is the largest law enforcement training facility in the United States. FLETC has its central training headquarters near Brunswick, Georgia, and has an annual budget of over $100,000. The IPA in Artesia, New Mexico, is a satellite-training center of FLETC. The FLETC's most current data, for fiscal 1999, indicate that 3,758 individuals graduated from the IPA in Artesia, or about 7% of the 25,168 officers were trained by FLETC that year.

The IPA offers a fourteen-week Basic Police Training Program as well as four weeks of Basic Detention Training; one week of Basic Radio Dispatch Training; ten weeks of Basic Criminal Investigator Training; one week of Criminal Investigation and Police Officer In-service Training; one week of Chiefs of Police In-service Training as well as Outreach Training (Indian country criminal jurisdiction; community policing, gangs, and domestic violence; use of force; patrol tactics and procedures; investigative techniques; and range officer safety and survival); and multiple advanced training programs. A twelve-week training program at the FBI National Academy is also available, as is one week of training at the Law Enforcement Executive Command College. The U.S. Attorney's Office and the Office of

Victims of Crime (OVC) also provide five one-week Regional Training Conferences yearly. Graduation data indicate that 34% of the officers trained at IPA come from the Great Plains; 32% from the Southwest; 20% from the Northeast; 7% from Oklahoma (Indian Territory) tribes; and 6% from the southeastern tribes (error factors accounts for differences from 100%).

In 1993, the National Native American Law Enforcement Association (NNALEA) was formed. It includes federal, state, country, local, and tribal police agencies. The objectives of NNALEA are (1) to provide for the exchange of ideas and new techniques used by criminal investigators; (2) to conduct training seminars, conferences, and research into educational methods for the benefit of American Indians in the law enforcement profession; (3) to keep the membership and public informed of current statute changes and judicial decisions as they relate to the law enforcement community; (4) to establish a network and directory consisting of Native American enforcement officers, agents, and employees; (5) to provide technical and/or investigative assistance to association members within the various aspects of law enforcement investigations; (6) to promote a positive attitude toward law enforcement in the American Indian community and other communities; and (7) to provide a support group for Native American offices, agents, and employees through a national organization.

Despite these advances, tribal policing remains a dangerous job. Kevin Gover, head of the BIA under the Clinton administration, told Congress that people living on Indian reservations fear for their safety and that of their families. While violent crime has been on the decline nationally in the United States, it has been on the increase in Indian country. The head of law enforcement for the BIA noted that one-person shifts and lonely patrols, hours from any backup, are the norm in policing Indian country. This situation has led to seventeen Indian police being killed in the line of duty during the 1990s alone.

The John F. Kennedy School of Government noted that the BIA police have an image problem, given that not so long ago their mandate was to keep tribal members confined to the reservation, to forcibly remove children from their homes and place them in boarding schools, to ration food, and to support the policies of resident agents of the U.S. government. Essentially, Indian police, to many residents of Indian country, convey the image of an occupying army. The report calls for more financial support and greater cultural autonomy for Indian police, something not likely while they are under the strict scrutiny of the BIA.

CHAPTER 13

Sen Sgt Paul Mullett leaves a press conference at the Police Association building in Melbourne, Friday, Feb 15, 2008. Mullett, Police Association secretary, was investigated by the Office of Police Integrity (OPI) in a police corruption scandal. (Credit: © AAP Image/Julian Smith)

POLICE CORRUPTION

OBJECTIVES:

1. The student will learn about organizational and occupational deviance as they relate to the police.
2. The student will learn about various types of police corruption.
3. The student will learn about measures for police accountability in cases of corruption.
4. The student will learn about functionalist, conflict theory, and interactionist perspectives on police corruption.
5. The student will learn about police corruption on an international level.

The image of a police officer engaging in wrongdoing is a particularly compelling one for two reasons. A police officer charged with upholding and enforcing the law is the last person that we would expect to be breaking it. Second, it is expected that those who become police officers be held to a higher standard of behavior in comparison to the public, as the opening quote makes clear. Thus, shock and controversy often results when police corruption and brutality among other forms of police misbehavior or misconduct are uncovered. Reports dealing with "corrupt cops" and "brutal, rogue cops" are often mainstays of media presentations, and never fail to arouse anger and passionate calls for change and reform. Society expects its police officers to be men and women of character. It may even be said that society holds police officers to a higher ethical and moral standard than other professional fields. Since the police are expected to enforce the law, should society not expect them to obey the laws they enforce? Should this not include the police following legal guidelines such as the Bill of Rights, and the policies and procedures established by their own police departments? In this chapter, we will learn about one of the most common forms of police misbehavior, corruption. The next chapter will deal with another, less common, but more egregious form of such misbehavior, police *use of excessive force*.

Police organizations and those individual police officers who work for these organizations are expected to be protectors of the community and the citizens who employ them. When organizations and their officers function in a manner that violates normative expectations, they subvert the mission of the organization—in this case, the maintenance of social order within prescribed constitutional and ethical limits— sociologists refer to this phenomenon as *deviance*. When organizations and police officers go against the norm of providing fair and impartial service for all, they are violating the trust and responsibility that society has given them. The term *"deviance* refers to conduct which the people of a group are considered so dangerous or embarrassing or irritating that they bring special sanctions to bear against the persons who exhibit it. The only way an observer can tell whether or not a given style of behavior is deviant, then, is to learn something about the standards of the audience which is responding to it" (Erickson, 1966: 3). The preceding definition of deviance has been referred to as *achieved deviant status*. This simply means that individuals have been labeled deviant by something or some action that they have done (Adler and Adler, 1997: 13). Police organizations and officers achieve deviant status by carrying out particular actions that they are not supposed to or by failing to perform actions required or expected of them (i.e., errors of omission and commission).

OCCUPATIONAL AND ORGANIZATIONAL DEVIANCE

When we think about "bad" police officers, we often think about them in highly individualistic terms. This means that we often consider these to be unique instances wherein one or two "bad" police officers are discovered within a larger department or agency that is thought to be otherwise "good." There are many cases (as we shall see later) where this is essentially true. In these cases of **occupational deviance**, individuals

occupational deviance

Individuals who happen to be in the police force engage in activities that violate departmental policies, laws, and social norms, and misuse the powers of their office. Deadly force: The amount of force that causes death or has the potential to cause death.

who happen to be in the police force engage in activities that violate departmental policies, laws, and social norms, and misuse the powers of their office. One example of such occupational deviance is a police officer who, on his or her own, asks for a small payment to "forget about" a traffic ticket from a motorist who is caught speeding.

However, it is equally important to recognize that problems of police corruption and brutality may be larger than an individual officer. There are cases where entire sections within a police agency and the entire agency itself may behave in brutal and corrupt ways. Under these circumstances, it makes no sense to speak of "bad apples." Sociologists have coined the term **organizational deviance** to encompass more serious situations of this kind. It is often impossible in deviant organizations for individual members, who themselves may be well intentioned and honorable, to resist the "culture of corruption" that exists around them. In a telling example of the insidious nature of organizational corruption, Frank Serpico, a New York City police officer in the 1970s, was unable to change the corrupt collection of "protection" money by his colleagues in the precinct in which he worked. When he also sought to expose the practice he paid drastically, with his career.

According to Lundman (1980: 140–41), five conditions must be met before individual **police misconduct** can be attributed to a dysfunctional police organization. They are as follows:

1. It must be contrary to norms or rules maintained by others external to the police department.

2. The deviant action must be supported by internal operating norms that conflict with the police organization's formal goals and rules.

3. Compliance with the internal operation norms supportive of police misconduct must be ensured through recruitment and socialization.

4. There must be peer support of the misbehavior of colleagues.

5. It must be supported by the dominant administrative coalition of the police organization.

Generally, police departments have formal policies forbidding police officers from accepting gratuities such as free meals and discounts on merchandise. When police officers gain financially because of their position by accepting discounts for merchandise and free meals, then informal practices have subverted formal police department rules. Often, the support of fellow police officers, in violation of formal departmental policies, may make accepting such gratuities the informal "norm" among fellows. The socialized acceptance of these informal practices has its beginnings in the police academies, and continues throughout the officer's career. One major reason for the acceptance of police deviance, including corruption, is often referred to as the **"Code of Silence."**

Robert McCormick (2001: 100–108) developed the Normed Corruption Model and maintained: "that agency leadership and fair and consistent discipline shapes police officers' perceptions as to the probity of their job related behavior." Activities of

organizational deviance

Coined by sociologists to encompass serious situations occurring within entire organization. This behavior includes police brutality and corruption.

police misconduct

Unethical, unprofessional, or illegal behavior conducted by a police officer.

code of silence

Police officer's failure to report police misconduct by officers.

officers who are not generally subject to disciplinary action when discovered become normed. There are several factors that have an impact on the level of normed corruption in a police agency. These include:

1. Political influence in which efforts to reform police agencies in communities in which there is a high level of political corruption, and little community interest or effort to eradicate it, are almost doomed to failure. Usually a new police chief with support from government officials has the best chance to eliminate systemic corruption.

2. Political leadership, which incorporates ethical leadership, is an important factor in reducing corruption. Effective leadership plays a vital role in controlling and eliminating corruption.

3. Recruitment and retention policies are important in reducing, controlling, and eliminating corruption.

4. Educational requirements are important in selecting quality applicants.

5. Police unions have interfered in aggressive investigations of criminal acts committed by police officers. While acknowledging that officers can organize themselves, efforts need to be made to reduce the interference of police unions in corruption investigations (McCormick, 2001: 100–108).

Code of Silence

The "Code of Silence" requires that police officers look the other way when they observe their fellow officers involved in acts of deviance. Frequently, these violations occur in police agencies where managers do not recognize the existence of fellow officers involved in deviant behavior, or fail to take the appropriate steps to stop such behavior (Lundman, 1980: 140–141). Skolnick and Fyfe (1993: 110) write that the "Code of Silence" exists and that it "typically is enforced by the threat of shunning, by fear that informing will lead to exposure of one's own derelictions, and by fear that colleagues' assistance may be withheld in emergencies." These authors believe that in reality, police officers will not deny assistance to fellow officers who may have informed on fellow officers in emergencies. They suggest that it is imagined or that officers are paranoid when they believe that fellow police officers will not come to their aid when they need assistance. According to Skolnick and Fyfe (1993: 112), "The Code of Silence, then, is not one that is enforced by assassins lurking in dark alleys or arranging for drug dealers to terminate cops who inform. The police Code of Silence is an extreme version of a phenomenon that exists in many human groups. It is exaggerated in some police departments and some police units, because cops so closely identify with their departments, their units, and their colleagues, that they cannot even conceive of doing anything else."

The Mollen Commission (Pooley, 1994), which investigated police corruption in New York City in the 1990s, considered the "Code of Silence" there to be alarming. They found the Code strongest in areas where corruption was the strongest. They believed that the "Code of Silence" was also powerful in crime-ridden precincts where police officers depended upon one another for their safety. The Commission found that the "Code" influenced honest police officers in the precincts where their willingness to inform was most needed. The relative success of the "Code of Silence" can be attributed to the real or assumed consequences for violating it. The Commission concluded that police officers who violated the "Code of Silence" by reporting corruption or other illegal behavior may be harassed and ostracized or may themselves become the target of complaints and possibly physical threats, and are often made to feel they will be left alone when they need assistance from fellow police officers. This assumption, of course, was what Skolnick and Fyfe (1993) were criticizing. The Commission reported that the "Code of Silence" fuels corruption since corrupt police officers feel invulnerable and protected (53).

Learning the "Code" begins in the police academy where instructors may inform recruits never to be rats and never to turn in a fellow officer. The Mollen Commission found that police officers would often accept blame for acts of misconduct they did not commit, or find that the confidentiality of their information about misbehavior by fellow officers had been violated even though they were told they would be protected. The Commission found that police officers often considered reporting acts of misconduct to be more serious and dangerous than the actual misconduct that happened.

The "Code of Silence" thus leads to a "blue fraternity" that creates an "Us vs. Them" mentality. The "Code of Silence," according to the Mollen Commission, insulates and protects corrupt officers from being turned in and punished for acts of misconduct. The public, the citizens served by the police are frequently considered to be trouble to them and not a supporter but an enemy. The "Us vs. Them" mentality can also be directed against fellow officers who pose a threat. A good example of this is the Internal Affairs Unit, which is viewed as a group that is "out to get" the street police officer. The Mollen Commission found the "Code of Silence" and the "Us vs. Them" mentality present when corruption was found. This helps explain how groups of corrupt officers can openly engage in corruption for long periods of time with impunity (60). William Hyatt, a former federal prosecutor, had the following to say about the police "Code of Silence": "The law enforcement code of silence, covering all of the things that an officer learns but cannot discuss, leads to a natural reticence to disclose any information about a fellow officer" (2001: 96).

Ellwyn Stoddard (1995) found that such an informal "Code" exists within police agencies that support and even condone such acts of corruption. Stoddard found that inappropriate acts such as corruption are prescribed socially within police organizations. For example, when recruits are indoctrinated into the police subculture by their police trainers the idea that their personal safety is dependent on their fellow officers is ingrained into them. Further, since police recruits are generally unfamiliar with police procedures and policies they become dependent upon the guidance of senior officers. Police officers, similar to other members of society, want to be accepted by their colleagues. Rookie officers who by chance observe veteran officers commit legal or departmental violations have the option of either being quiet about the incident or reporting it to a supervisor. Of course, if the rookie officer reports the violation of the senior officer, this, in all probability, will cause the rookie officer to have problems with other fellow officers. When rookie officers report veteran officers for violations, they not only lose the confidence of their colleagues but also of their superiors. It does not take the rookie officer long to realize that all police officers make mistakes, and if he or she wants his fellow officers to be quiet about his or her mistakes, then he or she must maintain silence about the mistakes, including legal and departmental violations.

The "Code of Silence" and the "Us vs. Them" mentality appear to be ingrained into American policing. As part of the police subculture, the "Code," to some extent, has been accepted by all police officers. The "Code of Silence" should not be considered a phenomenon that is new to the police culture. It appears to go back to the last century but seems to have grown with the policing philosophy that the police are crime fighters and are the authorities on how to control crime. Since the 1930s when the police adopted the primacy of the crime fighting role and image, their belief that they are primarily good guys and that nonpolice are the bad guys has become stronger. Therefore, if you are not one of the good guys you cannot understand police work since only police officers can understand what police work is about. It is not uncommon to hear police officers say that their commanders and administrators have forgotten what police work is all about. The narrow concept that only street police officers, patrol officers, and detectives can understand police work may be a contributing factor to the "Us vs. Them" mentality and to the "Code of Silence." As we enter the first decades of the twenty-first century, we can watch on television and read in our daily newspapers that the "Code of Silence" still exists as the Los Angeles Police Department's Rampart Area corruption incident (*Time*, 2000) makes clear.

Types of Police corruption

Police corruption can be found throughout U.S. police departments. Corruption can be explained as monetary gain obtained from not performing a legal duty or responsibility as a police officer. For example, in Atlanta, officers were arrested for extorting money from drug dealers and shaking down citizens for police protection. In the late 1990s, the Los Angeles Police Department (LAPD) experienced a corruption scandal that made national and international headlines. One of the Los Angeles police officers signed out cocaine for evidentiary use in court, but the cocaine was never returned. It was found out that the officer had no justifiable reason for signing out the cocaine. The district attorney filed the following charges against that particular officer, Rafael Perez: possession of cocaine for sale, grand theft, and forgery. The investigation of this officer revealed that he had close associations with drug dealers. Some of his past arrestees claimed that he planted evidence on them. Perez then made a deal with the district attorney to receive a lesser sentence of incarceration for which he turned in fellow corrupt officers (see *Time,* 2000).

Police corruption includes these forms of misconduct: "Free or discounted meals or services; kickbacks payments in the form of money, goods or services that a law enforcement agent receives for directing people that he comes in contact with" (Hyatt, 2001: 77–81):

- **Free or Discounted Meals or Services:** Such meals and services are often available to either uniformed law enforcement officers upon showing their badge. ...

- **Kickbacks:** Kickbacks are payments in the form of money, goods, or services that a law enforcement agent receives for directing people that he or she comes in contact with toward a particular service provider.

- **Opportunistic Thefts:** This form of theft is the taking of money or property from arrestees, burglary scenes, and unprotected properties by the officer during the course of duty.

- **Shakedowns:** This form of deviance consists of the taking of money or property from an arrestee caught with the fruits of a crime.

- **Bribes Related to Cases:** This broad category covers everything from the acceptance of a cash payment for not writing a motorist a traffic ticket to an officer accepting money for shading his testimony in a felony trial in order to give the defendant an opportunity to be acquitted.

- **Protection of Illegal Activities:** Protection of illegal activities takes two forms. The most common form is the acceptance of bribes in order to allow certain victimless crimes, such as illegal alcohol or drug sales, prostitution, and gambling to operate unmolested by law enforcement activity. The other is when police officers provide physical protection to drug dealers during drug transactions.

- **Internal Payoffs:** This is internal bribery in which officers pay one another to either acquire good assignments or avoid unpleasant ones.

- **Payment for Protection:** Taking bribes not to enforce the law from individuals who are committing crimes.

Degrees of Corruption

Historically, the police appear to have been involved in corruption since the New York State legislature established the New York City Police Department (NYPD) in 1844, arguably the first police department in the United States. Records indicate that the police were involved in corrupt activities, such as extortion, from the NYPD's earliest days. In the approximately 160-year history of the NYPD a major corruption scandal has occurred approximately every twenty years. Usually a crime commission will be created and will make recommendations to eliminate police corruption. At times some of the recommendations are implemented, but over a period of time, administrators, commanders, and supervisors become lax, or may not want the publicity that goes with combating police acts of corruption. Although many cities, large and small, have corruption scandals, the largest cities in America get the most attention. New York City, Los Angeles, Miami, Houston, Detroit, and Chicago are cities, which make the news headlines in this manner. While studies of corruption are usually conducted in big cities, we should be aware that police corruption occurs in many places. The smaller cities appear to be immune to exposure to acts of corruption, or at least the national media does not give them attention.

Various degrees of corruption exist. Some forms of corruption are considered more serious than others. For example, in the 1970s the New York City police officers coined the term "grass-eaters" and "meat-eaters." Police officers who are not actively soliciting illicit payments are called "grass-eaters" when they accept gratuities from construction contractors, tow-truck operators, and gamblers. When officers aggressively seek out financial gains from gambling, drugs, and prostitution that yield a substantial financial gain they are referred to as "meat-eaters" (Knapp Commission, 1973: 65). Although the terms "grass-eaters" and "meat-eaters" may not be as much in vogue these days, the concepts are as accurate today as they were in the 1970s when they were coined. The Knapp Commission concluded interestingly that the "grass-eaters" are the heart of the problem. Their greater numbers tend to make corruption "respectable." They also encourage the "Code of Silence" that brands anyone who exposes corruption "a traitor" (4). The Knapp Commission's conclusions on grass-eaters resonate even today. The "grass-eaters" give respectability to corruption by taking gratuities coming their way. If "grass-eaters" stop accepting gratuities and recognize that their gratuities (even if by the happenstance of police work) should not be accepted, corruption may decrease. Corruption definitely will not decrease if "grass-eaters" and "meat-eaters" continue in their corrupt ways.

The Knapp Commission (67–68) outlined five factors that contribute to police corruption:

- *Character of the officer*—This is the most important factor that determines whether the officer bucks the system and refuses all corruption money; goes along with the system and accepts what comes his way; or outdoes the system, and aggressively seeks corruption-prone situations and exploits them to the extent that it seriously cuts into the time available for doing his job. The officer's character will also determine the kind of grafts he accepts. Some officers, who don't think twice about accepting money from gamblers, refuse to have anything to do with drug pushers. They make a distinction between what they call "clean money" and "dirty money."

- *Branch of the department to which an officer is assigned*—A plainclothesman, for example, has more, and different, opportunities than a uniformed patrolman.

- *The area in which an officer is assigned*—At the time of the investigation certain precincts in Harlem, for instance, comprised what police officers called "the Gold Coast," because they contained so many payoff-prone activities, numbers, and drugs, being the largest.

- *The officer's assignment*—For uniformed men, a seat in a sector car was considered fairly lucrative in most precincts, while assignments to stand guard duty outside City Hall obviously was not, and assignment to one sector of a precinct could mean lots of payoffs from construction sites, while in another sector bar owners were big givers.

- *Rank*—For those officers who do receive payoffs, the amount involved generally increases with the rank.

Although the Knapp Commission's recounting of factors that influence police corruption dates back forty years, this does not make them obsolete. Obviously, the character of police officers always has to be considered an important factor in the ability to refuse or to perform an act of corruption. All departments want to employ police officers with integrity and the backbone to avoid committing acts of misconduct. The branch of the department that officers are assigned to plays a major part in corruption opportunities. In New York City, during the period investigated by the Knapp Commission, plainclothes officers had greater opportunities for committing corrupt acts. These same opportunities may exist for officers in other police departments. Opportunities for corruption often depend upon the city, the culture of the city, size of police force, crimes committed in the city, and organizational structure of the department. Police officers recognize that an officer's assignment can be an opportunity to be involved in corruption. Not all assignments afford police officers the opportunity to commit corrupt acts, for example, by standing guard at a city council meeting. It has also been generally accepted that the higher the rank the more influential and important the officer. Therefore, it is not unusual for higher-ranking officers to receive more corrupt payments more often than lower-ranking officers.

The War on Drugs and the continuing popularity of illegal drug use provide police officers with many opportunities for corrupt activities. These include: keeping money confiscated in drug arrests, selling drugs, planting drugs on persons arrested, giving informants drugs, and accepting money from drug offenders. Although police-officer involvement in drug corruption is still uncommon, in the past several decades it has accounted for the largest percentage of police corruption. For example, many Southern sheriffs allegedly protect drug dealers. In Savannah, a Georgia police sergeant operated his own drug ring. In the same city, an officer provided police intelligence information to a drug dealer. A quick search of our nation's newspapers will reveal that police officers in rural, suburban, and urban police departments have often given in to the temptation of taking money illegally from drug dealers.

One New York City police officer described police corruption to the Mollen Commission, appointed in the 1990s to investigate the matter, in this manner: "Police officers view the community as a candy store, I know of police officers stealing money from drug dealers, police officers selling stolen drugs back to drug dealers. I also know of police officers stealing guns and selling them. I know cops committing perjury to conceal their crimes" (Pooley, 1994: 17). The Mollen Commission found a group of corrupt cops known as the *Morgue Boys* who rampaged through black and Latino neighborhoods, snorting, stealing, and dealing cocaine, and selling protection to drug dealers (Pooley, 1994: 19). In a police precinct in Harlem, New York, 25 percent of the precinct officers were deemed corrupt. These corrupt officers were selling drugs, and protecting drug dealers (Klauss, 1994a: 1). In one incident, a police officer struck a drug dealer in the head, took his cocaine, then shot, and seriously wounded him. Other police officers, over a three-year period, made $60,000, stealing cash from drug dealers and selling drugs, while others accepted payoffs from drug dealers (Klauss, 1994b: 24).

Theories of Corruption

There are several theories as to why police officers become corrupt. Delattere (1989) hypothesizes three causes for corruption. First, there is the society-at-large concept in which society contributes to police corruption by giving gratuities to police officers. Second, the structural or affiliation concept involves the view adopted by police officers, because behavior of misconduct becomes accepted as appropriate within the police agency. Third is the "rotten-apple" view, by which a few police officers are always likely to get involved in corruption (71–78) regardless of the organization. Sherman sees "police corruption as the outcome of legal, institutional, and social arrangements rather than as the results of a few 'bad apples' (morally weak officers) who spoil the reputations of otherwise honest departments (1985: 251). In a study conducted by Carl Klockars et al. (2000: 1–2), the researchers suggest that contemporary police corruption theories are based on four organizational and occupational dimensions. They are:

- **Organizational Rules.** The first dimension concerns how the organizational rules that govern corruption are established, communicated, and understood. In the United States, where police agencies are highly decentralized, police organizations differ markedly in the types of activities they officially prohibit as corrupt behavior. This is particularly true of marginally corrupt or *mala prohibita* behavior, such as off-duty employment and acceptance of favors, small gifts, free meals, and discounts. Further complicating the problem, the official policy of many agencies formally prohibits such activities, while they are unofficially supported firmly by supervisors and administrators who permit and ignore such behavior so long as it is limited in scope and conducted discreetly.

- **Prevention and Control Mechanisms.** The second dimension of corruption emphasized in contemporary approaches is the wide range of mechanisms that police agencies employ to prevent and control corruption. Examples include education, proactive and reactive investigation of corruption, integrity testing, and corruption deterrence through disciplining of offenders. The extent to which agencies use such organizational anticorruption techniques varies greatly.

- **The Code.** The third dimension of corruption, inherent in the occupational culture of policing, is the "Code" or "The Blue Curtain" that informally prohibits or discourages police officers from reporting the misconduct of their colleagues. The parameters of the "Code"—precisely what behavior it covers and to whom its benefits are extended—vary among police agencies. For example, the "Code" may apply to only low-level corruption in some agencies and to the most serious forms of corruption in others. Furthermore, who and what the "Code" covers can vary substantially not only *among* police agencies but also *within* police agencies. Particularly in large police agencies, the occupational culture of integrity may differ substantially among precincts, service areas, task forces, and work groups.

- **Public Expectations.** The fourth dimension of police corruption that contemporary police theory emphasizes is the influence of the social, economic, and political environments in which police institutions, systems, and agencies operate. For example, some jurisdictions in the United States have long, virtually uninterrupted traditions of police corruption. Other jurisdictions have equally long traditions of minimal corruption, while still others have experienced repeated cycles of scandal and reform. Such histories indicate that public expectations about police integrity exert vastly different pressures on police agencies in different jurisdictions.

It is important to recognize that occurrences of police corruption are not endemic to the United States alone, and that they happen in other countries, as our section on police corruption internationally makes clear.

ACCOUNTABILITY

Perhaps the most common public response when instances of police deviance such as corruption and brutality come to light is the call to hold the offending individuals and agencies accountable for their actions. Police managers, commanders, supervisors, and police officers are responsible to a variety of entities for their behavior, their policies, procedures, and the behavior of all police personnel in a police organization. Police organizations, through their administrative structures, have the responsibility to hold officers involved in deviant behavior accountable. Officers who swear an oath to uphold the laws of our federal and state government should be held to a higher standard than the law violators of our society. Ideally, those selected to enforce our society's laws should be the crème of our society. If police officers violate our laws and the policies of their police organization, how can they justify their own right to enforce the laws of any given society? Over the years, several internal and external mechanisms have been proposed and developed to hold officers involved in deviant behavior accountable. The strategies currently in vogue to restrain and judge police officers involved in deviant occupational behavior consist of invoking a "Code of Conduct," the deployment of Internal Affairs Units, the formation and overview of **Civilian Review Boards** (or Civilian Oversight), the use of the criminal courts, and civil liability procedures.

Codes of Conduct

The first step in controlling police deviance is the direct inculcation of ethical behavior. All individuals selected for police work are asked to subscribe in word and deed to a "Code of Conduct," or a moral philosophy that deals with behavior—either good or bad behavior. A police officer's behavior or a police organization's practices can be judged as being either ethical or unethical. One criminal justice author defines ethics as "the study and analysis of what constitutes good or bad behavior" (Pollock, 1998: 6). Another author on police provides the following definition: " principles of acceptable rules of conduct for a particular individual or group as mandated by law, policy, or procedure" (Goodman, 1998: 3).

Although specific actions or the behavior of police officers may not be in violation of the law or a police department policy or procedures, this does not mean that the specific act or behavior of the officer is ethical. Unethical actions or behavior do not necessarily have to be in violation of the law. For example, the accepting of gratuities from an individual who wants you to recommend his cousin whom you do not know for a police job may not be a crime, but could be considered unethical.

Police officers who are sworn to uphold the law must be expected to conduct their behavior in an ethical manner. Good police officers will keep themselves in check by following the Law Enforcement Code of Conduct as urged by the International Association of Chiefs of Police (IACP). This Code of Conduct dates back to 1957, and a revised version was adopted by IACP members unanimously in 1991. Police officers not only take an oath to enforce the laws of the nation and their respective states, but are also asked to adhere to the Law Enforcement Code of Conduct. The first step in police accountability can be the self-imposed accountability of police officers to conduct themselves in a professional manner by following the Law Enforcement Code of Conduct. While these codes are useful in educating officers regarding behavioral expectations, they run the risk of being ignored or being thought of as nothing more than good advice. They also lack any "teeth" in terms of enforcement and punishment.

Internal Affairs Units

Middle-sized and larger police departments provide citizens with a mechanism within the department that allows the latter to complain against police officers. Generally, this unit is referred to as Internal Affairs (Davis, 1997). The commanding officer of the Internal Affairs Unit often reports directly to the police chief. This is done to keep the chief abreast of all complaints and findings and to remove internal police political pressures. The Internal Affairs Unit conducts an administrative investigation of an employee for the purpose of carrying out administrative actions. Upon the completion of an investigation into alleged wrongdoing, the findings usually can be classified under one of four dispositions (Trasher, 2001: 397):

- *Unfounded*—The incident of misconduct did not occur;
- *Not Involved*—The employee was not present or not involved at the time the incident of misconduct occurred;
- *Exonerated*—The incident occurred, but actions taken by the employees were lawful and proper;
- *Not Sustained*—There is insufficient evidence to prove or disapprove the allegation;
- *Sustained*—The allegation is supported by sufficient evidence.

If an allegation is sustained, the chief is then left with the responsibility of deciding what action to take against the officer involved. One drawback of this method of accountability is that while it may be useful against individual (i.e., occupational) deviance, it becomes problematic when entire units or departments are involved in corrupt practices. It will be difficult, or impossible, to collect evidence in the latter case.

Civilian Review Boards

The concept of a civilian (or citizen) review board can be traced to the 1930s. A Civilian Review Board is defined as "an independent tribunal of carefully selected outstanding citizens from the community at large" (Bopp and Schultz, 1972: 146). Civilian Oversight Boards, as they are sometimes called, consist of independent bodies of nonpolice officers drawn from the community. These boards review complaints from members of the public regarding police deviance and recommend action against offending officers. The idea of cities establishing Citizen Review Boards has recurrent popularity. Whenever the police are involved in turmoil, a Citizens' Review Board is recommended (if one does not exist already) to investigate and review police deviance.

Richard Terrill (1990) argues that, in recent times, other traditional procedures have not always worked to curb police deviance. He considers civilian oversight to be a suitable strategy for checking the excesses of police deviance. In the 1990s, thirty of America's fifty largest cities had some type of Civilian Oversight Boards (Terrill, 1990: 45).

Criminal Courts

In most democracies, the police can also be held accountable by the legal system for illegal acts in carrying out police duties. The U.S. legal system holds the police accountable for enforcing the law according to the guidelines established by the legislative branch and appellate court decisions. Our legal system also examines the manner in which the police enforce the law. The police are expected to enforce state and federal laws impartially and to protect the constitutional rights of all citizens. When they fail to do this, our courts can inform the police of their deviance and hold them accountable through punishment and the awarding of damages.

Courts review the procedures (e.g., stopping and questioning, arrest, search) carried out by the police officer for their legality. When a police officer fails to follow appropriate methods, a form of legal (or procedural) deviance, the trial judge has the duty to advise the police officer. Such legal deviance could jeopardize the police officer's case. For example, all of a police officer's reports pertaining to the case have to be accurate and truthful. If the police officer fails to meet this legal requirement, his or her competence as a police officer may be damaged in future cases. Furthermore, if it is proven that the police officer lied, then perjury charges can be leveled, and the officer punished. This can be extended to units and departments, if warranted by a review of their procedures. The trial plays important roles in making certain that police officers do not commit acts of corruption under the cover of the authority given to them legally.

Civil Liability

In the 1970s the U. S. Supreme Court began using *Title 42 U.S. Code, Section 1983,* to deal with police deviance in violation of citizens' constitutional rights. Section 1983 forbids police officers who, in their official capacity, function as agents of the state government, to use any state law, ordinance, regulation, or custom as a method of denying citizens their constitutional rights.

Title 42 of the United States Code, Section 1983, deals with procedural remedies rather than substantial remedies. The law provides an avenue for the redress of violations of federal constitutional rights, as addressed in the Bill of Rights, and specific rights, as guaranteed by federal statutes. The U. S. Supreme Court considers Section 1983 to have the following meaning (Nahmond, 1986: 4): "The very purpose of Section 1983 was to impose the federal courts between the States and the people, as guardians of the people's federal rights—to protect the people from unconstitutional action under color of state law, 'whether that action be executive, legislative, or judicial.'"

Police officers are agents of the government, and ultimately, it is a governmental agency that employs them, and is deemed responsible for their actions. County and city governments are sued for acts of police deviance committed by officers employed by them. Governments, not individual police officers, have "deep pockets"—money to cover the lawsuit, because they have a tax base to raise the money from. Generally, police officers are not well-off financially and the ability for those offended against to collect funds from them may prove difficult, if not impossible. "Jury awards and settlements now total tens of millions of dollars each year nationwide" (Anderson, 2000: 129). One by-product of county and city governments being sued appears to be a closer examination by these entities of all police procedures and policies often leading to more risk-aversive requirements. In the last several decades many instances of police deviance have usually led to more administrative and supervisory police discretion. For example, police officers in Wichita, Kansas, must obtain approval from their superiors before they make any arrest.

Acts of police deviance have led to more control over the authority and autonomy of individual police officers. In general, and in contrast to other countries, the police in the United States do not run wild. For the most part they are held accountable for behavior considered deviant by our legal system. Although police deviance, for the most part, is not all that common, it may appear so because media coverage has become more common and widespread than in past decades. One possible consequence of this increased coverage is that police officers involved in deviance will recognize that deviant and illegal acts or those in violation of decency standards are less likely to be tolerated by society. See the study in the box on "Perceptions of Police Misconduct" by Ronald Weitzer and Steven A. Touch (2004).

A STUDY OF PERCEPTIONS OF POLICE MISCONDUCT

This study on perception of police misconduct comes from a national survey conducted in 2002 of white, Hispanic, and African American residents of metropolitan areas having a population of 100,000 or more. Findings indicate that blacks are more likely to have negative views, while whites are least likely, with Hispanics falling in between. African Americans believed that police misconduct occurs very often, with the vast majority holding the view that it frequently occurs in their city or neighborhood.

Whites are less likely to believe that police engage in misconduct than African Americans and Hispanics. Younger whites and younger black respondents perceive more police misconduct at the city level. City-dwelling whites are more likely than suburban whites to perceive police misconduct in their city and neighborhoods. All three groups in high crime neighborhoods believe that police misconduct occurs in their neighborhoods. This seems to be true of blacks and Hispanics who are more likely to live in areas plagued by serious crime. This study indicated that race structures citizen's perceptions of police misconduct.

POLICE CORRUPTION: THREE SOCIOLOGICAL PERSPECTIVES

What would the three sociological perspectives that we have become familiar with—functionalism, conflict, and interactionism—make of the irony of those who are supposed to prevent and control certain forms of deviance, themselves acting in deviant, corrupt ways? Functionalists would see such behavior as indicative of dysfunctions that have crept into police departments. They would argue that police corruption exists due to failures in administrative policies and the socialization of individual officers. From their perspective, the fact that agencies identify these behaviors as unacceptable, and try to stamp them out, is indicative of the striving for ethical and functional police practices. Given this view, functionalists believe that clear policies and procedures, better socialization and training, as well as accountability are needed to curb the many problems associated with police deviance.

From a conflict perspective, police corruption is to be expected. Remember that for conflict theorists, the police are not a neutral entity who enforce the law, and maintain order without fear or favor. In fact, they are paid for and represent elite segments in a society. Even though rules and regulations may exist that forbid the police from acting in corrupt ways, this is mostly eyewash to give the impression of acting impartially. In controlling and suppressing the nonelite in a given society or community, the police step over the line. Generally, these cases of police deviance are not dealt with any severity for a reason. The elite and their lackeys (police administrators, judges, etc.) do not really care, if the police act in such ways as long as it is not against them.

Finally, from an interactionist perspective, a lot of attention would be devoted to considering the nature and meanings of acts that are defined as police corruption. With just about all forms of police corruption, there are differences in interpretation. Is it wrong for the owner of a diner to offer reduced prices or free coffee to police officers, because he or she would like to enhance the feelings of safety of other patrons by having law enforcement officers around at night? Many police officers would note that they did not ask for the free coffee or for reduced prices, but that they appreciated them. At the same time they would suggest that they would not go out of their way to overlook it, if the owner of the diner was selling drugs, or engaged in running a prostitution ring from that location. Would you, as an individual citizen, see this as an instance of police corruption, or would you not? How could the same event get interpreted in two totally different ways? Interactionists would be interested in these perceptual differences and where they stem from.

POLICE CORRUPTION INTERNATIONALLY: INDIA

Verma (2000: 264) notes: "Corruption within the Indian police is well recognized and pervasive. Corruption exists within every rank from the constable to the chief of police and in every police department of the country." There are many acts of misconduct and corruption identified with India's police forces that function as centralized (or national) entities. These include systematic extortion from those enmeshed within the criminal justice system (victims, witnesses, suspects, perpetrators); demands for weekly payments from businesses in the jurisdiction of a police station; and the suppression of charges and cases as a result of bribery and political pressures, etc. The Indian police have also developed a reputation for high-handedness

and brutality in dealing with the public. For example, it is commonplace to learn from India's mass media that suspected offenders and "terrorists" have been killed in euphemistically termed "encounters" with the police, or that they died by their own hands while held in jail. Often these extra-legal encounters and suicides of suspects while under police custody are nothing more than events staged by the police themselves to eliminate individuals who, for whatever reason, have become "inconvenient" to the police, or to their political masters.

India is a new nation-state (it became independent from the United Kingdom in 1947) that is still undergoing the process of nation-building and national

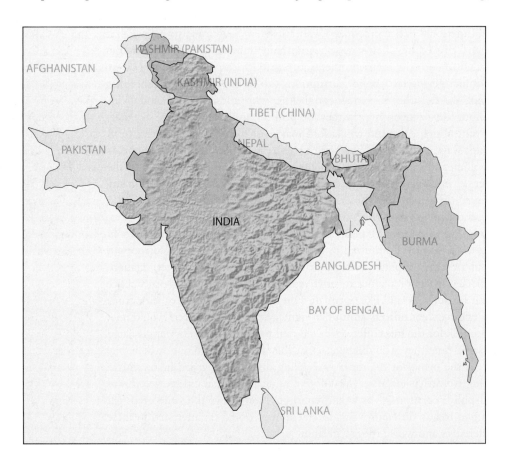

identification. However, its experiences exhibit commonalities with those of the older, more established police forces of the United States in terms of the nature (if not necessarily the extent) of police corruption. It is therefore important that these democracies search for solutions to the common problems associated with police deviance that crop up in the deployment and activities of police forces.

Having learned about corruption as a form of deviance in India, let us take a historical view of the same phenomenon in Australia. The United States, India, and Australia all share a common British colonial and police heritage. Their experiences with police corruption and its particular forms, however, appear different.

 # SUMMARY

In this chapter, we learned that deviance is a concern of modern policing. The concept of police deviance includes both individual occupational deviance and organizational deviance. At times entire police organizations may be deviant. This occurs when the deviance becomes acceptable practice throughout the entire police organization. This means that entire units or sections can be involved in acts of brutality or corruption. It is often impossible in deviant organizations for individual members, however well intentioned and honorable, to resist the "culture" of deviance that exists around him. Police misconduct falls under the umbrella of police deviance. All police misconduct involves acts of wrongdoing that are unacceptable under federal and state laws, departmental policies, and procedures. Acts of police misconduct can be unethical or immoral, but yet not be criminal in nature. Society expects police officers to be people of character who will obey the laws they swear to enforce and not be law violators. One element of police deviance, which allows police officers to be involved in police misconduct, is the "Code of Silence." This code requires that police officers look the other way when they observe their colleagues involved in acts of misconduct. Often, police misconduct occurs in police agencies, when managers refuse to recognize the existence of police

involved in deviant behavior, or when they fail to take the appropriate steps to eliminate the deviance. Police deviance can include police misconduct such as accepting free meals, kickbacks, petty thievery, shakedowns, bribes, and providing protection for illegal activities. Other deviant behavior by police officers includes corruption, which in some cities can be a serious problem. Various forms of corruption exist such as taking money from drug dealers and gamblers to look the other way rather than enforce the law that police officers swear to enforce. Another form of police deviance is the "use of excessive force" by police officers often referred to as "police brutality." It is difficult to know how widespread and how often incidents of police brutality occur. However, it does occur, and the media periodically brings this to our attention. The "use of excessive force" is closely associated with "**deadly force**." Deadly force occurs when a police officer commits an act that either causes the death of someone or has the potential of causing the death of someone. Both police and society can make serious efforts to eliminate and control deviant behavior by police officers. This occurs through strategies such as "Codes of Conduct," Internal Affairs investigations, Civilian Review Boards, and the criminal courts. Finally, we learned about the nature of police deviance in India.

KEY TERMS

Citizen Review Board: An independent tribunal of carefully selected outstanding citizens from the community at large to investigate and review police misconduct.

Code of Silence: Police officer's failure to report police misconduct by officers.

Deadly force: The amount of force that causes death or has the potential to cause death.

Use of Excessive Force: The use of more force to subdue a subject than is needed.

Police misconduct: Unethical, unprofessional, or illegal behavior conducted by a police officer.

Occupational deviance: Individuals who happen to be in the police force engage in activities that violate departmental policies, laws, and social norms, and misuse the powers of their office.

Organizational deviance: Coined by sociologists to encompass serious situations occurring within entire organization. This behavior includes police brutality and corruption.

REVIEW QUESTIONS

1. Describe the various types of corruption.
2. Describe police accountability.
3. Explain the sociological aspects of police corruption.

DISCUSSION QUESTIONS

1. Can police corruption be easily controlled?
2. If the police were held accountable for their behavior, would corruption exist?
3. Should it be expected that corruption could be committed by police officers?

REFERENCES

Adler, Patricia A. and Peter Adler (1997) *Construction of Deviance: Social Power, Context, and Interaction,* Second Edition, Albany, NY: Wadsworth Publishing Company.

Anderson, David C. (2000) "Policing the Police." Pp. 129–140 In Terrence J. Fitzgerald (ed.) *Police in Society.* New York: H. W. Wilson.

Bopp, William J. and Donald O. Schultz (1972) *Principles of American Law Enforcement and Criminal Justice.* Springfield, IL: Thomas.

Cooksey, O. E. (1991) "Corruption: A Continuing Challenge for Law Enforcement." *FBI Law Enforcement Bulletin* (September): 5–9.

Davis, Richard J. (1997) *Monitoring Study: A Review of Investigations Conducted by the Internal Affairs Bureau.* New York, NY: Commission to Combat Corruption.

Delattere, Edwin J. (1989) *Character and Cops: Ethics in Policing.* Washington, DC: American Enterprise Institute for Public Policy Research.

Erickson, Kai T. (1966) *Wayward Puritans: A Study in the Sociology of Deviance.* New York, NY: Allyn and Bacon.

Goodman, Debbie (1998) *Enforcing.* Upper Saddle River, NJ: Prentice-Hall.

Hyatt, William D. (2001) "Parameters of Police Misconduct." In M. J. Palmiotto (ed.) *Police Misconduct: A Reader for the 21st Century.* Upper Saddle River, NJ: Prentice-Hall.

Klauss, Clifford (1994a) "Bratton Says Corruption Sweep Involves Dozens More Officers." *The New York Times* (April 17).

Klauss, Clifford (1994b) "12 Police Officers Charged in Drug Corruption Sweep: Bratton Sees More Arrests." *The New York Times* (May 3).

Klockars, Carl B. (2000) *The Measurement of Police Integrity.* Washington, DC: U.S. Justice Department.

Lundman, Richard J. (1980) *Police and Policing: An Introduction.* New York, NY: Holt, Rinehart, and Winston.

McCormick, Robert J. (2001) "Police Perceptions and the Norming of Institutional Corruption" of Police Misconduct." In M. J. Palmiotto (ed.) *Police Misconduct: A Reader for the 21st Century.* Upper Saddle River, NJ: Prentice-Hall.

Nahmond, Sheldon H. (1986) *Civil Rights and Civil Liberties Litigation.* New York, NY: McGraw-Hill.

Pollock, Joycelyn M. (1998) *Sand Criminal Justice: Dilemmas and Decisions.* Belmont, CA: West/Wadsworth.

Pooley, Eric (1994) "The Extraordinary Story of How an Underfunded and Unloved Team of Mollen Commission Investigators Unearthed the Dirtiest Corruption of Them All: Untouchable." *New York Times* 27, July 11.

Sherman, Lawrence W. (1985) "Becoming Bent: Moral Careers of Corrupt Policemen." In F. A. Elliston and M. Feldberg (eds) *Moral Issues in Police Work.* Totowa, NJ: Rowan and Allanheld.

Skolnick, Jerome H. and James J. Fyfe (1993) *Above the Law.* New York, NY: The Free Press.

Stoddard, Ellwyn R. (1995) "The Informal 'Code' of Police Deviancy: A Group Approach to 'Blue Coat Crime.'" Pp. 185–206 In Victor E. Kappeler (ed.) *The Police and Society: Touchstone Readings.* Prospect Heights, IL: Waveland Press.

Terrill, Richard J. (1990) "Alternative Perceptions of Independence in Civilian Oversight." *Journal of Police Science and Administration* 17, 2: 77–83.

The Knapp Commission Report on Police Corruption (1973) New York: George Brazillier.

Time (2000) "Time and Again, I Stepped Over the Line: If Rafael Perez is Telling the Truth, an L.A. Cop Scandal will cost the City Millions and More." *Time* 135, March 6: i10, p.25.

Trasher, Ronald R. (2001) "Internal Affairs: The Police Agencies' Approach to the Investigation of Police Misconduct." In M. J. Palmiotto (ed.) *Police Misconduct.* Upper Saddle River: Prentice-Hall.

Verma, Arvind (2000) "Cultural Roots of Police Corruption in India." *Policing* 22, 3: 264–279.

POLICE DEVIANCE IN AUSTRALIA

Tim Prenzler

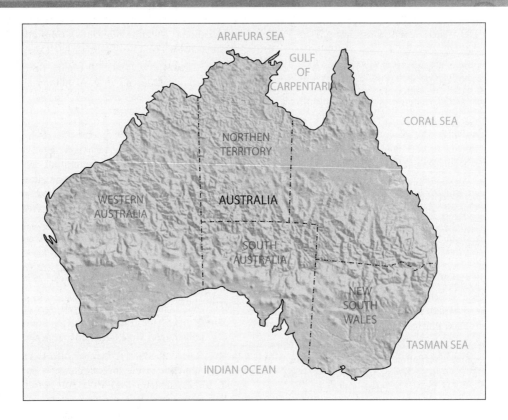

Australian policing has been blighted by the same problems of corruption and misconduct that have been common in many countries. There has not been the same degree of brutal suppression of dissent by "secret police" as occurred in many authoritarian regimes, although Australian police have also engaged in forms of unjustified political surveillance of citizens. Overall, however, there appears to be nothing distinctive about police deviance in Australia compared with other democracies. This underscores the common opportunity structure and cultural pressures that have existed in the modern form of policing.

Australia was settled by the British in 1788, and inherited a mixed model of policing. The English Peelian ideal of preventive, consensus-based, policing—emphasizing minimal force, judicious discretion, and impartiality (Reith, 1975)—sat uneasily with the militaristic colonial model of the Irish constabulary. Policing in the new colony of New South Wales was marked by significant disorganization that facilitated cases of extreme malpractice. The first police were marines who neglected their duty, stole goods, and sexually abused female convicts. The New South Wales Corps that replaced them in 1795 became known as "The Rum Corps," when it took control of the trade in spirits. Subsequent attempts to form civilian police required the recruitment of ex-convicts, with consequential conflict between convicts and the new police (Bryett, Harrison, and Shaw, 1997).

Outside urban centers, the frontier environment necessitated the creation of an armed and mounted police force, whose responsibilities included the violent suppression of indigenous people—often by native police units. Increasing professionalism came with colonial self-government from the mid-nineteenth century, but improvements in organization and training were marred by violence against striking workers during major industrial strikes in the 1880s and 1890s. Puritan restraints on gambling, alcohol, prostitution, and abortion created demand for organized corruption. There is considerable uncertainty about police integrity from the period of colonial government through nationhood (1901) to the 1950s. Research on this topic shows fairly high levels of dismissals of officers for misconduct while also highlighting continuous allegations and suspicions of corruption (Finnane, 1999).

The first major exposé of systemic corruption was made by the Fitzgerald Inquiry in the state of Queensland in the late 1980s. (Australia has a state-based policing system.) The Fitzgerald (1989) Commission revealed a long-standing racket, reaching up to the Commissioner, concentrated in police protection of prostitution and gambling. Criticisms were also made of police fabrication of evidence, excessive force in public order policing, and cover-ups of corruption. The most extensive revelations of corruption occurred in very recent times in New South Wales as a result of the Wood Commission of Inquiry from 1994 to 1997. It is probable that up to that time there had been continuous organized police corruption in Sydney, given its wealth and importance as a major port with numerous entertainment venues. There is fairly strong evidence of corruption networks in Sydney involving politicians in the 1960s and 1970s (Hickie, 1985). By the time of the Wood Inquiry police misconduct appeared to be occurring independently of politicians, and liberalization of vice reduced the size of protection rackets associated with liquor and gambling. Nonetheless, Wood's (1997) findings were focused on protection of gambling, drug trafficking, and the sex trade. He also identified extensive malpractice in the form of fabrication of evidence, assaults on suspects, opportunistic protection of criminals, and interference with prosecutions, extortion of criminals, opportunistic thefts, acceptance of gratuities, drinking on duty, absence from duty, false overtime claims and disability retirements, and specific issues like police failure to act against paedophiles.

Allegations of misconduct have varied considerably amongst the remaining police departments, with particular notoriety applying to Western Australia and Victoria (Prenzler and Sarre, 2002). A major corruption inquiry began in Western Australia in 2002. Victorian police have managed to avoid the scrutiny of a royal commission despite numerous scandals over "payback" shootings of criminals, shootings of mentally ill people, political surveillance, sex discrimination, and harassment of women both within and outside the police organization, the abuse of strip searching, and harassment of police whistle-blowers. The most organized form of corruption exposed in the Victoria Police was a kickback scheme operating from the 1970s to the 1990s involving preferential notifications by police to emergency security hardware installers.

Consistent with trends in other Western countries, the period from the 1960s in Australia also saw the development of a more general critique of unethical police practices covering claims such as under-policing of domestic violence and sexual assault, harassment of racial and ethnic minorities, harassment of minor drug users, neglect of white-collar crime, overzealousness in the use of force (including dangerous high speed vehicle pursuits), and "cronyism" in internal promotions and assignments. Many of these problems relate directly to the fact that Australian policing (again, like its counterparts in many countries) has been dominated by poorly educated white males, with a highly insular and defensive organizational culture.

In response to the corruption problem, Australia has become a major site of innovation in corruption prevention with strategies such as integrity testing, drug and alcohol testing, covert surveillance, complaints profiling, and external oversight (Prenzler and Ransley, 2002). All jurisdictions now have civilian agencies charged with reviewing police investigations of complaints, investigating more serious complaints, recommending disciplinary action, maintaining a general watchdog role against corruption, conducting research, and developing policy on contemporary issues, such as use of pepper spray and high speed pursuits. These bodies are often criticized for being weak and deferential toward police. Nonetheless, they appear to have an essential role in corruption prevention, especially in stopping traditional forms of organized graft, and in providing a counter to the tendency of police organizations to cover up problems.

In summary, it is difficult to define the levels of deviance in Australian policing in its 200-year history. There certainly have been cases of entrenched and extensive corruption, and a documented array of other forms of deviant practices. At the same time, police have provided an essential service, and untold numbers of officers have served with integrity and distinction.

References

Bryett, K.; A. Harrison and J. Shaw (1997) *The Role and Function of Police in Australia.* Sydney: Butterworths.

Finnane, M. (1999) "From Police Force to Police Service? Aspects of the Recent History of the New South Wales Police." In D. Dixon (ed.) *A Culture of Corruption.* Sydney: Hawkins Press.

Fitzgerald, G. (1989) *Report of a Commission of Inquiry Pursuant to Orders in Council.* Brisbane: Government Printer.

Hickie, D. (1985) *The Prince and the Premier.* Sydney: Angus and Robertson.

Prenzler, T. and J. Ransley (eds.) (2002) *Police Reform: Building Integrity.* Sydney: Federation Press.

Prenzler, T. and R. Sarre (2002) "The Policing Complex." In A. Graycar and P. Grabosky (eds.) *The Cambridge Handbook of Australian Criminology.* Melbourne: Cambridge University Press.

Reith, C. (1975) *The Blind Eye of History: A Study of the Origins of the Present Police Era.* Montclair, NJ: Patterson Smith.

Wood, J. (1997) *Royal Commission into the New South Wales Police Service, Final Report, Volume I: Corruption.* Sydney: Government of the State of New South Wales.

CHAPTER 14

A Jewish settler girl struggles with Israeli riot police as she is arrested during the evacuation of settlers from a Palestinian building in the West Bank town of Hebron, Sunday, May 7, 2006. Israeli police on Sunday evacuated dozens of Jewish squatters who took over a Palestinian home in the West Bank city of Hebron, in an important first test for Israel's new government and its plans to uproot tens of thousands of settlers. (Credit: © AP Photo/Kevin Frayer)

The authority of the police to use force represents one of the most misunderstood powers granted to representatives of government. Police officers are authorized to use both psychological and physical force to apprehend criminals and solve crimes. (Alpert and Smith, 1994)

POLICE USE OF EXCESSIVE FORCE

OBJECTIVES:

1. The student will gain an understanding of the meaning of the term use of force.
2. The student will learn about the various forms of police brutality.
3. The student will have an understanding of what is meant by deadly force.
4. The student will have an understanding of how police accountability affects their use of force.
5. The student will learn how functionalism, conflict theory, and interactionism view police use of excessive force.
6. The student will learn about police use of excessive force on an international level.

n the last chapter, we learned about the first of two forms of police deviance, corruption. In this chapter, we will examine a more controversial deviant action connected with the power to use force. As the quote above makes clear, illegal force, or more correctly, socially unacceptable use of force in actions is often referred to as **police brutality**, although the term in itself is controversial. Police brutality is defined as "the lawless exercise of force employed in excess" (Skolnick and Fyfe, 1993: xvi).

The **use of force** by the police can be defined as occurring "any time the police attempt to have citizens act in a certain way" (Roberg, Crank, and Kuykendall, 2000: 310). When does it become abusive? There are some who consider verbal abuse a form of police brutality, while others consider excessive force to consist solely of the excessive use of physical force. We begin to be concerned about such uses of force, when it is seen as excessive, or as an overreaction to a given situation. For example, a highway patrol officer politely asks to see your driver's license after stopping you on the highway. While there is force involved, you have no recourse but to comply; this is not seen as excessive. How about if the same highway patrol officer asks to see your license, while hitting you with a flashlight, and yelling obscenities? Here, the force used is definitely going to be seen as excessive, as there is nothing that indicates violence or resistance on the part of the motorist.

Incidents of police use of excessive force have included beating civil rights protestors, deliberate kicking and choking individuals while making arrests, and unprovoked use of deadly force when attempting to control riots and disturbances. Individual officers, a group of officers, or a large number of officers within the police department (thus pervading the culture of an entire police department) may carry out acts of excessive use of force. In the late 1990s, in Los Angeles, such excessive-force incidents even included officers who robbed banks, and shot drug dealers, and then planted weapons on them (*Time*, February 28, 2000; *Newsweek*, March 6, 2000; Walker, 2000).

As we saw in the last chapter, most occupations provide their practitioners with opportunities for misconduct, and police agencies and their officers are no exception. The opportunities for police officers to violate laws, and departmental policies discouraging the excessive use of force, are many. Techniques for accomplishing police operations often go hand-in-hand with the opportunities for such rule breaking. The socialization of police behavior begins in the recruit-training academy, where the police recruit is instructed into the "us" versus "them" mentality. With this attitude, the public becomes the enemy, and the only friends of a police officer are his fellow police officers. Many cultures, including the United States, encourage group and peer support, and police officers should not be considered any different from anyone else in this regard. From the day that the recruit enters training, he or she quickly learns that the support of fellow police officers is important to career success and future well-being as a police officer. The recruit quickly learns that it is generally best to look the other way when he or she sees fellow officers violating departmental rules and laws by using excessive force. The philosophy of "brother and sister" police officers in which the police subculture becomes a way of life can thus lead to police misconduct.

police brutality

More physical force used than is necessary to arrest someone.

use of force

Generally considered to be physical force used by the police. Some scholars consider that verbal abuse falls into this category.

DEMOCRATIC RIGHTS AND POLICE USE OF EXCESSIVE FORCE

Police officers hold a position of legal authority, control, and power over citizens. In democratic societies, it is not unusual for citizens to challenge laws they consider unfair or unjust, and thus challenge police authority. Examples of specific situations that can lead to police misconduct or accusations of police misconduct can include the following: mass demonstrations and sit-down strikes. Civil disobedience and direct confrontation with police authority may be encouraged, or may even be a part of the strategy of groups who intentionally want to confront the police. Democratic countries offer citizens redress when they believe that the police have been involved in actual or perceived police misconduct. The foundations of citizens' rights in American society are found in the U.S. Constitution, specifically in the Bill of Rights, which is consti-tuted by the first ten amendments to the Constitution. In 1789, the Bill of Rights was adopted by the Founding Fathers to protect citizens from governmental abuse by the federal government and its agents. In the twentieth century, the U.S. Supreme Court, to protect citizens from governmental abuse by the States and their agents, extended the applicability of the Bill of Rights to the States. The U.S. Supreme Court interpreted the "due process clause" of the Fourteenth Amendment as a protection for citizens against abuses by the State. Currently, the Bill of Rights protects citizens from both federal and state abuses, including policing misconduct. It should be remem-bered that local police, city, village, town, and county police officers are agents of the State, and the Bill of Rights applies to these police officers in their law enforcement authority.

When citizens directly challenge the authority of the police, it is often perceived by the latter as an attack on them. In confrontations between the police and citizens, the police often find themselves in many "no-win" situations. In such situations, the police are always open to criticism and formal charges of misconduct, regardless of how the situation was handled. The police are often attacked for violating the legal rights of citizens, because of the manner they used in enforcing the law. Although some of these accusations may be erroneous, the police have the responsibility to use their legal authority within prescribed legal and constitutional restrictions. Further, in any society, the police can be successful in maintaining social order and solving crime only with the cooperation of citizens. When the police lose the confidence of citizens, because they are perceived as brutal, or prone to unprovoked violence, the public will cease supporting the police in performing their law enforcement activities. This can include failing to providing information about crimes committed, refusing to serve as witnesses of crimes committed in their presence, or not supporting police when they want a salary increase and other benefits.

Police Use of Excessive Force as Misconduct and Deviance

Unlike the deviant behavior about which we learned in the last chapter, several types of police misconduct exist in which monetary, or material reward, or gain does not take place. According to Barker (2006), the range of police misconduct includes the following activities: perjury, sex on duty, sleeping on duty, drinking and using drugs on duty, and police brutality. When a police officer abuses people who he or she comes into contact with physically, this is likely to be criticized, and calls for corrective action from observers become loud. This, as we know, coincides neatly with how sociologists have defined the concept of deviance. You will recall that the meaning of the term "deviance" from the previous chapter is "conduct which the people of a group consider so dangerous or embarrassing or irritating that they bring special sanctions to bear against the persons who exhibit it," and that "the only way an observer can tell whether or not a given style of behavior is deviant, then, is to learn something about the standards of the audience which is responding to it" (Erikson, 1966: 3). Thus, police brutality can be defined as occurring when a police officer uses force in a way that the usual standards, as understood by the audience, in this case, the community, would consider excessive.

Incidents of police use of excessive force in making arrests and in controlling disturbances have occurred throughout history. Such incidents may be carried out by individual officers, a group of officers, or even involve the entire police department or a large number of officers within the police department. As we learned in the last chapter, Lundman (1980: 140–141) noted five conditions that must be met for individual (police) misconduct to be attributed to a dysfunctional (police) organization, for example, when occupational deviance becomes organizational deviance.

Those who are in command and those who have influence over the day-to-day operations of the department condone inappropriate or excessive use of force. One major reason for the acceptance of police use of inappropriate force is the "Code of Silence" that we became familiar with in the last chapter.

Police Use of Excessive Force and the Code of Silence

As mentioned earlier, the "Code" requires that police officers look the other way when they observe their fellow officers involved in acts of misconduct, in this case, brutality. Skolnick and Fyfe (1993: 110) write that the "Code of Silence" exists, and that it "typically is enforced by the threat of shunning, by fear that informing will lead to exposure of one's own derelictions, and by fear that colleagues' assistance may be withheld in emergencies." Skolnick and Fyfe (1993) believe that, in reality, police officers will not deny assistance to fellow officers, even those who may have informed on fellow officers in emergencies. They suggest that the fear upon which the "Code of Silence" appears based is imagined, or that officers are paranoid when they believe that fellow police officers will not come to their aid when they need assistance. According to Skolnick and Fyfe (1993: 112), "The Code of Silence then, is not one that is enforced by assassins lurking in dark alleys or arranging for drug dealers to terminate cops who inform. The police 'Code of Silence' are an extreme version of a phenomenon that exists in many human groups. It is exaggerated in some police departments and some police units because cops so closely identify with their departments, their units, and their colleagues, that they cannot even conceive of doing anything else."

FORMS OF POLICE EXCESSIVE USE OF FORCE

Incidents of the "use of excessive force" by police officers, or "police brutality," can be traced to early times in police history. In 1967, the President's Crime Commission (*Task Force Report: The Police:* 180) found that abuses in cities studied ranged from discourtesy to physical use of excessive force against people of all ages. The Commission further reported, "while allegations of excessive physical force receive the most attention, verbal abuse and discourtesy were probably greater irritants to community relations" (180). The same report found that many people, specifically minority groups, believe that the police are often engaged in excessive and unnecessary physical force. Similar to present-day efforts, the Commission was unable to determine exactly how serious a problem the excessive use of physical force was in U.S. police departments. However, although the Commission believed police brutality was a major problem, it was deemed not to be "systematic."

Barker (1986: 71) claims that when the public charges the police with excessive use of force, they are referring to any or all of the following actions by the police:

1. Profane and abusive language;
2. Commands to move on or go home;
3. Field stops and searches;
4. Threats;
5. Prodding with a nightstick or approaching with a pistol; and
6. The actual use of "physical force."

Most people would agree that it is inappropriate for police officers to use profanity and abusive language toward the general public. Although abusive language will not be good for police-community relations, should it be considered police brutality? The police have the authority to require people to move along, or request they go home, often for safety reasons. There are times when groups of individuals block entry into stores or the sidewalk, making it difficult for people to pass. The police also have the authority to tell juveniles to go home when communities have curfews.

Third Degree

Some forms of "police brutality" have also been referred to as the **third degree**. The term "third degree" came into vogue during the early decades of the twentieth century, and refers to use of excessive force during the questioning of suspects. Apparently, the term "first degree" presumably means the arrest, the "second degree" the transportation to a place of confinement, and the "third degree" the interrogation, which often means brutality (Skolnick and Fyfe, 1993: 43). In 1930, the American Bar Association's Committee on the Lawless Enforcement of the Law reported: "We can only say that the 'third degree,' in the sense of rigid and severe examination of men under arrest by police officers or prosecuting attorneys or both, is in use almost everywhere if not everywhere in the United States" (Skolnick and Fyfe, 1993: 45). The National Commission of Law Enforcement and Observance (the Wickersham

third degree

The use of physical force by the police to obtain a confession from a subject.

Commission), appointed by President Herbert Hoover in 1931, defined the third degree as "the inflicting of pain, physical or mental, to extract confessions or statements was widespread throughout the United States" (Skolnick and Fyfe, 1993: 45). In 1947, the President's Commission on Civil Rights, appointed by President Truman, made similar findings of excessive physical abuse by the police (181). The U.S. Civil Rights Commission, in 1961, concluded, "police brutality is still a serious problem throughout the United States" (181).

Although it appears that the third degree, or police brutality, does not occur to the extent that it did in the early decades of the twentieth century, it would be unrealistic to assume that it does not occur at all. Incidents of third-degree questioning have occurred not only in poorly administered police departments, which lack concern about how their officers treat people, but also in departments that are managed well and concerned about the treatment of citizens they serve.

Major Incidents of Police Use of Excessive Force

The last decade of the twentieth century saw numerous incidents of excessive use of physical force by police officers. Such incidents have continued into the twenty-first century. The first incident of excessive use of force that received national and international attention in the 1990s was the Rodney King incident. This event took place on March 3, 1991, in Los Angeles, California. The incident began at approximately 12: 40 a.m. when two California Highway Patrol (CHP) Officers detected King speeding on the freeway. Apparently, King's car passed the CHP car from the rear. The CHP officers paced the King vehicle. The officers activated their emergency equipment, and signaled for King to stop. King failed to stop, and continued to drive, and ran a stop sign, and a red traffic light. Later, King explained that he failed to stop, because he was afraid of getting a traffic summons, which could result in his probation (for an earlier robbery conviction) being revoked. The CHP officers notified the LAPD that they were pursuing a vehicle at a high rate of speed. King finally stopped his automobile along a curbside, where he was ordered out of his car. While this was taking place, police officers from other agencies arrived at the scene. There were two passengers in King's car who were ordered to get out of the car. They complied, and were taken into police custody. Initially, King refused to leave the automobile, and was struck with a Taser. When King finally came out, he was struck in the head with nightsticks, and kicked several times by police officers. It appears that King was struck approximately fifty-six times by police officers. There were anywhere from twenty-one to twenty-seven police officers who were witnesses to or participants in the beating of King. The injuries sustained by King consisted of a broken cheekbone, a fractured eye socket, missing teeth, kidney damage, skull fractures, external burns, and permanent brain damage (Christopher Commission, 1991).

What made the King-beating incident significantly different from earlier alleged incidents of police brutality was that a private citizen videotaped this incident. This videotape eventually fell into the hands of Cable News Network, which showed the King beating in the United States and throughout the world. The incident clearly shows excessive use of physical force by police officers at its worst. When brutality is alleged, often a police administrator investigates, and takes appropriate action based upon what is discovered. There is no doubt that the King beating gave the LAPD a black eye. Similar incidents, discussed later in this section, that occurred in the 1990s, further damaged the reputation of the LAPD.

Several years after the King incident, another scandalous act of excessive use of force occurred on the eastern coast of the United States. On the morning of August 9, 1997, several New York City police officers responded to a fight taking place outside of a club in Brooklyn. When the police officers arrived, one Abner Louima, in attempting to break up the melee, became drawn into the conflict. During the fight, one officer was punched, and it was believed that Louima was the culprit. Louima was taken into custody. On the way to the 70th precinct, police beat Louima with their fists in their patrol vehicle. While at the precinct, Louima, who was handcuffed, was taken to a restroom where a police officer rammed a two- to three-foot stick into Louima's rectum. Within a short period of time an ambulance was called, and Louima was hospitalized. A nurse reported the incident to the Police Internal Affairs Unit. Within hours of the report, the Louima incident became a local and national sensation. Similar to the Rodney King incident, the Abner Louima incident discredited the public image of the NYPD.

There are parallels and differences between the Rodney King beating and the Abner Louima case. Rodney King had a criminal history, and failed to stop his vehicle when told to do so by police officers. The beating of King was a classic example of excessive use of physical force. The assault on Louima was bizarre; the lawyer of a codefendant of the officer who placed the stick up Louima's rectum condemned the act as defying "humanity," and labeled the officer who performed it as a "monster." Both the King and Louima cases were tried in Federal court eventually, and the police officers responsible were convicted of crimes. Other police officers were acquitted.

King and Louima were both African American men who were brutalized by white police officers. The acts of brutality by white police officers against black men cannot fail to raise the question of racism. Both the LAPD chief and the NYPD commissioner characterized these acts of police brutality as aberrations, and denied that racism played a part in these incidents. While police critics agree that these acts were aberrations, but only in that white police officers used excessive physical force against blacks—this received wide publicity, and the police officers were punished.

Deadly Force

The excessive use of physical force may lead to serious bodily harm, and even the death of an individual. When such a death occurs, *deadly force* has been used. Generally, police officers have the authority to use deadly force, to cause the death of another human being, when their life, or the life of another person is jeopardized. The police can trace their authority to use deadly force back to the Common Law of England, which was developed during the Middle Ages. Under Common Law, a police officer could, if necessary, use deadly force to apprehend someone who he believed committed a felony. The rationale behind this authority was that, until the nineteenth century, virtually all felonies were punishable by death. In a sense, an officer who killed someone committing a felony was doing the state a favor since the person, if convicted of a felony, would receive the death penalty anyway. Such use of governmental authority has been limited statutorily. Currently, very few crimes are punishable by death. For an individual to receive the death penalty, an offender must be generally convicted of murder in the first degree. Even this is not uniform throughout the United States; some states have outlawed capital punishment. Under these circumstances, police officers who use deadly force and kill criminal suspects, in effect, have more power and authority than even juries and judges. Arguably, the most serious punishment a person can receive is the loss of his or her life. Because of this, the use of deadly force by police officers has become a controversial issue.

Fyfe (1981: 376), a noted scholar on police use of deadly force, claims that controversy over deadly force can be attributed to "Presidential Commissions, police practitioners, radical criminologists, more traditional academics, social activists, law reviews, and popular writers." There are a variety of ways that "routine" police actions can lead to death. For example, neck-holds or chokeholds can cut the circulation or blood flow to the brain, and cause death. As another example, in 1985, the Philadelphia Police Department dropped an incendiary bomb from a helicopter onto a house that caught fire, resulting in the death of eleven members of a radical group known as MOVE. However, the most common way for the police to use deadly force is with a firearm.

The decision as to when police officers should draw their weapons has not been clearly defined nor has the question of when they should fire them. While both actions rest on the discretion of the officer, there exists a difference between drawing and firing a firearm. Well-trained police officers receive training to draw their weapons only when circumstances present a reasonable expectation that they will encounter life-threatening violence. Police officers in busy police districts will draw their weapons more often than they are fired upon. Sometimes, officers draw their firearms when they respond to violent crime. Police officers who make arrests for serious crimes may have their weapons drawn to obtain quick compliance from suspects. Competent police officers know it may be unwise to display firearms to the mentally disturbed or those behaving illogically. It is an open question as to whether the display of an officer's firearm serves to stimulate violence rather than discourage it. It should be mentioned that each year there are a number of police officers that are shot with their own firearms (Skolnick and Fyfe, 1993: 41–42).

Periodically, shootings by police officers result in major unrest within the community served by them. On February 4, 1999, in the Soundview section of the Bronx, four NYPD officers, who were members of the Street Crime Unit, shot and killed Amadou Diallo, an immigrant from Africa. The four officers fired forty-one bullets, with nineteen penetrating Diallo's body. The victim was unarmed and standing alone in the vestibule of his Bronx apartment building; Diallo was shot by police officers standing no more than twenty feet away from him. This killing became a scandal with outcries of racism, again as a result of white police officers killing an African man. Immediately, following Diallo's death, the building became a shrine, with flowers and messages of condolence and anger lining the entryway (Kolber, 1999: 50). On February 25, 2000, a mixed-race jury of seven men and five women found the four police officers not guilty of second-degree murder, reckless endangerment, and manslaughter, and criminal negligent homicide in Diallo's death. The jury believed that the police officers acted in self-defense. Further, the jury believed that the police officers feared for their lives (Cukan, 2000: 1–4). The verdict of not guilty was not well received, and for several days, demonstrations took place in New York City. Diallo's parents petitioned the United States Justice Department to investigate the case for possible civil rights violations. The U.S. Justice Department decided in 2001 that the civil rights of Amadou Diallo were not violated, and that federal charges would not be invoked against police officers involved in the death of Diallo.

Several factors exist that for generations have placed the use of deadly force by the police high on the public policy agenda. These factors include public perceptions regarding crime problems, the availability of handguns to the public, limited technology available to the police to apprehend fleeing suspects, conflicting community perceptions and values, and the potential for any police actions, including even proper ones, to result in a community disturbance (Geller and Scott, 1992: 13).

Appellate court decisions, statutory law, and departmental policies all provide guidelines that police officers are supposed to follow for deadly force to be justifiable. In 1986, the U.S. Supreme Court struck down the fleeing felon rule, which allowed police officers to use deadly force, i.e., to shoot to kill a suspect escaping from the scene of a crime. In Tennessee v. Garner (105 Supreme Court Reporter, 470 U.S. 901, 1701) the court stated:

> The use of deadly force to prevent the escape of all felony suspects, whatever the circumstances is unconstitutionally unreasonable. It is not better that all felony suspects die than escape. Where the suspect poses no immediate threat and no threat to others, the harm resulting from failing to apprehend him does not justify the use of force to do so.

Although the U.S. Supreme Court banned arbitrary shootings of an unarmed fleeing felon who presents no threat to the police officer or any citizen, the Court decision was not absolute. The Supreme Court, in *Tennessee v. Garner,* found that when a police officer has probable cause to believe a suspect is a threat that is likely to cause serious physical harm to either the police officer or another person, the officer can use deadly force to prevent escape. Geller and Scott (1992: 13) had the following to say about police shootings.

> The importance of police-involved shootings stems not so much from their frequency (they are rare compared with the hundreds of thousands of encounters each year between persons suspected of violating the law) but from their potential consequences. Any experienced police officer knows the potentially devastating effects of even justified shootings by police—loss of life and bereavement, risks to an officer's career, the government's liability to civil suits, strained police-community relations, rioting and all the economic and social crises that attend major disturbances. (1)

It is important to recognize that occurrences of police brutality are not endemic to the United States alone, and that they happen in other countries, as the description of similar problems in Israel makes clear.

In Chapter 13 we learned about several internal and external mechanisms for holding officers involved in deviant behavior accountable. These strategies include the following: formulating and teaching a Code of Ethics, using Internal Affairs Units, providing for public oversight through Civilian (or Citizen) Review Boards, criminal charges being brought against offending police officers, and civil liability proceedings.

POLICE USE OF EXCESSIVE FORCE: THREE SOCIOLOGICAL PERSPECTIVES

Let us use three sociological perspectives that we have become familiar with—functionalism, conflict, and interactionism—to analyze the excessive use of force by the police. Similar to corruption, functionalists would first point to the laws, policies, and procedures that have been laid down against such behavior as expressing how the police are to act functionally. Dysfunctional behavior such as police violence comes about, from their point of view, because of the lack of adequate training and the failings of other socialization efforts, formal and informal. When an organization is in a state of dysfunction, the larger community or society steps in to render it functional again. Thus, offending officers are disciplined and punished; training procedures are revamped; and messages about the unacceptability of excessive use of force are relayed. In addition, renewed efforts at improving police-community relations are mounted so that the police department becomes functional.

The conflict perspective takes a critical stance (see Fielding, 2005) and believes that the police represent the group that has power, prestige, and wealth in a given society. Their job is to keep the powerless, noninfluential, and poorer sections of that society from stepping over the line, and challenging those in control. Police brutality is an extreme example of the use of raw power to show those threatening an existing unequal social order that those in power can fight back. Especially in cases of police brutality, such actions dramatize to the poor and powerless that there is a violent and authoritarian side to policing that should not be challenged. Historical examples in the United States would be the violent confrontations by law enforcement in the South against African Americans during the Civil Rights era. Conflict theorists would also question why the poor and visible minorities (as we saw from the examples earlier in this chapter) are targeted for police violence.

Finally, from an interactionist perspective, a lot of attention would be devoted to considering the nature and meanings of acts that are defined as police brutality, or excessive use of force. As we have seen, with just about all forms of police deviance, there are differences in interpretation. When the video of the violent police response to Rodney King was shown, many members of the public interpreted it as a senseless beating of an unarmed individual by brutal police officers. Many police officers suggested that what those officers were doing was in response to actions by King that they interpreted as increasingly threatening. Each increase in threat perception was met with an increase in violent response. They argued that this is how police are trained to respond when they are confronted with a violent individual who refuses to obey or back down. How could the same event get interpreted in two totally different ways? Interactionists would be interested in these perceptual differences, and where they stem from.

Israel, a nation primarily consisting of Jewish settlers from other parts of the world, occupies an important area of the strife-torn Middle East. What does the internal use of force by the police mean in a country that is simultaneously involved in defending itself militarily?

POLICE USE OF EXCESSIVE FORCE INTERNATIONALLY: ISRAEL

The history of the Israeli National Police began with the formation of Israel as a separate country in 1948, and generally followed the philosophies and procedures of the British colonial police before them. Initially, it dealt with the massive problems caused by the out-migration of Palestinians and the in-migration of waves of Jewish settlers from other parts of the world. Historically, the Israeli police have always struggled with the twin issues of conventional crime fighting and threats to internal security as a result of Palestinian civil disobedience and acts of terrorism.

Observers of the Israeli National Police noted "a marked increase in media coverage of alleged police brutality" (Herzog, 2001: 419), and that possibly "deviant organizational messages of violence prevail" (420) in that force. Specific areas of concern associated with the brutal discharge of police functions in Israel

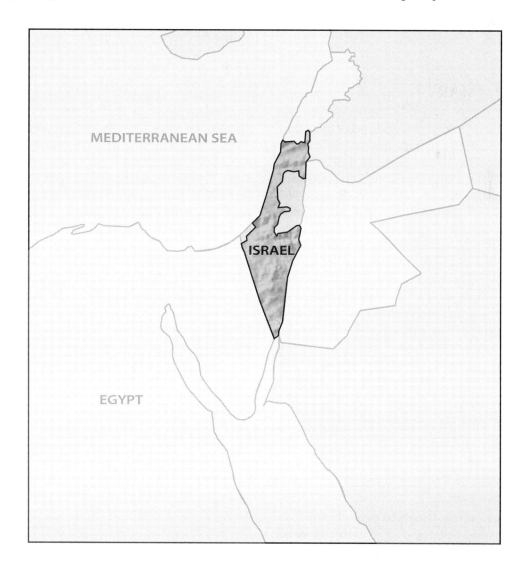

include: arresting drug offenders, dispersing violent demonstrations, and dealing with what the police refer to as "known offenders." Herzog (2001: 433) goes on to say that "the illegal use of force by Israeli police officers in general, and cover-up of such offenses by colleagues in the police department, are related to a deviant organizational subculture of the organization."

Based on a perceived increase in police violence, a Civilian Complaints Board was established by the Israeli police in 1992. Herzog (2002: 119), after examining trends in the illegal use of force by the police, concludes that they do not "seem to reflect actual worsening of police violence on the street, but (are) the result of wide public support for civilian involvement in the complaints system, procedural changes in that system, and of specific demographic changes in the Israeli population." The percentage of "sustained" instances of illegal use of force decreased after the Civilian Board was established. Given the common issues connected with **police use of force** in all democratic countries, it is important to note from the Israeli experience that some type of citizen oversight has the potential to reduce illegal instances of such use.

Finally, we turn briefly to recent policing reforms and use-of-force issues in an East European country that recently emerged from the shadow of the former Soviet Union—the Czech Republic (see accompanying Box).

 ## SUMMARY

In this chapter, we learned that while police officers are allowed to use force in certain situations, their utilization of excessive force in carrying out their work is a major concern and a form of misconduct and deviance. As we saw, police deviance includes both individual, occupational, and organizational deviance. At times entire police organizations may be involved in the excessive use of force against citizens. It is also a violation of the democratic rights of citizens. After learning the differences between use of force and excessive use of force (sometimes referred to as police brutality), we examined how the code of silence may be implicated in keeping such police violence hidden. As a result, it is difficult to know how widespread and how often incidents of police brutality occur. However, it does occur and the media periodically brings this to our attention as in the cases of Rodney King, Abner Louima, and Amadou Diallo. The "use of excessive force" is closely associated with "deadly force." Deadly force occurs when a police officer commits an act that either causes the death of someone, or has the potential of causing the death of someone. To eliminate and control deviant behavior by police officers, various accountability strategies such as codes of ethics, Internal Affairs investigations, civilian review boards, and criminal courts have been utilized. We examined the benefits and limitations of each of these strategies. We then applied the three major sociological analytic perspectives: functionalism, conflict, and interactionism to the issue of police brutality, and considered their conclusions. Finally, we learned about the nature of police use of excessive force in Israel and the success of civilian review there.

 ## KEY TERMS

Police brutality: More physical force used than is necessary to arrest someone.

Use of force: Generally considered to be physical force used by the police. Some scholars consider that verbal abuse falls into this category.

Third degree: The use of physical force by the police to obtain a confession from a subject.

REVIEW QUESTIONS

1. Discuss the various forms of police brutality.
2. Discuss accountability as it relates to police use of force.
3. Discuss deadly force as it relates to policing.

DISCUSSION QUESTIONS

1. Can deadly force ever be justified?
2. Do you think the Third Degree can be justified in the twenty-first century?
3. Do you really believe that police brutality exists today? Justify your answer.

REFERENCES

Alpert, Geoffrey P. and William C. Smith (1994) "How Reasonable Is the Reasonable Man?: Police and Excessive Force." *Journal of Criminal Law and Criminology* 85: 481–101.

Barker, Thomas (1986) "An Empirical Study of Police Deviance Other Than Corruption." In Thomas Barker and David Carter (eds.) *Police Deviance*. Cincinnati, Ohio: Anderson.

Christopher, Warren (1991) *A Report of the Independent Commission on the Los Angeles Police Department*. Los Angeles: City of Los Angeles.

Cukan, Alex (2000) "Jurors: The Only Issue Was the Law: Say Race Had No Part in Diallo Verdict?" *APBnews.com*. May 18.

Erikson, Kai T. (1966) *Wayward Puritans: A Study in the Sociology of Deviance*. New York, NY: Allyn and Bacon.

Fielding, Nigel (2005) *The Police and Social Conflict*. Second Edition. Portland, OR: Cavendish.

Fyfe, James J. (1981) "Observations on Police Deadly Force." *Crime and Delinquency* 27, 3: 376–389.

Geller, William A. and Michael S. Scott (1992) *Deadly Force: What We Know*. Washington, DC: Police Executive Research Forum.

Herzog, Sergio (2001) "Deviant Organizational Messages among Suspect Police Officers in Israel." *Policing* 23, 4: 416–438.

Herzog, Sergio (2002) "Police Violence in Israel: Has the Establishment of a Civilian Complaints Board Made a Difference?" *Police Practice and Research* 3, 2: 119–133. http://www.informaworld.com/smpp/content-db=all-content=a713743743

Kolber, Elizabeth (1999) "The Peril of Safety: Did Crime-Fighting Tactics put Amadou Diallou at Risk?" *New York Times*, May 22.

Lundman, Richard J. (1980) *Police and Policing: An Introduction*. New York, NY: Holt, Rinehart, and Winston.

Newsweek (2000) "How Do You Feel about Police Officers." March 6.

Roberg, Roy; John Crank and Jack Kuykendall (2000) *Police and Society*. Second Edition. Los Angeles, CA: Roxbury.

Skolnick, Jerome H. and James J. Fyfe (1993) *Above the Law*. New York, NY: The Free Press.

The President's Commission on Law Enforcement and Administration of Justice (1967) *Task Force Report: The Police*. Washington, DC: U.S. Government Printing Office.

Time (2000) "Time and Again, I Stepped Over the Line: If Rafael Perez is Telling the Truth, an L.A. Cop Scandal Will Cost the City Millions and More," *Time* March 6, 135, i10: 25.

Walker, Jesse (2000) "Gangsta Cops." *Reason* 31, 18: 13.

CZECH REPUBLIC POLICING, USE OF FORCE AND REFORMS

Tara O'Connor Shelley

The Velvet Revolution of 1989 ended the Communist era in Czechoslovakia, and in 1993, the country separated into two independent republics—the Czech Republic and the Slovak Republic (Ivković and Shelley, 2007). As a result of these events, reform of the Czech police was given immediate priority due to rising public expectations for a professionalized police force that would be respectful of democratic ideals and the desire for acceptance into the European Union (EU).

Immediate reform of the Czech police was critical to the success of the new democratic government. Prior to the Velvet Revolution, the Czech police were militaristic, and served the interests of the communist regime (Lundberg, 1992). Under this system of policing, it was not unusual for the police to violate human rights, ignore the service needs of the public, and to operate without transparency (Caparini and Marenin, 2005a; Caparini and Marenin, 2005b; Ivković and Shelley, 2007; Jenks, 2004). These human rights violations included excessive use of force to the point of police brutality and torture. To transform the police into a professional entity respectful of democratic principles and priorities, the Czech government passed lustration laws that called for the vetting of officers who were loyal to the prior regime and/or were members of the secret police (i.e., the Statni Bezpecnost or StB) (Jenks, 2004; Lundberg, 1992). Another pivotal aspect of reform was the passage of the 1991 Police Act that explicated the legal parameters for the authority and operation of the national police service under the Ministry of Interior. The Police Act (and subsequent amendments) also reinforced the importance of a service orientation, the protection of human rights, transparency, and accountability, all of which are central principles of a democratic system of policing (Bayley, 2001).

Following these initial reforms, the Czech police continue to respond to public and international pressure to further professionalize their services. Indeed, the Czech police have adopted community policing as a philosophy (Ministry of the Interior, 2002), and are in the process of implementing a service-oriented management approach through the use of the European

Foundation of Quality Management (EFQM) model. This model endorses social responsibility, partnerships, a customer orientation, and continuous learning and adjustments after systematic evaluations (EFQM, 2002). In 2005, the police adopted a Code of Ethics that emphasized the need for the police to be accountable to the rule of law and to report any form of misconduct committed by fellow officers (Ivković and Shelley, 2007).

The Czech police are also making improvements in equipment acquisition and the use of innovative technologies. Drastic improvements were required, given that in the early 1990s, the national police service (consisting of some 23,000 officers at the time) possessed a mere twenty-two cars equipped with radios, three radio-telephones, twenty-two bulletproof vests, and no central computer to process crime reports (Jenks, 2004). Due to these initial deficiencies it will be some time before the Czech police are fully equipped, and in the position to take advantage of the range of technological innovations available in the modern police industry. Indeed, it was not until 2004, that the Czech government purchased an integrated automated fingerprint identification system (IAFIS) for the police to enter and access data in the European Union's EURODAC centralized fingerprint identification system (Czech Republic, 2004).

Despite making significant progress in the reform of the Czech police, members of the Czech public, the international community, and a number of human rights organizations continue to have concerns about the police. Most of these concerns relate to police abuse and misconduct during large public protests (e.g., the 2000 International Monetary Fund or IMF, and World Bank meetings held in Prague); their recent use/misuse of wiretaps (particularly involving high-ranking government officials); biased, abusive, and negligent treatment of members of the Roma population (an ethnic minority comprising approximately 2 percent of the Czech Republic); and general corruption and misconduct issues (e.g., the acceptance of bribes). Although corruption is a problem that plagues many Czech institutions (Transparency International, 2005a), some feel the problem is particularly problematic among the Czech police (Transparency International, 2005b), and that the police/Interior Ministry are incapable of resolving corruption problems without bias (League of Human Rights, 2006).

Given the range of issues previously discussed, the future of Czech policing is certain to involve additional reform due in large part to rising public expectations, and international pressure from the European Union and human rights organizations. Thus, in the near future, one can expect reforms and recruitment programs that involve the diversification of the Czech police force to include members of ethnic and minority populations (particularly the Roma, Vietnamese, and Ukrainians), the improvement of police and minority relations through the use of liaisons and community policing/EFQM initiatives, and an increase in human rights and diversity awareness training in Czech police academies. It is also plausible that pressure from the Czech public and human rights organizations (particularly the League of Human Rights in Prague) will eventually convince the Czech police and Interior Ministry to vest external oversight of alleged police corruption and misconduct to another government institution and/or private entity.

It is particularly promising that some of the above-mentioned reforms are already in the early stages of implementation; however, it is likely that the Czech police will continue to experience human rights and misconduct problems with the Roma population until the Czech population and government first deal with larger social issues involving the Roma (i.e., social inequality, social isolation, and xenophobia) (Fawn, 2001). Despite these lingering problems, the Czech police are considered to be well on their way to successful democratization and professionalization (Caparini and Marenin, 2005a; Ivković and Shelley, 2007). If this trajectory of progress continues, the Czech police have the ability to serve as a model for police agencies undergoing reform in emerging democracies.

References

Act of the Czech National Council of 21 June 1991 Regulating the Police of the Czech Republic (No 283/1991). Retrieved on February 20, 2009, from http://www/mvcr.cz/dokument/index.html#z106

Bayley, D. (2001) *Democratizing the Police Abroad: What to Do and How to Do It.* Washington, DC: National Institute of Justice, U.S. Department of Justice.

Caparini, M. and O. Marenin (2005a) Crime, Insecurity, and Police Reform in Post-Socialist CEE. *The Journal of Power Institutions in Post-Soviet Societies.* Issue 2. Retrieved on February 18, 2006, from http://www.pipss.org/document330.html

Caparini, M. and O. Marenin. (2005b) "Reforming the Police in Central and Eastern European States." Pp. 217–242 In Fields, C. B. and R. H. Moore, Jr., (eds.) *Comparative and International Criminal Justice: Traditional and Nontraditional Systems of Law and Control.* Second Edition. Long Grove, IL: Waveland Press.

Czechoslovakia Police Repression (1987). Retrieved on October 12, 2009, from http://www.photius.com/countries/czechoslovakia/national_security/czechoslovakia_national_security_police_repression.html

"Czech Republic National Police Buy Enhanced Automated Fingerprint Technology as Country Joins European Union" (June 7, 2004). TMCnet. Retrieved on January 17, 2007, from http://www.tmcnet.com

European Foundation for Quality Management (2002) *The Fundamental Concepts of Excellence.* Belgium: EFQM. Retrieved on October 25, 2006, from http://www.efqm.org

Fawn, R. (2001) "Czech Attitudes towards the Roma: 'Expecting more of Havel's country'?" *Europe-Asia Studies* 53: 1193–1219.

Ivković, S. K. and T. O. Shelley (2007) *Police Integrity and the Czech Police Officers.* Manuscript submitted for publication.

Jenks, D. (2004) "The Czech Police: Adopting Democratic Principles." Pp. 23–44 In Caparini, M. and O. Marenin (eds.) *Transforming Police in Central and Eastern Europe.* Muenster, Germany: Lit Verlag/Somerset, NJ: Transaction Publishers.

League of Human Rights. (2006) *Police Misconduct.* Prague: League of Human Rights. Retrieved on October 25, 2006, from http://www.llp.cz

Lundberg, K. (1992) *The Czech Republic: Police Reform in a New Democracy* (Case Program). Cambridge, MA: Harvard University, Kennedy School of Government.

Ministry of the Interior (2002) *National Strategy on Policing Minorities. Resolution and Referential Report. Ministry of the Czech Republic.* Retrieved on February 4, 2006, from http://www.mvcr.cz/dokument/index.html

Transparency International. (2005a) *Corruption Perceptions Index.* Retrieved on February 26, 2006, from http://ww1.transparency.org/cpi/2005/cpi2005.sources.en.html

Transparency International. (2005b) *Transparency in the Police.* Retrieved on February 26, 2006, from http://www.transparency.cz

The mayor of the small Canadian town of Cornwall, Ontario, goes into hiding; nightly shootings occur across the waterways of the St. Lawrence River; smuggling related killings take place; rumors exist of tobacco company complicity, but fears of a growing organized crime network focus on Aboriginal communities armed and potentially violent "pirates," Asians, and other profit-seeking racketeers. Another major organized crime market is created. The policing and political response targets the most vulnerable criminals, while other media focus on the spread of various types of ethnic-based crime. The cigarette companies walk away . . . almost. Seven years later the attention turns toward corporate "suppliers" of the illegal commodity, giving new meaning to the phrase "targeting upward." (Beare, 2003: 189)

Anders Persson, a Swedish police officer assigned to Interpol's human trafficking unit, is seen working at his desk during an interview with the Associated Press, Tuesday, Oct. 16, 2007 at Interpol's headquarters in Lyon, central France. The international police organization, working off tips from people who responded to a global appeal for help, said on Monday that it has identified a suspected pedophile shown in Internet photos abusing young boys. (Credit: © AP Photo/Laurent Cipriani)

POLICING THE GLOBE

OBJECTIVES:

1. The student will learn how to think about crime and policing globally.
2. The student will learn about major forms of transnational crime.
3. The student will understand how policing transnational crime is carried out.
4. The student will learn how functionalism, conflict theory, and interactionism view the globalization of policing.
5. The student will learn about global policing as it operates on an international level.

n the quote above, Margaret Beare (2003: 189) begins her discussion of tobacco smuggling (from the United States where it is cheaper to Canada where it is relatively more expensive) with the above true scenario that speaks to the internationalization of both societies and crime. First, let us stipulate that cigarette smuggling (however large-scale) is probably not going to be atop anyone's list of "serious" crime. Second, the smuggling involved here (that takes advantage of a difference in prices between two friendly, neighboring countries) occurs along a border that was long thought to be safe. Third, the repercussions of this international (or more accurately, transnational) crime involve not just the usual considerations regarding perpetrators and victims, but a whole host of local, national, and bilateral consequences. For example, should the United States make more of an effort to prevent such smuggling? What should Canada's stance in this matter be? Think about both these questions in the context of what the United States has been urging other countries to do when it perceives itself as being victimized by transnational criminal activity, e.g., with regard to music and movie digital piracy (the illegal copying and distribution through CDs, DVDs, or over the Internet, which generally constitute infringements of copyright). Finally, the occurrence of global crime raises a number of issues, most obviously here (and the main point of Beare's contribution), the blurring and mingling of concepts such as organized crime and corporate crime. To illustrate, let us say an American company (i.e., chartered and registered in the United States) is implicated in long-term criminal activity abroad (bribing foreign officials, engaging in toxic dumping, maintaining an unsafe work environment for its employees, etc.). What does this pattern of operation do to our definitions of what constitutes organized crime (generally thought of as involving an organization whose central activity is crime) and corporate crime (generally when a company is involved in legitimate business, during the course of which it happens to do something illegal)? Our endeavor in this chapter is to discuss the growing phenomenon of transnational crime and to describe the existing police response to it. As you can imagine, this will take us far from the relative comfort of what we know about local police departments to span literally the entire world of policing (see Haberfeld and Cerrah, 2007), while also discussing along the way states, provinces, countries, and regions of the world, and their crime problems and their police forces.

THINKING ABOUT CRIME GLOBALLY

It has become commonplace to refer to people today as living in a global society or global village. **Globalization**, as we learned at the beginning of this book is the increasing interconnectedness of the economies, peoples, and to a lesser extent, the politics of various countries of the world. There are both positives and negatives to this contemporary trend (see Boli, Ellottt, and Bieri, 2004 for a complete survey of globalization issues). More specifically, the intention of a speaker who invokes the global village metaphor is to describe one of three processes. First is the movement of individuals from one country or world region to another for economic or political reasons (e.g., from Ireland

globalization

The increasing interconnectedness of the economies, peoples, and to a lesser extent, the politics of various countries of the world.

to the United States and Canada; from South and South East Asia to the Middle East). Second, the speaker may be discussing economic globalization (e.g., American airplanes being sold to Korea; call centers in India handling technical support services for computer owners in the United States). Third, the speaker may be referring to international communication networks, such as those involving telecommunications, multinational satellite broadcasts, and e-mail, as well as the Internet.

Fascinating as each of these processes may be, we should, however, be careful in trying to understand the meaning of crime while speaking globally. Criminal behavior is conceived of differently from society to society, and has varying national consequences. Let us take four aspects of this observation. First, the frequency of crime varies across countries, with poorer countries generally experiencing (or at least reporting) lower rates of crime. The modernization hypothesis (Shelly, 1981) regarding crime argues that as a country undergoes economic development (i.e., industrialization and urbanization), its crime rate increases. Thus, underdeveloped countries experience more crime as a consequence of the process of becoming modern (while simultaneously seeing a lessening of some other social problems: Ritzer, 2004). Second, economic development and accompanying affluence will bring about their own set of crime problems. For example, the increased availability and use of automobiles as a result of economic growth results in a rise in motor vehicle theft as a form of crime in a society that may previously have been kept at fairly low or nonexistent levels. At the same time, developed societies are also able to marshal the resources necessary to deal with (if not completely, do away with) the rising rates of crime.

Third, along these lines, Ritzer (2004: 4) notes that it is "only with affluence that people come to conceive of certain things as problems." Here one might consider views regarding slavery and indentured servitude that are often seen in preindustrial societies. In contemporary industrialized and affluent societies, these practices are almost universally condemned and criminalized with severe associated punishments. Fourth, we should pay attention to the fact that developed affluent societies may be more "at risk" to the consequences of specific criminal events and crime in general. We can consider what this means in terms of either a minor criminal event or a major one. Think about the "haul" a burglar would be able to steal from a poor peasant's home in an underdeveloped country, and compare it to what could be stolen from even a lower-class household in a developed country. The range, number, and value of possessions in the latter case are going to be larger. In thinking of this issue using a major criminal event, Ritzer (2004) points out that while the consequences of the bombing of the New York City World Trade Center on September 11, 2001, were heavy, both in terms of personnel and resources for the United States (a highly developed country), the return bombing of Afghanistan would cause lesser damage, simply because its economy was smaller. Both these points are another way of saying that when you have little, you have little to lose due to crime.

Having considered the differences in meaning and implication of global crime, let us look at some of the global forms of crime and disorder that call for a police response involving more than one sovereign nation. It should be mentioned here that most of our attention will focus on what Adler, Mueller, and Laufer (2004) define as **transnational**

transnational crime

Global forms of crime and disorder that call for a police response involving more than one sovereign nation.

international crimes

Major criminal offenses, so
designated by the community
of nations for the protection
of interests common to all
mankind, such as genocide and
mass human rights violations.

crimes as opposed to **international crimes**. The latter term refers to "major criminal offenses so designated by the community of nations for the protection of interests common to all mankind" (Adler, Mueller, and Laufer, 2004: 403), such as genocide and mass human rights violations. Generally, the police forces of any given country are much more likely to be dealing with transnational crime and much less likely, if ever, to be dealing with international crime.

TRANSNATIONAL FORMS OF CRIME

Mueller (2001: 14) quotes the *Fourth United Nations Survey of Crime Trends and Operations of Criminal Justice Systems Report* that defines transnational crime as consisting of "offenses, whose inception, prevention and/or direct or indirect effects involved more than one country." He also observes that while it is possible for individuals to commit transnational crime, such offenses usually involve organized activity of some sort. Gregory (2000) provides a well-researched account of three types of crime that were among the first to evoke historically a more or less international (or at least involving more than one state) response. These include piracy on the high seas as early as the sixteenth century; slavery and slave-trading through kidnapping individuals in one location, and selling them at another in the late eighteenth century; and drug trafficking of mood-altering substances (e.g., opium, cocaine) grown in one country, and sold at another beginning with the early twentieth century. Of the three mentioned, two (sea piracy and drug trafficking) forms of criminality exist today, and are of transnational concern, while a third (slavery) persists in a somewhat modified form (human trafficking for economic or sexual purposes).

While not an exhaustive list, Mueller (2001; see also Adler, Mueller, and Laufer, 2004) offers the following, based on categories developed by the United Nations, as incorporating most contemporary forms of transnational crime. Again, it should be clear that many of these offenses can, of course, be committed domestically; the added cross-national dimension often adds to the severity of the crime and the seriousness of its costs and consequences.

Money Laundering

This is the process used by criminals to convert funds acquired illegally (e.g., by selling illegal drugs; proceeds obtained by disposing stolen goods; or as a result of bribery) into what appears to be legitimate income that can be used for legal purposes such as investment and purchase. Since financial institutions are generally regulated by national governments, doing this in two countries (e.g., depositing money stolen in Uzbekistan in a Swiss bank account) has clear advantages. This crime is implicated in many of the other offenses to be discussed below, given that "legitimizing" the gains from criminal activity is a constant concern for perpetrators. Police departments, regulatory agencies, and commercial fraud investigators are all interested, and heavily involved in the prevention and detection of these offenses.

Illegal Drug Trafficking

As mentioned above, drug trafficking involves the movement of mood-altering substances from their points of origin to their points of consumption. The extensive growth of opium poppy in Afghanistan and Myanmar, and coca in Colombia, and their export to the United States where they are consumed in the form of heroin and cocaine, respectively, are examples of this transnational crime. Between the grower and the user is a vast network of individuals and groups operating worldwide that buys, transports, processes (e.g., turning the raw opium to finished heroin), and distributes the drug in question. Police agencies at all levels, national (e.g., the Drug Enforcement Administration), state (e.g., Highway Patrol), and local (often in the form of Joint Drug Task Forces), are involved in responding to drug trafficking.

Corruption and Bribery

In the global economy, corporations operate in many different countries and under many different guises (e.g., the Ford Motor Company owns Volvo, generally identified with Sweden; computer chips produced in Taiwan and Malaysia power computers that are sold with the Apple or Hewlett-Packard brand names). In many countries, to obtain the requisite operating or export licenses or permits, as well as contracts, government officials from the local to the national levels often ask and receive bribes. To compete, other companies have to offer similar inducements leading to a pervasive, corrupt economic and business environment. Police agencies may sometimes be involved in investigating, and may help in the prosecution of these offenses.

Infiltration of Legal Business

Although not in itself a crime, buying a legal business may be deemed criminal, if it is used as a means for laundering money that may have been acquired illegally. For example, an organized crime group may buy a number of automobile dealerships. The purchase is financed through drug trafficking profits that are thereby laundered. The dealerships could then serve as "fronts" for the disposal of stolen automobiles, and in time may be a means for the owner or his family to turn into legitimate business owners. Police agencies at all levels would, of course, be interested in knowing about and tracking the infiltration of organized crime groups in legal businesses.

Fraudulent Bankruptcy

A business (often one that has been infiltrated by organized crime groups) may declare bankruptcy for its subsidiary in a given country, while remaining profitable elsewhere. It may have been part of a deliberate strategy to move assets and money elsewhere, and to intentionally defund and close down a given unit. Thus, the bankruptcy is not due to an adverse business climate or competitive losses. In essence, it defrauds the host country of revenue and taxes, and its citizens of employment. While police departments do not typically track bankruptcy declarations, fraudulent ones are likely to be sometimes investigated.

Insurance Fraud

Locally, unscrupulous individuals scam insurance companies by filing fraudulent claims, for example, involving staged accidents, exaggerated injuries, questionable property losses, and higher medical or emergency bills (often for minor to nonexistent injuries). The same scams may be carried out internationally, given that insurance companies operate globally. For example, a multinational corporation can claim insurance for losses suffered at a foreign plant, which may have been deliberately faked. At the other end, it is possible for fraudulent insurance companies to collect premiums from customers in one country as payment for policies they falsely claim are backed by real insurance companies whose headquarters just happen to be offshore, and therefore do not meet their financial obligations. Given their overseas locations the companies are probably beyond the reach of state insurance and local law enforcement authorities.

Computer Crime

Since computers can be, and these days often are, linked through the World Wide Web that connects them with other computers across the globe, this form of communication can also serve as a means for committing transnational crime. In addition to the illegal downloading of copyrighted material, such as software, music, books, and movies, the Internet facilitates the spread of disabling computer viruses, and allows individuals to hack into supposedly "secure" computer networks containing sensitive information that may be private, governmental, and commercial. Add to this the role of computer networks in facilitating other traditional crimes as varied as gambling, pornography, confidence games (see the later section in this chapter on the Nigerian fraud), and hate crimes by connecting interested parties with information and contacts needed for the commission of these offenses, locally and across national borders. Cyber crimes call for a great deal of ingenuity and versatility on the part of law enforcement in terms of learning, investigation, and prevention.

Intellectual Property Theft

As mentioned above, the theft of copyrighted material is greatly facilitated by the global reach of the World Wide Web. However, this is not the only form that transnational intellectual property crime takes. Music CDs and movie DVDs can be mass produced in one country cheaply and illegally, and then sold in another at a price that does not include any profit for the company that originally commissioned the work, or for the artists who performed in them. Similarly, books can be printed or copied, and sold cheaply across geographic borders without any recourse for the authors or publishers. Along the same lines, computer software and scientific and pharmaceutical product formulae may also be exploited illegally for profit. Most victims of intellectual property theft are likely to be looking for recompense, and not criminal punishment, and therefore, not generally likely to involve police agencies.

Illicit Arms Trafficking

Legitimate producers of weaponry and other arms for military purposes are authorized to sell their wares by the government of the country where they are located to other specific countries, often with the stipulation that they be used for defensive purposes. Mueller (2001: 17) notes, however, that the illegal trade in arms "is performed by an apparently small group of wholesalers, assisted by larger groups of retailers, located at relatively few illicit arms trading hubs." Most worrisome, from a law enforcement perspective, is the added possibility of nuclear material that may later become "weaponized," being trafficked and thereby falling into the hands of rogue governments and terrorist groups. These governments and terrorist groups can then proceed to use these illicit arms against their fellow citizens, or for purposes of destabilizing other countries.

Terrorism

Similar to many other offenses mentioned in this chapter, terrorism (generally thought of as the intentional and indiscriminate use of cruelty against and killing of public targets for the purpose of spreading fear and to advance political or social objectives) may be localized, or may operate transnationally. Local examples include the many incidents of terrorism carried out by members of the Irish Republican Army in Britain; by Kashmiri separatists in India; by guerrillas in Sri Lanka; the 1994 bombing of the Murrah Federal Building in Oklahoma City, and the 1996 Atlanta Olympics bombing in the United States. As is well known about the largest act of terrorism on American soil, hijackers (mostly from Saudi Arabia) boarded, and redirected four airplanes (which were undertaking coast-to-coast flights, and therefore had nearly full fuel tanks), crashing two of them into the twin towers of the World Trade Center in New York City and one on the Pentagon (home of the U.S. Defense Department) in Washington, DC. The fourth plane, which was also reportedly headed for the capital, crashed in Pennsylvania before reaching its target due to actions taken by passengers on board. The objective was to bring terrorism home to the United States, and to make its citizens suffer for American policies and actions abroad. Rather than sophisticated weapons and technical superiority, the hijackers were armed with simple box cutters, and had taken lessons on flying airplanes. This incident has led to a massive revamping of the priorities of American law enforcement at federal, state, and local levels to emphasize homeland security. At the same time, preventing and dealing with the threats posed by terrorism while simultaneously maintaining traditions of dissent and free speech as well as operating without violating human rights, remain at the crux of the dilemma confronting democratic criminal justice (see Chadwick, 1997; Turk, 2003).

Aircraft Hijacking

The illegal commandeering of airplanes for the purpose of either demanding ransom payments (the celebrated case of D. B. Cooper in the 1970s who jumped out a plane using a parachute with the ransom money), or for making a political statement (such as happened with Pan Am Flight 103 that exploded over Lockerbie, Scotland, killing all its passengers, or others whose passengers were released after the demands of the hijackers were met or negotiated) has been a feature of much of the late twentieth century. It should be noted that the frequency of such hijacking attempts has declined, due mainly to increased security procedures at airports, even before the events of September 11, 2001 (which demonstrated that previous views of hijackers as being interested in negotiating are not always accurate), discussed above.

Sea Piracy

As mentioned earlier, this age-old offense, which is considered the first to result in multinational cooperative law enforcement efforts, continues to exist in certain parts of the world, particularly in and around Central and South America, South East Asia, and West Africa. The International Maritime Bureau, a organization set up by commercial shippers, defines the crime as follows: "Piracy is the act of boarding any vessel with an intent to commit theft or any other crime, and with an intent or capacity to use force in furtherance of that act." In most incidents of piracy, pirates intercept ships during their voyages on the high seas, or while they are waiting to dock at various ports, and loot them for money, goods, and other valuables. Although it does happen, it is rare for the ship itself to be commandeered, its occupants kicked out, and for the vessel to be used or sold by the pirates. Governments of the countries within whose territorial waters these incidents take place may often be unable or unwilling to patrol and police the seas to prevent them. Joint patrols utilizing the navies or coast guard units of neighboring countries are often carried out to prevent or arrest pirates. Other than in port cities and in the coast guard, law enforcement in general has little occasion to deal with this form of transnational crime.

Hijacking on Land

While the hijacking of an aircraft is a spectacular event and covered extensively by the media, land hijackings (involving delivery trucks carrying shipments of merchandise for delivery) is rarely covered. Interestingly, the term hijack (meaning the forcible robbery from, or seizure of a vehicle in transit) was originally meant to denote land-based crimes of this kind. Trucks carrying valuable merchandise (food, electronic equipment, cigarettes, etc.) are stopped, perhaps at gunpoint, and then driven to another country where the contents are sold, and the truck is disposed off. Porous borders (e.g., between countries that constitute the European Union, in Eastern Europe, and among various countries in Africa) and the complicity of bribed border guards and government officials obviously contribute to the growth of this transnational crime. This crime is of particular interest to highway police and their equivalents in countries where the offenses originate, where the hijacked vehicles pass through, and where it finally ends.

Human Trafficking

Individuals choose to migrate from one country to another for a variety of social, cultural, economic, and political reasons. They may do so legally following procedures established by the receiving country. Individuals may choose to flout these rules, and enter a given country illegally. In doing this, they may sometimes receive the assistance of organized criminal groups that do this for payment. The United Nations differentiates the illegal flow of people from one country to another into smuggling and trafficking. Human smuggling is defined as "the procurement of illegal entry of a person into a state of which the latter person is not a national with the objective of making a profit." Illegal immigrants to the United States from other countries who may enter the country through the Canadian and Mexican borders, or along the coasts without the proper documents, because they wish to live and work in this country, belong in this country. Human trafficking is defined as "the recruitment, transportation or receipt of persons through deception or coercion for the purposes of prostitution, other sexual exploitation or forced labour" (Graycar, 1999). Women from Russia and other East European countries who are forced into prostitution in other parts of Europe and in Asia belong to this category of crime. Mameli (2002: 67) argues that transnational police cooperation can help reduce forced prostitution, or what he refers to as the "virtual enslavement of a growing number of women into the global prostitution market" from the former Soviet Union. While both are illegal, clearly, human trafficking, since it involves "deception, coercion . . . prostitution . . . sexual exploitation or forced labor" is of more concern. Similarly, while the former involves some degree of choice on the part of the individual illegal immigrant, organized crime groups are heavily involved in both human smuggling and trafficking.

Human Organ Trafficking

Ghoulish and horrifying as it may sound to us, there is a thriving illegal international trade in human organs (such as kidneys, livers, lungs, and hearts) and tissue, which pairs those buying (e.g., an individual who can afford the money needed and is willing to travel to another country to have a kidney transplant performed) and those who are selling (i.e., another individual who is poor and in desperate need of the money gained from allowing the removal of a kidney). As an example it has been reported reliably that large slums exist in the Philippines where many people have sold their body parts. Similarly, tendons and tissue, removed illegally from South African cadavers were transported, via South Korea, to New York (and reportedly sold for more than $2,500 per unit). There is also the case of villagers from Moldavia who were tricked into going to Turkey (under false pretenses of obtaining employment), but on reaching their destination, were forced to "donate" their kidneys. Given its shadowy and usually consensual nature, obviously, this type of transnational crime can only be tackled by utilizing the cooperation of police agencies at all levels and in different parts of the world.

Art and Cultural Object Theft

These two forms of transnational crime are related and taken together, although the harm referred to in each type is slightly different. Fine arts objects (e.g., paintings, rare books, sculptures, etc.) are the form of property stolen in the first category. The second refers generally to the theft of antiques and other objects, such as may be found in a museum devoted to a nation's history or its culture (e.g., if someone stole the original copy of the U.S. Declaration of Independence or Native American artifacts). As mentioned above, there is some overlap between the two categories in that a piece of fine art may also be considered an important part of a country's heritage (e.g., if, as happened in 1911, when someone stole the famous Mona Lisa painting from the Louvre in Paris). According to **INTERPOL**, the art black market is among the top three or four largest international criminal enterprises (a list that includes drug trafficking, money laundering, and illicit arms trafficking). While the actual theft may be carried out by individuals, organized crime groups are almost always implicated in the smuggling and ultimate sale (usually to a private collector) of a valuable and highly prized object. Given the value of various pieces of fine art and the wealth of those who may have owned it, insurance investigators and private detectives (who may have specialized knowledge of the world of art and cultural objects) are often employed in tracking the stolen item. However, police agencies may become involved in investigating and compiling information for the criminal processing of the offender, his or her networks, and the buyer of the object. In addition, given that most cultural objects are publicly owned and displayed, police departments are likely to be involved in investigating such thefts from the very beginning.

INTERPOL

The International Criminal Police Organization.

Environmental Crime

The environment consists of literally everything in the natural world that surrounds human beings. Environmentalists and other activists have long decried the exploitation, degradation, and depletion that human beings have visited upon these irreplaceable natural resources (the atmosphere, forests, the earth, rivers, seas, other species, etc.). International attention to these problems has begun only recently, but continues to be controversial in that many countries feel that economic growth requires them to exploit natural resources. However, transnational environmental crime is a fact of contemporary life. For example, a flourishing illegal trade in various protected endangered species (e.g., rhinoceros which is killed for its horn) exists. Hazardous wastes are disposed in other countries (whose politicians and bureaucrats have been bribed), often oblivious to their deleterious effects on the land and water. Ozone-depleting substances (e.g., chlorofluorocarbons or CFCs) continue to be produced and sold, wreaking havoc on our common atmosphere. Finally, illegal logging (and the cutting down of irreplaceable, old-growth forests) continues in various parts of the world where the local leadership may be powerless or corrupt to such an extent that they cannot or will not stop these environmental depredations. Part of the problem here is that the environmental issues mentioned above do not stop at the borders of nations. However, given that crime and justice issues are dealt with in terms of national jurisdictions, unless countries (and their national law enforcement agencies) cooperate together, it is virtually impossible to deal with this important form of transnational crime that threatens the very environment in which we live and breathe.

Other Offenses Committed by Organized Criminal Groups

This last category is clearly a residual one. However, the movement of automobiles stolen in one country and sold in another may be included here as an example of such offenses. Reportedly, thieves steal automobiles in the United States and Canada, and these are then smuggled by organized crime groups to the Far East, the Caribbean, and South America where they are sold. Given the differences in record keeping and a lack of common databases for vehicle identification and tracking, it becomes virtually impossible to trace the stolen vehicle in the other country. While automobile theft victims may be able to recoup their losses or get replacement vehicles, the insurance industry suffers from huge losses as a result. It is difficult to assess the degree of cooperation among police agencies internationally in dealing with transnational auto theft. However, the presence of global positioning system devices in many automobiles may assist in the prevention of theft of and ultimate recovery (if stolen) of such vehicles.

GLOBAL POLICING AGAINST TRANSNATIONAL CRIME

Sheptycki (2002: 323) argues that "policing is no longer a set of practices embedded in the sovereign nation-state, but rather has become transnationalized and greatly differentiated." This is evident at many levels. For example, police in one country are often called upon to assist other countries in forming and training their own police forces (see Clegg and Whetton, 2000, on assistance by Britain to developing countries). Next, the ideas embodied in slogans such as "zero tolerance" (see Ismaili, 2003) and enforcement strategies such as "intelligence-led crime control" (Maguire, 2000) diffuse from one country to another with ease and speed. While these may assist in giving policing in different countries a degree of uniformity of conduct and operating ideology, they do little to deal with the kinds of transnational crime we discussed in the earlier section.

Di Gennaro (2001: 259) finds, "Over the last 20 years, there has been a growing preoccupation with transnational crime. Initially, it was only the criminologists who gave it serious attention, but in those early days the phenomenon had not acquired the gravity characterizing it in recent years. Today, public opinion, alerted by its grave and flagrant manipulations, is keenly aware of it. The media focus strongly upon it and politicians declare an intense concern about it." However, he goes on to say that the practical outcome in terms of action against transnational crime is depressing in that it has been lacking. He cites approvingly the formation of the European Office of Police (**EUROPOL**), and suggests that this involves taking a first step toward "a firm integration between the national police forces" (Di Gennaro, 2001: 266), about which we will discuss further below. First, let us turn our attention to the organization that embodies the hope that transnational crime may be tackled in a manner that transcends national borders, INTERPOL.

INTERPOL or the International Criminal Police Organization, according to Deflem (2004: 124), is "arguably the most discussed and least understood international police organization," and was formed as a result of deliberations during

EUROPOL

European Office of Police.

the International Police Congress in Vienna in 1923. Difficulties arose within the organization and its membership during the Second World War, and the body was reorganized in 1946. In 1949, it gained consultative status with the newly formed United Nations Organization (later becoming an intergovernmental organization in 1971), and then proceeded to modernize its constitution. Finally, a new INTERPOL General Secretariat was inaugurated in Lyon, France, in 1989.

INTERPOL currently has 182 member countries, and is financed by their governments through annual contributions. It is governed through a fairly complicated organizational structure with a secretary-general (usually a senior national police official from one of the member countries) as its chief executive. This individual is nominated by an executive committee for a five-year term and is then confirmed by a two-thirds majority of the General Assembly. The secretary-general runs the day-to-day operations of the General Secretariat, and is responsible for the implementation of the decisions of the General Assembly and the executive committee.

In addition to its headquarters at the General Secretariat in Lyon, INTERPOL operates five regional offices in Harare, Abidjan, and Nairobi (in Africa); Buenos Aires and San Salvador (in South America); and a liaison office in Bangkok (for Asia). However, any given police agency in a member country cannot deal with INTERPOL or another member country directly. This has to be done through a National Central Bureau (NCB) consisting of national law enforcement officers (in the case of the United States, it is the Federal Bureau of Investigation). The NCB acts as the coordinator of those agencies in the respective countries that may require assistance with investigations elsewhere in the world, and with locating and arresting fugitives (sometimes involving the regional offices mentioned above).

What does INTERPOL do in terms of coordinating among police agencies internationally and fighting transnational crime? It provides the following services to the police agencies of member countries through their NCBs (based on INTERPOL, 2004):

- Secure global police communications services such as the new I-24/7 communications system.
- Operational data services and databases for police covering key data such as names of individuals, fingerprints, photographs, DNA, identification and travel documents, and INTERPOL notices.
- Operational police support services for priority crime-fighting areas such as international fugitives, terrorism, drug trafficking, organized crime, etc.
- Alerting police in member countries regarding wanted persons via Interpol notices, such as the Red Notice (an international request for the provisional arrest of an individual, pending his or her extradition).
- Working groups that bring together experts to develop and promote best practice and training in crime investigation and analysis.

Having reviewed the organization and services provided by INTERPOL, it is clear that the organization, while serving a worthwhile coordinating function, has no independent powers and cannot act without the consent and involvement of its member nations and their police forces. In other words, it is still a conglomerate of individual countries, any one of which may stymie steps and actions that the individual country does not care for, e.g., such as in cases pertaining to environmental crime.

A more regional example of international police cooperation is EUROPOL (mentioned earlier), which began operating in 1998. According to Occhipinti (2003: 2), in addition to exchanging information regarding transnational crimes of concern to the European Union (EU), EUROPOL also does the following. It "assists in the fight against international organized crime by analyzing crime data, alerting national police forces in the member states about criminal trends and links among crime groups, and helps the police in different EU countries to coordinate their investigations, arrests, and other anti-crime efforts in general." At the same time Occhipinti (2003) appears to express some regret that EUROPOL (at least for now) is not a supranational FBI. While EUROPOL is a relatively new organization with a diffuse and uncertain future, it appears that it may overtake the older INTERPOL, given the higher level of underlying political integration among members of the European Union in terms of dealing with various forms of transnational crime.

POLICING THE GLOBE: THREE SOCIOLOGICAL PERSPECTIVES

How would the three sociological perspectives we have followed in this book, functionalism, conflict, and interactionism, view the internationalization of crime and police responses to it? A functionalist would look at society and its various parts as a system that adapts to changing circumstances and situations. Thus, the police part of that system has now been confronted with the challenge of dealing with crime in its transnational dimensions. The existence of international organizations such as INTERPOL and EUROPOL would be seen as responses to the challenges posed by the internationalization of crime. The functionalist would also note that there is usually a lag in time before systems become aware of new challenges, and then go on to adapt to them. The fact that we are still struggling to face up to and deal with the international aspects of crime would be interpreted as an example of this lag.

Critical about society and its components such as the police, the conflict theorist will have another viewpoint. He or she is likely to note that even internationally power and privilege are held by an elite group that wishes to preserve and continue its dominance. The international elite are connected together, because they went to elite colleges together, hold leadership positions in their native countries that put them in touch with others in parallel positions in other countries, meet at international gatherings, and develop friendships and business connections. The ability to utilize the police in each of their countries and to invoke the cooperation of INTERPOL or other regional police groupings belongs to those individuals who are likely to use it against their common enemies and not use it against their friends. A prominent example of the latter occurred in the late 1980s when the United States provided sanctuary to the deposed former dictator of the Philippines, Ferdinand Marcos, who had looted his country, because of his long-standing relationship with various U.S. politicians and leaders. With regard to terrorism, the conflict theorist would note that at the insistence and based on the support of the United States, a faraway African country, Tanzania, "took significant steps to establish a National Counter-terrorism Center. The purpose of this Center was to build Tanzania's capacity to prevent and respond to terrorist attacks. The Center included members of the police and military" (U. S. Department of State, 2006). Why are the political and crime-related priorities of the United States being urged upon and implemented in Tanzania? This happened because the United States has the power to do so. Thus, for a conflict theorist, it would not matter much whether crime became an international, as opposed to a national, concern that some people would benefit from, and that others, far more numerous, would not.

The language, words, and meanings that are associated with international crime and police response would fascinate an interactionist. Categories of crime, in general, are notorious for being defined, understood, and enforced differently from society to society. Let us take the example of terrorism. Many terrorist groups consist of individuals who are thought of as thugs and criminals in one country, and heroes in another. For example, in Sri Lanka, the late leader of the Liberation Tigers of Tamil Eelam (LTTE), who were fighting for a separate country for minority Tamils on the island, Velupillai Prabhakaran, was a wanted violent terrorist. However, he derived support and admiration from the majority ethnic Tamils in the neighboring state of Tamil Nadu, India. The Tamil Nadu police are sometimes implicated in helping the LTTE, and in expressing admiration for its leader. How can one ensure international cooperation and action under these circumstances, when meanings vary so much?

Finally, we consider one specific form of transnational crime that is derived from the country of Nigeria. We have not discussed crime and policing in African countries before, so here is an example of the interconnectedness of crime and policing in our globalized world that originates from that continent.

 # POLICING THE GLOBE INTERNATIONALLY: THE NIGERIAN SCAM

You are checking your e-mail and notice one that appears to be from another country, one that is economically in transition or troubled politically (e.g., one that had a coup d'etat or some other violent change in government). It is a very formal letter (often in very stilted and official language) and requires an urgent response from you. As you read further, you notice that it appears to be from a bank or government official saying that you (or your business) could profit by accessing a large sum of money (usually, many millions) that the official knew had been squirreled away by a former head of government (who is now dead or exiled) or enterprise (e.g., a government-owned petroleum monopoly that is being dismantled or privatized). In exchange, the official asks you for details of your bank accounts so that money transfers can be made into them, and so that you will be able keep a generous percentage of the amount so moved. Sometimes you are asked for some advance money (to be wired to another country) so that transfer arrangements may be initiated, or key local officials bribed. The writer almost always emphasizes that the entire transaction poses no risk to you.

You may have heard of Internet scams of this sort and therefore delete that e-mail thinking it is just another piece of unwanted spam. However, someone else (and all that the scammer sending the mass e-mail needs is just one victim for now) responds to the tempting offer of money for nothing and provides the bank-account information asked for. That person (in addition to losing advance money) soon finds his or her account balances withdrawn electronically by someone in another country (not necessarily where the original e-mail came from, or the country where the bank official said the millions were located). He or she has fallen victim to a very common Internet-based fraud.

In January 2004, Dutch police in Amsterdam arrested fifty-two individuals who were suspected of having perpetrated this now well-known "Nigerian e-mail" fraud on Internet users in other parts of the world. This international confidence game is also referred to as the Nigerian or "419" scam. The number refers to the particular section in the Nigerian Criminal Code defining criminal fraud of this sort, although it is safe to say that the Internet dimension to this crime was most probably inconceivable to those who codified it originally. This is a version of an old confidence game known as an "advance fee" fraud. In the original form of the fraud, the scammer, usually acting along with other members of a criminal group, obtains money or goods from a company or its representative, through deception. "Victims' addresses are obtained from telephone and e-mail directories, business journals, magazines or newspapers," according to Smith, Holmes, and Kaufmann (1999: 2).

The scam has, in the past, targeted a given business or company, either by mail, fax, or phone. A group based in Nigeria (or nowadays elsewhere), or individuals pretending to be, or representing important government officials made a business proposal in a letter, through a fax or by a phone call. They claimed that they had access to a large amount of over-budgeted money, almost always in American dollars. The proposal entailed the wire transfer of the overbudgeted dollars to a bank account outside of Nigeria, which is that of the targeted company. While a plausible explanation was usually given for the transfer (to provide for the former dictator's family, to set up a joint venture in another country), the basic appeal (as in many confidence games) was clearly to the intended victim's greed. The person receiving the letter or fax was generally promised large (sometimes up to 40 percent) of the money transferred, as a commission, for the use of the bank account whose information was being requested. When the targeted victim showed some interest in the proposal, he/she was then asked to provide paperwork (often signed blank stationery with the company letterhead, blank invoices, telephone and fax numbers, and in particular, information pertaining to relevant bank accounts) to make the transaction happen, and for the money to be transferred. The paperwork and account information was then used to move money from the victim's account to ones controlled by the scammers who then promptly disappeared.

Further wrinkles to this scam involved one or more of the following: asking the victim to deposit money into a specified bank account to help cover expenses, or bribing Nigerian officials; more money being bilked from the victim due to (often unspecified) "complications" that were holding up the transaction; luring the victim to Nigeria for a meeting to complete the money transfer where his or her passport was confiscated and returned only on the payment of more money; and to add insult to injury, after the victim realized that his

or her money was gone, someone pretending to be an "official" would get in touch with the victim on the pretext of investigating the case, or helping the victim get back the money which was lost, which would then cost more money.

As in the case of victims of other confidence games, the incidents often would go unreported due to the victims' embarrassment at their own gullibility, and sometimes because of fear of reprisals or guilt in having participated in illegal activity. In the United States, the Secret Service was tasked specifically in the late 1990s with tackling this particular form of criminal activity.

Finally, we consider how police can cooperate across borders, and look at how the continent of Europe has moved in this direction (see accompanying Box).

 ## SUMMARY

In this chapter, we began with an examination of how new forms of transnational crime challenge our traditional conceptions and definitions of crime. The impact of globalization has made crime an international, in addition to a national, regional, and local, concern. Among the forms of transnational crime that we considered to understand police responses to them are the following: money laundering, trafficking in illegal drugs, corruption and bribery, infiltration into legal business for criminal purposes, fraudulent bankruptcy, insurance fraud, computer crime,

intellectual property theft, illicit arms trafficking, terrorism, aircraft hijacking, sea piracy, hijacking on land, trafficking in humans and human organs, theft of art and cultural objects, environmental crime, and the operations of organized crime groups. We learned about international efforts to combat these crimes by groups such as INTERPOL and EUROPOL. Finally, we considered the nature and implications of one new and widespread form of international crime, the so-called Nigerian scam that takes place using the Internet.

 ## KEY TERMS

EUROPOL: European Office of Police.

Globalization: The increasing interconnectedness of the economies, peoples, and to a lesser extent, the politics of various countries of the world.

International crimes: Major criminal offenses, so designated by the community of nations for the protection of

interests common to all mankind, such as genocide and mass human rights violations.

INTERPOL: The International Criminal Police Organization.

Transnational crime: Global forms of crime and disorder that call for a police response involving more than one sovereign nation.

REVIEW QUESTIONS

1. What are the major forms of transnational crime?

2. Describe how INTERPOL and EUROPOL operate to deal with various forms of international crime.

3. What is the Nigerian (or "419") scam and how does it illustrate the effect of globalization on policing?

DISCUSSION QUESTIONS

1. Which sociological perspective on global policing discussed in this chapter do you most agree with? Please explain why.

2. Do you think the structure of policing currently is able to deal with the challenges posed by global crime? Support your answer with reasons.

3. Since September 11, 2001, the United States has been concerned with international terrorists attacking domestically. How can U.S. policing respond to this challenge at the national, state, and local levels?

REFERENCES

Adler, Freda; Gerhard O. W. Mueller and William S. Laufer (2004) *Criminology.* Fifth Edition. New York: McGraw Hill.

Beare, Margert (2003) "Organized Corporate Criminality: Corporate Complicity in Tobacco Smuggling." Pp. 24–46 In Margaret Beare (ed.) *Critical Reflections on Transnational Organized Crime, Money Laundering, and Corruption.* Toronto, Canada: University of Toronto Press.

Boli, John; Michael A. Elliott and Franziska Boeri (2004) "Globalization." Pp. 389–415 In George Ritzer (ed.) *Handbook of Social Problems: A Comparative International Perspective.* Thousand Oaks, CA: Sage.

Chadwick, Elizabeth (1997) "Terrorism and the Law: Historical Contexts, Contemporary Dilemmas and the End(s) of Democracy." *Crime, Law and Social Change* 26, 4: 329–350.

Clegg, Ian and Jim Whetton (2000) "UK Government Assistance to the Police in Developing Countries." *Crime Prevention and Community Safety* 2, 2: 7–23.

Deflem, Mathieu (2004) *Policing World Society: Historical Foundations of International Police Cooperation.* New York: Oxford University Press.

Di Gennaro, Giuseppe (2001) "Strengthening the International Legal System in Order to Combat Transnational Crime." Pp. 239–268 In Phil Williams and Dimitri Vlassis (eds.) *Combating Transnational Crime: Concepts, Activities and Responses.* London: Frank Cass.

Graycar, Adam (1999) *Human Smuggling.* Hong Kong: Centre for Criminology, University of Hong Kong.

Gregory, Frank (2000) "Private Criminality as a Matter of International Concern." Pp. 100–134 In James W. E. Sheptycki (ed.) *Issues in Transnational Policing.* London: Routledge.

Haberfeld, M. R. and Ibrahim Cerrah (2007) *Comparative Policing: The Struggle for Democratization.* Thousand Oaks, CA: Sage.

INTERPOL (2004) *INTERPOL—A Fact Sheet* http://www.interpol.com/Public/Icpo/FactSheets/FS200101.asp (Retrieved on December 20, 2004).

Ismaili, Karim (2003) "Explaining the Cultural and Symbolic Resonance of Zero Tolerance in Contemporary Criminal Justice." *Contemporary Justice Review* 6, 3: 255–264.

Maguire, Mike (2000) "Policing by Risks and Targets: Some Dimensions and Implications of Intelligence-Led Crime Control." *Policing and Society* 9, 4: 315–336.

Mameli, Peter A. (2002) "Stopping the Illegal Trafficking of Human Beings: How Transnational Police Work Can Stem the Flow of Forced Prostitution." *Crime, Law and Social Change* 38, 1: 67–80.

Mueller, Gerhard O. W. (2001) "Transnational Crime: Definitions and Concepts." Pp. 13–21 In Phil Williams and Dimitri Vlassis (eds.) *Combating Transnational Crime: Concepts, Activities and Responses.* London: Frank Cass.

Occhipinti, John D. (2003) *The Politics of EU Police Cooperation: Toward a European FBI?* Boulder, CO: Lynne Rienner Publishers.

Ritzer, George (2004) "Introduction." Pp. 3–13 In George Ritzer (ed.) *Handbook of Social Problems: A Comparative International Perspective.* Thousand Oaks, CA: Sage.

Shelly, Louise I. (1981) *Crime and Modernization: The Impact of Industrialization and Urbanization on Crime.* Carbondale, IL: Southern Illinois University Press.

Sheptycki, James W. E. (2002) "Accountability Across the Policing Field: Towards a General Cartography of Accountability in Post-Modern Policing." *Policing and Society* 12, 4: 323–338.

Smith, Russell G.; Michael N. Holmes and Philip Kaufmann (1999) "Nigerian Advance Fee Fraud." *Trends and Issues in Crime and Criminal Justice 121.* Canberra, Australia: Australian Institute of Criminology.

Turk, Austin T. (2003) "Confronting Enemies Foreign and Domestic: An American Dilemma." *Crime & Justice International* 19, 71 (March): 16–18.

U. S. Department of State (2006) *Country Reports on Terrorism: Chapter Five-Country Reports—Africa Overview.* http://www.state.gov/s/ct/rls/crt/2005/64335.htm (Retrieved on July 4, 2007)

INTERNATIONAL POLICE COOPERATION: A CASE OF EUROPE

Milan Pagon

EUROPE

As crime and crime-related problems are getting increasingly globalized, the need for cross-border and international cooperation among police forces is greater today than it has ever been in the past. While international police cooperation is not limited only to countries within the same region, it is only normal that cooperation of those countries is more frequent and intensive than that with more distant countries. Therefore, this cooperation, its extent, and forms might be different in different parts of the world. As an example of such cooperation, we will take a look at international police cooperation from the European perspective, as presented through various sources on the Internet.

The broadest form of the European countries' international police cooperation is their involvement with the **International Criminal Police Organization—INTERPOL.** This organization, in existence for the last eighty years, has a mission to promote international police cooperation, that is, to help officers from different police forces, countries, languages, and cultures to cooperate with one another and work together to solve crime. Because of the unbiased role INTERPOL must play at the international

level, its Constitution does not allow it to engage in any activity of a political, military, religious, or racial character. INTERPOL deals only with international crime and not with national crime, that is, crimes that overlap one or several member countries. It does not deal with crimes that are planned and committed in just one country, or with the ensuing investigation for the perpetrators if it is contained in the same country. INTERPOL's work covers many specialized areas, but its current work is largely related to public safety and terrorism, organized crime, illicit drug production and trafficking, weapons smuggling, trafficking in human beings, money laundering, financial and high tech crime, and corruption. It receives, stores, analyses, and circulates criminal intelligence with its member countries. INTERPOL is the second largest international organization after the United Nations, with 181 member countries spread over five continents. Every member country has an INTERPOL office called a National Central Bureau that is staffed by its own police. This bureau is the single point of contact for foreign governments requiring assistance with international investigations and adequate contact information, when confronted with different police structures in other countries. INTERPOL officers do not travel around the world to investigate cases in different countries. Each member country employs its own officers to operate on its own territory and in accordance with its own national laws. Each member country can also send officers to serve a tour of duty at the Organization's Headquarters in Lyon, France.

Many of the European police chiefs are members of the **International Association of Chiefs of Police (IACP).** Founded in 1893, the association's goals are to advance the science and art of police services; to develop and disseminate improved administrative, technical, and operational practices and promote their use in police work; to foster police cooperation and the exchange of information and experience among police administrators throughout the world; to bring about recruitment and training in the police profession of qualified persons; and to encourage adherence of all police officers to high professional standards of performance and conduct. The IACP's International Policy Committee sponsors international executive policing conferences every year.

Previous international conferences have addressed topics, such as terrorism, multinational policing efforts, and the application of community-oriented policing and technological advances in both crime and crime fighting. The conferences provide an ideal forum for these and other topics, as well as networking, exchanging ideas, capitalizing on lessons learned, and furthering professional growth for the members.

In addition to their involvement with INTERPOL, the European countries felt the need for closer cooperation within the European Union (EU), instigated by a free movement of people and goods within the EU territory. Improved police cooperation measures were first written into the **Schengen Agreement** signed in 1985 by some member States of the European Union. The "Schengen" police cooperation measures provide for mutual assistance and direct information exchange between police services, cross-border surveillance and pursuit of suspects, and improved communication links and information exchange via central law-enforcement agencies. In addition, a **Schengen Information System (SIS)** has been operational since 1995. It is a computer network system containing information on wanted persons and stolen objects. Two member States of the EU—Ireland and the United Kingdom—have not lifted border controls with other Schengen/EU States, but the United Kingdom has been authorized to take part in aspects of the Schengen Agreement that deal with cooperation between police forces. Ireland has made a request for a similar authorization. Two non-EU States—Iceland and Norway—have also subscribed to the Schengen Agreement.

A more recent addition to European police cooperation is **EUROPOL,** which is the European Union organization for cross-border coordination between EU national law-enforcement agencies (mainly national police forces, immigration and customs authorities) of the member States. Based in The Hague, Netherlands, EUROPOL is essentially a central police office for the support of member States by collation, analysis, and dissemination of information. It started in January 1994 as the EUROPOL Drugs Unit (EDU). In 1995, the EU Council of Ministers adopted an act to draw up the establishment of a European Police Office. Following the ratification by all EU member States of the Europol Convention, the organization took up its full activities on July 1, 1999. EUROPOL deals with an enormous range of law-enforcement issues, including drugs and

stolen vehicles; illegal immigration networks; trafficking in human beings, including child pornography and sexual exploitation of women; forgery of money and money laundering; smuggling of radioactive and nuclear materials; and terrorism. At the heart of the service is a vast computer database that helps national law-enforcement agencies across the EU share information on known and suspected criminals, and on stolen objects. The database is currently being developed, and when completed, will provide authorized law-enforcement officers in all EU member states with instant access to the shared data files.

Another form of European police cooperation at a top-management level is the **European Police Chiefs' Task Force**. It was created in 2000 by the EU to develop personal and informal links between the heads of the various law-enforcement agencies across the EU, to exchange information, and to assist with the development of more spontaneous interaction and closer cooperation between the various national and local police forces and other EU law-enforcement agencies. The creation of informal links at a high level between EU law-enforcement agencies should help to drive a more spontaneous interaction and closer cooperation between national and local police forces in EU member states in the continuing fight against crime.

Police cooperation in Europe is not limited only to operational cooperation. It also extends into the realm of police training. **CEPOL**, or the **European Police College**, is intended as an academy for the training of senior and middle-ranking EU law-enforcement officials. Set up initially as a network of existing training institutes, CEPOL began to offer courses on European policing in 2001. It is due to become a full-scale European Police College, with a permanent seat of its own, in a few years' time. CEPOL will train the next generation of police officers to work and cooperate at a European level with their counterparts from other EU law-enforcement agencies. Senior police officers from the EU's candidate countries will also be encouraged to attend CEPOL training schemes.

Due to changed circumstances within Europe, the EU was forced to extend its police cooperation into the area of peacekeeping by creating the **European Rapid Reaction Force (ERRF)**, a civilian peacekeeping force to help manage crisis situations and control conflicts in countries external to EU borders. The new peacekeeping force will be staffed by some 5,000 specially trained personnel drawn from police forces across Europe. The new force is operational in 2009. Police officers with the ERRF are trained in international peacekeeping, using interactive practice methods, as well as via training programs with strong human rights content. Skills training in problem-solving and prevention techniques also assume a priority in the training program.

Within the EU, we can see more than just efforts to increase police cooperation among individual states. The EU is also trying to establish a common strategy to fight against organized transnational crime, realizing that governments acting individually cannot address the newly emerging problems adequately. A strategy has been defined at the EU level—the 1997 action plan to combat organized crime. As a result, many concrete steps have already been taken by the EU Council of Ministers to fight against organized transnational crime. A new EU institutional framework to fight against organized crime was put in place following the entry into force of the Treaty of Amsterdam on May 1, 1999. It provides for the development of common actions in the field of police and judicial cooperation in criminal matters, while preserving member States' responsibility for maintaining law and order and safeguarding internal security. Since globalization is a general process that affects the whole world, and not only the EU, the fight against organized crime cannot limit itself to the EU borders. Measures have been taken to enhance international cooperation, especially with the countries that are candidates to accession. In this context, the EU and the seven candidate countries signed a Pre-Accession Pact on Organized Crime in 1998. All these efforts are also aided by various EU programs in the area of police cooperation and the fight against organized transnational crimes.

These programs are (or were) intended to contribute to an improvement in the cooperation between authorities and people engaged in the fight against and the prevention of organized crime. The **Falcone** (1998–2002) and **Hippocrates** (2001–02) programs are complementary to specific programs on judicial cooperation (**Grotius**), and police and customs cooperation (**OISIN**), as well as cooperation against trafficking in human beings, and the sexual exploitation of children (**STOP**). These programs will be merged into one single program from 2003 onwards. The new program is called **AGIS** (named after a king of ancient Sparta). It ran from 2003 till 2007. Its purpose is to help legal practitioners, law enforcement officials, and representatives of victim assistance services from the EU member States and candidate countries to set up Europe-wide networks, exchange information, and best practices. It also aims at encouraging member States to step up cooperation with the applicant countries and other third countries. AGIS will support transnational projects for a maximum duration of two years.

European Union Crime Prevention Network (EUCPN) has been set up to improve the sharing of crime-prevention information and best practices, mainly among the EU's member States. Its objectives are to supplement and facilitate national crime-prevention initiatives, while drawing attention to topics of common interest. The network shall also develop cooperation with applicant countries, third countries, and international bodies.

Finally, in addition to the official police cooperation among governments and police agencies, there is also cooperation among police officers on an individual level. The International Police Association (IPA) is one of the most unique and interesting social organizations in the world. This fraternal organization is dedicated "to unite in service and friendship all active and retired members of the law enforcement service throughout the world." The IPA strives to enhance the image of the police in its member countries, and to facilitate international cooperation through friendly contacts between police officers of all continents. Membership—open to any serving or former police officer—now exceeds 290,000 officers in over fifty countries, and is steadily rising. The purpose of the organization is strictly cultural, social, and recreational. At no time does the IPA take part in any matter of departmental policy, discipline, or unionism. The IPA creates an opportunity for cultural exchange and contacts on a local, national, and international level.

As shown in this overview from the European perspective, international police cooperation has many levels and many forms. They can be truly international or more continent-, region-, or content-specific. A common theme in all these efforts is a realization that only together—by cooperating, helping, and sharing— might we be successful in our efforts to prevent crime, improve safety and security, and promote human rights, freedom, justice, and peace in the world.

References

A Common EU Approach to the Fight against Organised Transnational Crime. http://europa.eu.int/comm/justice_home/fsj/crime/wai/fsj_crime_intro_en.htm.

AGIS. http://europa.eu.int/comm/justice_home/funding/agis/funding_agis_en.htm.

Building Personal Links between Police Chiefs across the EU. http://europa.eu.int/comm/justice_home/fsj/police/chief/wai/fsj_police_task_force_en.htm.

EU-Level Cooperation Crucial for National Police Forces. http://europa.eu.int/comm/justice_home/fsj/police/wai/fsj_police_intro_en.htm.

European Police Office Now in Full Swing. http://europa.eu.int/comm/justice_home/fsj/police/europol/wai/fsj_police_europol_en.htm.

International Association of Chiefs of Police. http://www.theiacp.org.

International Police Association, Canadian Section. http://www.ipa.ca.

Interpol—An Overview. http://www.interpol.int/Public/ICPO/InterpolOverview.pdf.

Justice and Home Affairs. http://europa.eu.int/comm/justice_home/fsj/external/wai/fsj_external_intro_en.htm.

National Police Training Institutes Connected across the EU. http://europa.eu.int/comm/justice_home/fsj/police/college/wai/fsj_police_college_en.htm.

New Peacekeeping Force Staffed by Police Officers from across EU. http://europa.eu.int/comm/justice_home/fsj/police/peacekeeping/wai/fsj_police_peacekeeping_en.htm.

Spreading Knowledge of Successful Crime Prevention Initiatives across the EU. http://europa.eu.int/comm/justice_home/fsj/police/network/wai/fsj_police_crime_prevention_en.htm.

CHAPTER 16

Clearly and despite police officers' affinity for the status quo, policing is a dynamic and ever-changing field. In simple terms, change plays a vital role in policing. Changes in norms and culture, economy, politics, technology, and the law among many other things, help to transform the environment in which the police work. (White, 2007: xiv)

Finnish police officers patrol outside Tampere Hall during the EU foreign ministers and Mediterranean countries council in Tampere, Finland, Monday, Nov. 27, 2006. The EU opens two days of talks with Israel and its Arab neighbors Monday to preserve what remains of the Mideast peace process and push ahead with broad economic assistance to boost chances for peace. (Credit: © AP Photo/Yves Logghe)

THE FUTURE OF POLICING

OBJECTIVES:

1. The student will learn why it is important to think about the future of policing.
2. The student will learn about six major contemporary trends that will affect the future of policing.
3. The student will learn about the implications of these trends for police practice and change.
4. The student will learn how functionalism, conflict theory, and interactionism are likely to view the future of policing.
5. The student will learn about the future of policing on an international level.

We have looked at various aspects of policing, and now it is time to identify a few relevant trends and to project what will happen with them in the future, as policing changes along with the world around it. It would be difficult, if not ridiculous, to claim that we have the ability to predict with accuracy the future of any given facet of human affairs. This holds true for the world of policing. What we can do instead is to understand the lessons of history regarding some current trends in policing, and then provide informed speculation as to where these trends might take policing in the short-term future. In this chapter, we have chosen to focus on what the future may hold for a number of important current trends in policing: police professionalism, the impact of population change on policing, privatization of police services, greater access to technology, and the resulting **rising expectations** regarding policing, community involvement in policing, and the internationalization of police activity. Let us take each of these issues in turn.

....
rising expectations

Higher public expectations regarding how policing will be delivered, and assessed in the future.

PROFESSIONALISM

The concept of police professionalism can be traced to 1829 when Sir Robert Peel established the London Metropolitan Police. The Peelian Principles are guidelines that provided the foundation for police professionalism. However, the early British conception of professional policing did not initially achieve a strong hold in the United States. Although it is often claimed that the American conception of policing was obtained directly from Britain, this does not appear to be completely accurate. Even though initial ideas regarding policing were obtained from the London Metropolitan model, the United States developed its own brand of policing as a result of its own historical experiences.

Attempts at making the public and society recognize that policing should be considered a profession can be traced to the early period of the twentieth century. During the first decades of the twentieth century, the International Association of Chiefs of Police (IACP) was formed. The IACP encouraged the idea of police professionalism. This made what was ostensibly an association that represented police chiefs of departments large and small, a major advocate for the field of policing in the U. S. police during this period, define police professionalism almost exclusively as involving administrative and managerial efficiency. Beginning in the 1920s and well into the 1950s and 1960s, the field of policing came under the influence of pioneers such as August Vollmer, O.W. Wilson, and J. Edgar Hoover. As a result of their efforts, the "crime fighter" image that continues to affect public perceptions of the police was born.

During the decade following World War II, the concept of professionalism (and relative efficiency) became primarily associated with California, and specifically, the Los Angeles Police Department, under the leadership of William H. Parker who became the chief in 1950. Parker emphasized administrative and police service efficiency. Since Parker assumed the chief's position following a corruption scandal, he implemented policies and guidelines that, while streamlining internal procedures, also served to keep police officers away from the community. To this day, many who identify themselves closely with the ideal of police professionalism consider Parker to be the chief who most exemplified it. However, some also suggest that as a result of his relentless focus on police discipline and procedure, a communication gap ensued between the police and community. Some of Parker's innovative operational procedures that contributed to professionalizing his department include the following (Schults and Beckman, 1987: 129):

- The formation of an internal affairs division to investigate citizens' complaints of misconduct;
- The coauthorship of Board of Rights procedures guaranteeing the separation of police discipline from politics;
- The creation of a bureau of administration, which included two new components: the intelligence and the planning and research divisions;
- The establishment of an intensive community relations program;
- The deployment of a fleet of patrol helicopters; and
- The enactment of a strict firearms use policy that included an internal review of all weapons discharged.

The IACP and the related work of pioneers such as Vollmer, Wilson, Hoover, and Parker did contribute greatly to improve the quality of policing of the U.S. police. However, these improvements in quality cannot be argued as having resulted in the successful **professionalization** of the police, or in the field being now recognized as such by the public. For one, the police have moved away from emphasizing their image as autonomous and professional crime fighters in favor of greater community involvement through community-oriented and problem-oriented policing. Second, the traditional professions (for which there is a consensus regarding their status) are law, ministry, and the field of medicine. For a field to be considered not an occupation, but a profession, minimally, a distinct body of knowledge, education, and research are generally required. Using this criterion, the police are only beginning on the long road toward achieving the status of a mature profession. Currently, U.S. police officers are obtaining college degrees, and receiving recruit (or academy) training as well as advanced training. Police officers are also being certified by state agencies to work as police officers. Those police officers that do not follow the state laws and policies lose their certification to work as police officers.

Another recent movement toward obtaining police professionalism has been the **accreditation** of police departments. A joint effort of the four major police organizations created the Commission on Accreditation for Law Enforcement Agencies in 1979. Four organizations in the United States, the IACP (whose pioneering role was discussed above), the National Organization of Black Police Law Enforcement Executives (NOBLE), the National Sheriffs' Association (NSA), and the Police Executive Research Forum (PERF) have had as their goal the development of law enforcement standards and the demonstration, through an accreditation process, that law enforcement agencies could voluntarily meet professionally recognized criteria (www.calea.org, 2003).

professionalization

The process by which occupations become professions by acquiring a distinct body of knowledge, education, and research.

accreditation

The development of law enforcement standards and to demonstrate through an accreditation process that law enforcement agencies could voluntarily meet professionally recognized criteria.

Today police officers are certainly educated and trained better than in the past. Police agencies also submit themselves to the process of obtaining accreditation as colleges, universities, hospitals, and law schools do. Police agencies and individual police officers will, of course, strive to improve themselves and their public image in the future. It is reasonable to assume that in the not too distant future all police officers will be expected to have a college education before they are hired, and that command staff will be expected to have a graduate degree. Police departments are also likely to be expected to obtain accreditation. The result of failing to obtain accreditation (particularly, in the context of comparable departments being successful) will be local community questioning of the "low" standards under which their department may currently be operating. Given this likelihood, it is likely that achieving recognition for policing as a profession will be a slow and long-term undertaking.

POPULATION DIVERSITY AND WORKFORCE TRENDS

The population of the United States has been changing constantly since its inception. Contributing to changes in U.S. population trends have been the changing economic, social, and political circumstances, specifically, in terms of the Industrial Revolution and overall shifts in work and employment of various kinds.

At the eve of World War I, the U.S. population was divided into three large groups; 54 percent native white stock; 34 percent foreign white stock; and 12 percent nonwhites. The majority of nonwhites were African Americans, with about one-half percent being Chinese, Japanese, and Native Americans (Easterlin, 2000: 632–633). From World War I to 1950, it was observed that the white population was becoming more homogenous. The descendants of foreign-born whites from earlier decades were being assimilated into the dominant culture of the United States. During this period, more Americans moved to urban areas. By 1950 approximately one-third of the black population lived in the North and West. There was also a substantial decrease in immigration in the period between World War 1 and 1950. However, the racial makeup of the population remained about the same as it had been on the eve of World War I. The major economic change during these decades was the decline of agriculture (farming, ranching) and the rise of industry (factories, machinery) as a source of livelihood for most Americans. The United States became a country of city dwellers (Easterlin, 2000: 641–643) and industrial workers and managers.

In the mid-1960s, the U. S. Congress passed the 1965 Amendment to the 1952 Immigration and Nationality Act, which shifted the country's immigration policy from quota allocation based on nationality origins (which was weighted toward European countries) to quota allocations based on need of any one of the three considerations: labor skills, reuniting families, and political refugees (essentially removing racial or national-origin preferences). Additional legislation in 1980 and 1990 was passed by Congress to modify eligibility criteria. The revised immigration laws provided for an increase of immigrants. From three million prior to the 1965 Act, immigration rose to seven million in the 1980s. Also, the immigration patterns changed from earlier, when the vast majority was coming from Europe to the large proportion now moving from Latin America, Philippines, Vietnam, Korea, China, and India (Easterlin, 2000: 651–653).

As a result, the United States experienced unprecedented population diversity. From 1970 to 1990 the United States also saw a population shift in terms of race/ethnicity. In 1970, the white population was 84 percent compared to 76 percent in 1990. The African American population in 1970 was 11 percent compared to 12 percent in 1990; the Hispanic population in 1970 was 5 percent compared to 9 percent in 1990; the Asian population was about one-half percent in 1970 compared to 3 percent in 1990; and the Native American Indian population in 1970 was less than one-half percent compared to 1990 when it was slightly less than one percent (Easterlin, 2000: 142, 202–203).

The 2000 Census of the United States reveals that the population of the country stood at 281 million, and that the population growth was almost 38 million people between 1990 and 2000. This population increase was the largest in U.S. history, although this varied significantly according to the region of the country. The West had the highest growth rate with almost 20 percent; the South had a growth rate of 17 percent; the Midwest had a growth rate of almost 8 percent, while the Northeast had a growth rate of 5.5 percent. The last census also revealed that the majority of Americans lived in ten states with California, Texas, and New York having the largest populations, with more than 80 percent of Americans living in metropolitan areas (Census 2000 Brief, 2000).

The population of the United States in the last census found that the population was 77.1 percent white, 12.9 percent African American, 12.5 percent Hispanic, and 4.2 percent Asian. In addition, females comprised 50.9 percent of the population compared to 49.1 percent males (www.census.gov).

The United States has a multicultural society that has gone through several ethnic and racial changes throughout its history. The racial and ethnic makeup of the United States has never remained stagnant. As multiculturalism reshapes the United States, it should be expected that these changes will be reflected in U.S. police departments. In 1990, Robert Trojanowicz and David Carter published an article in the *FBI Bulletin*, entitled "The Changing Face of America." The gist of this article was that the United States was changing and becoming decidedly multicultural. The changing face of the United States that these authors address has continued as the 2000 Census reveals. Police departments in the decades ahead can expect to have a substantial increase in the number of African Americans, Asians, and Hispanics as police officers and as individuals that they will come into contact with in performing various functions. In addition, it should be expected that females will play a larger and more important role in policing than they have in the past. The dominance of white males will, as a result, be decreasing in police matters, while the roles of females and the other ethnic groups increase correspondingly. In the not too distant future, the current majority may become the numerical minority, and the current minority groups may become the numerical majority. As minorities become assimilated into the American cultural system, unforeseen problems will be occurring that have not been anticipated. The police will have to adapt to a changing multicultural society. However, there is reason to believe that just as policing shifted during the early part of the twentieth century, from one dominated by males having particular ethnic backgrounds (primarily, Irish Americans and Italian

Americans) to white males (of all ethnic backgrounds), it should be possible for parallel changes to occur in the twenty-first century. Such changes would involve greater participation in police departments by people of all racial and ethnic backgrounds, and women. These changes would occur at both line and officer levels.

PRIVATIZATION

For decades, many observers have noted that the United States has essentially been served by two police systems. The two police systems are the government or public police who are under the control of the State and the private police or private security who are employed and supported by private individuals and companies. Interestingly, during the nineteenth century, the private police were much more professionally advanced than the public police. For example, many observers have identified the National Detective Agency under the leadership of Allan Pinkerton as the forerunner of the modern Federal Bureau of Investigation. The private police were instrumental in establishing the armored car industry, the burglary alarm system, and the provision of private security guards.

There are more private police in the United States than public police. The private police numbers will definitely be growing in the coming decades. When the growth of the U.S. economy slowed (such as in the very early 1990s and early 2000s), some communities looked for an alternative means for public safety. When there are financial cutbacks and stagnant budgets, as has occurred in the first years of the twenty-first century, the expectation is that the affluent, businesses, and those neighborhoods of the community concerned about their safety play a larger role. The observation about public policing made by the well-known *Hallcrest Report* several decades ago is as valid today as at the time that it was made. The *Hallcrest Report* states: "Law Enforcement resources have stagnated and in some cases are declining. This mandates greater cooperation with the private sector and its private security resources to jointly forge a partnership on an equal basis for crime prevention and reduction. Law enforcement can ill-afford to continue isolation and, in some cases, ignore these important resources" (Cunningham and Taylor, 1985: 275).

The role of the private sector in performing many of the functions generally associated with the public police has increased substantially, and is expected to increase in the decades ahead. Private police have become involved in numerous ways. They function as alarm monitors, and are the first responders to intrusions when burglary and robbery alarms go off. The private police thus respond in lieu of the public police. In addition, the private police can be a volunteer police organization under the supervision of the county sheriff or the local police chief. A volunteer police organization can function as a nonprofit, tax-exempt, private organization under state law. Such an organization will have a board of directors with limited police powers. The volunteer police organization can free the public police to perform police work that is more "serious." For example, they can check vacant houses while residents are on vacation, or direct traffic when the public police are swamped or otherwise unavailable at a given time.

Future decades will see an increase of private police as a security force used for public housing, private housing (as in gated communities or areas where entry and exit are controlled), directing traffic, and providing security and crowd control for civic events and publicly owned buildings. The guard force will be used for the management of parking enforcement. Private police can even perform patrol functions. A good example of this is in San Francisco. There, private police attend the city's police academy to qualify as peace officers; they are armed, uniformed, and are given police powers. The private police respond to service calls in their area just as public police officers do. The key difference is that the private police officers work for a business establishment rather than for a government entity. The preceding form of private policing has been occurring in San Francisco for some time, and this can be expected to increase, especially in affluent neighborhoods.

Currently, many cities have gated communities, which often have their own private security force. There may be a single entrance gate, with a private police officer allowing only approved individuals (e.g., residents and their invited guests) into the community's area. In addition, these private security officers function partly as the public police by responding to service calls from their residents. Not only do cities utilize private security police for building protection but the federal government does so as well. Generally, private security personnel protect county and state buildings and Federal Court Houses. The federal government has even farmed out the background investigations to private police business and retired FBI agents, who function as private investigators.

The transfer of functions traditionally performed by public police officers will be increasing in the coming years. Governments may contract out some of the services currently carried out by the staff of public police departments, such as record keeping, property management, data processing, and so on. It is clear that policing activities traditionally done by public police offices will be transferred (to a limited extent) to the private police. One important reason for this change seems to be that the United States's local, state, and federal governments do not want to provide benefits such as health and retirement pensions. In addition, government at all levels would like to decrease the budgets and payroll to keep taxes down for the millions of Americans who think they pay too much in taxes. If the American people do not want to substantially decrease the role of the public police, those running the government would not mind, particularly if it makes them look good to the voters.

Bayley (1994: 144) suggests that reducing the public police role in crime prevention activities (implied here by showing how in the future, some of these functions may be privatized, and replaced by a more specialized focus on crime-fighting professionalization) will result in "inequities in protection." To a large extent, we see that such inequities already exist, with the rich and businesses that can afford them, already enjoying the protection of both private (security) and public police. The challenge of the future may be to provide private policing (that a given jurisdiction may contract out to companies in the business of security) that will be regulated and assessed for quality purposes (perhaps by negotiating highly specific performance contracts). It is possible, in this regard, that public police and private police will develop a closer partnership to fight crime, maintain order, and provide service in the twenty-first century. It is clear that more recent attempts to bridge the gap between the public and private police have proven more or less successful, and a closer working relationship between the two, even though there may be misgivings, is all but inevitable.

TECHNOLOGICAL INNOVATION

In the first decade of the twenty-first century, it would be safe to say that the U.S. police have become substantially wedded to technology. Of course, the advance of technology in policing corresponds to the advancement of technology in the rest of American society. The parallel tracks between American society and the police in terms of the adoption and use of technology may be changing in the future. The police may be pioneering technological applications and usage that the rest of society will then follow. At least, that is the hope of progressive police administrators and organizations.

The National Institute of Law Enforcement (NILE) was created in 1968 to focus on research and development aimed at improving policing (Travis, 1995: 1–2). NILE, now known as the National Institute of Justice (NIJ), cooperated with other agencies on the development of riot control agents, night vision equipment, nonlethal bullets, and personal communications (Travis, 1995: 2–3). In 1971 the NILE established the Law Enforcement Standards Laboratory (LESL) under the auspices of the National Bureau of Standards, part of the Department of Commerce. The purpose of LESL has been to develop scientifically based, voluntarily commercial, manufacturing standards so that police agencies could select both high-quality and low-cost equipment. Also, it requires the laboratories to be certified in cases where equipment items can be evaluated according to those standards (Travis, 1995: 3).

During the late twentieth century, the police made great strides in technological sophistication. Advances that occurred during this period include concealed weapon detection, interactive stimulation trainers, mobile sensor platforms, sniper identification, and urban mapping. In the coming decades new technologies are likely to be developed, and older technologies improved so rapidly that it may be difficult for most police departments to keep up with all of these advances. Police departments will thus, in all probability, have difficulties obtaining all the latest technological advances, specifically in terms of the financial affordability of these constantly updated innovations, not to mention new products and services.

The current police use of available technologies has not only substantially increased, but embraces more complex applications as well. Current use includes a variety of applications such as computer-assisted forensics, biometrics, digital imaging, expert systems, training simulators, and various surveillance approaches routinely used by police departments (Nunn, 2001a: 259). The basic categories of police technological application are as follows (Nunn, 2001a: 261):

- **Biometrics:** the use of biological parameters to control people and places.
- **Monitoring:** the direct or remote observation of people, places, and machines.
- **Imaging:** analog or digital pictures of people, places, and evidence.
- **Communications:** expanded audio and video communications among agencies and agents.
- **Decision support:** smart computer software capable of assisting human decision-making.

- **Record keeping:** the maintenance of analog and digital databases for retrieval, as needed.

- **Weaponry:** the use of lethal and nonlethal weapons.

Unique measurements of different components of the human body are used in biometrics as a means of identification. Biometric tools commonly used in the first decade of the twenty-first century by law enforcement include fingerprints, DNA testing, retina scans, and facial recognition. There are two classifications for biometric technologies. The first group includes the use of fingerprint or palm characteristics, and the recent development of facial structure measurements, retinal blood vessel patterns, or DNA. It also includes finger images; palms, finger, and hand geometry; ear shape; and body odor (Nunn, 2001a: 262).

During the 1990s states established the Automated Fingerprinting Identification System (AFIS) to process fingerprints submitted by police agencies. Although AFIS was a great improvement over the old human process of matching prints with a suspect, it still needed improvements. AFIS was a fragmented system that lacked coordination and centralization. In 1999 the Federal Bureau of Investigation started the Integrated Automated Fingerprint System (IAFIS) that shortened the time to link fingerprint databases from several days to hours (Nunn, 2001a: 264).

IAFIS served to advance the centralization and coordination of fingerprint databases, and along with other advances and future advances will increase the sophistication of investigations and policing in general. An example of such application is in the Las Vegas (Nevada) Police Department, which has combined fingerprint digitalization with digitized mug shots (photographs) in a system called MAIN (Metro Automated Identification Network). The U.S. Immigration and Naturalization Service has established a kiosk-based biometric system that uses handprints to verify the identity, and expedite the flight processing for international travelers in several American Airports such as Los Angeles, Newark, Miami, and Kennedy in New York City (Nunn, 2001a: 264).

Monitoring system technologies that involve the direct or remote modeling of people and spaces have been developed. Software systems that monitor the movements of individuals under house arrest or on probation exist now. Technological advances are allowing eavesdropping on (or capturing a screenshot of) monitor displays from computers or the use of software programs inserted into a computer to log online activity. Law enforcement currently uses software technology, known as DIRT (Data Interception by Remote Terminal), to gather evidence from alleged child pornographers and hacker groups that threaten the security and integrity of computer networks. While the DIRT surveillance system is analogous to wiretapping a telephone, it is in effect designed to monitor data input into a personal computer by using a Windows operating system (Nunn, 2001a: 266).

Imaging technologies can help deconstruct scenes of crime and disorder that have been captured earlier, or while the violations are in progress. Imaging technologies examine and document crime scenes and photos from still and video cameras. This technology can decode information that has been embedded invisibly within space and hidden physical barriers. These physical barriers function as actual walls and partitions, or simply poorly resolved physical images in existing photographs and video imagery (Nunn, 2001b: 20).

....

heterodyning

A form of technology that
uses weak fluorescent emissions from organic molecules
to tag crime scenes evidence
normally invisible to the naked
eye.

Several approaches utilizing imaging technology include a method developed by
the Sandia National Laboratory, New Mexico, which created a method known as
heterodyning, which "uses weak fluorescent emissions from organic molecules to tag crime
scenes evidence normally invisible to the naked eye" (Nunn, 2001b: 20). The U.S. Department of Energy produced laser-induced fluorescent imaging (LIFI) that can spot fluids or
fingerprints at crime scenes. Also, the Goddard Space Center in Greenbelt, Maryland,has
developed methods to use near earth asteroids as well as rendezvous spacecraft to scan
crime scenes. The Marshall Space Flight Center in Huntsville, Alabama, developed video-
images stabilization registration (VISAR) that eliminates noise and image jitters in videos
to create a clearer picture of suspects and scenes (Nunn, 2001b: 20–21). This trend toward
technology will only increase and enhance policing in the coming decades.

With specific reference to communication technology, police acquisition and
utilization has made enormous gains in the latter part of the twentieth century. In the
1960s police officers that walked beats for the most part only had call boxes, or used
a public telephone to make contact with Police Headquarters. If they ran into trouble
while on their walking beat, they had to hope that some citizen would call Headquarters to request assistance. Also, the police officer leaving the police car in the 1960s to
respond to a call left the most efficient method of communicating with Headquarters
behind. Today, police officers are in constant contact with Headquarters when they
leave their cars, walk a beat, and ride a bicycle or a horse. Officers have access to
sophisticated two-way communications to be in constant contact with Headquarters.

Computer Aided Dispatching (CAD), currently in use with caller identification and
incorporating location identification with dispatchers having individual workstations, has
also proven to be more efficient than in past decades. Today, dispatchers have grids at their
disposal to define jurisdictions between several police departments and to determine geographical areas of police beats and to compile statistics. In addition to CAD, police officers
may have mobile data terminal / computers linked to CAD, which allows patrol officers
to query drivers'-license files and the National Criminal Information Center (NCIC).

Another form of technology that assists line police officers and managers are in-car
videos (ICV). The ICV systems are activated when the police vehicle turns on its emergency lights, video taping every incident wherein an officer stops a vehicle or a member
of the public provides an unbiased and accurate record that can be reviewed later by
supervisors and attorneys (Maghan, O'Reilly, and Ho Shon, 2002). Knowing that they
are being videotaped may also serve as a check on inclinations that individual officers
may have for anger toward or abuse of individual citizens who are being stopped.

THE FUTURE OF POLICING: THREE SOCIOLOGICAL PERSPECTIVES

We have learned much about the police and different ways of analyzing their existing role in society using three sociological perspectives: functionalism, conflict, and
interactionism. It is now time to consider briefly how these three perspectives would
view the future of policing in society. From a functionalist perspective, policing in the

future would be viewed through the lens of its utility and usefulness for society. As new changes arise (e.g., workforce diversity), the police will respond with innovations and adaptations (targeted recruitment of individuals from varying ethnic groups). Some of these changes will be useful or functional to society, and would be retained. Others would be inefficient or dysfunctional for society, and would be discarded or modified (e.g., the move away from a professional model of policing to one emphasizing involvement with the community). Thus, the system adapts to ongoing opportunities and challenges in the environment, picking and retaining what it finds useful. Policing, as we understand, was itself a response to challenges that existed in the past, and what we see as changes in its form is the response to more recent changes.

It would be safe to say that from a conflict perspective, the future of policing is not going to be as rosy as portrayed above. Conflict theorists view the police, as we have seen, as mostly instruments of those who hold the power and resources in a given society or community. Thus, the likelihood for the future is that the police will continue in this role. Given that premise, it is unrealistic to assume that the police will suddenly become concerned about the fate of the poor and powerless in the future, and train their attention on crimes committed by the rich and powerful. A more cynical reading of police behavior in this regard would be to say that even when they appear to be targeting the elite for their crimes and transgressions, the police do this so that people in society believe that the police and leadership of a society are unbiased. The few rich and powerful individuals so targeted are let off with relatively lighter punishments, and the trust of the general public in the essential goodness and impartiality of the police (and the social system they represent) is reaffirmed.

Finally, interactionists will continue to look for the nature and meanings of situations where the police are involved with the public and among themselves, and attempt to figure out how these have changed or not changed over time. One of the issues we have looked at in this chapter is police professionalism as a model that has evolved into more community-oriented policing. The interactionists would be interested in identifying where this changed rhetoric leads to in the future. Would the police continue to emphasize clearance rates and response times (major hallmarks of the professional model), while claiming at the same time that they are doing community policing? Further, interactionists would be interested in knowing whether members of the public have noticed these supposed changes in police behavior and interactions with the public, and if these are also reflected in the communication media of the future (Web logs, Internet sites, in addition to newspapers, cable and satellite television).

THE FUTURE OF POLICING INTERNATIONALLY

In an address to the International Section of the Academy of Criminal Justice Sciences, McKenzie (2004: 6) describes two incidents of cyber crime that happened on the same day. First, there was the havoc caused by a fourteen-year-old boy in the United Kingdom hacking into an American defense computer "bringing things to a standstill." Second, McKenzie (2004) describes the case of a computer virus whose quick spread knocked out machines in a number of countries. You can understand the local, regional, national, and global issues that these two incidents raise. Let us first take the minimal issue of jurisdiction. In the past, the police at the location where the crime occurred were responsible for its investigation. Given the two crimes mentioned above, can we tell in whose jurisdiction the crime occurred? Was it where the hacker lived, or where the program for the virus was written (Country A), or was it where the harm or damage from the crime resulted (Country B)? Even if we determine who should investigate and prosecute, the next question would be under whose law (Country A or Country B)? What do we do with the situation in the second crime wherein a number of nations are involved? Crime situations such as this are only going to become all too common in the future, necessitating international police cooperation on a hitherto unprecedented scale.

Koenig and Das (2001: 6–11) identify a number of existing methods by which such needed cooperation may be achieved. These include **bilateral agreements** (between two countries, say between the United States and Mexico), **multinational agreements** (generally between countries who constitute a regional grouping, e.g., the Nordic Council, consisting of Sweden, Denmark, Finland, Iceland, and Norway, or a historical bloc, e.g., countries who are members of the British Commonwealth), and **multilateral or global agreements** (those involving a large number of countries, e.g., the International Criminal Police Organization or INTERPOL and various organs of the United Nations, specifically the Criminal Justice and Crime Prevention Branch). Given the pace of globalization both in terms of communication, computer networks, and rapid mass transport, it is likely that police at all levels in the future will be informed of and able to access these agreements as and when a crime has been committed across borders.

Some international police cooperation (mainly through INTERPOL) already exists. Chatterton (2001: 343) notes that as early as in 1992, "more than one million messages were transmitted through the Interpol network, and 400,000 communications involved European member states . . . 140,000 files on international offenders or on criminal cases with international ramifications were opened at the Interpol General Secretariat." Such international cooperation, as already exists, is therefore only likely to expand and deepen in the near and long-term future. It is possible that the police officer of the future will be able to access these networks, either through a national nodal agency or even directly with a fellow police officer in another country.

PUBLICS, COMMUNITIES, AND RISING EXPECTATIONS IN THE FUTURE OF POLICING

In this chapter, we have considered a number of issues that pertain to the future structure and functions of policing. First, we have suggested that the police are going to be pursuing professionalization of both individual officers and departments by choosing to upgrade and meet high standards (in education and performance) that are the hallmarks of other occupations recognized as professions. Second, the police will have to reflect and relate to multiculturalism and diversity in the population that it serves and from which it draws its personnel. Third, we have noted that this will occur in the face

bilateral agreements

Agreements for police cooperation among two countries.

multilateral (or global) agreements

Agreements for police cooperation involving a large number of countries.

multinational agreements

Agreements for police cooperation between countries who constitute a regional grouping (e.g., the Nordic Council), or a historical bloc (e.g., members of the British Commonwealth).

of a surge in the privatization of what have always been understood to be core police functions (patrolling, first response) externally, or those closely identified with public organizations internally (record keeping, data processing, etc). Fourth, the rapid pace of adoption of new technologies as well as their wider range and applicability can be expected to change how police officers and departments will go about their work in the future. Fifth, police cooperation across international borders and spanning the entire globe can be expected to grow. This will occur both in response to crimes that take place in a given location, but where the offender has transported himself or herself to another part of the globe, and to crimes that may be committed across national jurisdictions (e.g., Internet financial swindles, piracy on the high seas, human or drug trafficking, environmental crimes, toxic product dumping, etc.).

Probably, the most vital implication of the combined effects of the above for the future of policing is the one we have chosen to focus on last. Taken together, these trends suggest that a revolution of **rising expectations** in how policing will be expected, delivered, and assessed in the future may be in sight (see Home Office, 2008). American policing can no longer be insular, provincial providers of all of the governmental functions currently associated with them. The public will instead expect their police professionals to solve crime problems (see, for example, Toch and Grant, 2005) with competence and certainty. The police will be racially and ethnically diverse, highly qualified educationally, working in state of the art departments; focused on more important or serious crime issues; able to bring the latest in a vast range of available technologies to bear on crime questions; and, to do so at a national, international (or transnational) basis, as needed. Clearly, all of the above goes beyond the level of current public expectations regarding the police, particularly in terms of quality, and may have indeed been raised as a result of the currently popular community-policing model.

The history of policing alerts us to the double-edged nature of rising public and community expectations. The technologies associated with the automobile (allowing the police to travel great distances), the telephone (allowing citizens to contact the police dispatcher and to communicate their need for police services), and the two-way radio (allowing the officer in a police car to respond quickly by automobile to a citizen's call for service on being instructed to do so by the dispatcher) resulted in increasing public expectations about police departments and personnel. In the middle of the twentieth century, U.S. policing responded to these rising expectations by adopting the professional model that served to separate them from the public they served. As many police historians have noted, dissatisfaction with the professional model resulted in attempts to involve the community more in policing. Perhaps, the rising expectations that current trends are likely to engender in the public and the police may result in a new separation between the professional police (in their newer, more narrowly focused, but highly trained, technical and international roles) and citizens. An extreme version of this may be envisioned if we think of future police officers as akin to physicians and police stations as paralleling hospitals or clinics. As individual citizens, we may avail ourselves of the services of these professionals only when needed (e.g., when victimized by crime), but with the expectation that a higher likelihood exists that they will solve the problem. Will that new era in policing be accompanied by the meeting of these raised expectations?

With the above question in mind, in the accompanying Box, we look at the future challenges of policing the nation of Finland, a previously isolated country now undergoing integration into the world economy and more immigration than it has been used to.

 ## SUMMARY

The final chapter of this book takes a look at what the future of policing is most likely to be. Given that we cannot forecast or predict every eventuality that may take place, we have chosen to focus our attention on how some major trends may play out in the future. In turn we consider what the future holds for the idea of police professionalism, the impact of population change on policing, the privatization of some police services, the availability of greater access to technology, and the resulting rising expectations regarding policing,

increasing community involvement in policing, and the internationalization of police activity that we had discussed in detail in Chapter 14. Finally, we consider how all of these trends, individually and collectively, are likely to affect the future activities and efforts of police departments. We end with the question of whether police departments of the future will be able to meet the rising expectations of the public for highly efficient, timely, responsive law enforcement; order maintenance; and service.

 ## KEY TERMS

Accreditation: The development of law enforcement standards and to demonstrate through an accreditation process that law enforcement agencies could voluntarily meet professionally recognized criteria.

Bilateral agreements: Agreements for police cooperation among two countries.

Heterodyning: A form of technology that uses weak fluorescent emissions from organic molecules to tag crime scenes evidence normally invisible to the naked eye.

Multilateral (or Global) agreements: Agreements for police cooperation involving a large number of countries.

Multinational agreements: Agreements for police cooperation between countries who constitute a regional grouping (e.g., the Nordic Council), or a historical bloc (e.g., members of the British Commonwealth).

Professionalization: The process by which occupations become professions by acquiring a distinct body of knowledge, education, and research.

Rising expectations: Higher public expectations regarding how policing will be delivered, and assessed in the future.

 ## REVIEW QUESTIONS

1. What does police professionalism and agency accreditation mean?
2. What are the consequences of rising community expectations on the future of policing?
3. How has policing in Finland changed due to the country's emergence from isolation, and its current integration into the world economy?

DISCUSSION QUESTIONS

1. Which sociological perspective on the future of policing discussed in this chapter do you most agree with? Please explain.

2. What functions of the police, if any, may be successfully privatized in the future? What functions, if any, are unlikely to be?

3. Do you agree with the idea that policing in the future will be based on agreements among countries? If so, what form would these agreements take? Which is likely to be more successful and why?

REFERENCES

Bayley, David H. (1994) *Police for the Future.* New York: Oxford University Press.

Census 2000 Brief (2000) *Population Change and Distribution 1990–2000.* Washington, DC: U. S. Department of Commerce, U. S. Census Bureau.

Chatterton, M. R. (2001) "Reflections on International Police Cooperation: Putting Police Cooperation in Its Place—An Organizational Perspective." Pp. 136–172 In Koenig, Daniel J. and Dilip K. Das (eds.) *International Police Cooperation.* Lanham, MD: Lexington.

Cunningham, William C. and Todd Taylor (1985) *Hallcrest Report.* Boston, MA: Butterworth-Heinemen.

Easterlin, Richard (2000) "Growth and Composition of the American Population in the 20th Century." Pp. 121–135 In Haines, Michael R. and Richard H. Steckel (eds.) *A Population History of North America.* Cambridge, United Kingdom: Cambridge Press.

Home Office (2008) *Building Communities, Beating Crime: A Better Police Service for the 21st Century.* London, United Kingdom: Home Office.

McKenzie, Ian (2004) "Content of Ian K. McKenzie's Luncheon Presentation." *ACJS International Newsletter* 4, 1: 5–8.

Koenig, Daniel J. and Dilip K. Das (2001) *International Police Cooperation.* Lanham, MD: Lexington.

Maghan, Jess; Gregory W. O'Reilley and Phillip Chong Ho Shon (2002) "Technology, Policing and In-Car Videos." *Police Quarterly* 5, 1: 34–57.

Nunn, Samuel (2001a) "Cities, Space, and the New World of Urban Law Enforcement Technologies." *Journal of Urban Affairs* 23, 3–4: 27–54.

Nunn, Samuel (2001b) "Police Technologies in Cities: Changes and Challenges." *Technology in Society* 23: 223–245.

Schults, Donald O. and Eric Beckman (1978) *Principles of American Enforcement of Criminal Justice.* Second Edition. Sacramento, CA: Custom.

Toch, Hans and J. Douglas Grant (2005) *Police as Problem Solvers.* Second Edition. Washington, DC: American Psychological Association.

Travis, Jeremy (1995) Criminal Justice Science and Technology Program, *National Institute of Justice: Research in Action.* Washington, DC: National Institute of Justice.

White, Michael D. (2007) *Current Issues and Controversies in Policing.* Boston, MA: Pearson Allyn and Bacon.

POLICING IN FINLAND: THE CHALLENGE OF THE FUTURE

Michael Palmiotto

The primary purpose of police agencies throughout the world is to maintain order in their country, states, provinces, and municipalities. The Finnish police can trace their development to the early nineteenth century. They were established for the sole purpose of maintaining public order. Like all police agencies in the world, the Finland police are expected to be reactive and respond to citizen calls dealing with crimes or emergencies. Their mission is to maintain social order in society. One of the biggest challenges that the Finnish police will face in the future is how to go about carrying out their responsibility to safeguard the country's social system, and to maintain order and security, while not impinging on an individual citizen's rights. The police are responsible for maintaining public order by enforcing laws with minimum infringements of people's rights, and to ensure that citizens' rights to do their job are not denied any more than necessary.

For example, the police are responsible for maintaining order in public places. They do so by patrolling, responding to calls, and overseeing major events. One of the responsibilities given to the Finnish police is the protection of what they call "domestic peace." The Finnish concept of domestic peace applies not only to residential premises but also to business premises, offices, schools, and other similar institutions and their grounds (Finland Police, 2009). Breaches of domestic peace include the following (Finland Police, 2009):

- A person enters somebody's home and refuses to leave.

- An invited guest starts behaving in a manner that the hosts consider inappropriate, and refuses to leave as requested.

- An occupant in a block of flats creates such a noise that other occupants cannot sleep properly.

- A customer creating a disturbance in commercial premises or offices refuses to leave when requested to do so by staff.

Unlike the United States, Finland has National Police Units, Provincial Police Units, and Local Police Units. At the national level, Finland has a National Bureau of Investigation (KRP), Security Police, and a National Traffic Police. The National Bureau of Investigation investigates major crimes. The Security Police are responsible for national security and investigation of related crimes. The National Traffic Police are responsible for traffic safety (Law Enforcement in Finland, 2009).

As can be seen, an already complex set of tasks, such as the above, is being made increasingly difficult by the lessening of the geographical isolation that Finland enjoyed in the past. Finland is currently well integrated economically with its Scandinavian neighbors such as Sweden, Denmark, and Norway, as well as with other European countries. Further, in the past four decades, Finland has welcomed ethnic Finns from the former Soviet Union, Chilean refugees, Vietnamese "boat people," Bosnians, and Albanians, all of whom were fleeing political repression and bloody wars in their homelands. How will a fairly homogeneous and socially isolated country respond to the movement of large numbers of "others" in and out of the country, particularly in terms of its policing structure and processes? Political, economic, social, and technological changes have affected and changed Finnish conceptions of their society and its police force.

References

Finland Police (2009) http://www.poliisi.fi/home.nsf/pags/75 cc458BC370038500?open document, obtained December 12, 2009.

Law Enforcement in Finland (2009) http:// www.answers.com. topic/law-enforcement-in-finland, obtained December 12, 2009.

INDEX